*Games Real Actors Play*

# Theoretical Lenses on Public Policy

Series Editor, Paul Sabatier

*Games Real Actors Play: Actor-Centered Institutionalism in Policy Research,* Fritz W. Scharpf

*Other People's Money: Policy Change, Congress, and Bank Regulation,* Jeffrey Worsham

*Policy Change and Learning: An Advocacy Approach,* edited by Paul A. Sabatier and Hank C. Jenkins-Smith

*Institutional Incentives and Sustainable Development: Infrastructure Policies in Perspective,* Elinor Ostrom, Larry Schroeder, and Susan Wynn

*Parties, Policies, and Democracy,* Hans-Dieter Klingemann, Richard I. Hofferbert, and Ian Budge

# *Games Real Actors Play*

Actor-Centered Institutionalism
in Policy Research

*Fritz W. Scharpf*

WestviewPress
*A Division of* HarperCollins*Publishers*

*Theoretical Lenses on Public Policy*

Copyright © 1997 by Westview Press, A Division of HarperCollins Publishers, Inc.

Published in 1997 in the United States of America by Westview Press, 5500 Central Avenue, Boulder, Colorado 80301-2877, and in the United Kingdom by Westview Press, 12 Hid's Copse Road, Cumnor Hill, Oxford OX2 9JJ

A CIP catalog record for this book is available from the Library of Congress.
ISBN 0-8133-6879-0 (hc.)    ISBN 0-8133-9968-8 (pbk.)

The paper used in this publication meets the requirements of the American National Standard for Permanence of Paper for Printed Library Materials Z39.48-1984.

10      9      8      7      6      5      4      3      2      1

*To Marlene*

# Contents

# Tables and Figures

# Acknowledgments

This book has received a good deal of help. My largest debt is to my colleague and codirector Renate Mayntz, who not only shares the credit for formulating the framework of "actor-centered institutionalism" (Mayntz/Scharpf 1995a) but who also, more than anybody else, has influenced my way of thinking about and of doing social science research. I have profited so much from our collaboration and discussion over more than a quarter of a century precisely because we have continued to see the world through sufficiently distinct lenses to make agreement something that was to be striven for rather than to be taken for granted. In the same spirit, I cannot claim, except where otherwise noted, that Renate would approve of all that is in this book, even though she has read all of it and given me the benefit of her comments.

My second debt is to the students at the University of Konstanz who responded to the ideas presented here in two seminar courses, one before the serious writing began, the other after a first draft was completed. At that stage I also received valuable comments from Kjell Hausken at our institute. The next push came then from Margaret Levi at the University of Washington, Seattle, and Adrienne Héritier at the European University Institute, Florence, both of whom agreed to review the second draft from the critical but on the whole sympathetic perspective of colleagues dealing with similar challenges in their own work. Their comments encouraged me to insist more boldly that theoretically disciplined explanations can be achieved even when we study potentially unique policy interactions and that a framework for policy research must reflect the normative as well as the positive dimensions of its subject. Around the same time, Marlene Brockmann did me the favor of going over the whole text with the red pencil of the professional writer and editor. If the result is at all readable, the credit must go to her.

The greatest influence on the substance and style of the book came from Paul Sabatier, the editor of the "Theoretical Lenses" series. He suggested the present format at a time when my plans were still malleable, and he also did me the favor of going through the manuscript, practically sentence by sentence, with editorial suggestions on every chapter and again on later versions of chapters that he had disliked initially or where I had initially disliked his comments. Given his superb editorial skills and his ever tactful insistence, I usually ended up liking what he did. I can only hope that he will also like the final version.

This book could not have been completed without the help of two institutions. All of the research was done at the Max Planck Institute for the Study of Societies in Cologne, Germany, where I profited from the efficient library services of Susanne Hilbring and her staff and from numerous discussions among colleagues and visiting fellows. When it was time to concentrate on serious writing, Yves Mény allowed me to spend four months in 1995 and another month in the spring of 1996 in splendid isolation at the Robert Schuman Center of the European University Institute. The actual production of the final manuscript was then placed in the competent hands of Christina Glasmacher, Christel Schommertz, Oliver Treib, and Lars Schubert at the Max Planck Institute.

I thank them all.

*Fritz W. Scharpf*

# Introduction

Politics is about many things. But foremost among these, in modern democratic polities, is the function of selecting and legitimating public policies that use the powers of the collectivity for the achievement of goals and the resolution of problems that are beyond the reach of individuals acting on their own or through market exchanges. The academic disciplines of political science and political sociology are also about many things. But among their foremost concerns is, or ought to be, the contribution that they could make to the understanding and the improvement of the conditions under which politics is able to produce effective and legitimate solutions to policy problems.

This book is about a set of conceptual tools that have proved their use in this endeavor. They will be discussed here within a framework that Renate Mayntz and I have implicitly used in our joint and separate work since the beginning of the 1970s, and that we have recently explicated and decided to name "actor-centered institutionalism" in a jointly authored article (Mayntz/Scharpf 1995a). The approach proceeds from the assumption that social phenomena are to be explained as the outcome of interactions among intentional actors—individual, collective, or corporate actors, that is—but that these interactions are structured, and the outcomes shaped, by the characteristics of the institutional settings within which they occur. An overview will be presented in Chapters 2 and 3. For the basic focus on actors interacting within institutions, we do not claim originality. On the contrary, we are convinced that many colleagues doing empirical policy research are implicitly working with similar assumptions, working hypotheses, and research strategies. Nevertheless, it seemed useful to explicate systematically and to reflect upon what has been implicitly assumed—and the positive response to our article in the German profession suggests that we are not alone in this belief.

It must be pointed out, however, that the framework as such is more general than are the purposes of this book. It also includes conceptual tools for the analysis of social differentiation (Mayntz 1988) and of large technical systems (Mayntz/Schneider 1988; Mayntz 1993) that I have not drawn upon here. Instead, this book places greater emphasis on the usefulness of analytical tools that are, in a broad sense, of a more game-theoretical nature than is necessarily implied by the more general framework.

In this regard, it is also fair to warn the reader that empiricists have not responded with great enthusiasm to a series of articles, published under the common title of "Games Real Actors Could Play," in which I have tried to show how, and with which modifications, game-theoretical models could be usefully employed in empirical policy research (Scharpf 1990; 1991b; 1994).[1] One reason for this may have been that I was doing two things at the same time—trying to persuade game theorists of the need to modify and simplify their analytical models in order to make them more useful tools of empirical research and trying to persuade fellow empiricists that it would be worth their while to invest time and effort in mastering a forbiddingly technical literature. This book is another attempt to restate, on a less technical level, the argument that was addressed to empirical policy researchers as well as to expand it so as to cover not only constellations to which the theory of noncooperative games could be directly applied but also a fuller range of interactions that we are likely to encounter in empirical policy research.

But before I launch into the major purposes of this book—to explicate the framework of actor-centered institutionalism and the analytical tools associated with it—I think it necessary to spell out in some detail the peculiar characteristics of empirical policy research and of the conditions under which it must be practiced. They differ significantly from the usual conditions of empirical and theoretical work in political science and political sociology. Unless they are well understood, either policy researchers are likely to be misled by the canons of "normal science" in empirical research, or their work will be unjustly criticized for violating these canons. In the remainder of this Introduction, I will discuss two of these special characteristics—the interaction of positive and normative research and the relation between problem-oriented policy analysis and interaction-oriented empirical research. A third characteristic—the ubiquitous "small-numbers" problem—will then be dealt with in Chapter 1.

## AN EXAMPLE

To give the reader a fuller appreciation of the arguments that follow, I find it best to think of the study that first persuaded me to use game-theoretic analyses in my own empirical work. It is summarized in the article reprinted in Appendix 1, but for readers who may dislike starting a book by reading its appendix, I begin with an abstract of the summary.

In the early 1970s all Western industrialized countries were confronted with dramatic changes in the international economic environment that tended to produce conditions of "stagflation" for the rest of the decade: On average, economic growth in the countries of the Organization for Economic Cooperation and Development (OECD) was less than half of what it had been in the preceding decade, and unemployment as well as inflation were twice as high. More interesting from a policy-research point of view is the fact that individual countries differed greatly on the two scores of economic performance, inflation and unemployment, that had the greatest political salience in the 1970s (see Appendix 1, Table A1.1). This is an interesting variance that calls for an explanation.

But even though inflation and unemployment were of high political salience in the 1970s, it could well have been the case that public policy had little or no influence and that differences were fully explained by variations in the policy environment and in economic starting conditions. Thus it was first necessary to identify the causes of the general decline of economic performance and those (combinations of) policy measures that potentially could, and did in fact, affect the outcomes in question. To do so, it was necessary to refer to macroeconomic analyses that had identified the first oil-price shock of 1973–1974 as a proximate cause of stagflation. The twelvefold increase, within the course of a few months, of the price of an essential resource of modern economies necessarily added a massive cost push to already high levels of inflation, while the additional purchasing power that had to be transferred to the oil-producing countries left, at least in the short run, a huge gap in the aggregate demand for the goods and services produced in the industrialized countries. The result was a combination of cost-push inflation and demand-gap unemployment for which national macroeconomic policy was ill prepared. Using conventional tools of fiscal and monetary reflation or deflation, it could only hope to alleviate one problem by exacerbating the other. More attractive outcomes could only be obtained if, in addition to government fiscal policy and central-bank monetary policy, it was also possible to enlist union wage policy in a concerted effort to deal with economic stagflation. In that case, union wage restraint could be employed to contain cost-push inflation, while fiscal and monetary policy (if they were able to act jointly) could then reflate aggregate demand to maintain full employment without causing excessive inflation.

My own research focused on four countries—Austria, Britain, Sweden, and West Germany—all of which were economically in fairly good shape at the beginning of the crisis in 1973, and all of which were initially governed by social-democratic parties with a strong preference for maintaining full employment and a secondary interest in avoiding high levels of inflation. At the end of the 1970s, however, only Austria had succeeded in maintaining both full employment and relative price stability, and Britain had done poorly on both counts. Sweden had done best on employment but suffered from high rates of inflation, and Germany had combined the lowest rates of inflation with the greatest increase in unemployment.

Since economic analysis had identified fiscal, monetary, and wage policy as having an effect on the outcomes in question, the search for explanations had to concentrate on actors controlling the use of these policy instruments. At the highest level of abstraction, these were governments controlling taxing and (deficit) spending, central banks determining interest rates and the money supply, and unions controlling wage settlements.[2] For each of these actors, it was also possible to specify the rank order of preferences over the range of feasible outcomes. However, since the "government" was vulnerable to election returns, it was also necessary to include the potential responses of the electorate in the analysis.

The basic explanation uses a model of two connected games, one played between the government and the unions, the other between the government and the electorate. In the first game, as long as the government remained firmly committed to full employment, the unions would prefer high wage increases, which would further escalate inflation. In the second game, however, the electorate might respond to runaway inflation by voting for a "monetarist" opposition party that would give priority to price stability rather than full employment. For the unions, this would constitute the worst-case outcome. Anticipating it, they might opt for wage moderation in order to avoid the political failure of a government that tried to maintain full employment.

In principle, these two connected games were being played in all four countries. But the game form obviously did not determine the outcomes. What differed among the countries were the institutional settings within which the games had to be played in reality. Thus the ultimate explanation focuses on three sets of institutional factors. First, there were significant differences in the way in which one set of actors was constituted in the four countries: Wage policy in Austria, Sweden, and West Germany was conducted by a limited number of centralized industrial unions, whereas wages in Britain were set in highly decentralized collective-bargaining processes involving more than 100 separate unions that were often competing for membership. Second, in Austria, Britain, and Sweden, the mode of interaction between the government and the central bank was an asymmetrical one, facilitating the hierarchical coordination among fiscal and monetary policy choices, whereas for Germany the *Bundesbank* had to be modeled as an autonomous player that was able to pursue its preferences unilaterally. Finally, in Austria, Britain, and Germany, the unions had reason to fear the electoral defeat of relatively weak social-democratic governments by opposition parties with a stronger commitment to price stability, whereas in Sweden the bourgeois coalition government continued to favor full employment since, after forty years of social-democratic rule, it could not see itself presiding over the first postwar rise of mass unemployment.

If we bring these factors together, we get the following thumbnail sketch of an interaction-oriented explanation: In Sweden unions were strong and organizationally centralized, but they saw no reason to practice wage restraint as long as the new bourgeois government coalition found itself politically compelled to continue full-employment policies at almost any cost—which explains the coexistence of full employment and high rates of inflation. By contrast, even though British unions had reason to fear a change of government and a switch to monetarist policies, their fragmented and decentralized organization made wage restraint extremely difficult to achieve. Thus, fearing electoral responses to runaway inflation after the "social compact" had failed in 1977, the Labour government began to fight inflation through monetarist strategies and was finally replaced by Margaret Thatcher's Conservatives in 1979. This explains the coincidence of high rates of inflation and relatively high unemployment in Britain. In Austria, however, a politically threatened social-democratic government was able to count on the support of strong and centralized unions in order to achieve an ideal "Keynesian concertation" among fiscal, monetary, and wage policies that did maintain full employment and reasonable price stability. In Germany, finally, government and unions were equally capable of concerted action. But since the independent central bank was unilaterally pursuing restrictive monetary strategies,[3] Germany suffered a steep rise of unemployment while achieving the lowest rate of inflation.

## THE IMPORTANCE OF THINKING GAME-THEORETICALLY

The explanations developed in the study I have just summarized were essentially game-theoretical. As it turned out, this was the aspect that was most puzzling even to friendly reviewers and critics of the study. Apparently, most colleagues interested in empirical policy research were either unaware or highly skeptical of the usefulness of such explanations. Moreover, some of the game theorists themselves, whose models I had sought to apply, not only were uninterested in empirical applications but also explicitly rejected the claim that their analytical algorithms could be used to explain interactions in real-world choice situations (e.g., Selten 1985; Binmore 1987).

In my view, this state of affairs is unfortunate, since the game-theoretic conceptualization of interactions seems uniquely appropriate for modeling constellations that we typically find in empirical studies of policy processes: These usually involve a limited number of individual and corporate actors[4]—governments, ministries, political parties, unions, industrial associations, business firms, research organizations, and so on—that are engaged in purposeful action under conditions in which the outcomes are a joint product of their separate choices. Moreover, these actors are generally aware of their interdependence; they respond to and often try to anticipate one another's moves. In other words, the game-theoretic conceptualization of strategic interaction has a very high degree of prima facie plausibility for the study of policy interactions.

At the same time, these interactive conditions are most likely to be ignored by disciplines such as welfare economics or systems analysis that are primarily involved in substantive policy research. They tend to ascribe policy choices to a unitary "policymaker" or "legislator" rather than to strategic interactions among independent actors. By the same token, even when policy must change the behavior of other actors to become effective, the conceptualization of that intervention is likely to be decision-theoretic rather than game-theoretic. The policymaker, in other words, is assumed to be engaged in a "game against nature" in which policy instruments are supposed to achieve causal effects in a "policy environment" that

is either passive or characterized by a fixed reaction function that can be anticipated and manipulated by well-designed policy instruments. The most famous
example of the deficiencies of this decision-theoretic perspective is the failure of
Keynesian macroeconomics to heed Michael Kalecki's (1971) early warning that
initially successful fiscal and monetary full-employment strategies would produce inflation and stagnation if labor and capital would, in response, change
their wage-setting and investment behavior. The implication is that if political
scientists will not introduce the game-theoretic perspective into policy research,
other disciplines are even less likely to do so.

The reluctance of empirically oriented political scientists to use game-
theoretic concepts seems to have two reasons. First, game theory is a branch of
applied mathematics, and much of the literature, written by mathematicians for
other mathematicians, not only *seems* forbiddingly technical but *is* in fact practically inaccessible to the uninitiated. Moreover, empiricists who have nevertheless
ventured to look behind the veil of technical difficulties are generally repelled by
the extreme unrealism of the assumptions that they have encountered.

Like all variants of rational-choice theory, game theory starts by assuming perfectly rational actors. Thus in introductory treatises on noncooperative game theory the assumptions are that actors will single-mindedly maximize their own self-
interest, that they do so under conditions of complete information, and that their
cognitive and computational capacities are unlimited. These are, in fact, exactly
the assumptions on which neoclassical microeconomics has been built. There,
however, they are relatively innocuous since the mathematically sophisticated theoretical apparatus of the "invisible hand" is allowed to do its work, as it were, "behind the backs" of relatively simple-minded subjects, whose quasi-automatic responses to relative-price changes are then aggregated into theoretically interesting
macroeconomic outcomes. Game theory, by contrast, at least in its rational-
analytic version that is of interest here, *must impute to the actors themselves all information and all solution algorithms that are used by the analyst.* Moreover, as the
original assumption of omniscience is relaxed in models allowing for incomplete
and asymmetrical information, the demands on the assumed computational capacities of the actors are again increased by orders of magnitude and thus to levels
that seem completely unattainable by any real-world actors (Scharpf 1991b).

It is because of these extreme demands on the cognitive capabilities of the assumed actors that game theorists are generally unwilling to claim explanatory (as
distinguished from normative) validity for their models. For the same reason, in
political science, game theory seems to have appealed mainly to political philosophers and analytical theorists but hardly to practitioners of empirical policy research. Since I regard this as unfortunate, I would now go further than I did in
the "Games-Real-Actors-Could-Play" articles mentioned earlier: *In order to profit
from the game-theoretic perspective, empiricists neither need to become mathematicians nor need they assume actors who are either omniscient or have at least unlimited computational capacities. It is sufficient that the basic notions of interdependent*

*strategic action and of equilibrium outcomes be self-consciously and systematically introduced into our explanatory hypotheses.* If that is the frame of attention and interpretation, then everything else can, in principle, be left to empirical research and the development of empirically grounded theory. Nevertheless, it helps to be aware of a few basic concepts, distinctions, and presentational conventions.

To begin with the latter, it is useful to be able to switch between two equivalent forms of presenting a simple game—the "normal form" and the "extensive form." The first, which I will use more frequently, represents the choice situation as a matrix or a table in which the strategies of one player are represented by rows, and those of the other player by columns, while the payoffs are numbers entered in the cells at which strategies intersect. The extensive form uses a tree-like representation of the players' moves, and it lists the payoffs at the end point of each sequence of moves. It is most useful when players are not assumed to move simultaneously but rather one after another, and it also can more easily be used to represent the moves of more than two players.

In saying this, I have also introduced the fundamental concepts of game theory—*players, strategies,* and *payoffs.* The concept of player may apply to any individual or composite actor that is assumed to be capable of making purposeful choices among alternative courses of action; strategies are the courses of action (or sequences of moves) available to a player. A game exists if these courses of action are in fact interdependent, so that the *outcome* achieved will be affected by the choices of both (or all) players. The third fundamental concept, payoffs, represents the valuation of a given set of possible outcomes by the preferences of the players involved. In the presentation here, these payoffs will be ranked ordinally, so that in Figure I.1, for example, the number 4 symbolizes the best outcome from the perspective of a player and the number 1 the worst possible outcome. For an illustration I will use the macroeconomic coordination game played between a monopolistic "Union" and a monetarist "Government" (or an independent central bank) in the example discussed earlier. Other, more familiar game constellations and their strategic implications will be more fully discussed later, in Chapter 4. What matters here is the general approach to the game-theoretical representation of interactions.

On the left-hand side of Figure I.1 is the normal or matrix form of representation. The two players are named "Government" and "Union," respectively. Each has two strategies. The Government player may choose between the upper row (i.e., reflating aggregate demand) and the lower row (deflating demand), whereas the Union player's choice between a moderate and an aggressive wage policy is represented by the left and right columns. Their respective payoffs are listed in the cells of the matrix, with those for Government located in the lower left and those for Union in the upper right-hand corner. An inspection of these cells reveals that if Government chooses to reflate the economy (upper row) and if Union chooses wage moderation (left column), both players will receive their second-best payoff (3, 3), but if Union chooses aggressive wage strategies it will

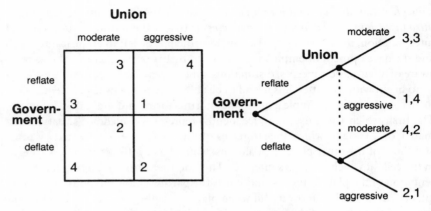

FIGURE I.1    "Monetarist" game in normal and extensive form

receive its very best and Government its worst possible outcome (1, 4). However, if Government switches to deflation an aggressive Union would receive its worst possible payoff, and it would then be in its own best interest to switch to wage moderation. Since this would be the outcome most preferred by Government, the game may "lock in" on this outcome in the lower-left cell.

Exactly the same information is contained in the "extensive form" or tree representation of the game on the right-hand side of the figure, with the payoffs of the Government player listed first. However, before these game constellations can be used for predictive or explanatory purposes, two further distinctions are necessary. First, the players may be involved in a *noncooperative* or a *cooperative* game. These labels are often misunderstood. A cooperative game is simply one in which binding agreements among the players are possible before each makes his or her choice, whereas in a noncooperative game anything that may be said before the move is just "cheap talk." Thus, in the usual case of games with "complete" information, the players will be informed about all elements of the game—that is, about the other players involved, their available strategies, and the payoffs that would result from each strategy combination—but they cannot know, at the moment of their own choice, which strategy others will choose. In the cooperative game, by contrast, strategies may be chosen jointly and by binding agreement. A look at Figure I.1 shows that in the absence of binding agreements, a monetarist Government has reason to choose unequivocally a deflationary strategy, in which case Union will be forced to choose wage moderation out of its own self-interest. From Government's point of view, there would therefore be absolutely no reason to seek agreement with Union (and Margaret Thatcher never did so).

The situation had been different for Thatcher's Labour predecessors, who would have very much liked to have reached a binding agreement with the unions that would have allowed the government to continue its full-employment

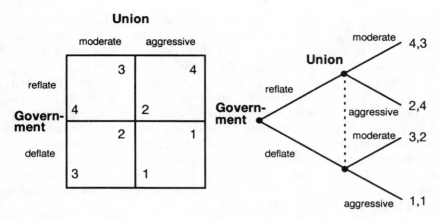

FIGURE I.2    "Keynesian" game in normal and extensive form

policy while the unions would do their part to combat inflation (Figure I.2). But at that time British unions did not have the institutional capacity to commit themselves to longer-term wage moderation, whereas in Austria institutional conditions allowed an effective agreement to be reached in which Government and Union strategies converged on the upper-left cell of the figure.

The second important distinction applies only to noncooperative games. It is between *simultaneous* and *sequential* games. In a simultaneous game, each player must select his or her own move without knowing the strategy choice of the other player. In a sequential game, one player may (or must) move first, and the other player will then move in the knowledge of that choice. Obviously the extensive game form on the right-hand side of the figure is particularly well suited to representing sequential games. If it is to be used for representing simultaneous choices, the dotted line between the second player's choice points in the figure would indicate that he or she must choose without knowing the first mover's choice.

The difference between simultaneous and sequential moves may or may not make a difference for the outcome that will be chosen in a noncooperative game. In the monetarist game represented in Figure I.1, it does not make a difference. Government will always choose its deflationary strategy, since the outcomes that it can achieve thereby are considered superior in all respects to the outcomes attainable through reflation. In the "Keynesian" game of Figure I.2, by contrast, sequence could make a difference. If the union moves first and chooses an aggressive wage settlement, then the Labour government may be blackmailed into reflating the economy to avoid mass unemployment even if that might lead to excessive rates of inflation. If Government has the first move instead, it may opt for deflation in the hope that Union will then avoid the worst-case outcome in the lower-right cell by switching to wage moderation in time before the next election. For Prime Minister Jim Callaghan, however, that gamble did not work.

This background is all that is needed to appreciate the fundamentals of game-theoretic thinking, which can be summarized in two concepts: *strategic interaction* and *equilibrium outcomes*. The first implies that actors are aware of their interdependence and that in arriving at their own choices each will try to anticipate the choices of the others, knowing that they in turn will do the same. In the noncooperative game constellation the implication might be an infinite regress of ever more contingent anticipations. This is not the case, however, if the game has one or more equilibrium outcomes. These are outcomes in which no player can improve his or her own payoff by *unilaterally* changing to another strategy. In the monetarist game matrix of Figure I.1, the equilibrium outcome is in the lower left-hand cell. Even though the payoffs (4/2) are unattractive for the Union player, Union cannot unilaterally improve its own situation while Government sticks to its preferred strategy choice.

In the context of empirical research, the explanatory power of these concepts should not be underestimated. They provide the basis for counterfactual "thought experiments" that systematically explore the outcomes that would have been obtained had the parties chosen other, equally feasible courses of action. If it can be shown that the actual outcome was indeed produced by strategy choices that, for all parties involved, were the best they could do under the circumstances, then this form of explanation has a persuasiveness that is not easily matched by alternative explanatory strategies (Tetlock/Belkin 1996).

I will have more to say about this in Chapters 4 and 5. Here I will merely point out that the concepts of strategic interaction and of equilibrium outcomes, though originally developed in the theory of noncooperative games, have a theoretical significance that is of much more general application. There are perhaps not many real-world interactions in which all the specific assumptions of noncooperative game theory are strictly fulfilled, and there is a much larger variety of modes of interaction that play a role in policy processes. Their discussion will be the subject of most of this book. But regardless of which mode of interaction is actually employed, the outcomes achieved can always be examined with a view to their equilibrium characteristics.

## PROBLEM-ORIENTED AND
## INTERACTION-ORIENTED POLICY RESEARCH

This book focuses on the potential contribution of political science and political sociology to policy research. But our disciplines are not alone in their concern with public policy, nor is it reasonable to think of them as the "master disciplines" in the field of policy research—even though we will often find ourselves organizing, using, and reviewing the policy-relevant contributions of other disciplines. It is thus necessary to identify more precisely the specific contribution that we can make in a field that depends on interdisciplinary cooperation or, at least, a well-understood division of labor among the policy-relevant disciplines. In doing so, I distinguish between "problem-oriented" and "interaction-oriented" policy research.

Problem-oriented research is concerned with the causes of policy problems, with the potential policy solutions, and with their likely effects on the initial problems and on the wider policy environment. In the stagflation study discussed earlier, for example, I had to rely on macroeconomic research to provide the problem-oriented analysis that did identify the oil-price shock as a proximate cause of cost-push inflation and demand-deficient unemployment and that pointed to the combination of fiscal and monetary reflation plus union wage restraint as the most effective policy solution to the stagflation problem. In other areas, contributions to problem-oriented policy research might come from a great many other disciplines—from criminology in the case of crime prevention, from epidemiology and immunology when the issue is the reappearance of contagious diseases, from sociology and psychology when a "war against poverty" is on the political agenda, or from the chemistry of stratospheric reactions when the destruction of the ozone layer is the problem under scrutiny. In this context, political science as a discipline has no specific role, even though there may be policy problems in which policy researchers who happen to be political scientists will organize multidisciplinary analyses or synthesize contributions of other disciplines that did not directly focus on the problem at hand.

But once the problem has been analyzed and potentially effective solutions identified, the specific contribution of political science and political sociology, for which I use the label "interaction-oriented policy research," comes into its own.[5] In the example discussed earlier this contribution did focus on the question why some countries did, and some did not, adopt the macroeconomic policy combinations that would have been effective in combating stagflation. Its importance is best appreciated in contrast to the dominant (but rarely explicit) "benevolent-dictator perspective" of most substantive policy analyses whose job is done when the causes of a problem have been correctly identified and a technically effective and cost-efficient solution proposed. The adoption and implementation of such solutions is then thought to be the responsibility of "the government" or some other unitary "policymaker" who ought to have the means and the will to put the best policy recommendations into practice.

Political scientists and sociologists, by contrast, should be interested in the fact that many or most of these well-designed policy proposals will never get a chance to become effective. The reason is that public policy is not usually produced by a unitary actor with adequate control over all required action resources and a single-minded concern for the public interest. Rather it is likely to result from the strategic interaction among several or many policy actors, each with its own understanding of the nature of the problem and the feasibility of particular solutions, each with its own individual and institutional self-interest and its own normative preferences, and each with its own capabilities or action resources that may be employed to affect the outcome. In other words, what I said in the preceding section about the importance of game-theoretic thinking is at the core of the specific contribution of political science and sociology to policy research.

The focus of our explanations, therefore, is on the interaction among purposeful actors—which, as the example discussed earlier illustrates, often means highly organized collective and corporate actors. This perspective is open to two principal objections, one from macrosocial systems theory, the other from methodological individualism. The first denies the theoretical relevance of human agency, focusing instead on macrosocietal characteristics such as functional differentiation and the "autopoiesis" of operationally closed systems of function-specific communication (Luhmann 1984). As a macroperspective it has little to offer for the explanation of specific policy choices.

By contrast, the challenge from methodological individualism is more relevant. It is certainly true that in the final analysis only individual human beings are capable of intentional action, and it is also true that interaction-oriented policy research would be impossible if explanations had to be sought at the individual level in every case. In the political process, however, the most relevant actors are typically acting in the interest, and from the perspective, of larger units, rather than for themselves. This allows us to simplify analysis by treating a limited number of large units as composite (i.e., aggregate, collective, or corporate) actors with relatively cohesive action orientations and relatively potent action resources. Nevertheless, we must be able to revert to the individual level whenever it becomes empirically necessary to do so. Thus the "micro foundations" of our analyses at the meso and macro levels will remain a constant concern. The conditions under which composite-actor concepts can be usefully employed in interaction-oriented analyses will be discussed in Chapter 3.

Moreover, these larger units—political parties, labor unions, government ministries, central banks, and so on—are operating within institutional settings in which they are much less free in their actions than autonomous individuals might be. They are themselves likely to be constituted by institutional norms that not only define their competencies and other action resources but that also specify particular purposes and shape the associated cognitive orientations. As a consequence, these policy actors are also likely to find themselves in relatively stable "actor constellations" that can be analyzed with the help of the game-theoretic concepts that I introduced earlier. Actor constellations will be further discussed in Chapter 4. In addition, the institutional setting also defines the modes of interaction—unilateral action, negotiations, voting, or hierarchical direction—through which actors are able to influence one another and to shape the resulting policy choices. The discussion of these modes of interaction will occupy the latter part of this book, Chapters 5 through 9.

## NORMATIVE AND POSITIVE ISSUES IN POLICY RESEARCH

Policy research requires not only a specific division of labor between problem-oriented and interaction-oriented analyses but also a more direct interaction between positive and normative investigations than is otherwise common in the social sciences. In the opening paragraph of this Introduction, I indicated that in the context of policy research, political science and political sociology should contribute to the understanding and improvement of the conditions under which politics is able to produce effective and legitimate solutions to policy problems. Both criteria are of course evaluative, but the first seems more amenable to purely positive research, whereas the second does appear more normative. However, as every lawyer knows, the validity of a rule depends not only on its proper derivation from higher-order norms but also on the positive judgment that it could be effectively realized in practice.[6] Conversely, to judge a policy effective requires not only information about its empirical consequences but also normative assumptions about what should be considered a problem and what would constitute a good solution. In short, the clear-cut division of labor between political scientists engaged in empirical research and positive theory and others concentrating on normative political theory cannot be maintained in policy-oriented research. Focusing on effectiveness *and* legitimacy, we are necessarily involved as much in identifying and explicating appropriate normative standards as we are engaged in collecting and interpreting empirical information. While it goes without saying that we must not confuse the one with the other, we cannot hope to avoid normative issues by focusing exclusively on the positive aspects of a policy issue.

For an illustration, take the example presented earlier. On its face, it is exclusively concerned with an empirical puzzle: Why is it that under the stagflation conditions of the 1970s some countries suffered from high rates of unemployment or high rates of inflation or both, while others did well on both counts? Assuming that at the time everyone agreed that full employment and price stability, if they could both be had, were good things and that uncontroversial statistical indicators were available to measure the degree of success or failure, normative issues do not seem to have great salience. But now assume further, if only for the sake of argument, that success could only be achieved by countries with "neocorporatist" institutions, allowing governments and the associations of capital and labor to reach negotiated agreements on the concertation of fiscal, monetary, and wage policies. If this were empirically true, as I argue that it is, it raises an issue of democratic legitimacy that was seriously debated at the time (Brittain 1977; Panitch 1980): How can governments remain democratically accountable if their policy comes to depend on the agreement of associations that are not also accountable to the democratic sovereign? Conversely, when we are trying to assess whether it is reasonable to think that the European Union (EU) suffers from a fundamental "democratic deficit," the normative dimension seems to be clearly dominant. However, as I will argue in Chapter 9, the empirical consequences of this unresolved issue do in fact limit the capacity of the EU to deal effectively with a range of critical policy problems.

Both of these examples are intended to show that policy issues can rarely be fully treated in policy research without attending to both the positive and the normative dimensions involved. But how should we deal with these normative issues? I leave aside the possibility that we merely wish to assert our own moral valuations or political preferences, which as citizens we are of course free to do. In that case, professional ethics would require us to lay open these preferences and to draw a clear line between findings of fact and the expression of personal valuations. If we should fail to do so, presumably the competitive environment of policy research will provide sufficient incentives to colleagues whose public criticism will damage our professional reputation (Kirchgässner 1996).

The question remains of how we should handle normative issues if we are not trying to play politics on our own account (or on the account of a particular client) but instead are seriously committed to the maxims of "scientific objectivity" or, at least, "neutrality." Here it is useful to distinguish between the *criteria of "good" policy* on the one hand and the *legitimacy of the policymaking system* on the other. In the first instance, we will often be able to refer to generally shared and uncontroversial criteria of policy success or failure, as was assumed in the stagflation example for full employment and price stability in the 1970s. When that is not the case, we may benefit from the characteristic division of labor between problem-oriented and interaction-oriented policy research discussed earlier. If substantive analyses should be the primary responsibility of another discipline, such as economics in the case of macroeconomic policy or the natural sciences in the case of environmental policy, then political scientists will not have to assume responsibility for defining their own criteria.

But often that will not suffice. Problem definitions and potential solutions may be controversial in scientific discourse as well as in political debate. In that case, the philosophically appropriate solution would be a procedural one, requiring public discourse conducted under the ground rules of an "ideal speech situation" (Habermas 1981; 1989), in which arguments asserting private self-interest as such would have no standing and the only admissible criterion would be the "common good" (Elster 1986). In practice, of course, we must often do research on issues where not only self-serving arguments but also different visions of the "common good" continue to compete against one another. Under such conditions policy research, in analogy to the role of legal scholarship and judicial review in the search for just legal rules (Habermas 1992, 324–348), may (and often does) attempt to anticipate, and to approximate, the outcome on which a hypothetical ideal discourse might converge. Even then, however, its role is more likely to be that of an advocate rather than that of a court of last resort. This is as it well should be.

For political scientists, however, the difficulty is reduced by the fact that they will not primarily be involved in disputes over the substantive goodness of public policy. Their professional competence is mainly on call when issues of *legitimacy* are in dispute. Remember, moreover, that we are still in the context of policy research. The issue therefore will not usually concern regime legitimacy in the broadest sense but rather the legitimacy of specific structures and procedures through which policy is being produced. Often such issues are thought to be the province of constitutional law, which, however, is here in need of positive theory and empirical information that cannot be produced within the "autopoietic" communications system of legal discourse (Teubner 1989; Teubner/Febbrajo 1992). The criterion must, again, be the notion of a "common good." But what is to be judged now is not the substantive quality of a particular policy choice but rather the *general* capacity of particular policymaking institutions to produce policy choices that are likely to approximate the common good. These are indeed judgments for which political science and political sociology have a unique professional competence.

In order to arrive at such judgments, however, we must make use of a number of distinctions. Policies that are in everyone's interest or that agree with everyone's preferences require no additional legitimation. Legitimacy becomes problematic only if the interests of some are made to suffer or if some are forced to act against their own preferences, as is true of taxes or of the military draft. To legitimate such policies, it is necessary to claim that they serve the common good. But the notion of a "common good" must remain inescapably controversial unless the *simultaneous relevance of two dimensions, welfare production and distribution,* is acknowledged. If it is accepted, then issues will be greatly clarified, and often it will be relatively easy to achieve agreement about which solutions are superior or inferior in the welfare dimension. Once it is clear which services and transfers should be tax financed, or whether the draft is necessary or not, debate can then focus on the definition of the appropriate criteria of distributive justice. I will return to these issues at the end of Chapter 4.

What is important here, however, is that these are not the judgments that we need to make ourselves. Focusing on legitimacy, we are not concerned with the rightness of individual policy choices but with the capacity of policy systems to reach good choices. This capacity can be assessed at a more abstract level with the help of the analytical tools presented in this book. Since the question will occupy us throughout Chapters 4 through 9, I will only suggest here that the capacity varies with the type of policy problem that needs to be resolved, with the constellation of policy actors, and with the institutionalized modes of interaction. The implication is that certain types of policy systems are generally capable of dealing with specific types of problems—and generally incapable of dealing with certain other types of problems—in ways that could satisfy the dual standards of welfare production and distributive justice. Thus, to use the example presented earlier, the Austrian system of "corporatist" negotiations facilitated the concertation of fiscal, monetary, and wage policy, whereas the German system, which allowed the central bank to act unilaterally, was less able to achieve a welfare-maximizing resolution of the stagflation crisis of the 1970s. These, I suggest, are clarifications that are uniquely within the professional competence of political science and political sociology.

## OVERVIEW OF THE BOOK

It should be emphasized again that although specific examples will be used throughout the book, the focus will be on the presentation and discussion of conceptual tools that can be used in empirical research rather than on the presentation of particular empirical findings or specific theoretical explanations.

Chapter 1 continues the explication of the special conditions of policy research that was begun in this Introduction. There the focus is on the peculiar relationship between empirical work and (positive) theory that differs from the canons of "normal science" in empirical research. The problem arises from the extreme complexity of the factors affecting policy interactions, which makes it difficult to discover "empirical regularities" and which also makes it unlikely that a sufficient number of cases could be found to allow the statistical testing of multivariate hypotheses. The conclusion is that in the absence of powerful procedures for hypothesis testing, we need to make greater investments in the theoretical quality of the working hypotheses we use. Moreover, since we also cannot deduce our working hypotheses from comprehensive theories, we need to combine more limited partial theories or well-understood "mechanisms" in modular explanations of complex cases. This approach is aided by a "framework" within which the theory modules that are relevant for interaction-oriented policy research can be located.

Chapter 2 provides an overview of the framework of actor-centered institutionalism. It proposes to explain policy choices by focusing on the interactions among individual, collective, and corporate actors that are shaped by the institutional settings within which they take place. Institutionalized rules, varying from one place and one time to another but relatively invariant within their domain, are thus the major sources of the regularities that we are able to discover and use in our explanations.

In Chapter 3 the focus is more narrowly on the concepts of actors. It is shown under which conditions and for which purposes it is useful to employ composite actor concepts—that is, aggregate, collective, and corporate actors—in analytical models and empirical research. In addition, the chapter discusses categories for describing the action resources and the action orientations of such actors. With regard to orientations, actor-centered institutionalism departs from standard rational-actor assumptions by emphasizing socially constructed and institutionally shaped perceptions and by distinguishing among three dimensions of preferences, namely (institutional) self-interest, normative orientations, and identity-related preferences.

Chapter 4 then presents the central concept of actor constellations. It describes the relationship in which the actors involved in policy interactions find themselves vis-à-vis one another with regard to their strategy options and with regard to their outcome preferences. In its information content, the concept of actor constellation is equivalent to the information contained in game matrices—but without the assumption that the actors are involved in a noncooperative game. The matrix can thus be taken as a static representation of the divergence and convergence of action preferences and thus of the level of conflict involved in a given interaction. The claim is that a thorough understanding of the underlying constellation is an essential precondition for the explanation and prediction of interaction outcomes. Discussion focuses on the explication of a number of "archetypal" constellations and on the possibilities of simplifying complex real-world constellations to the point at which they can be validly represented by relatively simple game matrices. The chapter concludes with a discussion of "interaction orientations," defined as subjective redefinitions, in light of the nature of the relationship, of the payoffs received by ego and alter, respectively.

The remaining chapters deal with four different modes of interaction, namely, unilateral action, negotiated agreement, majority voting, and hierarchical direction. The claim is that a given actor constellation may still result in different policy outcomes if the mode of interaction differs. The modes of interaction, in turn, need to be described in structural and in procedural terms.

Chapter 5 then deals with "unilateral action" under the structural conditions of "anarchic fields" or "minimal institutions." It introduces a distinction among three different modes: noncooperative games, Mutual Adjustment, and Negative Coordination. They differ primarily in the degree of foresight that is ascribed to the actors and in the need to respect protected interest positions. The chapter concludes by discussing the highly problematic welfare and distributional implications of all modes in which outcomes are determined by the unilateral actions of interdependent actors.

Chapter 6 discusses "negotiated agreements" under the structural conditions of minimal institutions, networks, regimes, and "joint-decision systems." In the procedural dimension, the chapter introduces the distinctions among "Spot Contracts," "Distributive Bargaining," "Problem Solving," and "Positive Coordination." It is shown that the implications of negotiated agreements for welfare production are generally positive, whereas standards of distributive justice will be realized only in the restricted sense of "equity" that tends to reproduce the initial distribution of bargaining power.

Chapter 7 focuses on interactions whose outcome is determined by majority voting. Since it is possible here to impose collectively binding decisions over the objections of a dissenting minority, the legitimacy of majority rule becomes a major issue. For the reasons mentioned earlier, conclusions must depend on normative as well as on positive judgments. First, it can be shown analytically that voting by majority will neither have positive welfare consequences nor approximate distributive justice if self-interested voters are assumed. Second, normative theories of "deliberative democracy" would avoid these dismal implications by postulating that voting should merely register the conclusions of public-interest–oriented discourses. But it can be shown, as a positive proposition, that the theory of deliberative democracy must fail if the institutionalized role of competitive political parties and interest organizations is acknowledged. What might work, in normative theory as well as in positive practice, is a "jury model" of democracy in which public-interested voters respond to the advocacy of self-interested and competitive political parties. However, given the inherent limitations of public attention, this model could satisfactorily cope only with a very small number of well-defined policy issues. The conclusion is therefore that the majority principle is not generally capable of legitimating collectively binding decisions that violate the preferences of a minority. What it may do instead is to legitimate the exercise of hierarchical authority in the democratic state.

Chapter 8 then focuses on binding decisions imposed by hierarchical direction within organizations and within the state. If the holders of asymmetric power could be assumed to have complete information and to be motivated by the public interest, then hierarchical coordination could assure both welfare production and distributive justice. It is then shown that the information problem associated with hierarchical coordination can be resolved only under very restrictive assumptions, whereas the mechanisms of democratic accountability may indeed assure a reasonable approximation of public-interest orientation among the governors of constitutional democracies.

Chapter 9, finally, discusses the conditions of the "negotiating state." Internally, the fact that hierarchical coordination is increasingly replaced by "negotiations in the shadow of the state" can be shown to be conducive to public-interest–oriented policy outcomes that suffer less from information deficits than would be true of hierarchical direction. Externally, however, increasing economic globalization and transnational interdependence will weaken the hierarchical authority of the nation-state and hence its capacity to assure welfare production and distributive justice. This loss of national problem-solving capacity is unlikely to be compensated for by policies adopted in transnational negotiations.

## NOTES

1. Another indication of the dominant sense of the profession is the fact that on both sides of the Atlantic the work of the few political scientists who are presenting game-theoretic analyses of empirical policy interactions at a high level of technical competence, such as George Tsebelis (1990; 1994) and Otto Keck (1987; 1988), is still considered a methodological specialty rather than part of the mainstream of empirical policy research.

2. In the "Keynesian" climate of the 1970s, wage increases could be "passed on" to consumers, so that firms had little reason to resist union demands.

3. The explanation implies that a restrictive monetary policy neutralizes the economic effects of any attempt by the government to practice fiscal reflation.

4. It is true, as Paul Sabatier, for one, keeps reminding me, that the number of actors involved in policymaking, and especially in policy implementation, may be quite large. Nevertheless, it will often be possible to use valid simplifications, to be discussed later in Chapter 4, in order to reduce the actor constellation to manageable proportions.

5. The reverse is equally true: Substantive policy analysis must have done its job before political science is able to answer any policy-relevant questions. Thus I have argued that countries with "neocorporatist" institutions did have a comparative advantage under the stagflation conditions of the 1970s, whereas that advantage disappeared in the economic environment of the early 1980s (Scharpf 1991a). Though that particular conclusion has been challenged (Garrett 1995; but see Moses 1995), the general point remains that we need to know what the policy problem and its requirements are before we can identify the factors that may cause a polity to do better or worse in that regard. Then, and only then, can political science research make a useful contribution to policy analysis.

6. On a more philosophical level, the same thought is expressed by the Kantian maxim "*Sollen impliziert Können*" (ought implies can).

# 1

# Policy Research
# in the Face of Complexity

In order to be pragmatically useful, the findings of interaction-oriented policy research should not only be case-specific and post hoc, in the sense in which that is true of historical research, but they should also allow lessons drawn from one case to be applied to others and, ideally, to produce lawlike generalizations with empirical validity. In the social sciences, however, this ideal is generally difficult to realize, and in interaction-oriented policy research it is nearly impossible.

## INTENTIONAL ACTION:
## BOUNDEDLY RATIONAL AND SOCIALLY CONSTRUCTED

The reason is straightforward: Policy is produced by human actors who are not merely driven by natural impulses or by the compulsion of external factors. Instead, public policies are the outcomes—under external constraints—of *intentional action*. Intentions, however, are subjective phenomena. They depend on the perceptions and preferences of the individuals involved. People act not on the basis of objective reality but on the basis of *perceived reality* and of assumed cause-and-effect relationships operating in the world they perceive. And people act not only on the basis of objective needs but also on the basis of preferences reflecting their *subjectively defined interests and valuations* and their *normative convictions* of how it is right or good or appropriate to act under the circumstances. Intentional action, in other words, cannot be described and explained without reference to the subjective "meaning" that this action has for the actor in question.

For social science research this condition creates an obvious problem, since we cannot directly observe subjective phenomena but always depend on what is at best secondhand information. Moreover, to say that intentions are subjective also suggests the possibility that they may be idiosyncratic, varying from one individual to another and from one time and place to another. If this were all that we could count on, a social science that is searching for lawlike regularities and for theory-based explanations and predictions would be not merely difficult but impossible. All we could aspire to do would be to describe what happened in histor-

ical narratives and perhaps to search for ad hoc explanations based on information about individual motives and worldviews of the actors involved that we
might infer from such unreliable sources as personal interviews, memoirs, and
contemporary documents. Since there would be no way in which we could apply
lessons from one case to another, our work would also lack pragmatic usefulness.

If, nevertheless, the social sciences do claim to discover regularities of human action that allow not only interesting descriptions of past events but also theory-
based explanations that are potentially useful for practical purposes, that claim presupposes the existence of mechanisms that, in some way, are able to structure, or to
standardize, the individual perceptions and preferences that we are likely to encounter in empirical research. In fact the social sciences have come to rely on two
such mechanisms, both of which depend at bottom on an evolutionary argument.

At one end of the social science spectrum are mainstream economics and
those variants of political science and sociology that have become committed to
the rational-actor approach. In the evolution of the human species, so it is assumed, there must have been a premium on accurate perceptions of the environment and on behavior that would increase the survival chances of the individual
and its progeny. As a consequence, rational self-interested action is thought to
have become genetically fixed as a universal characteristic. Among the social sciences proper, neoclassical economics depends most completely on this working
hypothesis. Economic actors are assumed to be exclusively motivated by economic self-interest—which is interpreted to imply the maximization of profits
for firms and the maximization of wealth for households. On the cognitive side
the corresponding assumption is that actors will perceive the economic environment in the same way that it is perceived by the scientific observer and that their
computational capacities are on the whole adequate to the task of selecting
courses of action that will in fact maximize their self-interest. When these assumptions are granted, choices will be determined by external conditions—
namely, by the available opportunities for investment and consumption, by their
relative prices, and by the actors' own budget constraints. Since data on these
conditions are, at least in principle, accessible to the researcher, neoclassical economics claims to explain and predict the behavior of economic subjects on the
basis of general laws combined with objectively available information.

For the world of competitive market economies, the assumptions of neoclassical economics may indeed approximately describe the intentions of economic actors—and as the intensity of competition increases, their empirical plausibility
increases as well (Latsis 1972). Moreover, since empirical economic research does
not usually try to explain or predict individual choices but rather is interested in
the aggregate effects of large numbers of individual choices, random deviations
from the assumed central tendency do not much matter, and economics is, on the
whole, reasonably successful in explaining and predicting—*under ceteris paribus
conditions*—the responses of capital owners, firms, workers, and consumers to
changes in the relative prices of capital, raw materials and energy, labor, and
goods and services.

At the other end of the social science spectrum, cultural anthropology and mainstream sociology also make a claim to evolutionary foundations. But rather than the survival value of rational self-interested action in natural environments, they emphasize the extreme complexity and uncertainty of an environment constituted by other human actors whose subjective worldviews and preferences cannot be directly observed, as well as the enormous difficulties that individuals would have to overcome in communicating with each other and in coordinating their actions in social encounters. Human societies could only have evolved, so it is argued, because these difficulties are overcome through a "social construction of reality" (Berger/Luckmann 1966) that assures the convergence of cognitive orientations and through social norms and institutionalized rules that shape and constrain the motivations or preferences of all participants in social interaction. Culture and institutions, in other words, are necessary preconditions of human interaction. They allow individuals to find some sense in their otherwise chaotic worlds and to anticipate to some extent the otherwise unpredictable—and hence threatening—intentions of others with whom they must interact. Most important for our purposes, they also create the behavioral regularities that can then be discovered by social science research and used in theory-based social science explanations.

These two paradigms are usually presented in opposition to each other. In fact, however, they are not mutually exclusive. On the one hand, even if the underlying assumptions of culturalist approaches were granted, it would not follow that human action can be explained exclusively by reference to culturally "taken-for-granted" beliefs and institutionalized rules of "appropriate behavior." Human actors are not merely acting out culturally defined "scripts," nor are they rule-following automata—they are intelligent and they have views of their own and interests and preferences of their own, which sometimes bring them to evade or to violate the norms and rules that they are supposed to follow.

But on the other hand, neither is it realistic to think of human actors as always being omniscient and single-minded self-interest maximizers who will rationally exploit all opportunities for individual gain regardless of the norms and rules that are violated. Human knowledge is limited and human rationality is bounded, and hence much human action is based not on the immediate cognition of real-world data and causal laws but on culturally shaped and socially constructed beliefs about the real world. At the same time, most human action will occur in social and organizational roles with clearly structured responsibilities and competencies and with assigned resources that can be used for specific purposes only. In these culturally and institutionally defined roles, pure self-interest will not explain much beyond the choice of assuming, or refusing to assume, certain roles. But once a role has been assumed, action within that role is practically impossible to explain without reference to cultural and social definitions of that role and to the institutionalized rules associated with its proper performance.

Thus, while the rational-actor paradigm may capture the basic driving force of social interaction, its information content with regard to the operative intentions of human actors outside of the economic field is close to zero—unless we are able to resort to institution-specific information for the specification of actor capabilities, cognitions, and preferences. This is the gist of the framework of actor-centered institutionalism that will be presented in Chapter 2.

## MANY VARIABLES AND FEW CASES

From the point of view of generalizability, however, we are still far from home. Institutional definitions of capabilities, cognitions, and preferences are by no means universal in their substantive content. Cultural history and cultural anthropology have informed us about the enormous variability of what is culturally "taken for granted" from one place to another and from one time to another, and we also know from legal history, constitutional history, comparative law, and comparative government how much institutions do in fact vary in time and place. So if behavior is shaped by institutions, the behavioral regularities we can expect are also likely to vary with time and place. Hence the best that we could hope to discover is not the universal theories that are the aim of the natural sciences but, as the late James S. Coleman (1964, 516–519) put it, "sometimes true theories"—providing explanations, that is, that hold only under specific institutional conditions. In order to assess the domain of such explanations, we therefore must vary the institutional context in comparative studies.

If we do so, however, we confront the fact that the institutional factors that will plausibly affect policy outcomes can only be described in a multidimensional property space. For instance, even if we limit comparison to highly developed Western societies and democratic political systems, and even if we consider only institutions at the national level, the institutional settings that are known to affect policy processes can be described as being either unitary or federal, parliamentary or presidential, having two- or multiparty systems in which interactions are competitive or consociational, and with pluralist or neocorporatist systems of interest intermediation. In comparative political science research, these variables are assumed to be of general policy relevance, whereas others—for example, the autonomy or dependence of central banks or the existence of insurance-based or tax-financed health care systems—may need to be considered only in particular policy contexts. Worse yet, interaction effects among the characteristics listed are likely to be important: In the case discussed in the Introduction, it was clear that the beneficial effects of neocorporatist institutional arrangements could be undermined by the existence of an independent central bank. Similarly, federalism in a two-party system will generate effects that differ from federalism in a multiparty system (Scharpf 1995). Hence even the first-mentioned five dichotomies will amount to $2^5$, or 32, different institutional constellations that, for all we know, may differ significantly in their impact on public policy.

But that is not all. The effect of institutions on public policy is also likely to be modified by changes in the external policy environment. Thus while neocorporatist concertation was successful in avoiding both inflation and unemployment under the stagflation conditions of the 1970s, the same institutional factors lost most of their effect on economic policy outcomes in the economic environment of globalized capital markets in the following decade (see Appendix 1). Similarly, in the benevolent economic environment of the postwar decades, a wide variety of welfare-state institutions have been equally successful in providing social security at acceptable cost. In the economic environment of the 1990s, however, Continental welfare states relying primarily on payroll taxes to finance transfer payments seem to be in greater difficulty than Scandinavian welfare states that are financed from general tax revenues and that emphasize services rather than transfer payments (Esping-Andersen 1990).

For comparative policy research, this means that the potential number of different constellations of situational and institutional factors will be extremely large—so large, in fact, that it is rather unlikely that exactly the same factor combination will appear in many empirical cases. In the natural sciences this difficulty would typically be overcome through experimental designs that permit the isolation and systematic variation of a single factor—which we can rarely hope to do in policy research. The closest equivalent to experimental designs in empirical research are comparative studies using carefully matched cases selected according to the logic of the "most-similar systems" or the "most-different systems" design (Przeworski/Teune 1970). If the cases differ (or agree) only in one variable or in a very limited set of variables, it may indeed be possible to derive causal inferences with a good deal of confidence.

The "most-similar systems" design was in fact used in the example study discussed in the Introduction: All four countries, Austria, Britain, Sweden, and West Germany, were hit by the same external oil-price shock in 1973–1974; all were in fairly good economic shape in 1973; all had governments that acted from a Keynesian worldview and that had a clear political preference for maintaining full employment; and all had relatively strong and generally "cooperative" trade unions. Since these factors could be "held constant," it was then possible to identify the influence of just two sets of institutional variables—union organization and central-bank independence—on the policy choices that were in fact adopted. Hence quasi-experimental designs may indeed work in policy research. However, two caveats are in order.

First, as the full-length study amply demonstrates, the four countries did differ in a great many other respects that I have not mentioned here, and the actual courses taken were also influenced by historical "accidents" that could not be represented in a parsimonious theoretical model (Scharpf 1991a). Hence the effectiveness of the quasi-experimental design depends on the level of detail at which explanations are being sought. Second, and more important, the research design used here depends on exceptional circumstances that policy researchers cannot count upon. In the general case, comparative designs are much more likely to encounter cases that differ not only in a few institutional variables but also in external conditions, actor identities and capabilities, actor perceptions, and actor preferences. Under such conditions, "most-similar" and "most-different" systems designs will not reduce variance sufficiently to facilitate quasi-experimental solutions (King/Keohane/Verba 1994, 199–206).

By the same token, however, the usual social science methods of inductive theory development and statistical theory testing will also run into difficulties here. Even if we disregard the logical objections to inductive generalization (Willer/Willer 1973; John 1980), we have little opportunity to discover "empirical regularities" by observing large numbers of similar cases and we have even less opportunity to subject hypotheses generated through inductive generalization to statistical tests using data sets that are different from the original observations. Given the number of potentially relevant independent variables, we will usually not have the requisite number of cases to perform statistical tests, even if the number of observations is inflated by combining cross-sectional and longitudinal data in "pooled time series."[1]

Gary King, Robert Keohane, and Sidney Verba (1994) have, it is true, identified a range of useful and imaginative research strategies that could be employed to ease or to overcome the small-sample, or small-N, problem by generating additional observations at different levels or in different segments of complex cases. Unfortunately, however, this important work only helps to highlight the more fundamental difficulty that we encounter when trying to follow the methodological canons of empirically validated causal inference. It is best summed up in their discussion of a study searching for explanations of interstate cooperation in high-tech weapons development. Since only three cases could be studied, whereas there were seven potentially effective independent variables, the research design was judged to be indeterminate: It could not determine which of the hypotheses, if any, was true. Assuming that a sufficient number of additional case studies could not be carried out, the best advice that the authors can provide is "to refocus the study on the effects of particular explanatory variables across a range of state action rather than on the causes of a particular set of effects, such as success in joint projects" (King/Keohane/Verba 1994, 120).

More generally, King and colleagues have a consistent preference for designs searching for the *effects* of a particular explanatory variable rather than for the *causes* of a particular empirical outcome; in fact, all their methodological recommendations for coping with the small-N problem have this "forward-looking" character. Everything else being equal, this certainly is a highly plausible methodological preference. When one is looking forward from a particular independent variable to its potential effects, hypotheses can be formulated so as to control the length of the chain of causation that is to be covered before a particular effect is selected as the "dependent variable." If the chain is short enough (e.g., from X to $E_1$ in Figure 1.1), interaction effects from other variables are of course less of a problem than they are for hypotheses trying to cover longer distances (e.g., from X to $E_3$). Hence the number of cases needed for valid empirical tests is smaller,

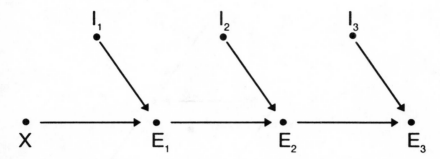

FIGURE 1.1    Forward-looking hypotheses (X = Independent variable; $I_1, I_2, I_3$ = Intervening variables; $E_1, E_2, E_3$ = Effects)

and at the same time, the number of available cases that are identical with regard to these two variables increases.

It may be quite feasible, therefore, to develop quantitative tests for hypotheses predicting the effect of various election systems on the number of political parties that will be represented in parliaments (Sartori 1994), but it would be much more difficult to establish empirically the existence or nonexistence of longer causal chains linking election systems to particular policy outcomes or, say, to democratic stability (King/Keohane/Verba 1994, 189–191).

In policy research, however, the questions that political scientists are expected to answer are typically *backward looking,* starting from an *explanandum* or a dependent variable at the other end of the hypothetical chain of causation. Here the expected end product is not the empirical confirmation or disconfirmation of single-factor hypotheses but rather explanations of particular policy choices or predictions of the political feasibility of particular policy options. As a consequence, the chain of causation considered cannot be arbitrarily shortened but rather must be long enough to reach from the dependent variable to pragmatically useful independent variables—that is, to variables that permit explanations that either identify causal factors that can be politically manipulated or that show that the outcome is/was beyond political control. Thus, for instance, it would not have been enough, in the study discussed in the Introduction, to show that inflation in the 1970s was controlled by union wage restraint; it was also necessary to identify the factors that enabled the unions in some but not all countries to practice wage restraint.

Moreover, and more important, backward-looking research designs not only may have to cope with longer chains of causation, but they also will have to cope with a larger number of such chains. A thought experiment will illustrate this. Assume that each node in a chain of causation is affected by two causal factors and that the investigation, forward or backward looking, will be limited to three steps in any chain. In Figure 1.1, illustrating a forward-looking design, therefore, $E_3$ would be treated as the ultimate dependent variable. Since we are interested in

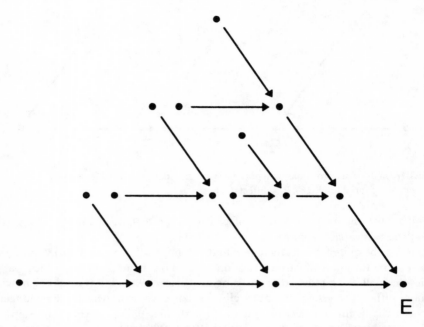

FIGURE 1.2    Backward-looking hypotheses (E = Effect to be explained. All other dots represent independent and intervening variables.)

identifying the effect of the independent variable X, we would only need to control for the intervening variables (but we would not explain these as well). This would require us to deal with six variables altogether that could influence $E_3$ (namely, X, $E_1$, $E_2$, $I_1$, $I_2$, and $I_3$). By contrast, a backward-looking design would under the same stipulations require us to trace back (for the same three steps) all chains of causation that have an impact on the dependent variable. In our thought experiment, this would require us to deal with fourteen independent and intervening variables altogether (Figure 1.2).

It is clear, therefore, that there are indeed good reasons for preferring research designs that test forward-looking hypotheses, but it is equally clear that in policy research this preference typically cannot be indulged. As a consequence, the difficulties we encounter are greater than is supposed by King and colleagues, and they are also not overcome by the (generally most convincing) recommendations that they have developed for coping with the problems of complexity and small numbers of observations.

A more promising way of coping with a plurality of independent variables seems to be the method of quantitative comparative analysis developed by Charles Ragin (1987), which uses truth tables and Boolean algebra to analyze the effect of a complete *set of combinations of "qualitative" independent variables* on a single dependent variable. From the perspective of policy research, its greatest advantage is that it is backward looking. The method necessitates a focus on a single, well-defined dependent variable—for example, a puzzling cross-national difference in policy outcomes; it can handle and reduce relatively large sets of independent variables; and by focusing on combinations of variables, it not only accommodates multicausality but also has no need to assume that variables are independent from one another. Moreover, Ragin's method has no difficulty with equifinality or functional equivalence that is, of course, ubiquitous in policy research: The same policy outcome is often produced in quite different (but not in all) institutional settings, and qualitative comparative analysis is able to analyze such conditions in a straightforward fashion.

A major problem remains, however. As the number of independent variables increases, the combinatorial approach generates an exponentially increasing number of different (potential) factor *combinations,* with the likely consequence that most of these will not have real-world counterparts in the available cases. Since some among these "missing cases" might well contradict the conclusions derived from the existing cases (which would then require a search for additional variables), the method becomes less definitive as the number of variables, and hence the percentage of missing cases, increases. Thus even though the quantitative constraints are not as tight as they are for statistical tests, the Boolean approach also depends on a more favorable relationship between the number of variables considered and the number of available cases than we can generally expect in empirical policy research. We must therefore conclude that by ordinary standards our opportunities, not only for theory development through empirical generalization but also for empirical theory testing, are quite limited in interaction-oriented policy research.

As a consequence, we seem to be confronted with a most unattractive dilemma. Researchers attempting to follow standard methodological precepts may find themselves compelled to reduce drastically the complexity of their hypotheses by focusing on a greatly reduced range of independent variables. From a hypothesis-testing point of view, this has the advantage of simultaneously increasing the number of "comparable" cases and reducing the number of observations needed to apply statistical tests. However, since the systematic effects of omitted variables cannot be controlled for, the results so obtained are of doubtful validity. More important, the insights that can be obtained by a methodology that requires us to ignore most of what we know, or could know, about the real world will not add much to our understanding of the past nor permit us to derive pragmatically useful predictions about the political feasibility of policy options.

## DESCRIPTION IS NOT ENOUGH

Alternatively, political scientists may, and often do, opt for historically descriptive studies of individual cases that are capable of representing the full complexity of the researcher's understanding of a particular situation. The detailed descriptions and narrative explanations that can be obtained in this fashion, relying on the relational logic of connected events and reconstructing precisely how one thing led to another in the specific case, are valuable in their own right—and not merely as preliminary heuristics in advance of more systematic and quantitative studies (White 1973; Danto 1985). As is true of good historiography, the insights gained in good case studies have a depth and persuasiveness that social scientists should not lightly dismiss in their quest for the elusive goal of generalizable empirical regularities and universal "scientific laws."

But, of course, the emphasis in the preceding sentence must be on the adjective "good." That is to say, the insights obtained in this fashion are not "self-correcting" (as would be true of quantitatively testable hypotheses) but rather depend very much on the personal capabilities and visions of the researchers who conduct this sort of study—not only on their diligence and resourcefulness in data collection but even more on their intuitive or experience-based understanding of how things may, and may not, happen in that particular province of reality, on their ability to distinguish the important from the insignificant, on their detective skills in constructing a coherent story that accounts for the available evidence, on their intellectual honesty in exploring alternative interpretations, and last but by no means least, on their literary skills in communicating what they have learned.

In short, case studies are difficult to do, not many can do them well, and the requisite skills, if they can be taught at all, are best acquired in an apprenticeship-like relationship. Moreover, in their reliance on narrative explanations, they also tend to overemphasize historically contingent sequences of events at the expense of structural explanations; thus, though they help us to understand the past, they do not necessarily improve our ability to anticipate the future; and, more generally, they do not contribute to the cumulative growth of a body of systematic knowledge about political structures and processes and their effect on the substance of public policy (Lustick 1996).

Thus if we consider pragmatic usefulness and cumulation as important criteria for policy research and more generally for the social sciences, we must go beyond descriptive case studies and narrative explanations in the search for systematic knowledge for which we can claim validity beyond the case at hand. That means that we must also accept the dual criteria of any scientific explanation: We need to have hypotheses that specify *a causal model showing why and how a given constellation of factors could bring about the effect in question,* and we need to have *empirical evidence that the effect predicted by the hypothesis is in fact being produced.* However, since our methods for subjecting hypotheses to quantitative empirical tests are inherently weak, this requires a shift of emphasis in the methodological discussion—away from the dominant focus on the quality of testing procedures and toward *a greater concern for the quality of the hypotheses that we bring to our empirical material.*

In the Popperian philosophy of science, the formulation of hypotheses is treated as a matter of minor importance; what matters is whether they are able to survive attempts at empirical falsification. And though King, Keohane, and Verba (1994, 99–114) do in fact devote a section to the discussion of rules for constructing causal theories, these rules remain entirely formal in the sense that they relate to the falsifiability, the internal consistency, the concreteness, or the desirable generality of the theories researchers are exhorted to invent—but not to the substance of such theories or the bodies of prior knowledge from which they might be derived. In a methodological treatise that claims to explicate the maxims of good research practice not only for the social sciences but also for science in general, that could hardly be otherwise. Nevertheless, the implication seems to be that the substance of hypotheses should somehow emerge from the untutored creativity or intuition of the individual researcher rather than being subjected to exactly the same professional discipline that is, rightly, demanded for the testing of hypotheses. This is an attitude that may have some justification where empirical tests can in fact be rigorous and conclusive; in fields where that is not true, it is indeed unfortunate.[2]

## FRAMEWORKS, PARTIAL THEORIES, AND MODULAR EXPLANATIONS

This book proceeds from the assumption that in a world that is exceedingly complex and in which we will often be studying unique cases, we must have a good idea of what to look for if we wish to discover anything worthwhile. Since a single data point can be "explained" by any number of regression lines, post hoc explanations are too easy to invent and usually (unless invented with the trained skill of the master historian) totally useless. The implication is that our search for explanations must be disciplined by strong *prior* expectations and that we must take the disconfirmation of such expectations as a welcome pointer to the development of more valid explanations.

It follows from what has been said that such expectations cannot be derived from any existing body of deductive theory—which would have to be, at the same time, of sufficiently broad scope to cover the immense variance and complexity of our cases and of sufficient specificity to contain hypotheses that can be directly applied in empirical work. It also follows that we cannot expect to develop broad theories of general application through induction from observed "empirical regularities." Moreover, we also cannot subject our expectations, however derived, to conclusive statistical tests. But where does that leave us in our search for disciplining expectations?

If we cannot have empirically validated theories that combine broad scope and empirical specificity, we nevertheless are not compelled to face each new case as if we had no prior expectations about how the world works. Instead, we should be able to explicate what the authors of "good" case studies always have in the back of their minds: a "framework" that organizes our prior (scientific and prescientific) knowledge about what to expect in the province of the world that is of interest to us, that emphasizes the questions that are worthwhile asking, the factors that are likely to have high explanatory potential, and the type of data that would generally be useful in supporting or invalidating specific explanations. In the words of Elinor Ostrom (1996, 4–5):

> Frameworks organize diagnostic and prescriptive inquiry. They provide the most general list of variables that should be used to analyze all types of institutional arrangements. Frameworks provide a metatheoretic language that can be used to compare theories. They attempt to identify the *universal* elements that any theory relevant to the same kind of phenomena would need to include. Many differences in surface reality can result from the way these variables combine with or interact with one another. Thus, the elements contained in a framework help the analyst to generate the questions that need to be addressed when first conducting an analysis.

Compared to a fully specified theory, a framework has less information content in the sense that fewer questions will be answered directly and more will have to be answered empirically.[3] Nevertheless, in comparison with the tacit expectations that all of us bring to our empirical research, an explicated framework is more easy to communicate and to criticize and hence to correct and to improve. At the minimum, therefore, it should provide us with a descriptive language that helps us to discover whether or not we are talking about the same thing and thus to compare assumptions, hypotheses, and findings across the variety of complex and unique cases that we are studying.

Beyond that, a framework should provide an ordering system that describes the location of, and the potential relationships among, the many partial theories or more limited "causal mechanisms" (Little 1991, 15–17) that we could in fact draw upon for the theoretically disciplined reconstruction of our nearly unique cases. While we cannot hope for comprehensive theories, our work is by no means devoid of theoretical elements on which we can draw for the explanation of specific, but limited, aspects of our cases. As Jon Elster (1989, viii) has put it: "The basic concept in the social sciences should be that of a mechanism rather than of a theory. . . . [T]he social sciences are light years away from the stage at which it will be possible to formulate general-law-like regularities about human behavior. Instead, we should concentrate on specifying small and medium-sized mechanisms for human action and interaction—plausible, frequently observed ways in which things happen." Thus, since we cannot rely on theories formulating "general-law-like regularities" to explain complex social phenomena, we should relax the criterion of comprehensiveness and work with "small or medium-sized mechanisms" instead. But that also implies that the complete explanations, which we nevertheless must strive for, can only be modular constructs, combining and linking several theoretical "modules" to account for complex and potentially unique empirically observed phenomena or events. The linkages among these modules could then be narrative, or they could themselves have the character of partial theories. But what would be the nature of these "small and medium-sized mechanisms"? In my view, there are two useful interpretations, one more analytical, the other more empirical.

The analytical variety could be described as *incomplete theories*—that is, as abstract models based on logical or mathematical deductions from specified assumptions but with unspecified empirical antecedents. Since our focus is on *purposive actors*, the models we rely on will generally have rational-choice flavor—that is, they will proceed from the assumption that actors will select their best available course of action under the circumstances, given their (institutionally shaped) preferences and perceptions. Moreover, since we assume—for the reasons discussed in the Introduction—that explanations must take account of *interactions* among purposive actors, the most useful analytic models will be of a game-theoretic nature, which, within the framework presented in this book, implies that they will combine the specification of a particular *actor constellation* and a particular *mode of interaction* with the specification of a particular *institutional setting*. One example of such a mechanism is Mark Granovetter's (1978) "threshold model," which explains the presence or absence of bandwagon effects by the distribution of preferences in a population of actors that respond to others' choices. Another is the "Tragedy of the Commons" (Hardin 1968), which explains the depletion of common-pool resources by the existence of a "Prisoner's-Dilemma" constellation in which actors interact in the mode of a noncooperative game and under minimal institutional constraints. A third example could be the "joint-decision trap" (Scharpf 1988), which explains the low capacity for institutional reforms when high-conflict constellations must be resolved through compulsory negotiations.

Many more examples will be presented in the following chapters. Two points must be emphasized, however. First, to speak of a "causal mechanism" implies that the model of the particular interaction has clear-cut behavioral implications.[4] But as we will see in the following chapters, many actor constellations will have several possible outcomes, or they will have no game-theoretic equilibrium at all. When that is true, the (theoretically valid) model will not have the character of a "causal mechanism" but rather will require the introduction of narrative elements for a complete explanation. Moreover, even when we can rely on models with high predictive power, they are likely to be of limited scope and will only represent certain subsets of the complex, multiarena and multilevel interactions that are characteristic of real-world processes of policy formation and policy implementation. Thus it is usually necessary to *combine* several such modules into a more complete explanation.

For an example, consider again the study discussed in the Introduction. In its full-length form (Scharpf 1991a), the complete explanation of policy outcomes in the four countries studied could not depend only on the "government-union" game. Since "the union" is not a unitary actor, the central module had to be complemented by a "union-union" module (with constellations among several unions representing either a game of coordination or a game of competition) and a "voluntary-organization module," reflecting the difficulties that unions face in maintaining the loyalty of their members. Similarly, in some countries "the government" could not be modeled as a unitary actor but had to be represented by a "government–central bank" module, which, again, was characterized by a specific actor constellation and a specific mode of interaction in a specific institutional setting. Finally, in all countries, the preferences of "the government" were strongly affected by a three-cornered "electoral game" characterized by a zero-sum constellation between the government and opposition parties and a connected positive-sum game with the electorate (which will be discussed more fully in Chapter 8). Many of these modules have good theoretical and empirical foundations in the available social science literature (Olson 1965; Crouch/ Pizzorno 1978; Pizzorno 1978; Streeck 1982; Marin 1990), so that they can be used with a good deal of confidence, whereas others needed to be constructed de novo within the framework presented in this book.

To step back from the example, it is obvious that the composite explanation of the course of events is likely to be unique for each country but that the modules employed in constructing it may reappear more frequently in other cases as well and thus are more likely to achieve the status of empirically tested theoretical statements. Even then, however, the *linkages* between these modules remain problematical. Though there have been promising efforts (Putnam 1988; Tsebelis 1990), it seems fair to say that good theoretical models of "connected games" (also referred to as "two-level games" or "nested games") are not yet generally available. Thus we will often depend on narrative, rather than analytical, connections between partial theories that have analytical as well as empirical support— which also means that the composite explanation itself remains vulnerable to charges of being ad hoc.

In the face of this difficulty, it may seem more promising instead to turn to a short list of more integrated and historically situated explanatory modules that try to capture the characteristic logic of empirically observable policy interactions in real-world institutional settings. In political science, such historically situated modules are often defined at the macro level of political systems.[5] Examples that come to mind include highly complex configurations such as the Westminster model of British parliamentarism (Wilson 1994), the consociational model of Swiss or Dutch democracy (Lehmbruch 1967; 1974; Lijphart 1968), the pluralist model of American politics (Dahl 1967), the joint-decision model of German federalism (Scharpf/Reissert/Schnabel 1976; Scharpf 1988), or the neocorporatist model of interest intermediation in the Scandinavian countries and in Austria (Schmitter/Lehmbruch 1979). These are perhaps best characterized as inductive generalizations of the understanding that can be gained through in-depth empirical studies of the complex functioning of particular political systems.

Within their original setting, the explanatory power of these complex, empirically grounded models tends to be high as long as the conditions originally identified remain stable.[6] The difficulties begin when such macro models and their associated hypotheses are transferred to other settings that seem similar but are not quite identical. In the absence of formalization and rigorous definitions, it is difficult to say when applications cease to be valid, and the temptation is great to find instances of currently fashionable models just about everywhere. The downside is that if the hypotheses are not borne out in the case at hand, this is often taken as "falsification" of the original theory rather than an indication of its misapplication.

One remedy for this tendency to diffuse and corrupt useful concepts might be to move from empirical induction to the analytical reconstruction of these macro modules with the help of more basic, analytical models.[7] Thus, for instance, neocorporatism in the field of macroeconomic policy could be analytically reconstructed as a tripartite negotiation system in which one party is a democratically accountable government while the other two parties are monopolistic unions and employers' associations whose power to act depends on the precarious loyalty of their membership. Furthermore, the actor constellation among these parties is characterized by the fact that the government has the option of unilateral hierarchical action but would much prefer a cooperative solution, whereas the constellation among the other two parties is characterized by the coexistence of distributive conflict with a common interest in cooperation. Given this analytical reconstruction, it would then be possible to assess the usefulness of stretching the concept to include "mesocorporatism" and "microcorporatism."[8]

But how, then, could we know whether the hypotheses that we bring to our case studies are in fact true and could support generalizable conclusions? The standard answer is that we should always treat our research as a "crucial case study" (Eckstein 1975) that tests the validity of the explanatory hypothesis employed. But in doing so, we must again proceed with caution.[9] Since the outcome of the case can only be explained by the composite model as a whole, nonconfirmation in the specific case may imply that a necessary element is lacking or that one of the elements or one of the linkages between elements was misspecified. Normally that would not be a good reason for throwing away the remainder of the composite model. Thus in the example study Germany would have appeared as a deviant case if the composite model (constructed from a comparison of the British and Austrian cases) had consisted only of the "government-union" and the "union-union" modules. All three cases can be explained, however, if the model is enlarged to include also a "government–central bank" module.

Thus if a model does not seem to work in the case at hand, we may first search for additional factors by which this case differs from previously explained ones. But not all factual differences will allow us to maintain the validity of the original hypothesis while reducing its generality. In exactly the same manner in which common-law courts must deal with divergent precedents, our "distinctions" must also "make a difference," which is to say that they themselves must be based on the identification of a causal mechanism that could *generally* produce the different outcome. In other words, we are constrained to base explanations, as well as exceptions, only on propositions that are intended as lawlike statements of general applicability. Hence if we cannot define a general rule that would justify the exception, we should indeed consider the original hypothesis as falsified.

None of these maxims can tell us which hypotheses to propose when we cannot draw on empirically validated theoretical models. For that we need an orienting framework that provides guidance to potentially relevant factors, causal mechanisms, and contextual conditions. In the social sciences, there is a wide variety of such orienting frameworks (usually labeled theories)—from macro-level systems theories, materialist theories, and structuralist theories through hermeneutic and social-constructionist theories and varieties of rational-choice theories all the way to behavioralist learning theories, and many more. Useful and illustrative overviews are readily available (e.g., Lave/March 1975; Greenstein/Polsby 1975; Little 1991; Finifter 1993), and I will not add to them here. Instead, this book is intended to explicate and illustrate one particular framework that Renate Mayntz and I have developed over the years and applied in empirical studies of policy formation and policy implementation inside government institutions (Mayntz/Scharpf 1975; Scharpf/Reissert/Schnabel 1976; Mayntz 1980; 1983), of policy interactions among governments, unions, and central banks (Scharpf 1991a), and of governance structures and processes in a variety of service sectors (such as health care, telecommunications, and research and development) that are characterized by high levels of state involvement (Mayntz/Scharpf 1995b). This framework of actor-centered institutionalism is characterized by its giving equal weight to the strategic actions and interactions of purposeful and resourceful individual and corporate actors and to the enabling, constraining, and shaping effects of given (but variable) institutional structures and institutionalized norms. Its elaboration will be a major purpose of this book. An overview will be presented in the following chapter.

## NOTES

1. This is generally true when we study policy *formation* at the macro or meso levels. In *implementation* studies, by contrast, it is often possible to collect data on a sufficient number of local jurisdictions to determine statistically the effect of *local variables* on the implementation of a national program. Since all these jurisdictions will be part of the same political, legal, and cultural system, many of the variables that in cross-national studies would generate excessive complexity can be considered constant.

2. A position similar to the one taken here is argued by Robert H. Bates, Avner Greif, Margaret Levi, Jean-Laurent Rosenthal, and Barry Weingast in their joint introduction to a book manuscript on "Analytical Narratives" presented for discussion at a workshop at Harvard University in January 1997.

3. In this information-theoretic sense, the difference between a framework and a theory is one of degree. In a theory more variables are replaced by constants. Thus, in comparison with the framework of Copernicus, Kepler provided a more information-rich theory of planetary orbits. Similarly, a rational-choice framework may merely postulate that human

actors will try to do the best they can under the circumstances in the light of their given interests and perceptions, whereas a rational-choice theory (like neoclassical economics) would specify interests (e.g., profit maximization) and perceptions (e.g., complete and accurate information processed by unlimited cognitive capacity). For that reason, of course, theories have a greater chance of being wrong.

4. Bates and colleagues, in their draft mentioned in note 2, have found a felicitous definition, describing a mechanism as a "structure of incentives" that (in a model) is able to generate specific outcomes.

5. Even at the macro level, the trade-off between complexity and variety may be difficult to resolve. Relatively "large" concepts—say, the Westminster model of competitive democracy—may organize a great deal of information, but their definitions will be multidimensional and their boundaries vague or contested (Sartori 1991; Collier/Mahon 1993). But if much simpler and less ambiguous concepts—such as the several hundred subtypes of "democracy with adjectives" that Collier and Levitsky (1994) have extracted from the literature—were used, the explosive increase of their number and variety would make inductive generalization practically impossible.

6. By the time Lijphart (1968) had described and analyzed consociational democracy, the model was already on its way out in the Netherlands. The same was true of most studies describing the macrocorporatism of the 1970s.

7. In Chapter 8 I try to do this for the Westminster and consociational models of democracy.

8. However, as we try to endogenize a larger number of interacting analytical models, we are likely to re-create our original problem of excessive complexity at the level of the module: Analytically, interaction effects among the elements may no longer be transparent, and empirically, the class of real-world phenomena, to which the more complex macro module applies in all aspects, will shrink and may, in the extreme case, again include only a single member. In other words, what we gain by using more integrated macro modules, we again lose in terms of transparency and empirical testability.

9. Obviously stochastic hypotheses cannot be tested in single-case studies. Thus everything said here relates to models that claim deterministic validity.

# 2

# Actor-Centered
# Institutionalism

Renate Mayntz and I have selected the label "actor-centered institutionalism" for the framework that has oriented our research since the beginning of the 1970s and that we first explicated in a volume that presented an overview of the work of our institute (Mayntz/Scharpf 1995b). The material contained in this chapter and the next therefore represents her thinking as much as it does mine. But we are not alone in recognizing the need to combine actor-centered and institution-centered approaches in an integrated framework. Others have chosen different labels to describe the same fundamental idea. Elinor Ostrom and collaborators (Ostrom/Gardner/Walker 1994), for instance, use an "institutional analysis and development" (IAD) framework to analyze the resolution of common-pool resource problems; Tom Burns and collaborators (Burns/Baumgartner/Deville 1985) speak of "actor-system dynamics" (ASD); and Michael Zürn (1992) prefers to call his framework "situation-structural." What these approaches have in common is an integration of action-theoretic or rational-choice and institutionalist or structuralist paradigms, which, in the confrontation between "economic" and "sociological" theories, are conventionally treated as being mutually exclusive.[1] What is gained by this fusion of paradigms is a better "goodness of fit" between theoretical perspectives and the observed reality of political interaction that is driven by the interactive strategies of purposive actors operating within institutional settings that, at the same time, enable and constrain these strategies. What is lost is the greater parsimony of theories that will ignore either one or the other source of empirical variation.

But as I pointed out in the previous chapter, this is a parsimony that we cannot afford in empirical policy research. Policy, by definition, is intentional action by actors who are most interested in achieving specific outcomes. Thus, unlike in some types of sociological theory, we cannot assume that they will merely follow cultural norms or institutional rules. We also cannot assume, however, as is done in neoclassical economics or in the neorealist theory of international relations, that the goals pursued or the interests defended are invariant across actors and across time. Rather, we know that actors respond differently to external threats, constraints, and opportunities because they may differ in their intrinsic perceptions and preferences but also because their perceptions and preferences are very much shaped by the specific institutional setting within which they interact.

If, in the case discussed in the Introduction, we attempt to explain the different economic and employment policy choices of European governments in the 1970s and early 1980s, it matters that the preferences and perceptions of Keynesian governments differed from those of monetarist governments (Hall 1992); but it matters equally that central bank policy was under government control in some countries and autonomous in others or that unions were able to develop their wage strategies within a highly concentrated and centralized institutional structure in some countries but not in others. Moreover, not only was the external environment of national economic policy changed radically by the oil-price shocks of the 1970s and the evolution of globalized capital markets, but the effectiveness of policy instruments was also changed as a consequence (Scharpf 1991a). Thus, at the most general level, we need a framework that conceptualizes policy processes driven by the interaction of individual and corporate actors endowed with certain capabilities and specific cognitive and normative orientations, within a given institutional setting and within a given external situation.

But it is important to keep in mind that a framework is not a theory. Theories are the more powerful the more they are able to substitute theoretically justified assumptions for data that would need to be empirically ascertained. Frameworks, by contrast, will only provide guidelines for the search for explanations. Neoclassical economics, for instance, uses *assumptions* to specify the relevant actors (firms and households), their preferences (to maximize profit, etc.), their perceptions (empirically accurate), and their modes of interaction (exchange at market prices between buyers and sellers, games against nature among sellers). For interaction-oriented policy research, however, I argued earlier that universalistic assumptions of this type would not be useful. Constellations are too variable and research interests too specific to benefit much from highly generalized proxies for empirical information.[2] And since policy research generally deals with few cases at a time, we also cannot profit from the speculation that assumptions, even if untrue in individual observations, may nevertheless define the central tendencies in large populations of similar cases (Friedman 1953).

The implication is that interaction-oriented policy research is more dependent on empirical data that must be collected specifically for each case than might be the case in neoclassical economics (or in the natural sciences for that matter). Worse yet, since actor-centered approaches must ultimately rest on intentional explanations that depend on the subjective preferences of specific actors and on their subjective perceptions of reality (Dennett 1981; Rosenberg 1988), the data required are not only hard to obtain but also may vary from one individual to another. The answer, however, cannot be total empiricism. To explain means to relate what appears puzzling to what is already known about the world—so if no relevant prior knowledge were available, we could only describe but not explain or predict. Hence it is also a function of our framework to point to bodies of pre-existing information that explanatory models could draw upon. Since these could not be provided by generalized and invariant assumptions, the framework of actor-centered institutionalism emphasizes the influence of institutions on the perceptions, preferences, and capabilities of individual and corporate actors and on the modes of their interaction.

## INSTITUTIONS, NOT ASSUMPTIONS, REDUCE EMPIRICAL VARIANCE

"Institution" is an ill-defined concept. Authors in the rational-choice tradition, among them Douglass North (1990) and Elinor Ostrom and associates (Ostrom/Gardner/Walker 1994), tend to focus narrowly on sanctioned rules that effectively change the costs and benefits that an actor can expect when following a certain course of action; others extend the meaning to include not only social norms and culturally stabilized systems of meaning but also social entities that are capable of purposive action (e.g., March/Olsen 1989). We prefer to reserve the latter meaning for terms like "organizations" or "corporate actors" and to restrict the concept of institution to systems of rules that structure the courses of actions that a set of actors may choose. In this definition we would, however, include not only formal legal rules that are sanctioned by the court system and the machinery of the state but also social norms that actors will generally respect and whose violation will be sanctioned by loss of reputation, social disapproval, withdrawal of cooperation and rewards, or even ostracism.

All of these definitions remain at an extremely high level of abstraction, which also is not significantly reduced by the introduction of functionally defined subcategories such as "boundary rules," "scope rules," "position rules," "information rules," and the like (Ostrom 1986; Ostrom/Gardner/Walker 1994). Inevitably such attempts at classification (including the efforts on which Harold Lasswell spent the latter part of his professional life [Lasswell/Kaplan 1950]) are overwhelmed by the variety of existing institutions. A complete systematization would have to account for the full range of legal rules—including public international law, conflict of law, the law of international organizations, national constitutional law, election law, parliamentary procedure, administrative law and administrative procedure, criminal law and criminal procedure, civil law and civil procedure, collective-bargaining law, labor law, company law, and so on—and it would also have to include the full range of informal rules, norms, conventions, and expectations that extend, complement, or modify the normative expectations derived from the "hard core" of formal legal rules. And even though they may be classified under abstract categories, the point remains that these rules are highly individualized *and that they produce causal effects only in their concrete shape.* The more abstract classifications, in other words, do not describe real phenomena, or aggregations of real phenomena, with properties of their own that can be expected to have explanatory power.

In our framework, therefore, the concept of the "institutional setting" does not have the status of a theoretically defined set of variables that could be systematized and operationalized to serve as explanatory factors in empirical research. Rather, we use it as a shorthand term to describe the most important influences on those factors that in fact drive our explanations—namely, actors with their orientations and capabilities, actor constellations, and modes of interaction.

For our purposes, institutions are the most important influences—and hence the most useful sources of information—on actors and interactions because, as I argued in Chapter 1, the actors themselves depend on socially constructed rules to orient their actions in otherwise chaotic social environments and because, if they in fact perform this function, these rules must be "common knowledge" among the actors and hence relatively accessible to researchers as well. Institutions have explanatory value because sanctioned rules will reduce the range of potential behavior by specifying required, prohibited, or permitted actions (Ostrom/Gardner/Walker 1994, 38). If the severity and certainty of sanctions is sufficient to render alternative courses prohibitively expensive, it may indeed be appropriate to say that, in game-theoretic terms, the set of feasible strategies is reduced to an institutionally defined subset. In the general case, however, it is more plausible to think that the positive and negative incentives attached to institutionalized rules will merely increase or decrease the payoffs associated with the use of particular strategies and hence their probability of being chosen by self-interested actors.

If nothing more were claimed for institutions, most rational-choice theorists would also qualify for membership in the institutionalist club. But institutionalism has more to offer. In policy research, we are dealing mainly with collective and corporate actors, such as political parties, labor unions, government ministries, central banks, or international organizations, rather than with individuals acting on their own account. These composite actors are institutionally constituted— meaning trivially that they were created according to preexisting rules and that they depend on rules for their continuing existence and operation. In a more profound sense, corporate and collective actors may be said to "exist" only to the extent that the individuals acting within and for them are able to coordinate their choices within a common frame of reference that is constituted by institutional rules. They define not only the membership of composite actors and the material and legal action resources they can draw upon, and thus the scope of their legitimate activities and the powers of the individuals who act for them, but also the purposes that they are to serve or the values that they are to consider in arriving at their choices. To a large extent, therefore, institutions not only facilitate and constrain a range of choices, but they also define how the outcomes achieved through such choices will be evaluated by the actors involved—and they will thus determine the preferences of these actors with regard to the feasible options.

Moreover, institutionalized responsibilities also influence perceptions. From organizational research we know that the departmental identity of actors shapes their "selective perception," not only by focusing attention on different phenom-

ena but by influencing views of the relative causal effectiveness of phenomena
that are jointly perceived (Dearborn/Simon 1958). A well-analyzed example was
the Cuban missile crisis, in which radically different interpretations of what was
going on and of what was the interest of the United States were explained by the
departmental identities of the participants (Allison 1971). Similarly, in the stagflation cases discussed in the Introduction it was clear that governments, independent central banks, and unions not only had different preferences but also focused their attention on different indicators of economic performance and
applied different causal interpretations to the phenomena that they did observe.
In game-theoretic terms, therefore, institutions not only constrain feasible strategies, but they also constitute the important players of the game and shape their
perceptions and valuations of outcomes in the payoff matrix. In short, the games
that are in fact being played in policy processes are to a large extent defined by institutions.[3]

Hence all variants of institutionalism rest on the assumption that the "rules
and systems of rules in any historically given society not only organize and regulate social behavior but make it understandable—and in a limited conditional
sense—predictable for those sharing in rule knowledge" (Burns/Baumgartner/
Deville 1985, 256). As I have tried to show in a previous article (Scharpf 1990),
this is an extremely important precondition of productive social interactions. If
actors did not know which options their interlocutors are considering and how
these interlocutors do in fact evaluate the outcomes that could be obtained
through interaction, they would be well advised to act on the basis of worst-case
scenarios and to resort to risk-minimizing "maximin" strategies. These are in fact
the strategies appropriate to constellations of pure zero-sum conflict, and if actors generally resorted to them in other constellations as well, all potential gains
from exchange and cooperation would be ignored and social production would
be reduced to zero. In other words, we owe the fact that societies are generally
productive and able to increase social welfare to the existence of mechanisms that
create relatively high degrees of mutual predictability or "common knowledge."
There are, as I have argued, several such mechanisms, but among them institutions are the most generalized, and the most public, sources of reliable information about the intentions we can expect, or not expect, from others.

At the individual level, moreover, it seems sufficient to conceptualize the effect
of norms by reference to the notion of a "social production function": Even if individuals were exclusively motivated by a desire to maximize physical well-being
and social approval (which is how Adam Smith defined self-interest), the proximate actions conducive to these ulterior goals would still be defined by the institutional settings within which they must pursue these selfish goals. Thus "to
maximize social approval, a judge must maximize justice" (Lindenberg 1989,
191) and, as I will argue at greater length in Chapter 8, to reduce the danger of
losing office, democratically accountable governments must attempt to adopt
public-interest–oriented policies.

From the perspective of empirical research, therefore, we will not gain much mileage from assumptions of self-interested action per se, but neither are we left with the unmanageable task of having to collect empirical data on the feasible options and the specific content of idiosyncratic perceptions and preferences in every case and for every actor. Instead, researchers can make use of the same institutional information that enables the actors themselves to interact with reasonable assurance that, by and large, they will know what is going on and what to expect of each other. Thus the fact that institutionalized expectations are able to create conditions of "common knowledge" is not only an essential precondition of productive social interactions, but it also reduces the information costs of empirical research. Once we know the institutional setting of interaction, we know a good deal about the actors involved, about their options, and about their perceptions and preferences. An institutionalist framework, in other words, provides a halfway position between a theoretical system that, like neoclassical economics, substitutes universal and standardized assumptions for empirical information on the one hand and purely descriptive studies of individual cases on the other. But two caveats are in order:

First, we must never forget that institutions vary cross-nationally and intertemporally. Parliamentary interactions in the U.S. Congress are worlds apart from interactions in the House of Commons; Swedish industrial relations differ in fundamental ways from British industrial relations (Crouch 1993); and Swedish industrial relations in the 1980s differed significantly from those in the 1960s (Scharpf 1991a). More generally, since institutions are themselves created and changed by human action—either through evolutionary processes of mutual adaptation (Schotter 1981) or through purposive design (Brennan/Buchanan 1985)—we have no reason to assume a convergence toward one "best" solution. Institutional development is path dependent in the sense that where you end up is strongly influenced by where you started from. Moreover, as economic historians have pointed out, mutual adaptation may "lock in" on any one of multiple equilibria, some of which may be Pareto-inefficient (a possibility for which the QWERTY layout of typewriter and computer keyboards has become the celebrated example [David 1985]), and the same may also be true of the purposeful choices of institutional engineering.

At any rate, once institutions are installed, and once actors have come to rely on their coordinating function, institutional change will be costly, and thus institutions are hard to reform or abolish, even if the circumstances that brought them about, and that may originally have justified them, no longer persist (Scharpf 1986). Thus in the absence of very rigorous selection mechanisms to weed out inferior solutions, institutional inertia tends to assure that, in general, "history is not efficient" (Etzioni 1988; March/Olsen 1989; Pierson 1996a; Hall/Taylor 1996). Within the present context, therefore, the implication is that empirical regularities that depend on the standardizing effects of institutions will not be universal but rather limited by time and place. Hence the substantive theories that could, at best, be generated within an institutionalist framework will necessarily have the character of "sometimes true theories" (Coleman 1964, 516; Stinchcombe 1968). They are able to explain outcomes within a given institutional setting but will not necessarily apply beyond its domain.

Second, we must remain aware of the fact that although institutions constitute composite actors, create and constrain options, and shape perceptions and preferences, they cannot influence choices and outcomes in a deterministic sense. Institutionalized rules, even if they are completely effective, will rarely prescribe one and only one course of action. Instead, by proscribing some and permitting other actions, they will define repertoires of more or less acceptable courses of action that will leave considerable scope for the strategic and tactical choices of purposeful actors.

Moreover, unlike the laws of nature, even binding rules may be violated by actors who are willing to pay the price of sanctions' being applied or who subjectively discount their incidence. More generally, the influence of institutions on perceptions and preferences, and hence on intentions, can never be complete. In modern societies the social backgrounds and socialization histories of individuals have become increasingly diverse, and explicit efforts to create organizational cultures that will "resocialize" individuals in the organizational mold are perhaps less a solution to than a symptom of the underlying heterogeneity. Moreover, it is well known that a change of incumbents in leading positions, even when they belong to the same political party, may have important effects on policy choices and outcomes. Thus a knowledge of institutions will tell us much about the options, perceptions, and preferences of given actors, but it certainly cannot tell us all.

Nevertheless, for many purposes institution-based information will be sufficient to derive satisfactory explanations, and it makes pragmatic sense to reduce levels of abstraction only gradually in the search for theoretical explanations (Lindenberg 1991). This implies that we should begin with institutional explanations and that we should search for information on more idiosyncratic factors only when the more parsimonious explanation fails. Thus it may be sufficient for some purposes to know whether monetary policy is under the control of an independent central bank or of an electorally accountable government, whereas for other purposes it may be necessary to investigate if and when monetary policymakers had become converted to Keynesian or monetarist perceptions of the role of macroeconomic policy (Hall 1989). Similarly, the search for specific forms of cognitive convergence or cognitive change—"groupthink" (Janis 1972), "advocacy coalitions" (Sabatier 1987), "epistemic communities" (Haas 1992), or "policy learning" (Jenkins-Smith/Sabatier 1993)—does have an important place in the institutionalist framework; but it seems pragmatically advisable to begin this methodologically very demanding (Axelrod 1976; Vowe 1993) search only when there are clear indications that the standard ascription of institutionally shaped perceptions and preferences will not provide satisfactory explanations.

However, access to information is only the first step in theory-oriented policy research. When we have the necessary information about initial conditions, we need to develop hypotheses about how these initial conditions could be transformed into the policy outcomes that are of interest. It is here that analytical models can be of great help—and it is here that the selection of appropriate models will make an important difference for the success or failure of empirical policy research. Since the framework that guides this selection is multidimensional and relatively complex, I will provide a brief overview in the following sections; the central elements will then be described in greater detail in subsequent chapters.

## THE BASIC EXPLANATORY FRAMEWORK

The primary business of interaction-oriented policy research within the framework of actor-centered institutionalism is to explain past policy choices and to produce systematic knowledge that may be useful for developing politically feasible policy recommendations or for designing institutions that will generally favor the formation and implementation of public-interest–oriented policy.[4] For that purpose, it is useful to remind ourselves of the linkage, discussed in the Introduction, between our own framework and the problem-oriented perspective of substantive policy analysis (see Figure 2.1).

### Actors

Within our framework, we need first to identify the set[5] of interactions that actually produces the policy outcomes that are to be explained. This set constitutes our unit of analysis. Only then can we identify the *actors,* individual and corporate, that are actually involved in the policy process and whose choices will ultimately determine the outcome. Actors are characterized by specific *capabilities,* specific *perceptions,* and specific *preferences.*

Capabilities must, of course, be defined relative to specific outcomes. The term is meant to describe all action resources that allow an actor to influence an outcome in certain respects and to a certain degree.[6] These include personal properties like physical strength, intelligence, or human and social capital (Coleman 1990, chapter 12); physical resources such as money or land or military power; technological capabilities; privileged access to information, and so on. What matters most in the context of policy research, however, are the action resources that are created by institutional rules defining competencies and granting or limiting rights of participation, of veto, or of autonomous decision in certain aspects of given policy processes.

Actors are further characterized by their specific action orientations. These characteristic perceptions and preferences may be relatively stable (as is assumed in rational-choice theories), or they may be changeable through learning and persuasion. At any rate, they will be activated and specified by the stimulus provided by a particular policy problem or issue, and they will refer to the desirable or undesirable nature of the status quo, to the causes of a perceived problem, to the efficacy and desirability of perceived courses of action, and to the outcomes

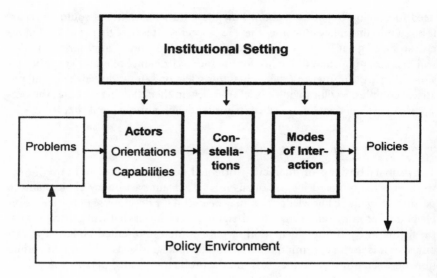

FIGURE 2.1    The domain of interaction-oriented policy research

associated with these. These orientations are also influenced by the institutional
setting. They will be discussed more fully in Chapter 3.

### Actor Constellations

If an actor were dealing exclusively with a natural or otherwise given environment,
then a complete description of that actor's perceptions, preferences, and capabilities would allow us to infer the course of action that is likely to be chosen—and a
complete description of the environment and its causal laws would allow us to
predict the outcome. However, as I said in the Introduction, it is unlikely that any
actor that is capable of unified action (a concept to be discussed in the next chapter) will be able to determine policy outcomes according to the actor's own perceptions and preferences and through the use of the actor's own capabilities. What
is determinative, rather, is the *constellation* among the plurality of actors that are
involved in policy interactions. The term needs some explanation, since it departs
from normal game-theoretic conventions. What is generally considered a "game"
must, in our terminology, be described by the combination of a specific "actor
constellation" and a specific "mode of interaction." This modular approach to
conceptualization seems useful because both aspects of the game can vary independently from one another, and both have explanatory power.

The *constellation* describes the players involved, their strategy options, the outcomes associated with strategy combinations, and the preferences of the players
over these outcomes. This description is fully represented by the game matrix. Thus

in the example discussed in the Introduction the actor constellations (involving governments and unions) are described by the matrices of the "monetarist" and "Keynesian" games in Figures I.1 and I.2, respectively. In the game-theoretic litera- ture, however, the constellations so described are usually associated with one spe- cific way in which the players are assumed to interact with one another—namely, in the mode of a "noncooperative game" in which all parties involved will choose their own strategies unilaterally. By contrast, our conceptualization assumes that in prin- ciple any given constellation could be played out in a variety of *modes of interac- tion*—not only as a "noncooperative game" but also as a "cooperative game" (when strategies are chosen by negotiated agreement) or as a "voting game" (when strate- gies are determined by majority rule) or as a "hierarchical game" (when the strate- gies of one or more actors can be determined by the unilateral choice of another actor). Conversely, of course, the modular approach also implies that any given mode of interaction (say, negotiated agreements) may be employed to deal with a great variety of actor constellations. In every case, the actual outcome will be af- fected by both constellations and modes, but useful knowledge can be accumulated and communicated by treating each dimension separately.

Within our framework, the concept of actor constellations serves two pur- poses. The game-theoretic representation allows us to describe and compare, at a very high level of abstraction but with great precision, extremely diverse real- world constellations. This descriptive language may allow us to discover empiri- cal regularities that otherwise might remain hidden under surface differences. Moreover, game-theoretic descriptions can be used to characterize different lev- els and types of conflict among the actors involved. Since political scientists have always thought that the level of conflict will affect the ability of political systems to attain satisfactory policy outcomes, having a more precise descriptive language will help us to formulate hypotheses about the demands that a particular policy issue is likely to place on the available capacities for conflict resolution. This might also allow us to respond to and reformulate Theodore Lowi's (1964) call for a political theory that will treat "policy" as an independent variable influenc- ing the types of "politics" that will be encountered.

What matters more in the present context is that the explicit conceptualization of actor constellations provides the crucial link between substantive policy analy- sis and interaction-oriented policy research. In principle we could take the prob- lem definitions and policy solutions produced by policy analysts and reclassify them in terms of their impact on the groups ultimately affected in a way that re- sembles our actor constellations.[7] A particular policy problem could then be de- scribed as a game of "pure coordination" or as a Prisoner's Dilemma game or as a game of "redistribution."[8] But it is important to realize that *these underlying prob- lem constellations are not the games that are being played in the policy process.* Pol- icy interactions do not usually take place among the members of the societal groups that are ultimately affected—even the electorate is different from the pop- ulation at large—but among specialized political actors. These may of course identify or sympathize to varying degrees with the groups directly affected, and they will themselves also be affected, directly and indirectly, by the policy problem in question, but *how* they are in fact affected will depend to a large degree on their institutional roles and their institutional self-interest.

Hence in order to link substantive policy analysis to interaction-oriented research, we need to *map the substantive policy problem onto the constellation of the policy actors involved.* This mapping will never be a perfect one-to-one representation, and the policy process will inevitably deal with problems that differ from the substantive problems at the societal level as they are defined by policy analysts or as they are experienced by the populations directly affected. In certain parliamentary settings, for instance, the class conflict between capital and labor may be treated as a coordination problem among coalition parties, whereas in others it will be acted out as a zero-sum conflict between the government and the opposition. Nevertheless, the normative expectation remains that policy processes should deal with the "real" problems of that society, and empirically there are also large differences in the degree to which policy processes do in fact "deviate" from their ascribed function.[9] As a consequence, interaction-oriented policy research also has an evaluative dimension in identifying systematic deviations and their causes and a prescriptive dimension in contributing to the design of deviation-reducing institutional arrangements.

### *Modes of Interaction*

Institutional design may influence the problem-solving effectiveness of policy processes through rules determining the constitution of actors and their institutional capabilities—which also affect their inclusion, and their strategic options, in the policy-relevant actor constellations. But the actor constellation still describes a static picture rather than the actual interactions producing policy outcomes. These can differ widely in character, and we describe these different *modes of interaction* by using the descriptors "unilateral action," "negotiated agreement," "majority vote," and "hierarchical direction." These will be discussed extensively in Chapters 5 through 8.

These modes of interaction are of course shaped by institutional rules regulating their use or perhaps, in the case of unilateral action, by the absence of such rules. However, the actual character of interactions is not only determined by specific rules defining, for instance, the formal steps that must be taken to reach a binding agreement or the procedures according to which issues can be brought to a vote. It is also affected by the larger institutional setting within which the interaction takes place. To describe these settings, I use the terms "anarchic fields and minimal institutions," "networks, regimes, and joint-decision systems," "associations, constituencies, and representative assemblies," and "hierarchical organizations and the state." These represent examples rather than analytical definitions. What they are meant to exemplify is the (bounded) variety of institutional arrangements that *minimally* permit a specific mode of interaction to be employed.

TABLE 2.1  Modes of Interaction

| | Institutional Setting | | | |
| --- | --- | --- | --- | --- |
| | Anarchic Field | Network | Association | Organization |
| Unilateral action | X | X | X | X |
| Negotiated agreement | (X) | X | X | X |
| Majority vote | – | – | X | X |
| Hierarchical direction | – | – | – | X |

The theoretical reason for using this seemingly convoluted approach to definition is reflected in Table 2.1. It is assumed that modes of interaction differ in their demands on the institutional capacity for conflict resolution and that institutional structures differ in their capacity to support different modes of interaction. Thus unilateral action could occur in the absence of any institutional structure, negotiations depend on structures assuring the binding character of agreements, and decisions by majority vote or by hierarchical direction depend on much more specific and demanding institutional arrangements. This suggests the idea of a possibility frontier, where the institutional setting constrains the modes of interaction that can be employed. Hierarchical settings are able to support all varieties of modes of interaction, whereas a self-organizing network could support neither the exercise of hierarchical authority nor decisions taken by majority vote.

What is more interesting, from a theoretical point of view, is the possibility that modes of interaction will change their character—and their capacity for the resolution of policy problems—from one structural setting to another. Take "negotiations" as an example: In the context of "minimal institutions" (meaning protection of property rights and the possibility of judicially enforced contracts), their problem-solving capacity will be very limited, whereas the existence of ongoing "network" relationships among the contracting parties will allow more demanding agreements to be reached. The situation changes again if negotiations occur "in the shadow of the majority vote" or "in the shadow of hierarchy," where one side could unilaterally impose its preferred solution if the attempt to reach a negotiated agreement should fail (Scharpf 1994). These implications will be further explored in Chapters 5 through 9.

### Actor Constellations and Modes of Interaction

If we now bring information about modes of interaction together with the discussion of actor constellations in the previous section, we have the beginnings of a conceptual scheme that allows us to discuss the capacity of given systems of policy interactions for dealing with given types of policy problems. It involves three steps. First, we must in fact be able to map the problem identified by substantive policy analyses into actor constellations among the actors actually involved in policy processes. In the example presented in the Introduction, that was done by translating the economic analysis of stagflation problems into "strategies" under the control of "unions" and "governments" and identifying the "payoffs" that each of these actors was likely to associate with the outcomes attainable by the respective combinations of union and government strategies.

This mapping will give us a highly abstract but at the same time very precise representation of the ways in which the actors involved diverge or converge in their preferences over the range of feasible outcomes. Thus, in the example, the game played between the unions and a monetarist government (Figure I.1) was characterized by more divergent preferences than the Keynesian game (Figure I.2). By itself, however, the level of conflict (however measured) that is inherent in a given actor constellation will not yet allow us to predict or explain either the difficulties of conflict resolution or the outcome that is likely to be reached. In order to do so, we would also need to take account of the mode of interaction among the parties involved.

In the example, I had assumed that interactions between the monetarist government and the unions were conducted in the mode of unilateral action, in which both sides would choose their strategies independently. Under those conditions the policy problem was resolved quasi-automatically in the government's favor, and to the unions' great disadvantage, by a convergence on the noncooperative "equilibrium" outcome in the lower-left cell of the matrix. But assume for a moment that the coordination between wage policy and government fiscal and monetary policy would need to be achieved by negotiated agreement (as was true in Britain during the short period of the "social compact" and as was generally true in Austria). In that case, an outcome in the lower-left cell of Figure I.1 would not have found the agreement of the unions, and the most likely compromise solution would then be located in the upper-left cell. The outcome would again have been different, at least in the Keynesian constellation, if the government had possessed the capability hierarchically to impose wage and price controls. In other words, for a given actor constellation, the expected policy outcome would differ if the institutionalized mode of interaction is varied—and conversely, a given mode of interaction would lead to effective policy solutions for some constellations but may fail to do so when confronted with other types of actor constellations.

The example is meant to illustrate the explanatory potential that we associate with actor-centered institutionalism: By systematically combining analyses of actor constellations with the analysis of modes of interaction, we will have extremely powerful tools for explaining the outcomes of specific policy interactions. Moreover, and even more immodestly, we expect that the same tools will also enable us to arrive at more general, and pragmatically useful, conclusions about the capacity of different types of institutional structures to deal effectively with different types of policy problems. These are large claims that can only be justified through the successful explanation of important puzzles in empirical policy research. The present book is not intended to do this. Its main concern is the presentation and explication of the tools that could be used in such work.

## NOTES

1. Burns et al. (1985, 7) appropriately characterize the integrative intent of their own approach by opposing it to James S. Duesenberry's famous quip that "economics is all about how people make choices. Sociology is about why they don't have any choices to make."

2. The neorealist theory of international relations, it is true, also tries to get much mileage out of assumptions specifying the relevant actors (nation-states), their preferences (to maximize relative gains in the balance of power), their perceptions (empirically accurate), and their mode of interaction (noncooperative games). It is clear that these assumptions, if generally correct, would greatly reduce the need for empirical data—but it has also been pointed out that empirical research has mainly found them to be very poor predictors (Moravcsik 1992 and the studies cited there).

3. There is a philosophically and psychologically important debate on whether these beneficial effects should be conceptualized as external constraints (or negative and positive incentives) that do not affect the intrinsic preferences of self-interest-maximizing actors, or whether norms and values should be construed as a type of actor orientation that is logically distinct from self-interest (Elster 1991)—with the implication that the intrinsic preferences of individuals may be transformed by the socialization effect of institutions. Freud (1915), for instance, distinguished sharply between the control of egotistic drives through positive and negative incentives (which would cease to be effective when controls are removed), and their "civilization" through the internalization of cultural norms. However, since we are not primarily concerned with individual action but rather with collective and corporate actors, whose goals can clearly be shaped by the rules that constitute them, the resolution of this dispute one way or another is not of paramount importance for policy research.

4. By contrast, we should not claim the ability to predict policy outcomes. Given the pervasiveness of "Cournot effects" (i.e., the accidental intersection of unrelated chains of causation) in social and political interactions (Lübbe 1975; Boudon 1984; Mayntz 1995), even theoretically well-founded predictions may turn out to be wrong—which does not invalidate the usefulness of the same knowledge for design purposes.

5. The plural form is used to indicate that there will often be separate interactions, such as voting in two chambers of a legislature, linked through negotiations in a conference committee, that produce the outcome.

6. This includes the ability of ego, who has control over outcomes that are of interest to alter, to influence alter, who in turn has control over the outcome that is of interest to ego. That is the essence of Coleman's concept of a political exchange (1990, chap. 6), which has strongly influenced the research on policy networks.

7. It has also been suggested that Theodore Lowi's suggestive typology of distributive, regulatory, and redistributive policies could be reformulated in terms of different types of

game constellations (Kellow 1988; Lowi 1988; Heckathorn/Maser 1990; H. Miller 1990). From the present perspective, what remains unclear is whether the reference is to constellations of societal interests or to constellations among actors directly involved in policy processes.

8. These characterizations are extremely useful for identifying those problems that are *not* likely to be dealt with effectively through the evolution of a Hayekian *spontaneous order* or through the *market* (defined by voluntary agreements under conditions of minimal institutions). In that sense they do, or they should, play a crucial role in substantive policy research.

9. Thus we do not start from the assumption, radicalized in Niklas Luhmann's theory of social systems, that the political system can, in any case, only solve its own political problems (Luhmann 1984; 1986).

# 3

# *Actors*

In the framework of actor-centered institutionalism, actors are characterized by their orientations (perceptions and preferences) and by their capabilities. What I have to say on the aspect of capabilities in this book can be extremely brief: They are obviously critical to any explanation of policy outcomes since, in the absence of action resources, even the most enlightened perceptions and preferences will fail to make a practical difference. From a theoretical point of view, however, capabilities appear to be highly contingent. On the one hand, policy actors may, under certain circumstances, benefit from employing any and all of the eight Lasswellian "values" (Lasswell/Kaplan 1950), from "wealth" and "power" all the way to a reputation for "rectitude," as action resources and instruments of political influence.[1] But which of them will be effective under which conditions depends so much on the specifics of the case and on situational factors that nothing worthwhile could be said in the context of a general framework.[2] On the other hand, in institutionalized interactions, at least some of the prepolitical endowments that actors may have are neutralized or superseded by the assignment of institutionalized competencies and veto rights. Thus the allocation of political power through general elections on the basis of equal votes will at least reduce some of the preexisting power differences in society, and the creation of a specialized agency within the machinery of the state may significantly increase the power resources of otherwise politically impotent groups. These institutional aspects are of course of central concern within the framework of actor-centered institutionalism, and they will be discussed throughout this book, but it does not seem useful to attempt a general classification here.

What need to be discussed under general aspects, however, are the conditions under which it is appropriate to apply actor-centered concepts to units that include several or many human beings. The issue is of no concern either to micro-level rational-choice theorists, who are firmly committed to the principles of methodological individualism, or to macro-level systems theorists, who can only ridicule the pretensions of actor-centered approaches that would need to account for "the billions of simultaneously acting actors" (Luhmann 1988a, 132). In actor-centered institutionalism, however, the question is of crucial interest. This discussion will be taken up first, after which I will explain the categories that we use to describe the perceptions and preferences of individual or composite actors.

## INDIVIDUALS AND COMPOSITE ACTORS

Although it is a truism raised to the status of a dogma by methodological individualism that in the final analysis only individuals can act, we know that, in law and in fact, individuals will often act in the name of and in the interest of another person, a larger group, or an organization. In Chapter 2, I simply assumed that it is empirically meaningful to treat aggregates of individuals as composite actors and to explain policy outcomes in terms of their preferences and strategy choices. The following sections will now explore the conditions under which these assumptions may or may not be empirically useful. In doing so, however, it will be necessary to deal with the two-level character of any conceptualization of actors above the level of individuals. When it is not used merely as a figure of speech, the notion of a composite actor implies a capacity for intentional action at a level above the individuals involved. However, since indeed only individuals are capable of having intentions, the capacity to act at the higher level(s)[3] must be produced by internal interactions. This implies that in principle the same empirical phenomenon must be analyzed from two perspectives: from the outside, as it were, as a composite actor with certain resources and a greater or lesser capacity for employing these resources in strategic action; and from the inside, as an institutional structure within which internal actors interact to produce the actions ascribed to the composite actor. For our purposes, this means that the concepts and hypotheses developed for the analysis of external interactions can in principle also be applied at the level of internal interactions within composite actors. This assures a greater conceptual unity within our approach.

The concept of composite actor would be pragmatically useless, however, and critics would be justified in denying that actor-centered approaches could have a place in social science theory above the micro level, if it were necessary to extend analyses to the level of internal interactions in every study. Indeed, the viability of actor-centered institutionalism as an empirical research program depends crucially on the assumption that the "architecture of complexity" (Simon 1962) of real-world interactions will allow us to treat larger units as actors whose choices may be explained in terms of factors defined at the level of the larger unit.

But what is implied if we treat an aggregate of persons as a composite actor? The answer depends on the purposes of the analysis. If the issue is the ability to conclude legally binding contracts, the law defines the types of "juristic persons" that are invested with the capacity to own and to alienate property rights, and it also defines which individuals, under which conditions, have the capacity to act in a legally binding way for a given unit and which acts, however performed, are to be attributed to which legal unit. In institutionalist social science research, we have good reason to take notice of these legal ground rules. However, they do not define our own research interests.

For us, the important implication is that we need to make use of composite-actor concepts in order to facilitate the task of explaining and predicting policy outcomes in actor-theoretic terms. In this we must remain alert to the fact that the collective units we may observe vary enormously in the degree of their integration and hence in the degree to which valid explanations may actually be decoupled from information about micro-level actors and their interactions. Appropriate distinctions will be introduced later. But even where decoupling is not appropriate, so that explanations must be based exclusively on information about micro-level choices, these choices may be similar enough to allow us to treat aggregates of individuals as a unit (even though not as a composite actor) in meso- or macro-level analyses. I begin with a discussion of this latter possibility.

### Actor Aggregates and Autodynamic Coordination

It is a common and entirely legitimate practice, in everyday parlance as well as in scientific analyses, to use *aggregate* categories for describing the parallel actions of populations of individuals who share certain salient characteristics. Thus it may be allowable to speak of "the farm vote" in discussions of U.S. presidential elections or of the risk of "capital flight" in a discussion of tax legislation. In this use of quasi groups or classes as shorthand descriptors for the choices of large numbers of individuals the explanation rests entirely on individual-level information about the preferences and the situational conditions of the microactors involved, and the more simple aggregate description is justified exclusively by the assumed empirical similarity among individual choices.

But the micro-macro link may also be more complex than a mere aggregation and thus theoretically more interesting. This is true in populations of actors who are not necessarily similar in their characteristics or preferences but whose utility functions are interdependent in such a way that certain acts by some will increase or decrease the likelihood that others will act in the same way. Examples include bandwagon effects in election campaigns, "bull" and "bear" phases or "bubbles" and "crashes" on the stock exchange, "pig cycles" of overproduction and shortage in agricultural markets, or fashions and fads in consumer behavior. The underlying mechanisms at the micro level can be described as forms of circular stimulation generating *autodynamic* processes that, at the aggregate level, will result in positive or negative feedback effects that may lead to upward or downward spirals or cyclical fluctuations of certain phenomena (Maruyama 1963; Masuch 1985; Mayntz/Nedelmann 1987; Tsebelis/Sprague 1989).

When preferences or the external conditions facing each actor are differentiated within a given population, the aggregate behavior may also be characterized by *threshold effects*, where the number of individuals who are more easily provoked to action must reach a certain minimum before the more resistant (or more fearful) members of the population will also respond (Granovetter 1978). This is a model that seems particularly appropriate for the explanation of revolutions or of the downfall of seemingly stable dictatorships.[4] Since the similarity of the actions of a great number of individual actors rests not merely on the initial similarity of their characteristics but is also reinforced through the feedback mechanisms, autodynamic coordination may achieve a much higher degree of coherence, and a greater persistence and dynamism, than could be expected from the mere aggregation of the action tendencies of similarly inclined individuals who are acting in isolation from one another. However, while the explanatory mechanism makes use of structural information about relationships among individuals and about the distribution of preferences within the population, it still remains true that only individual actors are considered and that these are assumed to be acting only from their individual action perspectives and with regard to their own expected payoffs. The aggregate effect is then a result of individual choices, but it is not itself an object of anyone's purposeful choice. In game-theoretic analyses, therefore, one should avoid ascribing strategic choices to actor aggregates such as "voters" or "peasants" or "urban dwellers." Nevertheless, they could be modeled as responding in a predictable fashion to the moves of (individual or composite) actors that are capable of strategic action.

### Collective and Corporate Actors

The term "composite actor" will thus be reserved to constellations in which the "intent" of intentional action refers to the joint effect of coordinated action expected by the participating individuals. In other words, the use of actor-theoretic concepts above the individual level presupposes that the individuals involved intend to create a joint product or to achieve a common purpose. Mere exchange relationships would not qualify, but a joint venture could. Beyond that definitional minimum, however, the degree of integration varies greatly among different types of composite actors. I find it useful to work with a further distinction between "collective actors" that are dependent on and guided by the preferences of their members and "corporate actors" that have a high degree of autonomy from the ultimate beneficiaries of their action and whose activities are carried out by staff members whose own private preferences are supposed to be neutralized by employment contracts (Coleman 1974; Mayntz 1986).

For collective actors, further distinctions may be characterized in two dimensions. The first describes the degree to which critical action resources are either held and controlled individually by the members or have been "collectivized" and are controlled at the level of the collective actor. An important empirical indicator is the existence of a staff and its relative importance for carrying out the activities of the collective actor. The second dimension reflects the fact that unlike individual or corporate actors, collective actors are not autonomous in the choice of the preferences that guide their actions but rather are dependent on the prefer-

**Reference of Action Orientations**

|  | | separate purposes | collective purpose |
|---|---|---|---|
| **Control over Action Resources** | separate | Coalition | Movement |
| | collective | Club | Association |

FIGURE 3.1    Types of collective actors

ences of their members. These, however, may either be related to the separate goals of these members or refer to purposes that can only be defined at the level of the collective.[5] Thus a logrolling agreement between two groups of senators in the U.S. Congress would further the separate purposes of both groups, whereas members of the "pro-life" movement must work for a common purpose. The resultant typology includes "coalitions," "movements," "clubs," and "associations" (Figure 3.1).

*Coalitions* are here defined as semipermanent arrangements among actors pursuing separate but, by and large, convergent or compatible purposes and using their separate action resources in coordinated strategies. Usually exit remains possible. Though the joint effect of concerted action is actively sought, the evaluation of common strategies is oriented to the individual utility of each of the component actors involved. In principle, therefore, coalitions must act by agreement, and they will be able to agree only on strategies that are perceived as furthering the separate self-interest of all members at the same time. Nevertheless, the longer-term advantages of membership in a given coalition may facilitate agreement to individual decisions that, when viewed in isolation, are unattractive to some members. In any case, however, though courses of action are chosen by the coalition as a whole, their effective implementation will depend on decisions made individually since critical action resources are held by coalition members individually.

*Movements* also depend entirely on the voluntary cooperation of their members, but they differ from coalitions in two important respects. On the one hand, their membership is typically so large and dispersed that coordination by negotiated agreement or even by voting may be a practical impossibility. On the other hand, the members of a movement typically share a moral or ideological commitment to a collective goal that may be pursued even at great sacrifices to individual members. However, as in coalitions, there is no institutionalized leadership structure,[6] and though a high degree of consensus may be achieved through public discussion about alternative courses of action, critical action resources—

in particular the active physical participation in collective action—remain under individual control. The implication is that movements may be able to coordinate on relatively simple, straightforward strategies but are at a disadvantage when confronted by an opponent with greater strategic flexibility—as was true when the triumph of the Paris Commune was turned into defeat by initially much weaker government forces (Haffner 1987).

*Clubs* share some of the features of coalitions, but they also benefit from the advantages of collectivized action resources. On the one hand, members of a club, like members of a coalition, are assumed to be motivated by individual self-interest and to evaluate the actions of the club in these terms; moreover, membership is voluntary and exit is generally not associated with high costs. On the other hand, membership typically implies regular contributions to a pool of collective resources, and it may also imply reliance on staff services for the provision of club goods. The necessary complement is a formalized decision structure, in which the competence to decide on the use of these collectivized resources is transferred from individual members acting individually to collective decision processes. Characteristic examples are private-interest organizations as well as international organizations of a service character (e.g., the OECD) with a "secretariat" and a central budget from which the actions that are in fact undertaken are financed.

*Associations,* finally, are integrated in both dimensions (Streeck/Schmitter 1985). Critical action resources are collectively held,[7] and choices are evaluated by reference to preferences defined at the level of the collective actor—and they may include a preference to influence and control the behavior of members. Membership may be voluntary or compulsory (as is true of some "corporatist" professional organizations). Nevertheless, associations are normatively defined as "bottom-up" organizations intended to serve the preferences of their members, who, in the language of principal-agent theory, are in the position of "principals," while the leadership and central staffs are treated as their "agents." In that spirit, not only are leaders supposed to be directly or indirectly accountable to the members, but also member preferences, where they are expressed, are expected to override the preferences of the leadership. However, most action resources are held by the association as such, and de facto control over their deployment rests with the leadership.

"Corporate actors," by contrast, are typically "top-down" organizations under the control of an "owner" or of a hierarchical leadership representing the owners or beneficiaries. Even if they have "members" in the formal sense, these members are not actively involved in defining the corporate actors' course of action but rather have at most the collective power to select and replace the leaders. At any rate, strategy choices are decoupled from the preferences of the membership. Moreover, they are also supposed to be decoupled from the private preferences of the bureaucratic staff that participates in preparing these choices and that must implement them. These staffs are expected to follow the rules adopted by central decision processes and the hierarchical directives of the leadership. Their own private interests are supposed to be neutralized by the employment relationship

TABLE 3.1 Overview: Aggregate, Collective, and Corporate Actors

| | Aggregate Actors | Collective Actors | | | | Corporate Actors |
|---|---|---|---|---|---|---|
| | | *Coalition* | *Club* | *Movement* | *Association* | |
| Action | Individual | Joint | Joint | Joint | Joint | Organization |
| Purpose | Individual | Individual | Individual | Collective | Collective | Organization |
| Resources | Individual | Individual | Collective | Individual | Collective | Organization |
| Decisions | Individual | Agreement | Voting | Consensus | Voting | Hierarchical |

(March/Simon 1958). The overall pattern of aggregate-, collective-, and corporate-actor characteristics is summarized in Table 3.1.

Corporate actors may thus achieve identities, purposes, and capabilities that are autonomous from the interests and preferences of the populations they affect and are supposed to serve. On the positive side, this allows a degree of effectiveness and efficiency that collective actors depending immediately on membership preferences could not achieve. On the negative side, the ever-increasing domination of the modern world by huge, powerful, and often nonaccountable corporate actors is indeed a nightmare vision for normative social and political theory (Coleman 1974; 1986). It is necessary to point out, however, that the distinction between collective actors and corporate actors is of an analytical character and that intermediate forms are empirically quite frequent.

Even more important from a theoretical and practical point of view are solutions that separately institutionalize structures of collective and corporate actors and combine these to serve complementary purposes. This provides opportunities to optimize both the membership-oriented accountability of the collective actor and the superior effectiveness and efficiency of the corporate actor. The primary example is of course the democratic state, which uses the associative structures of popular elections, party competition, and parliamentary responsibility of ministers to control the power of the bureaucratic machinery—which, however, is largely immunized against immediate interventions from political processes in its day-to-day operations. In a different model, the European Union combines the structure of an intergovernmental "club," whose central institution is the Council of Ministers, with the corporate-actor capabilities of the European Commission (Schneider/Werle 1990). Similar combinations are characteristic of many associations. In the typical case the associative structure will legitimate and control a top leadership, which in turn is expected to direct and control a bureaucratic staff. The bureaucratic organization itself is, on the one hand, the major action resource of the association, but on the other hand, it is also the most powerful instrument through which leaders are potentially able to control and exploit the association and its members. These are themes to which I will return later.

Empirically, to repeat, there are no sharp dividing lines separating the analytically defined categories of corporate and collective actors or the different types of collective actors. Nevertheless, these distinctions are useful for alerting us to the fact that the degree of integration of composite actors varies widely and that it is necessary in each instance to identify the conditions that may justify the simplifying assumption that a plurality of individuals could be treated, for certain purposes, as a unit actor.

## The Capacity for Strategic Action

It is still necessary, however, to identify more precisely the conditions under which actor-theoretic explanations can in fact be applied to composite actors. The ideal individual actor of rational-choice models is assumed to have the capacity for strategic action—which is to say that on the basis of accurate perceptions and adequate information-processing capacity, he or she is able to respond to the risks and opportunities inherent in a given actor constellation by selecting the strategies that will maximize his or her expected total utility. Clearly, if this model—or a "boundedly rational" version of this model—is to be applied to composite actors, its cognitive as well as its evaluative mechanisms must be respecified before they can be meaningfully employed.

In the *cognitive* dimension, composite actors depend on interpersonal information processing and communication. Strategic capacity is low if the individual members, or the subgroups, of a collective are committed to divergent or even incommensurable cognitive maps, and it increases as the worldviews and causal theories of relevant subgroups converge on common—and empirically true—interpretations of a given situation and of the options and constraints inherent in it. The preconditions, risks, and benefits of cognitive convergence are discussed in the literature on "groupthink" (Janis 1972), "advocacy coalitions" (Sabatier 1987; Sabatier/Jenkins-Smith 1993), and "epistemic communities" (Haas 1992), but the methodological difficulties of measuring the degree of convergence or divergence of the "cognitive maps" of individual and composite actors should not be underestimated (Axelrod 1976).

In the *evaluative* dimension, the capacity for strategic action presupposes the integration of preferences. In general terms, this implies a capacity to accept some losses in order to obtain larger overall gains (or to avoid larger overall losses). Integration has an intertemporal, an intersectoral, and an interpersonal dimension—the ability to forgo present satisfaction for future gain; the ability to trade one type of interest for another that is considered more important; and the ability to sacrifice the interests of some members for the greater benefit of the collectivity. Though these three aspects of strategic capacity are conceptually distinct, they all assume an interpersonal character when we are dealing with composite actors whose members may be affected differently by, and have different preferences with regard to, any given set of alternative courses of action.

We can thus conclude that the capacity for strategic action depends, on the one hand, on the preexisting convergence or divergence of (policy-relevant) perceptions and preferences among the (policy-relevant) members of the composite actor and, on the other hand, on the capacity for conflict resolution within the collective unit. Since differences in perceptions as well as differences in evaluative criteria will ultimately lead to differing preferences regarding the available courses of action, both can be represented by the conceptual tools discussed in Chapter 4, Actor Constellations.

At a given level of conflict, the strategic capacity of composite actors then depends on institutional conditions facilitating internal conflict resolution. These conditions are largely defined by the modes of interaction that will be discussed in subsequent chapters. Composite actors that must resolve internal conflict through negotiated agreement have a lower capacity for conflict resolution than actors that are able to resort to majority votes or to hierarchical decisions in the face of continuing disagreement. But one caveat is in order: Majority votes or hierarchical decisions may be highly effective in facilitating action in the face of conflicting preferences, but they may have disastrous consequences if they are used to settle cognitive conflicts based on different sources of information or divergent cause-and-effect hypotheses. Hence, since actual cases will vary in the divergence of either cognitions or preferences, we cannot generally ascribe greater or lesser strategic capacity to a particular type of structure.

Moreover, we also have to expect a tendency of empirical matching that reduces visible discrepancies between demands on conflict resolution and available capacities. Coalitions, for instance, are unlikely to form in the first place unless the participating actors are convinced that they have sufficiently convergent interests to make joint action an attractive prospect for all of them. When that is true, the transaction costs associated with internal negotiations may be low enough to permit the coalition to be a fully effective strategic actor toward the outside world. This, of course, does not rule out the possibility that an existing coalition may unexpectedly find itself confronted with an issue in which the interests of its members diverge to such a degree that the weak capacities for conflict resolution are overtaxed. But this is not the typical case, for then the coalition would not exist. Similarly, social and political movements have extremely weak capacities for conflict resolution, but they nevertheless may be able to achieve a considerable degree of strategic capability since the cognitions and preferences of their members are likely to converge on the basis of strong ideological commitments. By contrast, organizations with strong majoritarian or hierarchical capacities for conflict resolution, such as British political parties, may find themselves dealing with issues involving highly conflicting preferences (which other organizations would never be able to tackle in the first place).

Empirically, we are therefore likely to find composite actors that are by and large capable of strategic action in those areas in which they are routinely engaged—which implies that differences in strategic capability would show up primarily when existing collective actors are confronted with novel problem situations that cannot be handled successfully within the existing repertoire of strategies. Thus, in the example discussed in the Introduction, it took the oil-price shock of the early 1970s to expose characteristic strengths and weaknesses in the strategic capacity of Austrian, British, German, and Swedish unions, which previously had seemed about equally competent in dealing with their given environments (Scharpf 1991a). Within our approach these differences in strategic capability are to be explained by institutional factors shaping the internal interactions within given collective actors. Since they are analytically congruent to the factors affecting external interactions that will be the subject of the following chapters, I will not discuss them further at this point. Instead, I now turn to the question of how we propose to deal with the fact that actor-centered explanations must necessarily refer to subjective states of mind that are not immediately accessible to empirical research.

## ACTOR ORIENTATIONS

The major difficulty with actor-centered approaches is that they must, at bottom, rely on intentional explanations that are inevitably based on subjectivities (Dennett 1981; Rosenberg 1988). It is not in the real world but in the actor's mental image of the world that the attribution of causes and expected effects must be located; and actions are motivated not by actors' objective interests but by their subjective preferences. Moreover, for the reasons discussed in Chapter 1, we cannot simply stipulate invariant perceptions and preferences.

Since subjective action orientations cannot be directly observed, researchers will be tempted to infer them from the courses of action that are in fact chosen— a temptation that is dignified in economics by the concept of "revealed preferences." But whatever may be its status in economic theory (Sen 1977; 1986), if used as a methodological precept in empirical policy research, it could produce only tautologies instead of explanations.[8] Sometimes, in retrospective research, it may be possible to reconstruct the effective action orientations from contemporary documents or from a battery of interviews with participants. However, the reliable reconstruction of subjectivities is an extremely difficult and work-intensive task in empirical research (Vowe 1993); hence we again try to get as far as possible with simplifying, and generally institution-based, assumptions. In doing so, we benefit from disaggregating the complex notion of action orientations into its simpler component parts, which will be easier to link to institutionally determined or empirically observable indicators.

### Unit of Reference

Though it remains true that in the final analysis only individuals are capable of purposive action, the world of empirical policy research is populated by collective actors of all types and in particular by corporate actors. The apparent contradiction is resolved by the fact that individuals will not always act on their own behalf but may act in a representative capacity and that they have the ability to identify with and to act from the perspective of larger units—a family, a group, a nation, and above all, organizations of all kinds, including firms, labor unions, political parties, government ministries, and the state. From our point of view, therefore, the perennial controversy in political science about whether "the state" should be considered a meaningful concept resolves itself into an empirical question: The concept is useful to the extent that there are actors for whose orientation the state is the critical unit of reference.

For policy research, this implies that we need to relate individual behavior—which is all that we are able to observe empirically—to the appropriate (individual or social) unit of reference on whose behalf action is taken and from whose perspective intentional choices can be explained. In general, it is not difficult to do so, since we will typically be able to infer the appropriate reference unit from the social role that the individual in question is performing. Role positions are associated with role-specific norms and expectations, which will also define the social unit that is to be served by role-specific actions. At the same time, the willingness of individuals to assume such roles is generally assured through benefits of membership, of position, and of career opportunities that could not otherwise be obtained. At any rate, once a role is taken, expectations are generally supported by effective sanctions, ranging from social disapproval to exclusion and criminal prosecution. In most cases, therefore, individual self-interest as such would not be a useful predictor of role-related action; rather, what matters are the normative expectations addressed to specific roles and, above all, perceptions and preferences derived from the perspective of the social unit on whose behalf the action is performed. Thus, knowing that a particular individual acts as the president of the central bank and another as the chairman of the metal workers' union will already tell us much about the positions that they are likely to take when invited to a session of the "concerted action." Information about role-specific orientations is of course much more readily available than information about the idiosyncratic orientations of individuals.

Nevertheless, we need to remain alert to two difficulties. Individuals will often assume several roles on behalf of different reference units. Normally they will be able to keep the actions associated with these different roles separate from one another, as when the chief executive officer of a large corporation also serves on the board of governors of a private university. But there will also be situations in which the choice of one course of action will necessarily (and legitimately) be evaluated from the perspective of more than one reference unit. These evaluations will not necessarily lead to the same conclusion. One example is provided by the dual roles of members of the *Bundesrat* in German federalism (Scharpf 1995). As ministers or prime ministers of a federal state, they are supposed to serve the interests of their respective states; as party leaders, however, they are expected to maximize the electoral prospects and support the policy positions of their respective national parties. These role conflicts are particularly acute when the opposition at the national level holds a majority of seats in the *Bundesrat*. Under these conditions of "divided government," the opposition will often try to block the passage of government initiatives, whereas the interest of the states may be better served by financially attractive compromises than by visible policy failures. Similarly, state governments under the control of parties that form the federal government are also exposed to the conflicting expectations of party-political support for national policy initiatives and of defending the self-interest of their respective states. When these obligations interact, as they did in negotiations over the financial adjustments necessitated by German unification, the outcome may be impossible to predict, and any ex post facto explanation will need to disentangle these partly symbiotic, partly conflicting action perspectives (Renzsch 1994).

Moreover, we also must remain alert to the possibility that individual self-interest, or the idiosyncratic orientations of individuals (which are never quite absent in any case), may in fact become so important in the case at hand that our explanations will fail if we do not take them into account. This is most likely to be true in leadership positions that are less constrained by institutionalized routines, controls, and sanctions than other organizational roles.[9] Thus we have no theoretical scruples in acknowledging the possibility that the personal visions of Charles de Gaulle or Margaret Thatcher may need to be treated as important factors in theory-oriented policy research. However, according to Lindenberg's (1991) pragmatic maxim of "declining levels of abstraction" cited earlier, we try to get as much mileage as possible from the more easily available institutional information before we resort to an investigation of more idiosyncratic orientations.

### Cognitive Orientations

With regard to *cognitive orientations,* we generally start from the working hypothesis that actors' perceptions of directly observable facts will be empirically correct and that their hypotheses about what they cannot observe as well as about causal linkages will be shaped by theories prevailing at the particular time and in the particular institutional setting (Goldstein/Keohane 1993). Thus, unlike in neoclassical economics, we do not assume omniscient actors that are fully informed about the state of the world plus all objectively available options. We merely expect that the specific combinations of knowledge and ignorance tend to be shared among actors in institutionalized interactions—and that, for the same reason, they will be accessible to researchers as well. We depart from these assumptions of shared knowledge and ignorance only when we have specific reason to think that different actors were interpreting observable facts by applying different theories that would lead them to different strategic choices.

However, our central focus on the problem-solving capacity of policy processes must make us particularly sensitive to variations in the empirical validity of the perceptions and of the cause-effect hypotheses on the basis of which action is in fact taken. For our explanations it is of the greatest empirical interest whether and how perceptions depart from the best available knowledge (which will often be available only in hindsight). In particular, we need to ascertain to what extent the available courses of action, their likely outcomes, and their impacts on the respective preferences are correctly perceived. If freedom is defined as a perception of options among which choice is possible (Luhmann 1995), its range is restricted if available options are unknown. Even more important, in multiactor constellations, the compatibility or incompatibility of preferences, and hence the level of conflict, depends critically on the available options. In many highly conflictual negotiation situations the discovery of previously unknown "win-win solutions" may make all the difference between a policy impasse and effective action (Pruitt 1981; Thompson 1992). Hence learning processes must necessarily have an important place in our conceptualization of actor perceptions (Argyris/Schoen 1978; Macy 1989; Selten 1991).

Even then, however, we tend to downplay the importance of idiosyncratic perceptions in favor of working hypotheses that start from the assumption that policy-oriented learning, even if not diffused universally, is nevertheless likely to be shared in identifiable subsets of actors that can be characterized as "advocacy coalitions" (Sabatier 1987) or "epistemic communities" (Haas 1992). Within these subsets of actors, collective learning implies communication and often public debate. Thus even if we take policy learning into account, the difficulties of empirical research may be manageable, since the interpretative theories on which strategy choices are based are likely to be a matter of public record, at least for those actors who are required to justify their choices in public hearings, in parliamentary debates, in reports to the membership, or in the media. It has been our experience, at any rate, that generally the data that can be obtained relatively easily from public records and qualified newspaper reports correspond remarkably well with inside information that could only have been gained through access to operative documents, confidential interviews, or participant observation.

*Preferences*

Preferences are a different matter—mainly because the term itself is associated with complex and diverse connotations. For our own work, we have adopted a conceptualization that disaggregates the complex concept into four simpler components—"interests," "norms," "identities," and "interaction orientations"—in the expectation that it will be easier to obtain unambiguous empirical referents for each of the simpler concepts (Mayntz/Scharpf 1995a). Of these, the first three will be discussed here, the fourth in the next chapter.

This conceptual "modularization" has advantages for dealing with the fundamental complexity of actor motivations in empirical research. Unlike hard-core rational-choice approaches, we cannot simply stipulate self-interested preferences. Nevertheless, we recognize that the (institutional) self-interest of collective and corporate actors must be granted a special place in explanations of policy interactions. By separately specifying the other components that also may enter into the formation of preferences, we will be able to determine their potential salience in a given case. If it is low, then it may be quite sufficient to base explanations entirely on institutional self-interest, which is somewhat more easy to determine empirically.

*Basic Self-Interest.* The "self-interest" component is meant to describe the basic preference of actors for self-preservation, autonomy, and growth. For individuals, the operative implications may be identified by relating Adam Smith's definition of self-interest (physical well-being and social recognition) to the "production function" of social institutions within which this self-interest must be realized (Lindenberg 1989; 1991). Similarly, for corporate actors, self-interest can be identified with the conditions of organizational survival, autonomy, and growth[10]—which, again, depend on the institutional environment within which the organization operates. Thus organizational self-interest has different strategic implications for, say, a business firm operating in a highly competitive market, a labor union depending on the loyalty of a voluntary membership, or a research organization depending on its attractiveness for Nobel-prize candidates as well as on continuing financial support from the state budget or from industrial sponsors.

What matters here is that the specific requirements associated with the self-interest of collective and corporate actors[11] are relatively transparent, to other actors[12] as well as to researchers. We are defining "interests," that is, in a quasi-objective sense—which we are free to do, since we are not equating the concept with the full range of concerns that enter into the "preferences" that will ultimately determine an actor's choice among alternative courses of action.

*Normative Role Orientations.* The second component, "norms," is also defined in a quasi-objective way, relating to normative expectations addressed to the occupants of given positions. For our purposes, these expectations need not have the formal quality of legal rules, and effective sanctions may imply no more than social disapproval. What matters, again, is that they should be shared expectations among participants in an interaction which, for that reason, are also relatively accessible to the researcher.

It is also worth pointing out that norms, according to a basic logical distinction, may define either the antecedent *conditions* of particular actions or the *purposes* to be achieved thereby (Luhmann 1966). It is the former sense that is usually implied when rules are defined as constraints that either prohibit or require or permit specified acts (under specified conditions). For corporate actors, however, norms of the second type are of equal or greater practical importance. Since organizations are created and maintained to serve specific purposes, normatively specified organizational goals or missions are of obvious importance, even though it may be impossible to prescribe in advance the means—and even less specific actions—that should be used for the attainment of these goals. Nevertheless, these purposes are likely to be powerful arguments in the decision premises of organizations involved in policy processes—and they also allow researchers to infer without collecting large quantities of empirical data that, for instance, labor unions will generally be most concerned about real wages and job losses, whereas central banks will primarily focus on price stability (see Appendix 1).

*Identity.* There is no reason to think that either the diverse aspects of self-interest or the norms addressed to a specific actor should form a hierarchically integrated, logically consistent system; and we certainly cannot rule out conflicts between courses of action suggested by considerations of self-interest on the one hand and those dictated by normative duty on the other. Thus actors will often have to choose their effective preferences. Moreover, there will be choice situations for which neither self-interest nor generally held normative expectations will provide clear-cut guidelines. Finally, actors also have the capacity to adopt idiosyncratic interests and to follow self-defined rules. For all of these reasons researchers often cannot simply rely on standardized "institutional" information in order to identify effective actor preferences. But, again, what is a problem for empirical research must also be a problem for the actors involved, who will have a hard time making up their own minds in each individual case and an even harder time in making themselves predictable to others.

A partial solution to the problem of indeterminate preferences is provided by the formation of a specific "identity"—which constitutes the third component of our modular conceptualization of actor preferences. Actors, individual and composite, have the possibility of defining specific interests and norms for themselves, and—what is more important—they may selectively emphasize certain aspects of self-interest as well as certain rules and normative purposes from among those that generally apply to individuals or organizations of their type. In other words, actors have the possibility of defining a specific identity, which, if adhered to, will simplify their own choices and which, when communicated and believed, reduces uncertainty for other actors (and for researchers as well). A commitment to such a selective self-description may be considered a value in itself, but it also has utilitarian value. For the actors concerned, it will help to reduce the complexity and contingency of their own choices—or in the case of a "corporate identity" or a "corporate culture" (Meek 1988; Kreps 1995), of the choices of their members—and it will also inform other actors of what to expect from them. In that sense, a clearly defined individual or corporate identity reduces search costs internally and transaction costs externally and hence tends to increase the efficiency of interactions.

But greater efficiency comes at a price. In order to be effective, identities must be relatively stable over time, and they must restrict the range of feasible choices further than "objective" self-interest and externally imposed norms would have done. But what may be an advantage in a predictable environment may turn into a liability when the environment becomes more volatile and threatening and when a high degree of flexibility (including "moral" flexibility) may be a precondition of successful survival strategies. When that is so, the obstacles that would always stand in the way of strategy changes are considerably increased by the anticipated loss of personal or corporate identity. Volkswagen, for example, almost went under in the early 1970s because it was unable to cast off its air-cooled-rear-engine identity—and it was able to save itself at the last minute only because VW's chief executive officer, who had made the Beetle a world success, happened to be replaced by a successor who came from Audi, a recently acquired subsidiary with an equally strong corporate identity associated with front-wheel-drive water-cooled automobiles.

This is by no means an extreme example. Other firms have indeed gone out of business under similar circumstances, and the same has been true of political parties, labor unions, professional associations, religious organizations, research institutions, and many other varieties of corporate actors. Changing corporate identities implies discarding a large investment in moral commitments and cognitive certainties, which cannot be easy.[13] The least that it usually seems to take is a change of incumbents in top leadership positions. By reverse implication, however, individual and corporate identities must be considered as an extremely powerful *explanans*, or predictor, of choices that are underdetermined by more general considerations of interest and duty.

This concludes the survey of concepts that are useful for *describing* actor orientations. We speak of "describing" because—in empirical research—we do not have the freedom merely to *stipulate* perceptions and preferences in the way that rational-choice theories are wont to do. But neither do we consider it our task to provide a general theory that is able to *explain* the formation of perceptions and preferences. In fact we usually tend to take perceptions and preferences as given, just as is true of rational-choice approaches—except that we see a need to determine their content empirically and that we primarily rely on institutional information to facilitate that empirical determination.

This does not rule out the possibility that perceptions and preferences may change—and when that happens during the period we are studying, we must of course pay attention. In the case presented in the Introduction, that was true of the "reluctant conversion to monetarism" (Scharpf 1991a, 82) of the British Labour government under Callaghan. Where change in perceptions is important, we must investigate changing cognitive beliefs, causal theories, and "policy paradigms" (Hall 1992; 1993). We also do not rule out the possibility that preferences may change in the policy process itself as a consequence of "arguing" among the participants (Elster 1986; Prittwitz 1996).[14] But from a pragmatic point of view we prefer to cross that bridge when we come to it rather than to place the issue of exogenous or endogenous changes of action orientations at the very top of our research agenda.

## NOTES

1. These values include four "deference values" (power, respect, rectitude, and affection) and four "welfare values" (well-being, wealth, skill, and enlightenment), but of course even the latter will often be translated into political influence.

2. This is even true of the organizational factors emphasized by the "power resources" school of political economy (Korpi 1983), which have proven to be much less useful in the international economic environment of the 1980s and 1990s (Canova 1994).

3. It should be noted that the members of composite actors need not be individuals but will often be lower-order composite actors.

4. A recent example of a downward spiral under conditions of differentiated preferences is provided by the self-destruction of polyclinics in the East German health care system. Even though a large majority of the physicians employed there had expressed a preference for continuing in their present role, practically all of them were in fact in private practice within a year after German unification. The explanation, apparently, is not a change in the intrinsic preferences of the majority. But when the minority of doctors who always had wanted to set themselves up in private practice began to do so, the viability of some polyclinics seemed uncertain, so that more ambivalent staff members saw reason to follow suit, which again influenced the expectations of others, until, in the end, everyone feared being left behind in doomed polyclinics while in the meantime most patients would have become attached to those doctors in private practice who had started early (Wasem 1992).

5. The distinction of different orientations does not coincide with the standard economic distinction between "private goods" and "collective goods," which is based on the "objective" criteria of rivalry in use and excludability.

6. Movements directed by a charismatic leader are an entirely different matter with regard to their strategic capacities as collective actors. Analytically, they may be treated as "associations."

7. Nevertheless, members may retain control over some critical action resources. In collective-bargaining conflicts, for instance, the employers' association is legitimated to make binding decisions on conflict strategies, but lockouts must still be implemented by individual firms. On the union side, the same is true of the implementation of strike decisions.

8. Observed actions are explained by preferences that in turn are inferred from observed action.

9. Nevertheless, the occupants of leadership positions are also constrained by the functional requirements associated with such positions. Among these are the need to maintain the revenues of the state and other action resources (Levi 1988) and, of course, political requirements expressed best in Lyndon Johnson's famous dictum that "you've got to be re-elected to be a statesman."

10. We have no difficulty with the assumption of methodological individualism that the force driving organizational self-interest must be the self-interest of the individuals whose livelihood and career opportunities depend on the organization. But knowing the source of energy does not yet tell us the direction in which the organization will be driven.

11. Individual actors have of course much greater freedom in defining their own self-interest in idiosyncratic ways, and they may even ignore basic survival interests (which biologists would in any case locate not at the level of the individual but at the level of the gene—see, for example, Dawkins 1976; Campbell 1986).

12. Uwe Schimank (1995) has emphasized the "reflexive" nature of this linkage. Other actors will, as a matter of course, attribute these basic interests to individual and corporate actors and act on that assumption—which, in turn, stabilizes the actor's own commitment to these orientations.

13. Raising this difficulty to the status of a general theory, the "population ecology" school of organizational sociology assumes that organizations have "hardwired" strategies, implying that they will succeed or fail depending on the state of the environment but will be unable to learn and to adapt to external changes (Hannan/Freeman 1977; 1984).

14. I realized too late for discussion in the text that controversies about the stability or variability of preferences are sometimes purely semantic. As it is used here, at any rate, the concept of "preferences" refers to stable *criteria of evaluation,* not to the *intention* of choosing a particular strategy. There is no question that intentions may change if arguing provides new information about the likely outcomes of strategies.

# 4

## Actor Constellations

In Chapter 2 I introduced the concept of "actor constellations" as the crucial link between substantive policy analyses and interaction-oriented policy research. The basic idea was that the solutions (identified by substantive policy research) to a given policy problem must be produced by the interdependent choices of a plurality of policy actors with specific capabilities and with specific perceptions and preferences regarding the outcomes that could be obtained. Since the choices are interdependent, it is likely that no single actor will be able to determine the outcome unilaterally. What matters is the actor constellation.

In the present chapter I will begin by discussing a variety of characteristic or "archetypal" actor constellations. Since these are represented by simple and highly transparent two-by-two game matrices, it also becomes necessary to discuss the conditions under which this radical simplification of complex real-world constellations might be methodologically permissible. Next I will return to an issue that was mentioned but postponed in the previous chapter: Game matrices are usually taken to represent the worldviews of players who only care about their own payoffs. In real-world interactions, however, it is often the case that actors do care very much, positively or negatively, about the payoffs that others will receive. Thus it is necessary to show how these "interaction orientations" could be integrated into the analysis of actor constellations. The chapter concludes with a discussion of normative criteria by which the problem-solving capacity of different types of policy interactions can be evaluated.

### POLICY PROBLEMS AND ACTOR ORIENTATIONS

In the most general sense, anything that ego considers desirable (or undesirable) may become a policy problem if changes in the desired direction are possible in principle but cannot be achieved by ego acting alone because others are either causing the problem or have control over some action resources that are necessary for its resolution (Coleman 1990). Of course that does not imply that all of these problems need to be resolved through *public* policy, or for that matter through any kind of supra-individual arrangement. They may be resolved through noncooperative or cooperative interaction among the actors immediately involved, and they are in fact largely resolved through interactions in the market. But not all problems can be resolved in this fashion, and the market itself is also a major cause of societal problems. Some of these will come onto the agenda of public-policy processes, which, after all, have the manifest function of dealing with problems that cannot be resolved by individual action or by other mechanisms of social coordination. Focusing on the interpersonal (rather than the technical-instrumental) aspect of policy problems,[1] we may analytically divide these into three distinct groups that can be described as coordination problems, externalities and collective goods, and redistribution problems.

*Problems of coordination* may arise if individual actors would benefit from exchanging available objects (goods or services) or from producing objects that are compatible with each other or from collaborating in the joint production of objects that neither party could produce by itself. Though in principle individual actors ought to be able to resolve coordination problems through voluntary agreement among themselves, public policy may nevertheless play a crucial role in reducing distrust and the transaction costs of such agreements by defining property rights and protecting them through the law of torts, by defining a law of contracts that provides fallback solutions for incomplete agreements and by providing the legal machinery for the enforcement of contractual obligations, and by defining technical standards that assure the compatibility of products.

*Externalities and collective-goods problems* may arise if individual action produces negative or positive effects for others that will be disregarded by purely self-interested actors—which means that purely unilateral action would produce more negative and fewer positive effects than would be welfare optimal. If this process went unchecked, the result could be a Tragedy of the Commons (Hardin 1968), in which common resources are exploited and ultimately destroyed by rational self-interested actors. If property rights are well-defined, and if external effects are concentrated on small numbers of other actors, the law of torts or the law of contracts may permit satisfactory solutions to be reached through negotiations. As the number of affected parties increases, however, negotiated solutions will incur exponentially rising and eventually prohibitive transaction costs. Public policy could intervene to correct externalities either through regulations or by imposing negative incentives on the producers of negative externalities or providing positive incentives to the producers of positive externalities. Similarly, collective goods that would not be produced by individual self-interested action could be produced through organized collective action or through public provision. In either case, public-policy interventions could also take the form of facilitating and stabilizing cooperation and forms of effective self-regulation by the actors directly involved (Ostrom 1990; Ostrom/Gardner/Walker 1994).

*Redistribution problems*, finally, may arise under two conditions. On the one hand, there may be situations in which (otherwise attractive) policy purposes can only be attained at the expense of identifiable individuals or groups; on the other hand, the existing distribution of assets or life chances may itself become a policy issue. In the first case, the distributional issue will necessarily have to be resolved one way or another in the policy process. In the second case, societies differ greatly in the extent to which the inequalities of market-generated distribution are made a policy issue. But even in societies that have a high tolerance for inequality and that emphasize self-reliance, the state's power to tax and to regulate is used to ensure that those who cannot help themselves—the young, the sick, and the old—are provided with a minimum of resources.

These different types of policy problems could well be represented as game-theoretic constellations among the groups involved. What is important here, however, is that *these are not the games that are in fact being played in the policy processes* that we are trying to analyze. These different types of societal constellations will enter the policy process only to the extent that, and in the form in which, they are represented in the actor constellations through which public policy is in fact formulated and implemented.

The relationship between the orientations and capabilities of policy actors and the underlying societal interests is a complex one. In referenda and other forms of direct democracy, citizens may directly participate in policy processes, but in all other contexts, the individuals affected depend on complex structures of "interest intermediation" to have their preferences considered in policy interactions. For game-theoretical interaction analyses—as distinguished from the structural analysis of "policy networks" (Knoke et al. 1996)—this complexity can be quite overwhelming. For that reason it is useful to distinguish between a subset of primary policy actors (described as the "collective decider" by Knoke et al.) that are directly and necessarily participating in the making of policy choices and all other actors that may be able to influence the choices of these primary actors.[2] Only the former will be included in the definition of the "actor constellation."

But although the distinction simplifies analysis, it also highlights the tenuous relationship between policy actors and societal interests. Some members of the actor constellation may be directly representative of specific societal interests—as is true, for instance, of agrarian parties in Sweden or Switzerland or of the bipartisan "farm bloc" in both houses of the U.S. Congress. More generally, the dependence on elections is supposed to assure the responsiveness of democratically accountable governments to all societal interests, but in institutionally fragmented political systems certain policy actors may be specifically dependent on the electoral support of particular clientele groups. In addition, specialized policy actors—such as the Securities and Exchange Commission or the Environmental Protection Agency—may be institutionalized precisely to look after specific societal interests. However, not all interests depend on the institutionalization of "voice" in order to be heard in policy processes (Hirschman 1970). With the increase in transnational economic mobility, the "exit" option has increased the already disproportionate (Lindblom 1977) influence of capital interests on the

preferences of national policymakers, regardless of the organizational and political strength of the pressure groups and parties representing these interests.

At any rate, in translating policy problems into actor constellations, we cannot
simply treat societal interests as "inputs" into an undifferentiated "political system" that will "convert" them into "outputs" (Easton 1965); rather, we need to
show how particular policy actors with specific orientations and capabilities will
or will not include them in their own action orientations. Thus the fact that capital owners may worry about rising rates of inflation will find more resonance in
the policy system if the central bank is institutionally independent from the national government rather than under the control of, say, the Treasury of a Labour
government (see Appendix 1). Similarly, in Germany, the interests of physicians
in private practice have more influence on the policy preferences of the small
Liberal party than on those of the two larger parties, and they are best protected
when this party finds itself in a strong veto position in a coalition government
(Rosewitz/Webber 1990). In Sweden, by contrast, the similarly well-organized
physicians did not find powerful champions within the "corporatist" policymaking system that had an interest in taking up their cause (Immergut 1990; 1992).
Hence in assessing the responsiveness of the policy system to societal interests we
need to map these interests onto the action orientations of the primary actors involved in policy interactions.

## ACTOR CONSTELLATIONS

Interaction is a complex, multidimensional concept. In order to simplify presentation and analysis, it seems useful to distinguish between *actor constellations* and
*modes of interaction*. As I pointed out in Chapter 2, this distinction allows us to
use the analytical power contained in game matrices without committing ourselves to viewing the whole world in terms of noncooperative games. "Actor constellations" are meant to represent what we know of the set of actors that are actually involved in particular policy interactions—their capabilities (translated
into potential "strategies"), their perceptions and evaluations of the outcomes
obtainable (translated into "payoffs"), and the degree to which their payoff aspirations are compatible or incompatible with one another. The constellation thus
describes the level of potential conflict, but it does not yet include information
about the mode of interaction through which that conflict is to be resolved—
through unilateral action, negotiations, voting, or hierarchical determination.

### Archetypal Game Constellations

Actor constellations differ from one another, and in empirical research it is important that each one be carefully constructed on the basis of available data.
*There is no way in which generalized assumptions could here substitute for empirical
information.* In empirical research the abstract "strategies" ascribed to players

must be identified as (physically and institutionally) feasible courses of action that one or another of the actors could in fact take. The cells of the matrix then represent the (physical) outcomes that are expected to occur when specific strategy choices of interdependent actors intersect. It is only after we have identified these expected outcomes that we can begin to rank them according to the specific interests, normative preferences, and identities of the different actors involved. Game theory as such can provide no help in identifying outcomes and their valuation by the "players"; the empirical and theoretical work necessary to describe them must have been done by the researcher before it makes sense to draw up game matrices.

It is only after we have constructed the payoff matrix from our own empirical information that the theory of noncooperative games would help us in identifying potential equilibrium solutions. However, to repeat, we need not assume that a noncooperative game is being played in order to profit from the game-theoretic form of organizing the information that we have obtained. Even when we know that other modes of interaction, such as negotiations or voting, are being used, the game matrix still describes the "logic of the situation" (Zürn 1992; Zintl 1995) with which the actors must cope.

Moreover, in constructing and interpreting empirical constellations it is extremely helpful to be aware of a number of well-known game constellations that have received sufficient analytical and experimental attention to render their strategic implications highly transparent. The most simple among these are constellations of *pure conflict* (or zero-sum or constant-sum) games, in which one side must lose what the other side gains, and constellations of *pure coordination*, in which all actors can maximize their own payoff by agreeing on concerted strategies (Figure 4.1).

In real-world interactions, however, both of these simple constellations are extremely rare. Of much greater empirical importance are the so-called *mixed-motive games* (or variable-sum games) in which the preferences of players are partly harmonious and partly in conflict. Of these, four "archetypal" constellations have achieved the most notoriety, even among social scientists who otherwise profess to game-theoretic illiteracy. They are known by the nicknames of "Assurance," "Battle of the Sexes," "Prisoner's Dilemma," and "Chicken" (Figure 4.2).

In discussing the implications of these mixed-motive constellations, the strategies available to both players are conventionally labeled "cooperate" (C) and "defect" (D), depending on whether the strategy is intended to realize the common interest of ego and alter or to maximize the advantage of ego at the expense of alter.

In the Assurance game,[3] the players have a clear common interest in coordinating on C/C, which will provide both parties with their best possible payoff (4,4). In that sense the constellation is quite similar to a game of pure coordination. However, there is a certain risk involved: If, for whatever reason, the Column player chooses D instead of C, then the "cooperative" Row player will end up with the worst possible outcome (1,3). The game is thus a reminder of the crucial im-

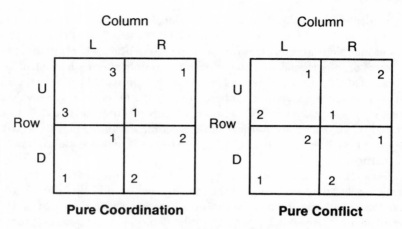

FIGURE 4.1    Constellations of pure coordination and pure conflict

portance of perceptions and of mutual predictability in social interactions. If the Row player is unable to trust Column's understanding of the common situation, it would be reasonable to choose D in order to avoid the worst-case outcome of C/D, and if Column should act from the same uncertainty, then both would end up with D/D, which is their second-worst outcome.

Battle of the Sexes[4] is a member of the large class of "games of coordination with conflict over distribution," which is very frequently encountered in real-world negotiations. Here the parties have a common interest in coordinating their choices so that one of the welfare-superior outcomes (4,3 or 3,4) is reached—but the Row player would prefer the first option and the Column player the second. When played out as a noncooperative game with simultaneous moves and without the possibility of prior communication, there is no way in which the players could be certain to reach either of the preferred outcomes. In fact, if both should choose to "cooperate" by opting for the outcome preferred by the other player, they would both end up with their worst possible payoffs (1,1).

Moreover, the difficulties would not disappear if communication and even binding agreements were possible, because now the parties would disagree over the choice among the two coordinated outcomes that differ in their distributive characteristics. Negotiations would thus be associated with high transaction costs. However, since both sides would still prefer the less attractive coordinated outcome over noncoordination, agreement is likely to be reached somehow.[5] If it is reached, then implementation of the agreement will not be a problem because even the disadvantaged party will have an interest to comply. Transaction costs would be greatly reduced, however, if Battle of the Sexes could be played as a noncooperative but sequential game. Now the party that has the first move could select its most preferred outcome, and in the light of that choice, it would then be in the other party's best interest to coordinate on the same outcome.[6] Battle of

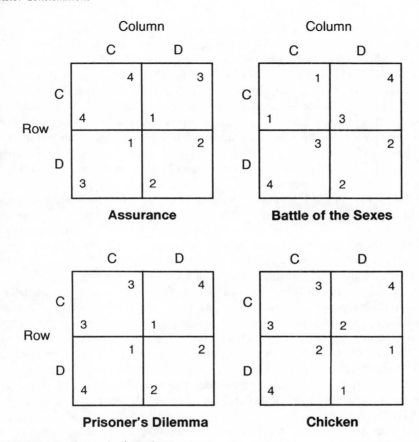

FIGURE 4.2    Four mixed-motive games

the Sexes thus illustrates the fact that communication and negotiations will not under all conditions lead to outcomes that are socially superior to unilateral and self-interested action (Genschel/Pluemper 1996).[7]

Next in Figure 4.2 comes the Prisoner's Dilemma,[8] which is so well known that an introduction seems less necessary than the warning to resist the temptation to interpret all social and political interactions in its terms (Wildavsky 1992). It has become the paradigm for "social traps" (Platt 1973; Messick/McClelland 1983) in which individually rational choices will produce collectively irrational outcomes. As an inspection of Figure 4.2-3 will reveal, for both players defection is the "dominant" strategy (i.e., the strategy that will produce higher payoffs, regardless of what the other side does), but when they both choose D, both will end up with their second-worst outcome (2,2). Nor can either of them unilaterally escape from this trap, since the choice of a cooperative strategy would create the risk of being exploited by the other side (at C/D or at D/C), resulting in the worst possible outcome for the "sucker" and the best outcome for the exploiter (1,4 or 4,1). All this is well known. Nevertheless, three remarks seem to be in order.

First, the original story that gave the game its name emphasizes the fact that the two prisoners are *unable to communicate* after the district attorney has offered to reward a unilateral confession. It is often concluded, therefore, that the Prisoner's Dilemma would be easily resolved if prior communication is possible. Though this intuition finds a good deal of support in laboratory experiments, it is not theoretically valid. Communication will indeed facilitate agreement on the "cooperative" solution (C/C). But in a noncooperative game, such agreements would not have binding force, and the Prisoner's Dilemma differs from Battle of the Sexes in that agreements are not self-enforcing. When the stakes are substantial (as they are not in laboratory experiments), the temptation to defect remains as high after a prior agreement as it was before. In the absence of an external mechanism that allows the parties to make *binding* commitments, communication in Prisoner's Dilemma constellations remains "cheap talk" that cannot eliminate the possibility of mutual defection.

That conclusion is challenged by a "folk theorem"[9] regarding *iterated games* that postulates that the pernicious character of Prisoner's Dilemma constellations will disappear if the same interactions are indefinitely repeated. Whereas the dilemma is inexorable in single-shot encounters between rational self-interested strangers, iteration permits each player to reward or punish the past moves of the other player. If this endogenous sanctioning capacity is then employed in "tit-for-tat" strategies, rewarding cooperation with cooperation and punishing defection with defection, then rational self-interested players are in fact able to achieve stable cooperation in the iterated two-person Prisoner's Dilemma (Axelrod 1984).[10]

Unfortunately, however, the tit-for-tat solution does not carry over from two-person games into *multiactor constellations*. As has been known for some time (Hardin 1971), the "collective-action problem" analyzed by Mancur Olson (1965) as well as the Tragedy of the Commons identified by Garrett Hardin (1968), or more generally, the production of public goods and of public bads, can be understood as large-number (or "n-person") Prisoner's Dilemma games. In all of these cases, free-riding is a dominant strategy for each individual actor that, if adopted by all participants, must lead to collectively suboptimal outcomes. However, even though many constellations may have the characteristics of indefinitely iterated games, tit-for-tat strategies will not solve the problem here. There are several reasons, but the most important is that the only endogenously available sanction—to punish defection by defecting oneself—cannot be targeted to the culprit in large-number situations: If all players defect in response to a single defection, then cooperation will never have a chance; yet if this defection is ignored, then cooperation is bound to unravel as more and more players will be tempted by the rewards of unilateral defection. Thus in order to stabilize cooperation in multiactor Prisoner's Dilemma constellations, noncooperative games, whether iterated or single-shot, will not be enough. What is needed, as Elinor Ostrom has shown in her studies of multiactor common-resource problems, are structures and processes of interaction that permit the adoption and enforcement of collectively binding decisions (Ostrom 1990; Ostrom et al. 1994).

When binding commitments are possible, however, agreement in the symmetrical Prisoner's Dilemma seems easy. Rational actors should of course prefer a secure and fair cooperative solution (3,3) to the certain prospect of mutual defection (2,2). It should be noted, however, that the symmetry suggested by the archetypal two-by-two Prisoner's Dilemma matrix involves a rather extreme (and often highly ideological) assumption. Real-world constellations will often allow for several "cooperative" solutions that may differ significantly in their distributive consequences (Heckathorn/Maser 1987). When that is so, the constellation will assume some of the characteristics of Battle of the Sexes,[11] implying that the common aversion to the outcome associated with mutual defection is not sufficient to assure agreement on one of the competing cooperative solutions. This model was used to explain the near-breakdown of international negotiations over banking regulations (Genschel/Pluemper 1996). Other examples might be "peace talks" in Northern Ireland, the former Yugoslavia, or the Middle East between parties who are war-weary but nevertheless have very different ideas about the content of a negotiated settlement (and who would rather continue to fight than capitulate).

Hence negotiated solutions will often be more difficult in practice than is suggested by the two-by-two matrix of the symmetrical Prisoner's Dilemma. By contrast, when decisions can be taken by majority vote (or by hierarchical rule for that matter), outcomes will be reached much more easily. But now the danger is exploitation: Whoever is able to impose his or her preferred solution will be tempted to choose not the cooperative solution (C/C) that is associated with the greatest overall benefit but an asymmetrical outcome (D/C or C/D) that maximizes that player's own gain at the expense of the losing side. These variants are a reminder of the fact that a given actor constellation (the Prisoner's Dilemma in this case) will lead to very different outcomes if the mode of interaction is varied.

In Chicken,[12] the last of our four archetypal mixed-motive games, agreements on a cooperative solution (C/C) are as plausible and as much threatened by unilateral defection as they are in the Prisoner's Dilemma. However, joint defection (D/D) here will produce not the second-worst but the worst outcome for both sides. This has important consequences for the victim of a unilateral defection. In a Prisoner's Dilemma situation, a player who retaliates by defecting in turn will receive a better outcome than a player who remains cooperative. In Chicken, by contrast, fighting back with this strategy will make things even worse (achieving that player's worst-case outcome). Thus Chicken is a good model of situations in which rational actors are vulnerable to the preemptive moves of aggressive opponents and in which their threats of subsequent retaliation would lack credibility.[13] Nuclear deterrence philosophy in its various versions during the cold war period grappled with this problem, and the Cuban missile crisis can also be interpreted in these terms. Even at a more mundane level, constellations are not infrequent in which "going to the brink" will pay—but only as long as the other side will not retaliate in kind. Within government coalitions, for example, an individual party may sharpen its political profile by provoking controversies with other members of the coalition, but the government would fall apart if other parties were to do likewise. The same can be true of conflict strategies between unions and employers when neither side actually wants a major strike. There is, as it were, a maximum level of overt conflict that an ongoing relationship can bear without coming apart, and if that maximum is exhausted by unilateral action, then the other side must either give in or initiate the war that neither side had wanted.

If Chicken is played as a sequential game, the first mover will always win at the expense of the other side. Under these conditions, there is thus a strong temptation to resort to preemptive strikes that mere communication cannot eliminate. Also, since fighting back will make matters even worse for the victim of an aggression, tit-for-tat strategies are less likely to be employed than is assumed in the Prisoner's Dilemma literature. Thus we cannot expect stable cooperation to result from infinitely iterated encounters. Nevertheless, in the symmetrical Chicken game both sides have similar opportunities of succeeding through preemptive aggression, and mutual aggression will hurt both sides. Thus a cooperative solution should be in the common interest of all parties, and it is likely to be achieved under conditions in which binding agreements are possible.

However, all games discussed thus far have shared two properties: The parties are assumed to have a common interest in avoiding maximal conflict, and the constellations are symmetrical in the sense that the preferences of both players are either identical or mirror images of each other. But of course neither of these conditions is necessarily fulfilled in real-world interactions. In fact, the first constellation presented in the Introduction (Figure I.1) of the game played between the unions and a monetarist government illustrates both possibilities. The government unconditionally prefers to pursue a tight-money policy (i.e., it will never "cooperate"), and the unions must moderate their wage demands (i.e., cooperate) in order to avoid their worst-case outcome.

In the literature, the nickname "Deadlock" is used to characterize still other constellations in which both sides will actually prefer mutual defection (D/D) over mutual cooperation (C/C). An example could be conflict in the last phases of a coalition government in which parties prefer to fight the election with their ideological positions intact rather than to compromise on an issue that is of high salience to their voters. Alternatively, consider an asymmetrical "Rambo" game in which the preferences of the Row player correspond to the Chicken game and those of the Column player to Deadlock. Here the Column player would of course prefer to win without a fight (2,4) but prefers a fight (D/D) over a compromise (C/C). For the Row player, however, a fight would produce the worst possible payoff outcome (1,3), so that capitulation without a fight (C/D) will become the most likely outcome among rational, self-interested players (Figure 4.3).

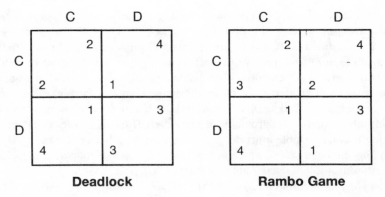

FIGURE 4.3    Deadlock and Rambo games

It may be useful to emphasize again that the actor constellations I have discussed in this overview do not represent an exhaustive typology. In fact, if preferences are strictly ordinal, ranging from 4 to 1 in every case, it is theoretically possible to identify seventy-eight two-by-two games that are structurally different (Rapoport/Guyer/Gordon 1976), and if restrictions on preference orderings are relaxed, the number of distinguishable two-by-two games rises to 66,645 (Fishburn/Kilgour 1990). With three or more players or three or more strategies, therefore, the astronomical number of potential constellations defies all attempts at systematization. And though it may be possible to classify games using a general measure of the level of conflict of interest involved (Axelrod 1970; Budge 1973), the measure proposed applies only to two-person games,[14] and even there it does not capture all strategic aspects that make game-theoretic analyses useful for empirical policy research in the first place (Mohr/Hausken 1996).[15]

Under these circumstances, we do well to content ourselves in empirical research with constructing our own matrices from the empirical data and contextual information that we have about the specific interactions we are studying, using the archetypal game constellations mainly to alert us to the potential variety of possible constellations. Moreover, since the strategic implications of these archetypes have been widely explored, analytically, empirically, and in laboratory experiments, we can use this literature to get a better sense of what might actually be implied in the constellation that we have before us.

## The Need for Simplification

A major problem remains to be addressed, however. As is done in much of the applied literature, I have discussed two-by-two games. Yet we know that the situations we encounter in empirical research will often involve a considerable number of actors, each of whom may have a large repertoire of actions to choose from and who also may have more than one criterion for evaluating the outcomes expected. When that is so, the game-theoretic representation of actor constellations would run into problems of exploding complexity (Scharpf 1991b), and any attempt to transform such constellations into the form of a two-by-two matrix with a single number representing each actor's payoff would seem to require more than merely heroic efforts. But what is a problem for the analyst would of course be an even greater problem for the actors involved. Purposeful action in strategic situations would simply be impossible if actors were required to solve large-numbers interaction problems in every case. Thus the fact that strategic interaction is at all possible must depend on one or the other of two mechanisms, *decoupling* and *aggregation,* which actors as well as analysts may use for the cognitive simplification of overcomplex constellations.

*Decoupling* implies that many of the interdependencies that could be made the object of strategic interaction will be either ignored or treated as part of a given environment *for the purposes of a particular policy interaction.* But what is ignored today, or in one arena, may be actively processed tomorrow, or in another arena involving the same or different actors, who, however, will be laboring under similar constraints on the range of interdependencies that they will be able to take into account. This is why consultants selling substantive policy analyses can always make money by pointing to glaring "coordination deficits" in any policy area to which they turn their attention. What they do not recognize is the effectiveness of forms of coordination that Charles Lindblom (1965) has described as "partisan mutual adjustment" (see Appendix 2). As I will show in the next chapter, these are not necessarily very welfare efficient, but as long as "synoptic" policymaking will fail in the face of explosive complexity, they are too valuable to be ignored. At any rate, in our reconstruction of policy processes, we need to be aware of the (shifting) boundaries through which the actors themselves have limited the complexity of their interaction.

The second mechanism, *aggregation,* was implied in the discussion of aggregate and composite actors in the preceding chapter. These are constructs that dramatically reduce the complexity of multiperson interactions for actors and observers alike. Often we are dealing only with a few large "corporate actors" to begin with, or we may benefit from the fact that large numbers of individual actors have conveniently organized themselves as "collective actors" into a limited number of coalitions, clubs, movements, or associations. Thus, for instance, hundreds of individual members of parliament will typically form a few relatively cohesive parliamentary parties that, moreover, will have combined to form a government coalition and the opposition. More generally, the mechanism of coalition formation is perhaps the most powerful simplifier of complex constellations for actors and observers alike. At the same time, the political process will rarely deal with large numbers of policy alternatives at the same time but will tend rather to focus on a limited number of options whose outcomes are evaluated in a single, highly salient issue dimension, in which preferences are easily identified.[16]

When that is so, representation of the actor constellation in the form of a small-numbers or even a two-by-two game may not imply any significant loss of information. This is true, I think, of the matrices representing union, government, and central-bank preferences under the stagflation conditions of the mid-1970s (see Appendix 1). But it is not always true. In some situations we may be dealing with multiactor constellations in which the actors have not (yet) organized themselves into large coalitions and with multidimensional outcomes that have not (yet) been integrated into a single criterion. This is most likely to be a problem when we engage in empirical studies of ongoing policy processes in which interactions have not yet run their course and in which perceptions and preferences have not yet become simplified and "frozen." Even then, however, we may achieve fairly good predictions if we proceed systematically, and use transparent methods, in our own anticipatory simplifications.

A method that I have found to be particularly useful might be called *hypothetical coalitions*. It implies that we divide a given population of actors into two potential groups, each of whose members share a common interest in a certain potentially salient aspect of the expected outcomes of policy interactions. The interaction between these hypothetical coalitions can then be represented as a two-person game in which outcomes are evaluated in a single dimension. The same can be done for alternative hypothetical partitions of the actor set, focusing on other aspects of the expected outcomes. Of course this does not yet tell us which of these potential coalitions, if any, will actually form. However, the number of empirically probable coalitions can be significantly reduced if we next proceed to an examination of their internal cohesion.

In order to do so, we must simply repeat the same operations at the level of the hypothetically identified coalitions. The point of this exercise is to determine whether the members of that subset of actors would in fact be able to agree on a common position or whether their coalition would founder on internal conflicts of interest over another issue raised by the hypothetically assumed common strategy. This sounds more complicated than it is in practice. For an illustration, consider an example from a recent article (Scharpf 1996) examining the chances of common European regulations in the fields of social welfare and industrial relations (Figure 4.4).

Analysis starts from the hypothesis that in the Council of Ministers of the European Union, the "rich" member states and the "poor" member states could be treated as hypothetical coalitions, each of them united by shared interests in maintaining or increasing their economic competitiveness. In the integrated European market, economically advanced countries with costly welfare-state regulations have reason to fear "social dumping" and the emigration of their industries to low-cost countries. Hence they would prefer common European standards at high levels of social protection. Less developed countries, by contrast, depending on low welfare costs in order to compensate for the lower productivity of their firms and other competitive disadvantages, could not afford to accept common regulations at such high levels of protection.

In this example it is assumed that the mode of interaction is "negotiated agreement," that is, that no common European regulation could be adopted unless it is

## Rich Countries

### Level of Protection

|               | high        | low          |
|---------------|-------------|--------------|

The figure is a 2×2 matrix:

|                          |       | **high**      | **low**       |
|--------------------------|-------|---------------|---------------|
| **Poor Countries** high  |       | 3 / 1         | 2 / 3   NA    |
| low                      |       | 2 / 3   NA    | 1 / 2         |

FIGURE 4.4   Social regulations in the European Union: Preferences of rich and poor countries for uniform European regulations at high and low levels of protection (NA = Nonagreement)

accepted by both coalitions. But the best outcome for the coalition of rich countries, namely, agreement on common regulations at high levels of protection (high/high), would be completely unacceptable for the coalition of poor countries. In fact, for the poor member states, even common European regulations at low levels of protection (low/low) would be less attractive than the nonagreement outcome (NA)—assuming that in the absence of agreement rich countries would continue to apply their expensive national regulations to their national industries. Thus, under the unanimity rule that applies to social regulations in the Council of Ministers, we would predict that common European rules are unlikely to be adopted.

But now let us assume, counterfactually, that social regulations could be adopted by majority vote in the Council of Ministers and that the coalition of rich countries with expensive welfare states would have the votes to impose common high-protection standards at the European level.[17] The question then is whether the members of this hypothetical coalition would be able to agree among themselves on a single substantive standard. In trying to answer this question, the issue shifts from the common interest in maintaining industrial competitiveness (which depends on the *level* of protection) to the choice among different *types* of regulation and thus to the fact that the highly developed European welfare states have adopted functionally equivalent but institutionally extremely diverse solutions. Uniform European rules would thus require a choice between the universalistic and tax-based Scandinavian models and the corporatist and insurance-based Continental models of social security (Esping-Andersen 1990) or between the legalist tradition of Continental industrial relations and the British

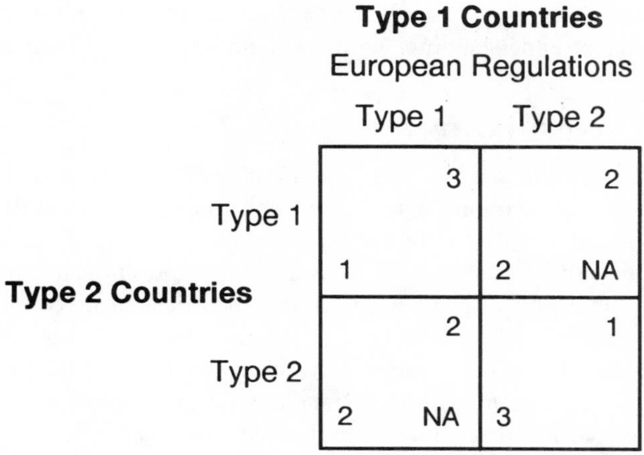

**Type 1 Countries**

European Regulations

Type 1     Type 2

|   | Type 1 | Type 2 |
|---|---|---|
| **Type 1** | 3 / 1 | 2 / 2  NA |
| **Type 2** | 2 / 2  NA | 1 / 3 |

**Type 2 Countries** (row label)

FIGURE 4.5     European harmonization of welfare-state rules

tradition of state-free collective bargaining (Crouch 1993). In either case the institutional adjustment imposed on those countries that would be required to change their systems would be forcefully resisted by politically powerful organizations whose institutional self-interest is symbiotic with the existing system. Thus the constellation of interests within the hypothetical coalition of high-welfare countries might be most plausibly represented by Figure 4.5.

From this analysis it is then possible to conclude that the hypothetical winning coalition of the rich welfare states will be plagued by considerable internal conflicts of interest. Whether these conflicts would ultimately prevent the coalition from forming will of course depend on the available alternative options in the case of disagreement. If the pressure of international competition is very great, even major institutional changes may become acceptable, as is true, for instance, in the privatization and liberalization of national telecommunication monopolies (Schneider 1995; Schmidt 1995). In the specific case, however, the political salience of institutional differences seems to be so high that even if decisions on the "social dimension" could be taken by qualified majority in the Council of Ministers, a common European welfare regime is unlikely to be adopted in the near future (Scharpf 1997).

This specific prediction may be open to challenge—but such challenges could be formulated and discussed within the same analytical framework. What matters here, therefore, is the suggestion that the method of hypothetical coalitions, if applied sequentially to different value aspects of multidimensional issues and to different levels or subgroups within a larger population,[18] makes it possible to analyze fairly complex constellations of preferences with the use of quite simple game matrices. In using this method, we should of course treat it as a tool to assist and expli-

cate our own understanding of a given situation rather than as an automated procedure substituting for understanding. But that should be true of all analytical tools.

## INTERACTION ORIENTATIONS

I now return to an issue that was mentioned but not discussed in the preceding
chapter. The actor orientations presented there all seemed to refer to the individual actor considered in isolation. But now that the central place of actor *constellations* in our conceptual framework has been established, it is time to consider also
the *relational* dimension of actor orientations. In neoclassical economics, it is
true, this is considered an irrelevant issue. There the postulated anonymity of actors in atomistic markets does indeed leave no room for relational considerations. Beyond that, however, it is much less plausible to assume (as is done in all
rational-choice theories) that actors are exclusively maximizing their own payoffs
and are totally unconcerned, positively or negatively, about the payoffs received
by other actors involved. In empirical research (as distinguished from normative
models of rational behavior), envy may play a role, friends may cherish each
other's gains, and enemies may gloat over each other's losses. In order to account
for these relationally defined preferences, I use the additional dimension of "interaction orientations" (Scharpf 1989; 1990; 1991a).

However, relational aspects may enter analysis either in objective or in subjective form. The first possibility arises in constellations in which gains to one party
will objectively increase or decrease the expected payoff of the other party. This is
assumed by the neorealist school in International Relations to be true of interactions among states. Starting from the premise that war is an ever-present possibility among nation-states and from the fact that *relative power* will determine
success or failure in military encounters, it follows logically that all interactions
among states must be evaluated from a "relative-gains" perspective: What matters, then, is not how much a particular state may gain but whether it gains more
or less than its opponent (Waltz 1979). Conversely, in a wartime alliance the victory of an ally should indeed be counted as a benefit to one's own side. Similarly,
the rules of the football game define a goal scored by one team as a loss for the
other, and the rules governing medical practice require physicians to give paramount consideration to the well-being of their patients—but not necessarily to
that of their colleagues. When these empirical or normative conditions are sufficiently stable and interpersonally known, there is no need for conceptualizing
"interaction orientations" separately. They should enter into the payoff specification of the normal actor constellation.

By contrast, the concept of interaction orientations should be used for *subjective redefinitions* of the "objective" interest constellation, leading to discrimination
among partners even when the factual consequences and the applicable norms are
identical.[19] Thus we may need to refer to interaction orientations in order to explain why, for instance, cooperation was and is generally more easy between the
United States and Britain than it is between the United States and France or why

the peace processes in the former Yugoslavia, the Middle East, or Northern Ireland remain so difficult long after it has become clear that all sides can only lose from the continuation of conflict. For the actors involved, that is to say, a relationship may assume a character of its own that affects the valuation of "real" gains and losses and that distinguishes this particular relationship from "objectively" similar interactions with other parties or with the same party at another time. In that sense, the concept serves the same individualizing purpose at the relational level that "identity" serves in the definition of individual preferences.

In order to describe the notion of interaction orientations, I use a conceptualization developed by social psychologists for the interpretation of seemingly anomalous results in game-theoretic laboratory experiments (McClintock 1972; Kelley/Thibaut 1978). Instead of assuming that subjects had either misunderstood the structure of "objective" payoffs designed by the experimenter or that they were unable to perform the appropriate calculations, Harold Kelley and John Thibaut interpreted consistently "anomalous" choices in clearly defined experimental situations as the transformation of a "given matrix" (describing the payoff the subject will in fact receive) into an "effective matrix," in which ego may also give some weight to the payoff that alter will receive (1978, 14–17, 137–166). The specific form of the transformation depends on how ego interprets the relationship with alter—and the considerable variance in the transformation of identical given matrices that is observed in experimental situations may be attributed either to ego's personality variables or to alter's previous behavior.

Regardless of how they are to be explained, the observed effective matrices can be generated by different transformation rules specifying how the payoffs of ego and alter in the given matrix are to be converted into ego's effective matrix. The generic form of these transformation rules is the function $U_x = aX + bY$ where $U_x$ is the total utility that is subjectively experienced by ego; X and Y are the "objective" payoffs received by ego and alter, respectively; and a and b are parameters varying between $-1$ and $+1$.[20]

In experiments it has been shown that the full range of theoretically possible transformation parameters, including intermediate values, may in fact occur in the responses of human subjects (Schulz/May 1989). However, the most frequently encountered interaction orientations can be described by rules in which the parameters are either zero or plus or minus one. They will generate the following (nonexhaustive[21]) set of five transformation rules:

*Individualism:* $U_x = X$. This rule describes the standard assumption of self-interest maximization of neoclassical economics and conventional rational-choice approaches. Only gains and losses to ego will be considered. In graphical representation (Figure 4.6) desirable outcomes for ego will be located to the right of the vertical axis.

*Solidarity:* $U_x = X + Y$. This rule defines the precondition of unrestricted cooperation. A gain to alter or a gain to ego will be equally valued. In graphical representation, desired outcomes for ego and alter will be located in the outcome space above and to the right of the northwest-southeast diagonal. This space in-

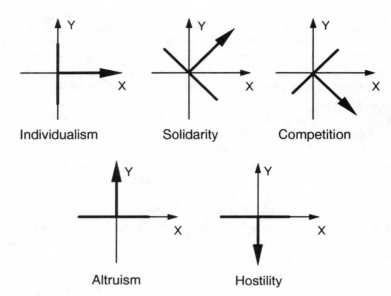

Individualism            Solidarity            Competition

Altruism            Hostility

FIGURE 4.6    Five interaction orientations

cludes, it should be noted, outcomes located to the left of the vertical axis, implying a real loss to ego, as long as they are justified by a larger gain to alter.

*Competition:* $U_x = X - Y$. This rule describes the psychological mechanisms of a need to win or of envy. It also describes the mechanisms of competition in sports, business, politics, and war. A gain to ego or a loss to alter will be equally valued. What matters is the difference between payoffs, or the relative gain of ego over alter. Thus a gain to ego will nevertheless be considered a loss if the gain to alter is still larger. Conversely, even if the outcome implies a loss to ego, it may still be counted as a relative gain if alter's loss is even larger. In the figure, desirable outcomes for ego will be located to the right and below the southwest-northeast diagonal.

*Altruism:* $U_x = Y$. This is the normative rule of the helping professions. A gain to alter will be considered as a positive outcome to ego, and ego's own payoffs are considered irrelevant for the interaction. This may—but does not necessarily presuppose—selflessness in the moral sense. In interactions with a patient, a doctor may act with exclusive regard for the patient's well-being precisely because his or her salary (or fixed honorarium) is not affected by the outcome of the treatment. In graphical representation, desired outcomes for ego will be located above the horizontal axis.

*Hostility:* $U_x = -Y$. This rule describes the psychological mechanisms of hate or of sadism. A loss to alter will be considered as gain to ego, and ego's own gains or losses are considered irrelevant. In graphical representation, desired outcomes for ego will be located below the horizontal axis.

In real-world policy processes, in the domestic politics of democratic states as well as in international relations, impulses toward altruism and hostility are generally constrained by the norms of political professionalism and of *raison d'état*. Actors who are accountable for the welfare of others are not expected to indulge in love or hate. Thus individualism, solidarity, and competition, and certain intermediate forms[22] are the most likely interaction orientations to expect. How they affect certain given matrices is illustrated, with regard to two of the archetypal game constellations discussed earlier, in Figure 4.7.

For an explication, consider the Prisoner's Dilemma. The "individualistic transformation" is of course identical to the standard matrix presented earlier—and thus to the "given matrix" in experimental social psychology. The matrix in the middle represents the "competitive transformation"—that is, the view that is obtained when the transformation $U_x = X - Y$ is applied to the payoffs in each cell of the "given matrix."[23] The new matrix so obtained represents a zero-sum game, in which what one side gains the other side must lose. In the matrix on the right, by contrast, which represents the result of a "cooperative" or "solidaristic" transformation (according to the rule $U_x = X + Y$), all aspects of conflict of interest are eliminated, and the players have a common interest in reaching the outcome that maximizes the sum of their payoffs without regard to which of them may get more or less individually. Two comments are in order.

First, compared to the strategic complexity of the original Prisoner's Dilemma, both the "competitive" and the "solidaristic" transformations represent radically simplified actor constellations. Competitive interaction orientations will transform all varieties of constellations into zero-sum games. Under these conditions cooperation, which would presuppose a modicum of common interest, is ruled out, and any communication received from the other is at best "cheap talk" but more likely an attempt at deception. When that is assumed, game theory provides a simple and unambiguous recommendation: In zero-sum games of this type, rational players should choose a "maximin" strategy, that is, the strategy that will *maximize the minimal payoff* that they can expect under worst-case assumptions. In the Prisoner's Dilemma, therefore, the Row player should choose the bottom row, where his or her minimum payoff would be zero, rather than the top row, where the minimum would be $-3$; and by the same logic, the Column player should of course choose the right-hand column.

A "cooperative" transformation, by contrast, will convert all kinds of actor constellations into "games of pure coordination" in which actors are only interested in coordinating their choices on a solution that produces the best combined payoffs. This is no problem at all in the Prisoner's Dilemma, where the upper-left cell contains the outcome that is best for both. In the Battle of the Sexes, however, there are two "best" outcomes, one in the upper-left cell, the other in the lower-right cell. But since the players are indifferent between these, communication should allow them to select one or the other.

The second comment has to do with the make-believe character of subjective "interaction orientations," which merely affect the actor's worldview but cannot change the real world. Even though the parties in a civil war may believe that the only thing that matters is defeating the other side, they will still have to mourn

## Battle of the Sexes

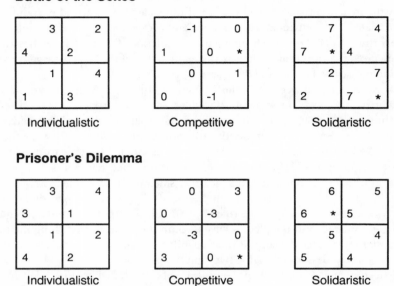

Individualistic                    Competitive                    Solidaristic

## Prisoner's Dilemma

Individualistic                    Competitive                    Solidaristic

FIGURE 4.7   Individualistic, competitive, and solidaristic transformations of two game constellations. Cells marked by an asterisk represent equilibrium outcomes in the transformed matrices.

their dead and live in the towns they destroyed. Thus it seems necessary to retranslate the strategy choices induced by the "delusions" of the transformation rules into the hard facts of the "given matrix." To do so, we need to compare the cells marked by an asterisk in the transformed matrices to the outcomes in the corresponding cells in the given matrix.

When that is done, the impression gained by an inspection of Figure 4.7 can be generalized: Actors who are (jointly!) "deluded" by a solidaristic orientation will generally find themselves well-off on the "morning after," when only the outcomes that they will in fact receive in real terms are considered. In particular, they will always do better than if they had found themselves caught in competitive interaction orientations. There, under the influence of worst-case assumptions, they would have had to pursue risk-minimizing strategies that would have ignored all opportunities for mutual gain through cooperation. When retranslated into the given matrices of a great variety of two-by-two game constellations, the outcomes so selected will never represent more than the second-worst payoffs for either player (and in some cases they represent the worst possible outcome).

Thus, if actors were able to choose their orientations (Sen 1970; 1977), they would be better off, in purely individualistic terms, if they could opt for solidarity—and could trust others to do likewise. But the ability to trust is of course the crucial problem. If one party acts from a solidaristic orientation while the other is motivated by competitive preferences, then the trusting party would be left with its own worst-case outcome in all games except the Battle of the Sexes, and the other side could always reach its own best or second-best outcome. In other words, being able to trust, and being trusted, is an advantage—but exploiting trust may be even more advantageous. Hence solidarity is a precarious inter-action orientation whose maintenance may depend on highly demanding indi-vidual and institutional preconditions and typically on high visibility and the availability of effective sanctions (Hechter 1987; Ostrom 1990). Competitive ori-entations, by contrast, are immune to disappointment and hence tend to be self-stabilizing.

For empirical research, the conclusion is therefore that we must remain alert to the possibility that interaction orientations may change. This is obvious in pri-vate relationships at the individual level, when, say, love turns into hate or com-petition into cooperation. But it is also a possibility at the level of highly orga-nized collective or corporate actors. It is true that Otto von Bismarck, in his memoirs, insisted time and again that states had interests, but neither hate nor love, in their relations with other states. But the fact that he needed to insist upon this point, even in a period of cabinet politics and before the arrival of mass democracy, emphasizes the purely normative, counterfactual nature of his exhor-tations. Surely the breakup of Yugoslavia cannot be explained without taking account of a "competitive" or "hostile" switch in interaction orientations, and similarly it is unlikely that peace processes will succeed unless interaction orien-tations switch back, if not to "solidarity" at least to "rational egoism." Empirical research would of course greatly benefit from having well-tested theories that are able to explain[24] and predict switches in interaction orientations. As long as we do not have them, we should at least remain attentive to the empirical impor-tance of interaction orientations and to their potential changeability.

## NORMATIVE ASPECTS

In the remaining chapters of this book I will discuss different modes of interac-tion, from unilateral action through negotiated agreements and majoritarian vot-ing to hierarchical determination. As I pointed out earlier, these modes are likely to have a significant effect on the outcomes of interactions in any given actor constellation. If, for instance, the constellation resembles a symmetrical Pris-oner's Dilemma, then unilateral action is likely to lead the actors into a "social trap"; but when negotiated agreements with binding effect are possible, the out-come is likely to be superior for all actors involved. At the same time, the mode of interaction actually employed is often the object of institutional design or may be chosen ad hoc by the parties involved. From a pragmatic point of view, therefore, it is important that policy research be able to describe and compare the effects of different modes of interaction in terms of the normative or evaluative criteria of "good" public policy suggested in the Introduction. These criteria have been implicitly used in the preceding discussion. They now need to be explicated further.

In the Introduction I suggested a dualistic standard for evaluating the influence of modes of interaction on policy outcomes.[25] Its *welfare-theoretic* dimension is defined in utilitarian terms; its second dimension is that of *distributive justice.*

The utilitarian welfare criterion implies that one outcome is to be preferred over another if it creates more aggregate value. In our game matrices this would be the outcome associated with the highest sum-total of individual payoffs. The reader should be warned, however, that the use of utilitarian criteria is controversial. There are conceptual difficulties involved in comparing different *types* of values, accruing at different points in *time* and *space* and benefiting different *persons.* These difficulties have given utilitarianism a bad name in philosophy (Höffe 1987), and they explain why modern welfare economics has more or less abandoned utilitarianism and is contenting itself with the criterion of *Pareto superiority,* which favors outcomes that improve value production in some respect (favoring particular types of values, at particular times and places, and benefiting particular persons) without reducing the satisfaction of any other value aspect. But once the opportunities for such "costless" gains are exhausted, modern welfare economics declares itself incompetent to judge the distributive issues involved in trade-offs among different value aspects on the "Pareto frontier."

One reason for this is related to the conceptual difficulty of collapsing values differing in type and in their temporal, local, and personal incidence into a single measure of aggregate utility. Pragmatically, however, it has always been assumed in economics that *individuals* are somehow capable of aggregating the benefits they receive from events differing in type, space, and time into a single utility measure and preference judgment. If we maintain that assumption, the difficulties, at the level of public policy, are reduced to their *interpersonal* dimension. They arise because choices among different types of values—say, education or old-age pensions—will provide benefits and impose costs on different groups, and the same is true of differences in time and place. If it were otherwise, more net benefit would always be preferred to less. Thus the critical issue, on which modern welfare economics refuses to take a stand, is the interpersonal distribution of costs and benefits—a refusal that is usually justified by one or both of two arguments.

The first asserts that science should avoid issues requiring value judgments. But even though it is true that distributive issues involve value judgments, the claim that these could be avoided in welfare economics is open to challenge. Though the criterion of Pareto superiority is defined without reference to distributive consequences, it is itself by no means value free since it postulates that all existing value positions should be protected. Moreover, since changes that are Pareto improvements may increase inequality, the standard also presupposes that *distributive consequences should not matter*—which is of course as much a value judgment as would be an explicit preference for any particular distributive outcome. Thus not much is gained in terms of value-free scientific purity by sticking to the Pareto criterion.

The second argument emphasizes the fact that the evaluation of distributive justice depends on interpersonal comparisons of utility that are considered impossible. Being locked into my own subjective world, it is indeed impossible for me to partake directly of your experience. But that truism cannot invalidate the human capacity for empathy. Imagining myself in your shoes, I could still assess *how I would feel in your place,* and I can compare this feeling to my own situation. Public-policy discourses are generally conducted at the level of such vicarious judgments, and policy issues are typically concerned with varieties of costs and benefits that rarely affect the innermost subjectivities of target populations and that hence are relatively robust with regard to empathetic comparisons (Binmore 1994). At any rate, since the policy process is inevitably concerned with value trade-offs, it seems more plausible for the policy sciences to work with the (utilitarian) welfare criterion proposed by Nicholas Kaldor (1939) according to which policy choices are minimally acceptable if the gains to the winners are high enough to permit full compensation to all losers (Figure 4.8).

In the figure, this is illustrated for the two-person case, where the welfare of X is measured on the horizontal and that of Y on the vertical axis, and where SQ represents the status quo. The northwest-southeast diagonal through SQ (where $X + Y = 0$) then represents the Kaldor criterion, and parallels to that diagonal can be interpreted as welfare isoquants, representing locations of outcomes producing the same level of aggregate welfare. Any outcome below and to the left of the diagonal through SQ, such as an outcome located at A, would be unacceptable, and policy outcomes would be the more attractive in welfare-theoretic terms the further out the welfare isoquant on which they are located. Thus the highly unequal outcome C would be preferred to the more equal outcome B because the gain to X is larger than Y's loss.

Like the Pareto criterion, the Kaldor criterion is thus silent on distribution. It merely requires gains large enough that the losers *could* be compensated, but it leaves the question of whether and how compensation should actually be carried out to the political process. It is clear, however, that the political process itself is continuously involved in distributive issues and also that these issues are inevitably debated and decided by reference to normative standards that are supposed to have general validity beyond the case at hand (Elster 1992; Rothstein 1992). And even if welfare economics may be silent on issues of distributive justice, it is equally clear that jurisprudence, philosophy, and normative political theory have made important analytical contributions to their clarification (Rawls 1971; Barry/Rae 1975; Barry 1989; 1995). The problem therefore is not the lack of criteria but rather their plurality.

Social psychology has identified at least three logically distinct definitions of distributive justice, labeled "equity," "equality," and "need" (Deutsch 1975; 1985). *Equity* refers to the equivalence of efforts, contributions, or sacrifices on the one

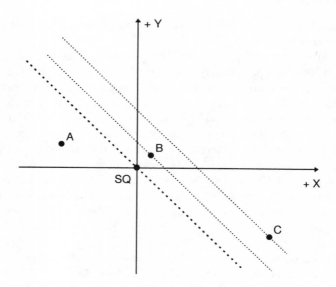

FIGURE 4.8    The Kaldor welfare criterion

side and rewards on the other side. Its criterion is proportionality, and its normative relevance is most obvious in all types of relationships involving exchange or
collaboration toward a common goal. *Equality* is understood as formal equality—in the sense of the "one-person-one-vote" rule governing elections. Its relevance is most obvious in the relationship of citizens to the democratic state.
*Need,* finally, is defined by special disabilities or disadvantages that justify positive
discrimination or, conversely, by special capabilities or an above-average "ability
to pay" that justifies the imposition of unequal burdens. It is obvious that these
different concepts of distributive justice need not necessarily compete with each
other—they seem to fit different "spheres of justice" (Walzer 1983). Nevertheless,
concepts of justice are likely to be contested, and Jon Elster's empirical studies of
the criteria applied to "hard choices" have shown a much greater variety and sophistication of the criteria applied to specific situations than could be derived
from the simple triad discussed here (Elster 1992). They have also shown, however, that ordinary citizens, judges, bureaucrats, and politicians are in fact capable
of working out normatively defensible solutions to difficult problems of distributive justice.

     As a consequence, our task as policy researchers is not to take over this job and
to announce, as it were, "scientifically" validated value judgments on specific distributional issues. What we can and should do, however, is to assess the extent to
which different institutional arrangements, and in particular different modes of
interaction, are conducive to the settlement of distributive issues in the light of
considered criteria of distributive justice. Exactly the same is of course our job

with regard to welfare-theoretic criteria, whether of the Paretian or Kaldorian variety. As will be shown in the following chapters, different modes of interaction will indeed differ significantly in both of these dimensions, and it is also possible to specify the conditions that would increase the chances that a particular mode of interaction will in fact produce outcomes that increase aggregate welfare and that reflect criteria of distributive justice.

In doing so, however, we must keep two things in mind: First, actor constellations differ greatly in the degree of difficulty that must be overcome in order to arrive at normatively acceptable outcomes. Games of pure coordination are easy to resolve in satisfactory fashion through any mode of coordination. By contrast, in a Chicken game there are much greater obstacles that stand in the way of a satisfactory resolution, and the difficulties would again increase under conditions corresponding to the asymmetrical conflict game of Figure 4.5. Thus when considering the implications of a particular mode of interaction, the actor constellations that it is required to deal with, and their characteristic difficulties, must be considered as well. As long as the European Community, for instance, was primarily engaged in realizing the common interest of member states in gaining access to a common market, the fact that its mode of interaction depended on the unanimous agreement among member-state governments was relatively innocuous—but it becomes deficient when issues requiring the resolution of major conflicts of interest among member states become more prevalent.

The second reminder concerns the fact that we will always be dealing with interactions among policy actors rather than with the underlying policy problems. Thus when we are comparing the welfare efficiency and distributive justice produced by different modes of interaction, we always should remain aware of the need to retranslate these outcomes into the terms of the original policy problems. With this in mind, in the following chapters I will examine the specific implications of four different modes of interaction—unilateral action, negotiated agreement, majoritarian voting, and hierarchical direction.

## NOTES

1. As I pointed out earlier, substantive policy analysis is characteristically conducted from a decision-theoretic (and by implication, from a single-actor) perspective. As a consequence, the interpersonal aspects that are constitutive of a public-policy problem are not always distinguished from analyses that merely advise actors of how their own action resources ought to be employed to the actors' best advantage.

2. Methodologically, this implies working with "connected games," in which interactions between one set of actors influence interactions among another set of actors (Tsebelis 1990).

3. The game is often illustrated by a scenario ascribed to Jean-Jacques Rousseau: A group of hunters sets out to catch a stag. If they stay together, they will all eat well. But if one of them gets sidetracked by the chance to catch a rabbit, he will eat less well and the others will go hungry. In that case, it is better for the others to chase their own rabbits as well.

4. The scenario that explains the nickname of the game assumes that she and he would love to spend an evening together, but while she likes boxing matches, he would prefer to go to the opera. Nevertheless, each would rather endure the less favored entertainment than spend the evening alone.

5. An important empirical example is provided by the research of Adrienne Héritier and her collaborators on "regulatory competition" in European environmental policy. The competition is among environmentally "activist" member states, all of which have a preference for common European regulations at high levels of protection. However, since their national "styles" of environmental regulation differ significantly (with Germany being committed to limiting emissions at the source and Britain having opted for air-quality standards), the costs of adjustment will be considerably lower for the country that can persuade the European Commission to adopt its own regulatory system. As it turned out, the Commission used German-type standards in the 1980s and switched to the British model in the 1990s, but in both periods agreement was ultimately reached through negotiations (Héritier et al. 1994; Héritier/Knill/Mingers 1996; Héritier 1996).

6. As Philipp Genschel (1995) has shown, this is the empirical pattern through which a high degree of coordination is achieved among the multitude of international standardization organizations in the field of telecommunications and information technology.

7. In an ongoing relationship, however, a fair solution (such as turn taking) may be a necessary precondition of reliable coordination. Otherwise growing resentment may cause the permanently disadvantaged party to adopt a competitive orientation, which will transform its perception of the game.

8. The game owes its nickname to a scenario in which two bandits suspected of bank robbery are arrested and kept in separate cells. The district attorney confronts each of them separately with the same proposition: If one, but not the other, will confess to the robbery, he will go free and the other will go to jail for ten years. If both confess, they will both go to jail for five years. If neither confesses, they will both be convicted of a minor offense and go to jail for one year.

9. "Folk theorems" are insights that game theorists have long been aware of even though nobody claims to have discovered them first.

10. More generally, a game-theoretic "folk theorem" postulates that in all indefinitely iterated noncooperative games, any outcome that is better for all players than the single-shot equilibrium may become an equilibrium solution—given a sufficiently low rate of discounting the future (Fudenberg/Maskin 1986).

11. The constellation could be represented by a modification of the standard Prisoner's Dilemma matrix in which the upper-left (C/C) cell contains not a definite outcome but another game to be played—in this case, a negotiated Battle of the Sexes. Nonagreement would then throw the parties back to the D/D outcome in the original matrix.

12. The name refers to a "game" reportedly played by American teenagers in the 1950s. Racing their cars toward a head-on collision, he who swerves first is "Chicken," but if neither does, both will crash.

13. In game-theoretic terms: In a sequential noncooperative game played with perfect information, the prior commitment of the second mover to a retaliatory countermove could not lead to a "subgame perfect equilibrium" (Osborne/Rubinstein 1994, 97–101; Selten 1965).

14. In constellations involving three or more actors, coalitions are possible, and hence the level of conflict will vary, depending on which of the theoretically possible coalitions are in fact formed.

15. Michael Zürn (1992) has introduced a classification of game constellations in international relations that is intended to reflect the likelihood that normative regimes will be created. He distinguishes among games of pure coordination, games of coordination with distributive conflict, dilemma games, and Rambo games. But again, this classification cannot capture all empirically relevant aspects of the constellations.

16. The point is well made by Otto Keck (1994, 211). Referring to the possibility of communication and agreement (albeit without the possibility of external enforcement) in iterated Prisoner's Dilemma constellations, he writes: "Agreement may transform a real situation with innumerable options and incomplete information about the action of the opponent into an ideal-typical situation with exactly two options (namely to honor the agreement or to defect) and complete information about the action of the opponent (on the basis of agreed-upon verification measures)."

17. Alternatively, and more realistically, one could assume that regulations at two levels could be adopted—high standards for the rich countries and lower standards for others.

18. In this respect the method of hypothetical coalitions is structurally equivalent to the concepts of "two-level games" (Putnam 1988) or of "nested games" (Tsebelis 1990), which also imply that interdependent interactions may be analytically decomposed into several simpler interactions that, however, remain causally connected. In Appendix 1 an example is provided in which the coordination game played between the government and the unions and the electoral game played between the government and different strata of the electorate (represented as actor aggregates) are connected by virtue of the fact that the state of the economy produced by the coordination game determines the government's chances of success in the electoral game.

19. The justification for this, as for any, conceptual distinction is purely pragmatic. For mathematical game theorists, who work with postulated payoffs, there is no reason to distinguish between objective and subjective components. In social-psychological game experiments, by contrast, the distinction is critical since the experimenter is able to control only the objective payoffs, but not their subjective reinterpretation by experimental subjects. In empirical research, finally, the distinction is useful because it corresponds to basic differences in access to information. "Objective" payoffs are not only likely to be more stable over time, but they also can be inferred from factual and institutional information that is generally accessible at low cost. When subjective reinterpretations matter, by contrast, different sources of information must be explored and generally more costly research methods will be called for.

20. The application of conversion rules assumes that the payoffs of both players can be added to or subtracted from one another—that is, that interpersonal comparison of utilities should be possible. This assumption is in fact quite reasonable for competitive interactions: What actors compete about, and what it takes to win or lose, is either defined intersubjectively by institutionalized rules of the game or it must be so defined by the actors involved (or in the case of one-sided envy, by one actor defining the criterion of comparison for him- or herself). In the case of solidarity these definitional aids are not available, but there we have the methodological option of staying with individually rank-ordered preferences and maximizing the average of individual rank-orderings.

21. Transformation rules not considered here include:

$U_x = -1X + 0Y$ (masochism)
$U_x = -1X + 1Y$ (self-sacrifice)
$U_x = -1X - 1Y$ (mutual destruction)
$U_x = 0X + 0Y$ (indolence)

Though historical examples may be found for each of these possibilities, they do not seem to occur frequently enough to merit systematic attention here.

22. There has recently been a considerable amount of discussion on the importance of "intermediate" forms of relative-gains orientations in the International Relations literature (Powell 1991; Snidal 1991; Grieco/Powell/Snidal 1993). The claim is that neorealist theory (which always assumes relative-gains orientations among states) could nevertheless explain some international cooperation if the assumption were slightly softened, say, to $U_X = X - 0.9Y$. At the analytical level the argument is of course tautologically true. The more important issue seems to be whether neorealist assumptions have sufficient empirical plausibility to begin with to make the examination of marginal modifications theoretically and empirically worthwhile. However, it might indeed be worthwhile to consider a softened version of the individualistic orientation in which ego gives some small weight to the interests of alter—say, $U_X = X + 0.1Y$. Real-world actors—out of a sense of human kindness, duty, or honor—are often willing to do small favors that will not cost ego very much but may be quite important to alter.

23. The coincidence of the "individualistic transformation" with the "given matrix" suggests that the individualistic assumptions of rational-choice approaches have indeed a theoretically privileged position. On the one hand, they represent a subjective interpretation of a given relationship, just like all other interaction orientations. On the other hand, however, they also describe the real consequences that an actor will have to live with as a result of the particular interaction. Whereas the world created by the other interaction orientations collapses when attitudes change, the given matrix describes the real world that will reassert itself, and that actors will have to deal with, on the "morning after"—that is, after love or hate, solidarity, or the competitive spirit has lost its capacity to redefine the situation.

24. A game-theoretic explanation of the switch to hostility in Serbian orientations is provided by Casella and Weingast (1995).

25. Elinor Ostrom (1996), in a paper that I saw only as this book was going to press, suggests that policy processes should be evaluated by six criteria, namely, "economic efficiency," "equity through fiscal equivalence," "redistributional equity," "accountability," "conformance to general morality," and "adaptability."

# 5

# *Unilateral Action in Anarchic Fields and Minimal Institutions*

In Chapter 4 I discussed how real-world policy problems may be mapped on constellations of actors with given preferences and given capabilities to generate a variety of "actor constellations" differing in the degree to which interests converge or conflict. The remaining chapters will deal with the modes of interaction through which these game constellations are converted into policy outcomes. This already suggests that we cannot restrict analysis to the solution concepts provided by the theory of noncooperative games but need rather to consider the full range of empirically possible modes, from unilateral action through varieties of negotiations and voting to hierarchical direction. As I pointed out in Chapter 2, these modes have a structural as well as a procedural dimension. The distinction is theoretically significant since the same procedure of interaction—say, negotiations—may be employed in quite different structural settings—say, in a market, in a network, in a parliamentary arena, or within a bureaucratic hierarchy (Table 2.1). The assumption is that these modes will change their character when employed in different institutional settings. Negotiations "in the shadow of hierarchy" differ in their problem-solving capacity from negotiations in a market setting.

A further assumption is that the institutionalization of different structures is associated with different degrees of difficulty or improbability. The default condition—or, more appropriately, the "background condition"—is the anarchic field in which actors respond to each other by mutual adjustment or in noncooperative games. Markets, though they also have some of the characteristics of unstructured fields, are institutionally more demanding since they depend on the prior definition and protection of property rights and on the exogenous enforcement of contracts. Networks may evolve from the same institutional foundations, but they are more effective, and at the same time more selective, than markets in facilitating cooperative interactions. By comparison, the establishment of an arena in which collectively binding decisions can be taken by majority vote, or by hierarchical direction, is institutionally much more demanding.[1]

## ANARCHIC FIELDS AND MINIMAL INSTITUTIONS

I begin with a brief discussion of the least demanding structural setting that permits no more than unilateral action. In a sense the "anarchic field" describes a
nonstructure, or an institution-free context, in which individual actors will interact with one another in the absence of a preexisting relationship, or of specific
obligations, between them. They are thus free to use all strategies within their capability, and they are constrained only by physical limitations and by the countermoves of other actors. They may communicate and conclude agreements, but
they are also free to break such agreements if it suits their interests. Robert Dahl
and Charles Lindblom (1953), in their pathbreaking attempt to systematize "basic social processes" more than forty years ago, introduced the term "field" with
the intention of showing that even under such conditions mutual adjustment
and "spontaneous field control" among independent actors may lead to a form of
ecological coordination. The same expectation is shared by Hayekian models
postulating the emergence of "spontaneous social order" from interactions
among self-interested individuals in an institution-free context (Schotter 1981).
In a less optimistic spirit, the neorealist theory of international relations also assumes that interactions among nation-states take place in an institution-free setting, conceptualized as the "anarchy of the international system" (Waltz 1954;
1979). Again, the assumption is that the freedom of unilateral action is effectively
constrained only by the limits of physical capabilities and by the anticipated
countermoves of other states—but now the conclusion is less benign: War is endemic in the international system, and interactions must therefore be governed
by the relative-gains logic of mutual distrust and generalized caution.

Within the nation-state, by contrast, actors will not usually deal with one another under conditions of anarchy. Their choices are—exogenously[2]—constrained by (at least) the minimal institutions of a legal system that protects certain interest positions against unilateral violation. Thus criminal law enforced by
the machinery of state prosecution and punishment protects interests in life, physical integrity, physical liberty, and property rights against intentional or negligent
violation, and the private law of torts extends the range of protected interests still
further and adds civil liability to the system of sanctions. In addition, the law of
contracts provides a system of rules that define the conditions under which agreements among private parties are treated as binding, and the law of civil procedure
provides a machinery for enforcing the contractual obligations so defined.

Property rights and legally binding contracts are also the (exogenously given)
minimal institutional conditions presupposed by economic theories of market
transactions among strangers. In addition, however, interactions in anonymous
markets are thought to be constrained by the existence of generally known market
prices that buyers as well as sellers will treat as exogenous determinants of their
agreements. Nevertheless, these are minimal institutional constraints that, in general, are only sufficient for facilitating "arms-length" interactions leading to "spot

contracts" for the exchange of well-defined goods or services in which promise and performance are not significantly separated in time. At any rate, given our interest in policy interactions, market exchanges will not concern us further. Instead, we have a considerable interest in the other modes of interaction that are possible within anarchic fields and minimal institutions. Among them, we distinguish noncooperative games, Mutual Adjustment, and Negative Coordination.

## NONCOOPERATIVE GAMES AND THE NASH EQUILIBRIUM

In game theory, it is a fundamental tenet that all forms of interaction should be reduced to the form of a noncooperative game (Nash 1953; Holler/Illing 1993). For empirical research, however, that is not useful advice. The different modes of interaction have their own characteristic capabilities and difficulties, and even if it were logically possible to reconstruct all of these in the conceptual language of the theory of noncooperative games, to do so would not be helpful for identifying and communicating the important differences between them. In one sense, however, noncooperative games are indeed fundamental: Regardless of the structures and modes of interaction they may be involved in, actors always have the option of falling back to unilateral action. It may be illegal or violate an agreement, but the fallback option of unilateral action cannot be taken away.

This is why game theorists, within their universalistic theoretical program, insist that all "higher" forms of interaction should be reconstructed as equilibrium outcomes of noncooperative interactions. From our empirical perspective, by contrast, what matters is the ever-present possibility that other modes of interaction may be accompanied by or degenerate into noncooperative games. For instance, in the field of international telecommunications, technical standards are generally produced through negotiations in international standardization committees. However, the firms involved still are able to produce nonstandardized equipment in the hope of succeeding in the market on their own—an outside option that, in this case, is judged to increase the efficiency of committee standardization (Farrell/Saloner 1988).

The theory of noncooperative games assumes that actors act on their own, without the possibility of binding agreements and with a single-minded interest in maximizing their own payoffs but in awareness of their interdependence with other actors and with complete knowledge of the available strategies and the associated payoffs of all other players. The important contribution that this theory has made to social science thinking is, first, *a clear focus on strategic interaction*—on the fact, that is, that the social situation generally cannot be modeled as a "game against nature" or against a passive environment but must rather be understood as an encounter among intelligent and resourceful actors who are likely to respond to any moves in order to improve their own situation. Second, the theory of noncooperative games adds analytical power to the intuition expressed in Carl J. Friedrich's famous "doctrine of anticipated reactions" (1937, 16), which, as I will argue later, is essential for both the effectiveness of democratic accountability and the effectiveness of hierarchical authority. Of even greater theoretical importance is the demonstration that mutual anticipation among rational actors need not lead into the infinite regress of "I think that she thinks that I think that . . . " but instead may produce stable equilibrium outcomes. In fact, the single most important idea that game theory has contributed to the social sciences is the concept of "Nash equilibrium" (Nash 1951), which is defined as a constellation of individual strategies in which no player could still improve his or her own outcome by unilaterally switching to another available option. For the four archetypal mixed-motive games discussed earlier, the concept is illustrated in Figure 5.1.

For example, in the Assurance game, C/C represents a Nash equilibrium in which both players would obtain their best payoff (4,4) and which neither has a motive to change. Nevertheless, there exists a second Nash equilibrium at D/D. It is much less attractive for both players (2,2), but if the Row player should unilaterally shift to C/D, the outcome would be even worse for Row (1,3), and the same reason would prevent the Column player from a unilateral shift to D/C. However, since both players have a preference for the outcome at C/C, mere communication between them would be enough to facilitate a *common* shift to that outcome.

This is not so in the Battle of the Sexes, which also has two equilibria, at C/D and D/C, but in which the players' preferences are not in agreement. Row will prefer D/C (4,3) and Column D/C (3,4). Yet if one of these outcomes should somehow be reached, even the disadvantaged party will not want to change it unilaterally. The asymmetry is even more pronounced in Chicken, where the Nash equilibria at C/D and D/C are solutions in which one of the players is severely exploited by the other (2,4 and 4,2). Nevertheless, the "compromise" solution at C/C, in which both players would get their second-best payoff (3,3), is not a stable equilibrium, since Row could do better by moving to D/C, and Column could move to C/D. Similarly, in the Prisoner's Dilemma the "cooperative" outcome at C/C (3,3) is not a stable solution, even though it would clearly be more attractive to both players than the only Nash equilibrium at D/D. In other words, even the weak Pareto criterion would be violated here.

Thus there is no reason to think that a Nash equilibrium should be either "efficient" in welfare-theoretic terms or "fair" in terms of distributive justice. It merely is an outcome that, once it is reached in one way or another, rational players are unable to leave through unilateral action. In particular, the existence of Pareto-inferior equilibria in actor constellations resembling the Prisoner's Dilemma provides a powerful explanation of the Tragedy of the Commons (Hardin 1968) and of a wide variety of "social traps" (Platt 1973; Messick/McClelland 1983). In the same way, political philosophers have been able to reconstruct the "Hobbesian condition" before the arrival of Leviathan as well as Rousseauian society before the social contract as equilibrium outcomes of a multiactor Prisoner's Dilemma (Runciman/Sen 1965; Sen 1969). In short, under conditions in which binding agreements or collectively binding decisions are not

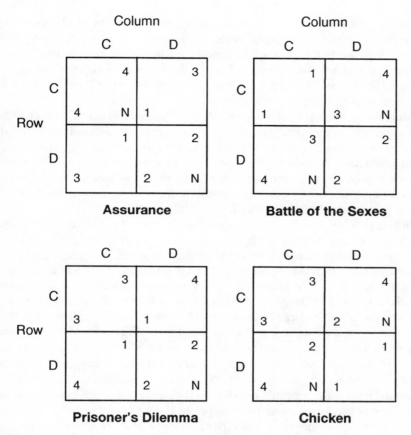

FIGURE 5.1    Nash equilibria (N) in four mixed-motive games

possible, the Nash equilibrium concept has the power of explaining stable out-comes—and the explanation is uniquely compelling in cases in which these out-comes seem unsatisfactory from the point of view of all the actors involved.

From an empirical point of view, however, the concept of Nash equilibrium may be able to explain the stability of particular outcomes, but it does not provide an algorithm that could explain why and how the players should reach a particular outcome. Outcomes are assumed to be stable if for all players involved the strategy selected is their best response against the best-response strategies of all other play-ers. Since that assumption, as we will see immediately, is of little predictive use, it is important to note that difficulties of *prediction* will not invalidate the Nash con-cept as a useful tool for the *explanation* of empirically stable outcomes.

That difficulties of prediction do in fact exist is evident in the four archetypal two-by-two games reproduced in Figure 5.1, of which three have two Nash equilibria. In Assurance, it is true, rational and completely informed players would have no difficulty in converging on the equilibrium at C/C, which for both of them is superior to the D/D equilibrium. In Battle of the Sexes and in Chicken, however, the players will strongly disagree in their preferences for one or the other of the two equilibrium solutions—and nothing in the Nash concept will tell them what to do under the circumstances.

Moreover, as is illustrated in Figure 5.2, not all games will have a Nash equilibrium outcome in pure strategies. There, if the status quo should be at Up/Left, the Row player could go for the big prize and move to Down, at which point Column would move to Right to gain the best outcome (which for Row would be the worst). Row could then improve things a bit by switching back to Up, which, being Column's worst-case outcome, would motivate Column to move Left—at which point the cycle could begin again.

In game theory, it is true, it is assumed that players will not be restricted to the "pure" strategies (choosing either "Up" or "Down," "Left" or "Right") discussed so far but may also resort to "mixed strategies," in which they use randomized combinations of their pure strategies.[3] When that is allowed, mathematical game theory assures us that all games will have at least one Nash equilibrium solution in mixed strategies (Dasgupta/Maskin 1986). It is not certain, however, that much is gained for empirical research by this mathematical demonstration. Unless players are involved in large numbers of identical interactions, it is unclear how a randomizing strategy that maximizes *expected* payoffs would make practical sense from their point of view. At any rate, it is hard to imagine real-world policymakers throwing dice—and if they did, we would be most unlikely to learn about it. Hence, since we could not observe the randomizing process itself, all we would see is the actual move that happened to be selected—which would of course give us no clue to the underlying strategy. Moreover, the outcome so achieved (in pure strategies, that is) by definition could not itself be a Nash equilibrium, and so if there were any chance of revision at all it would be unstable. Thus the concept of a mixed-strategy Nash equilibrium, though mathematically meaningful, allows us neither to predict nor to explain real-world outcomes. I suggest that we not include it in our theoretical tool kit for empirical policy research (Scharpf 1990).

This means, however, that there will be noncooperative interactions without equilibrium outcomes and, as Matthias Mohr has shown in computer simulations, the proportion of such cases will generally increase as the number of players involved, and the number of their strategies, increases (see Appendix 2). This is unfortunate, but it is probably quite realistic. The expectation that all human interactions, or all noncooperative interactions, should lead to stable equilibrium outcomes has no support in substantive social science theory. Many interactions will take place far from equilibrium, and they may continue, or be discontinued, without ever reaching an equilibrium outcome. For such processes the theory of noncooperative games has little predictive power. Its strength lies in providing

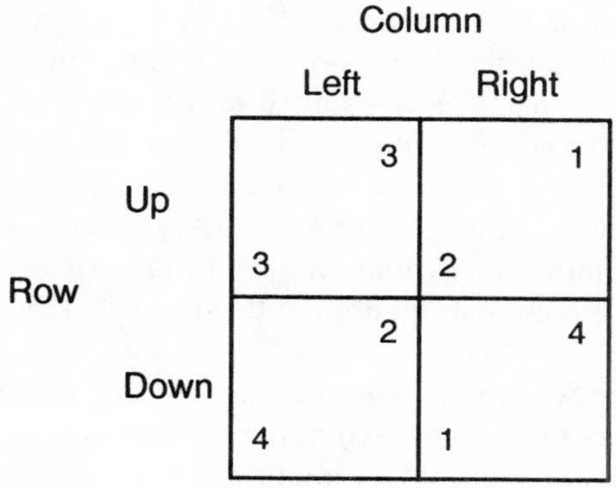

Column

Left        Right

FIGURE 5.2    Game without a Nash equilibrium in pure strategies

explanations for stable outcomes, and we ought to use it for purposes, and in constellations, where it is strong.

But even then, there are serious problems since, as we have seen, games that have any Nash equilibrium solution in pure strategies are quite likely to have more than one—and in complex game constellations or in iterated games, there may in fact exist very many equilibrium outcomes. Thus we need to return to the processes through which actors arrive at their strategy choices. Here game theorists have discussed a number of "solution concepts" that are highly plausible in some types of constellations but none of which is generally applicable or, if applicable, generally conducive to outcomes that are acceptable in welfare-theoretic terms.

The least controversial of these is the concept of *dominance.* It implies that in choosing between two strategies an actor should always select the one that provides for payoffs that are superior or equal to the payoffs provided by the second strategy for all options the other parties might exercise. The logic of this rule is impeccable, and it also has the great advantage that the solutions so obtained will certainly be Nash equilibria and that each player need only have information about his or her own payoffs in order to apply it. The disadvantage of the rule is its limited applicability. In the five two-by-two games reproduced earlier, only the Prisoner's Dilemma could be decided by the dominance concept—and there its application will produce a Pareto-inferior outcome. Nevertheless, the dominance rule will often help to eliminate some dominated strategies and thus help to simplify complex game matrices to more manageable proportions.

Similarly, the *maximin* rule is fully plausible only for a limited domain. It implies that a player should examine the expected payoffs for each of the strategy options and choose the one for which the minimum payoff is highest. The rule shares with dominance the great advantage that players need only know and analyze their own payoffs and do not depend on information about others' preferences. Normatively the rule makes good sense for game constellations of pure conflict, or zero-sum games, where it is reasonable to assume that the other party will do its best to inflict damage on one's interest position. Under these worst-case assumptions a rule of generalized caution will limit the maximum damage that could be done. Similarly, in games without a Nash equilibrium, maximin may provide a "satisficing" stopping point for parties that are frustrated by the infinite meandering of moves and countermoves. In the Prisoner's Dilemma it would lead to the same suboptimal equilibrium that is reached through the dominance rule.

However, the maximin rule is not theoretically satisfactory under more general mixed-motive conditions. Often, the outcomes so reached will not be Nash equilibria and hence may not be stable. More important, from a normative point of view, is the implication that players following the maximin rule must act under worst-case assumptions. If the constellation is not in fact zero sum, they may thus be required to choose inferior outcomes and to ignore attractive opportunities for mutual gain. The extreme case is illustrated by the Assurance game in Figure 5.1, in which maximin would require both Row and Column to opt for D, leaving both with their second-worst outcome and ignoring the much more attractive Nash equilibrium at C/C. Similarly, in the Battle of the Sexes maximin will prevent the parties from coordinating on one of the two preferred outcomes. In the Chicken game the situation is more complicated. Here if maximin were applied by both parties, then the outcome would be a mutually attractive compromise solution at C/C. However, since that solution is not a Nash equilibrium, it is unstable. Row as well as Column would be tempted to switch to D. If one player is able to move first, then the outcome would be highly asymmetric in his or her favor, but stable. However, if both move at the same time, both would end up with their worst payoff. Thus maximin here looks more like an opening move than a rule that will lead to a unique and mutually acceptable end state.

Similar problems are associated with all other solution concepts that are meant to simplify the strategy choice of individual actors (Colman 1982; Holler/Illing 1993). Hence we are ultimately left with the Nash concept, pure and simple. However, if it is used not as a characteristic of the solution but as a procedure for finding this solution, then it is much more demanding on the players than any of the rules discussed thus far. It implies not only that they should know their own strategic options and their own preferences but also that they should have "complete information" on the strategy options of all players, on the outcomes to be expected at the intersections of all strategies, and on the preferences that all players actually attach to these outcomes. On the basis of that information, they would then need to reconstruct the (multidimensional) game matrix and examine each of the potential outcomes with regard to the possibility that any of the players could improve his or her own payoff through a unilateral departure from that outcome. These cognitive difficulties will increase exponentially as the number of players and the number of their available strategies increase.

It is true, as I argued earlier, that in many situations the cognitive difficulties of these tasks will be reduced through the formation of macroactors and through reliance on institutional information. Collective and corporate actors are institutionally constituted, and institutions not only define the repertoires of their permissible strategies but also shape the interests and preferences in the light of which players will evaluate the potential outcomes that would be obtained at the intersections of these strategies. Moreover, policy interactions in open, democratic societies are generally accompanied by much public debate and more-or-less competent analyses of options and implications in the media.[4] Thus we can often assume that the (highly professional) actors whom we encounter in policy processes will have a relatively clear mental image of the game constellation.

However, the degree to which options and evaluations are shaped by institutions varies, and it is never perfect, even under the best of circumstances. Game theory, it is true, has developed "Bayesian" solution algorithms for games in which complete information is lacking (Harsanyi 1967–1968). But it is fair to say that the probabilistic calculations and the updating of expectations required by these algorithms are beyond the cognitive capacities of real-world actors. Moreover, even under the best of circumstances, the cognitive complexity of identifying Nash equilibria will rapidly increase to completely unmanageable dimensions as the number of independent players involved and the number of their permissible strategies increase beyond a very few (Scharpf 1991b). Even if all these difficulties were overcome, players would still be faced with the possibility that the game constellation may include multiple Nash equilibria, and nothing in the Nash concept would allow them to identify one of these on which they could expect all parties involved to converge.[5]

We thus have reason to conclude that real-world players will have difficulty in arriving at a specific Nash equilibrium through the rational anticipation of one another's moves. For empirical research, therefore, the domain in which the theory of noncooperative games will have *predictive* power appears to be narrowly circumscribed. It is most plausible in highly structured and frequently recurring interactions among a limited number of actors with a high capacity for strategic action, in situations in which a great deal is at stake, and in interest constellations with a relatively high level of conflict in which binding agreements are not generally possible. It is not surprising, therefore, that noncooperative game theory has gained its most important empirical strongholds in studies of international relations (Snyder/Diesing 1977; Snidal 1985a; Zürn 1992), of interactions in the legislative process (Shepsle/Weingast 1981; Tsebelis 1994), and of interactions among oligopolistic firms (Osborne/Rubinstein 1990; Holler/Illing 1993), whereas in many other areas of social science its application is viewed with much greater skepticism.

However, the fact that the domain of its predictive power is limited does not deprive the Nash concept of its explanatory power in the wider domain. Noncooperative interactions in the form postulated by the theory of noncooperative games—that is, interactions with perfect mutual anticipation but without the possibility of binding agreements—constitute only one among several possible modes of interaction and surely a highly improbable one. But the Nash concept, as I have suggested, does not postulate a particular way in which an equilibrium outcome should be reached—it merely specifies conditions under which outcomes are likely to be stable—and thus it does not depend on the specific cognitive and procedural assumptions generally associated with noncooperative game theory.

To express the same idea in terms of an empirical hypothesis: Regardless of the way in which a particular outcome has been reached—by ecological adjustment, through negotiations, through voting, or by hierarchical fiat—it is more likely to be stable if it meets the conditions of a Nash equilibrium. Conversely, if one or more of the players can still improve their own payoff by unilaterally deviating from a given solution, then that solution should be considered fragile. Of course such a post-outcome analysis must consider not only the original constellation of preferences but also the positive and negative incentives provided by the preexisting institutional framework on the one hand and produced by the interaction in question on the other. Thus if the unilateral departure from an agreement should imply the forfeiture of a valuable "hostage," cooperative solutions to a constellation that otherwise would have been a Prisoner's Dilemma may be stable even in the absence of external enforcement (Raub/Keren 1993). In other words, the Nash equilibrium is synonymous with "incentive-compatible" solutions (Hurwicz 1972; Gintis 1992)—which, of course, are as crucial to negotiated agreements as they are to hierarchically determined outcomes.

This does not imply that outcomes that are not Nash equilibria cannot occur. But it does suggest that where they are maintained, by moral commitment or by "enlightened" self-interest, they must be maintained against strong temptations. Take the example discussed in the Introduction and in Appendix 1: In the early 1970s, with governments committed to Keynesian full-employment policies, labor unions would achieve their best outcome by pushing for high wage increases. In the longer run, however, that outcome would produce runaway inflation, which would lead either to the electoral defeat of the government or, through anticipation of that possibility, to a monetarist switch of government policy— which would then entail rapidly rising unemployment. Anticipating this eventuality, therefore, it would have been in the longer-term interest of unions to maintain wage moderation while a Keynesian government was in power. But since that outcome was not a short-term Nash equilibrium, its maintenance depended on the capacity of unions to make internally binding commitments.

That was unproblematic in Austria, where large "encompassing" unions (Olson 1982) with a highly centralized decision structure could be treated as a unitary actor with the capacity for strategic choices, trading short-term disadvantages for longer-term advantages. In Britain, however, the more than 100 individual unions pursuing highly decentralized bargaining strategies could not be treated as a unified actor. Most bargaining units were much too small, individually, to have an appreciable impact on the rate of inflation. Thus if one of them practiced restraint while others continued to get high wage increases, inflation would continue and its members would suffer. However, if others were to reduce overall inflation through wage restraint, then their members would benefit all the more from high wage increases. In short, the constellation was a perfect instance of the large-number Prisoner's Dilemma; and the Nash equilibrium in this union-union game was a situation in which all unions found themselves compelled to maximize the short-term gains of their members.[6] Nevertheless, even in the United Kingdom effective wage restraint was practiced between 1975 and 1977 on the basis of a social compact among all unions and the Labour government. It drastically reduced wage increases for a year or two—but then collapsed in general frustration. The explanation seems straightforward: Since wage moderation was not a Nash equilibrium, commitment had to be achieved through massive moral appeals to "give a year to Britain,"[7] which, however, could not be indefinitely maintained against the institutional self-interest of craft unions with relatively high bargaining power and in the face of inevitable ambiguities and irritations encountered in the implementation of the agreement (Scharpf 1991a).

More generally, therefore, the implication is that the concept of Nash equilibrium is most useful for analyzing the *stability or vulnerability* of given outcomes rather than for predicting which specific outcome might be attained. In this restricted sense, however, it is of general importance in the social sciences. Even though it has been defined in the context of the theory of noncooperative games, its application is by no means restricted to noncooperative games but is as useful for the analysis of other modes of interaction.

## MUTUAL ADJUSTMENT

In any case, noncooperative games in the sense discussed thus far are not the only mode of interaction that may occur in anarchic fields or in minimal institutions. The mathematical theory of noncooperative games is based on assumptions that imply extremely high demands on the cognitive capabilities of human actors, individual or corporate. At the same time, however, there also exists a well-developed mathematical theory of evolutionary games, which completely dispenses with all cognitive demands since the behavior of its "actors" is assumed to be genetically programmed. It has made its career in population biology (Smith 1982), where the differing genetic endowments of individuals within a species are equated with game-theoretic "strategies," and where the reproductive success associated with a particular genetic trait is treated as its "payoff." If it is determined exclusively by the environment, evolution can be interpreted as a "game against nature"; however, if reproductive success depends on the interaction between genetically different types of individuals, the solution concepts of noncooperative game theory can be applied even though the "strategies" of the "players" are genetically fixed rather than strategically chosen. The same evolutionary version of game theory was applied in Robert Axelrod's (1984) computer simulation of different types of fixed strategies in indefinitely iterated Prisoner's Dilemma games; it has also been applied to the study of populations of (competing) organizations, again with the assumption that their organizational strategies are somehow hardwired (Alchian 1950; Hannan/Freeman 1977; 1984). But of course for actors capable of purposive action and of learning, the assumption of hardwired strategies is empirically even more unrealistic than the assumption of game-theoretic superrationality.

We thus have the seemingly paradoxical situation in which the theory of noncooperative games seems equally applicable to either superrational or totally nonrational behavior—but not to the ordinary empirical world of boundedly rational human action. The paradox ceases to be puzzling, however, once it is realized that both superrational and hardwired strategies have a general and precise definition that facilitates analytical modeling, whereas models of boundedly rational action would require the introduction of highly variable assumptions about the information that players are assumed to have, or to lack, and about the limits of their computational capabilities. Whereas there is only one way to be perfectly rational and only one way to be completely nonrational, there is an infinite number of ways of being nonperfectly rational. Hence any such assumptions not only would appear ad hoc but also would always be suspected of being post hoc, since "by cleverly choosing the nature of uncertainty . . . one may get out of game-theoretic analysis whatever one wishes" (Kreps/Wilson 1982, 276).

I believe, however, that it is possible to define a nonarbitrary minimum level of bounded rationality that must be met if the game-theoretic concept of Nash equilibrium is to be used for explanatory purposes. This minimum definition would have to assure that actors are likely to reach a Nash equilibrium outcome, if one exists, and that they will remain at that equilibrium for as long as the available strategies, the outcomes associated with them, and the preferences attached to these outcomes are not changed. In the article reproduced in Appendix 2, Matthias Mohr and I have borrowed Charles Lindblom's (1965) term "parametric adjustment" to describe a mode of interaction that is characterized by this minimum level of rationality. In the meantime, I have realized that this term, when taken out of Lindblom's context, is not conducive to easy communication, and I now prefer to use Lindblom's more generic term "mutual adjustment." But what matters is the definition rather than the label.

The first assumption for a minimum level of rationality is that each actor will at least know his or her own strategy options and the outcomes that can be attained by their use, provided all other actors maintain their present strategy choices. On that basis, the actor is also assumed to be able to evaluate attainable outcomes in the light of his or her own preferences. Finally, if the actor's own immediate payoff can be improved through the exercise of one of his or her own options, it is assumed that he or she will do so—and so will all other actors. With these assumptions, the biggest cognitive obstacle to empirical applications of noncooperative game theory is avoided: Players are required to know only their own options and payoffs but not those of other actors. Hence they also cannot anticipate the moves of other players; they are merely assumed to respond to the status quo that has been created by the past moves of all other actors.

The interactions that can be performed under these assumptions are best understood as *sequential games* in which, starting from a given status quo, actors will move unilaterally whenever they see a chance of improving their own payoffs. But since they are assumed to be myopic, they will have no overall strategy that anticipates all potential moves and countermoves of all players involved. For that reason, interactions will continue unless a Nash equilibrium happens to be reached. When it is reached, however, no actor will be able to do better by acting unilaterally, and then interactions will come to a stop.

Thus if no equilibrium (in pure strategies, of course) exists, the meandering of moves and countermoves may continue indefinitely (or be terminated arbitrarily). If a single Nash equilibrium exists, it will eventually be reached under stable external conditions, provided that actors have a recollection of past moves and will avoid infinite cycles by trying out second-best moves. When multiple equilibria exist, finally, the process of Mutual Adjustment will "lock in" on the first one that happens to be reached.

What we have here, therefore, is a baseline mode of interaction that does not presuppose complete information and that makes only minimal demands on the cognitive capabilities of actors but that still approximates the results that could be achieved in noncooperative games with complete information and involving fully rational actors: There is a high probability that a Nash equilibrium will be reached if one exists—and once reached, that it will be maintained.

Mutual Adjustment can thus be used as a model for explaining stable social outcomes in the absence of explicit coordination by agreement or binding decisions. In comparison with the assumptions of superrationality implied by the theory of noncooperative games, the informational and computational requirements on actors are drastically reduced. Any further reduction (if, for instance, actors did not know their own options or could not evaluate actual or expected outcomes in light of their own preferences) would no longer assure equilibrium outcomes. But what makes the model even more attractive from a theoretical point of view is the fact that any gain in information or computational capacity above and beyond these minimal requirements (if actors were to have more information about one another and better foresight) would not change the outcome. It would merely mean that Nash equilibria will be reached after fewer cycles of trial and error through better approximations of the cognitive operations assumed by noncooperative game theory. In that sense the present definition of Mutual Adjustment avoids the ad hoc nature of which bounded-rationality assumptions are usually accused. It specifies a well-defined (and empirically ascertainable) minimum level of rationality, and things will not change—for the purely explanatory purposes pursued here—if actors should in fact operate at a higher level of rationality (but within the confines of a noncooperative game).

From an empirical point of view, it is important to point out that Mutual Adjustment, as it is defined here, does provide a plausible baseline model for a great many social processes. Social and political encounters often have this character of long, drawn-out sequential interactions in which no one is able, at the beginning, to collapse the vagaries of future choice constellations into the complete, anticipatory "strategy" postulated by the theory of noncooperative games. Moreover, since the model only assumes that actors are informed about their own options and preferences, the a priori plausibility of the model is not restricted to two-person games or interactions among, at most, a very small number of actors who know each other very well. In fact, Mutual Adjustment as defined here specifies the processional preconditions under which Hayekian "spontaneous order" may evolve without explicit planning or political intervention (Schotter 1981). It is also the mode of interaction that can explain "lock-in" processes in the choice of technical solutions (David 1985; Arthur 1988), as well as the possibility of "network externalities" (Liebowitz/Margolis 1994) and other forms of "autodynamic" coordination among large populations of interdependent actors that were discussed earlier (Mayntz/Nedelmann 1987). Moreover, in contrast to more potent modes of coordination by binding agreements or collectively binding decisions, coordination through Mutual Adjustment does not prevent innovation or impede responses to changing circumstances. Actors do not lose their freedom of unilateral action, and they are able to exit from any lock-in outcome whenever they perceive individually attractive alternatives.

However, Mutual Adjustment will take time to reach an existing equilibrium outcome through successive moves and countermoves. Thus if external circumstances are changing, the process may never come to rest, even though equilibrium solutions may have existed originally. From this it would follow that, ceteris paribus, all forms of "evolutionary" or "autodynamic" social coordination or of Hayekian spontaneous order become more difficult as the rate of technological, economic, political, and social change accelerates. It would be interesting to speculate, nevertheless, whether the simultaneous evolution of worldwide systems of communication and worldwide economic exchange might also increase the speed of Mutual Adjustment at such a rate that even in the presence of continuous external change, social interactions may now benefit from (temporary) equilibria that previously were too short-lived to be realized. Just as the computer industry seems to be doing well with compatibility standards that are bound to become obsolete after two years at the most, we may now find that in a great many areas of activity, standards need not be stable for long in order to be useful for the coordination of social, economic, and political activities.

But this is speculation. What is more important to point out is that the potential efficiency, in welfare-theoretic terms, of Mutual Adjustment is limited to a certain class of policy problems, or actor constellations, which can be described as games of pure coordination and constellations resembling the Battle of the Sexes. Hence claims about the evolution of norms and social institutions or of "spontaneous order" necessarily presuppose that the underlying problems have the character of games of coordination, and the resulting "conventions" (like the rule to drive on the right-hand side of the road) are self-enforcing because it is in everybody's self-interest to observe them. When these conditions prevail, the lock-in on any Nash equilibrium will improve general welfare and social production. To be sure, that particular equilibrium may not be a "fair" solution in terms of distributive justice. Moreover, in welfare-theoretic terms, it may not be the best one that could have been attained originally, and its existence may impede the change to a better solution later (David 1985; but see Liebowitz/Margolis 1994). Nevertheless, even then the coordinated solution must be better for all concerned than a reversal to uncoordinated unilateral action—or else it would not be maintained.

Now, of course, games of pure coordination would be easy to handle in any type of coordination mechanism.[8] But this is not so for constellations resembling the Battle of the Sexes game and other games that combine gains from coordination with conflict over distribution. There, Mutual Adjustment not only is capable of achieving effective solutions in welfare-theoretic terms, but it may in fact be the most efficient mode of interaction in terms of the transaction costs incurred in the process. The coexistence of a common interest in coordination, and conflicting interests over distribution, creates difficulties of equilibrium selection in anticipatory noncooperative games, and it creates even greater difficulties when coordination must be achieved through negotiated agreement. Even when solutions can be imposed through voting or through hierarchical decision, the justification of an outcome that favors one side over another may involve protracted controversy.

All these difficulties disappear in Mutual Adjustment. Now, whoever has the first move is able to select the strategy that leads to his or her own best outcome;[9] and whoever moves next must respond in the best way possible to the situation created by the first mover. In constellations resembling the Battle of the Sexes, that means that the choice of the second mover will be adjusted so as to achieve perfect coordination, even if a different outcome would initially have been preferred. A good example is provided in international telecommunication by the interactions among standardization committees with specialized jurisdictions over subject areas that are technically interdependent (Genschel 1995). There, no attempt is made to coordinate the numerous committees through negotiations in a supercoordination committee; instead, each committee proceeds in its own work and at its own pace but remains informed, through overlapping membership, about the state of deliberations in related committees. Once it is realized that a particular committee will be first in finalizing a particular technical standard, the other ones take that standard as given and adjust their own work so as to assure compatibility.

When problems are in the nature of dilemma games or of games with high levels of distributive conflict, however, the welfare-theoretic implications of coordination through Mutual Adjustment are much less attractive. In multiactor constellations resembling the Prisoner's Dilemma, lock-in on the mutually damaging equilibrium is almost inevitable.[10] Thus the avoidance of the Tragedy of the Commons through the successful management of "common resource problems" (Ostrom 1990; Ostrom/Gardner/Walker 1994) depends on modes of interaction that have greater coordinative capacity. The same is true for actor constellations that involve a higher level of conflict than is true of the Battle of the Sexes or for constellations in which there exists no Nash equilibrium. In all these circumstances, what seems most deficient from a welfare-theoretic point of view is the fact that Mutual Adjustment lacks any mechanism that could prevent the players from inflicting damages on one another that exceed the gains that they could expect themselves. Thus there is no assurance that Mutual Adjustment will allow the actors to avoid outcomes that reduce rather than increase overall social welfare in comparison to a given status quo.

## NEGATIVE COORDINATION IN MINIMAL INSTITUTIONS

If the interaction mode is unilateral action, welfare losses in comparison to the status quo can be prevented if the institutional setting provides protection to the status-quo interests of other actors. This is not possible under the structural conditions of anarchic fields, but it is true under the conditions described as "minimal institutions." They presuppose the existence of criminal and civil law systems that effectively protect life, liberty, and property against unilateral violation. When these minimal institutional protections are in place, unilateral action changes its character to a mode that Lindblom (1965) has named "deferential adjustment" and that Renate Mayntz and I (1975) have described as "Negative Coordination." It is discussed at some length in Appendix 2, so I can be brief here.

Negative Coordination may appear in two forms: as a variant of unilateral action and as a variant of negotiated agreement. What matters in either case is the requirement that actors, in choosing their own courses of action, are required to avoid inflicting damages to the protected interests of other actors involved. In other words, Negative Coordination presupposes that the occupant of a protected interest position is able to block contrary action through the exercise of a veto. In the private sphere this protection is assured through the law of torts and criminal law sanctions against the violation of a wide range of specified interests. In the public sector, the legal protection of substantive interests is more limited, but network-like relationships and procedural veto positions[11] assure that Negative Coordination also plays a significant role in relations between public-sector institutions and between states in international relations.

In comparison to unilateral action in anarchic fields, Negative Coordination is attractive from a welfare-theoretic point of view because it avoids outcomes that

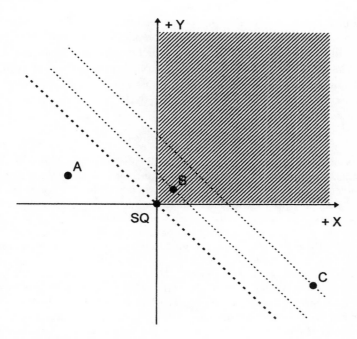

FIGURE 5.3    Negative Coordination

constitute overall welfare losses. Its attraction is limited, however, by its conservative bias, which prevents changes that are attractive from an overall social point
of view as long as they would violate the status-quo interests of a single veto actor. Figure 5.3, which was first introduced at the end of Chapter 4, illustrates the
argument for the two-actor case.

From a welfare-theoretic point of view, all outcomes located above and to the
right of the diagonal through the status-quo point (SQ) constitute improvements
of general welfare, and all outcomes below and to the left of the diagonal imply
welfare losses. Veto positions, however, preclude all outcomes to the left of the
vertical axis (if X has a veto) and below the horizontal axis (if Y has a veto). Now,
in the absence of a veto, Y could proceed to implement project A, which is attractive to Y even though its location below the diagonal indicates that it will entail
losses to X that are larger than Y's gain—and hence a loss of overall welfare. Negative Coordination would prevent this welfare loss since X would surely veto
project A. By the same token, however, project C would also be vetoed by Y, even
though here the gain to X would be larger than Y's losses. Thus the only project
that could be realized would be the one located at B.

More generally speaking, Negative Coordination would prevent some potential gains in utilitarian welfare from being realized by restricting policy choices to

solutions that are Pareto superior to the status quo. In the figure, these are locations in the northeast quadrant—which includes only half of the policy space above and to the right of the diagonal. If the number of independent veto positions is increased, Negative Coordination implies a rapidly shrinking policy space and an increasing immobilism, as the cumulation of vetoes will rule out more and more attempts to depart from the status quo.[12]

## NOTES

1. It should perhaps also be pointed out that discussion in the following chapters is explicitly about interactions *between* interdependent actors, not about the internal interactions *within* a collective actor, which were discussed in Chapter 3. However, given the formal parallelism of between-actor and within-actor interactions in our multilevel analyses, it can be assumed that much of what is being said here will, with appropriate adjustments, also help to explain interactions within corporate or collective actors. In actual case studies, we will therefore employ these same analytical concepts at several levels. An association, for instance, is considered a collective actor whose internal interactions (when they need to be empirically considered) may take place within an arena structure. In its external interactions, this association may then be part of a coalition (a higher-level collective actor) that was formed within a preexisting network structure in order to win a majority vote within the parliamentary arena. In this fashion, a relatively limited set of relatively simple conceptual tools can be employed to reconstruct and to explain quite complex and convoluted empirical interactions.

2. Unlike in neoclassical economics, rational-choice theories are of course much concerned with the problem of how the existence of institutions may be theoretically derived from the rational choices of purely self-interested individuals. For empirical policy research, however, this is not really much of a problem—we only need to recognize institutions where they happen to exist.

3. Thus in Figure 5.2 both Row and Column could use a randomizing device to determine their choices between Up and Down or Left and Right. By selecting the probability distribution that maximizes their expected payoff, given the choice of the other party, they will arrive at a Nash equilibrium in mixed strategies. In Figure 5.2 that would imply that both of the players assign a probability of 50 percent to each of their pure strategies, which would give each of them an expected payoff of 2.5.

4. It is nevertheless rare that analyses in the media are developed in explicitly game-theoretic terms, as was done, in a very enlightening column in the *Economist,* for the options that Prime Minister John Major and opposition leader Tony Blair might consider with regard to a referendum on the European Union ("Bagehot" 1994).

5. Game theorists have developed a series of concepts that will reduce the number of equilibria that will have to be considered. Thus it is plausible that Pareto-inferior equilibria will be ignored, and in sequential games it also seems reasonable to require that only "subgame-perfect" equilibria should be considered (Osborne/Rubinstein 1994). In a much more ambitious effort, John Harsanyi and Reinhard Selten (1988) have attempted to develop a general theory that, through a hierarchy of criteria, should lead to the selection of a unique equilibrium in each game. The prescriptive plausibility of some of these criteria is still in dispute among game theorists, and Harsanyi (1995) has in the meantime pre-

sented an updated version that avoids some of the objections raised in the literature. In any case, however, these concepts are purely prescriptive, and the authors do not claim that real-world actors could in fact go through these sequences of analytical operations to converge on a single outcome.

6. The example shows that in identifying self-interest there are two dimensions to consider: the level at which a composite actor is able to define its self-interest (skill-group or industry; local, regional, or national units), and the time horizon within which self-interest is to be defined. Whereas institutional fragmentation tends to go along with a short time horizon (if you are too small to affect future rates of inflation and unemployment, you might as well take what you can get now), large "encompassing" unions may choose to be either myopic or enlightened in their definition of self-interest.

7. The social contract thus could be explained by a "solidaristic" transformation of the payoff matrix in the terms discussed in Chapter 4.

8. Hierarchical coordination, it should be granted to Hayekian objections, might have difficulty using local (and tacit) knowledge that lower-level actors would be able to draw upon without difficulty in Mutual Adjustment.

9. Having the first move is an advantage in sequential games with more than one Nash equilibrium. In games with precisely one equilibrium, the sequence of moves will not affect the outcome; and in games without an equilibrium in pure strategies, the first mover is generally at a disadvantage.

10. Of course, strong social norms could prevent that. But if they were effective, we would not classify the actor constellation as a Prisoner's Dilemma.

11. In the German ministerial bureaucracy, for instance, where we originally discovered the mechanism (Mayntz/Scharpf 1975), policy initiatives are usually developed unilaterally by a single ministry, in response to the problems within its own sphere of responsibility or the demands of its own clientele, and with the use of its own policy instruments. But other ministries whose jurisdictions might potentially be affected must "sign off" before the initiative may be submitted to the cabinet for approval. In principle, of course, the cabinet may also decide to settle interministerial conflicts—but if all disputes were submitted to it, its agenda would be totally overloaded. Hence the procedural sign-off generally operates as an effective veto that forces the initiating ministry to modify its proposal in such a way that negative impacts on other ministerial jurisdictions are avoided.

12. For the three-actor case, represented by a three-dimensional figure, the policy space that is available under Negative Coordination would shrink to one-eighth of the total policy space, or one-fourth of the space in which welfare improvements are possible.

# 6

## Negotiated Agreements

Welfare losses that cannot be avoided in the modes of unilateral action can in principle be avoided in cooperative games—that is, under institutional conditions that not only provide legal or procedural protection for property rights and other interest positions but also assure the binding force of negotiated agreements. When that is the case, the Coase Theorem (Coase 1960) assures us that—regardless of whether property rights are assigned to one party or another—negotiations among rational (and fully informed) actors will lead to voluntary agreements that will realize all potential welfare gains among the participants, provided that transaction costs are negligible and that side payments or package deals are possible. What is more, these welfare-efficient outcomes are to be achieved by purely self-interested actors who, by definition, would not agree unless the expected outcome is more attractive, from their subjective perspective, than the outcome that could be expected without the agreement. From a normative point of view this is an extremely important claim that can be made for no other mode of interaction among self-interested actors—neither for unilateral action, nor for majority voting, nor for hierarchical decisions. This normative significance is not reduced by the fact that the Coase Theorem is only concerned with the maximization of aggregate utility or welfare and not with the distributive justice of negotiated outcomes. These are likely to be "fair" with regard to the alternative options available to the negotiating parties, but they will not correct existing inequalities of initial endowments.

By contrast, the normative significance of the Coase Theorem is indeed affected by the assumption of negligible transaction costs. The reason for this is of general significance for political theory: Obviously, the welfare claims of the theorem apply only among the actors who actually participate in a negotiation. Now if transaction costs were zero, negotiations could include all parties who are in one way or another affected by a policy problem. In that case voluntary agreement would be the only mode of interaction that is normatively defensible on welfare-theoretic grounds (Buchanan/Tullock 1962).

But if transaction costs cannot be neglected—and Ronald Coase, the founder of transaction-cost economics, was emphatic in his insistence that they not be neglected—they will rise exponentially with the number of independent participants (see Appendix 2). As a consequence, the size of actor-sets within which negotiated solutions can be reached is limited and likely to be quite small. In practice, it will often be much smaller than the population that is affected by a policy problem. When that is the case negotiators may well maximize their own welfare at the expense of the larger population and of overall welfare.

In the present chapter I first examine the causes of high transaction costs associated with negotiations. They are analyzed by reference to the "Negotiator's Dilemma" that arises from the need simultaneously to search for optimal solutions and to resolve distributive conflicts. I then proceed to distinguish four varieties of negotiations that differ in the extent to which the Negotiator's Dilemma is manifest. Third, I consider four variants of institutional settings that, to different degrees, facilitate overcoming the dilemma. Finally, I discuss the normative limitations of all negotiation systems when considered as modes of interactions in the policy process.

## PROBLEMS NEGOTIATORS MUST RESOLVE

In order to appreciate the importance of transaction costs, it seems useful first to discuss the problems negotiators will have to resolve in order to produce outcomes that satisfy the Coase Theorem. They include the difficulties of reaching an agreement and the problem of assuring the proper implementation of agreements. Since the implementation stage will not be reached unless an agreement has been concluded, the anticipation of implementation problems merely adds to the difficulties of reaching agreement in the first place. Nevertheless, the extent to which this is true can be clarified by a brief investigation of implementation problems.

### The Problem of Faithful Implementation

Since the outcomes associated with a faithfully implemented agreement must be superior, from the point of view of the parties involved, to the outcomes associated with nonagreement, the problem of implementation can be clarified by a simple distinction: In some constellations, the benefits that ego can expect from the agreement depend entirely on alter's contribution; in others ego cannot benefit unless its own contribution is also forthcoming. In the first case, the object of the agreement can be described as an *exchange;* in the second, it is *joint production.* Even though the agreement to be implemented was reached consensually, each party must still decide unilaterally whether to honor or to default upon its contractual obligations. Thus the choices faced at the implementation stage are best represented as noncooperative games (Figure 6.1).[1]

The first constellation would arise, for instance, in the implementation of a sales contract in which ego would profit from not paying the price as long as alter

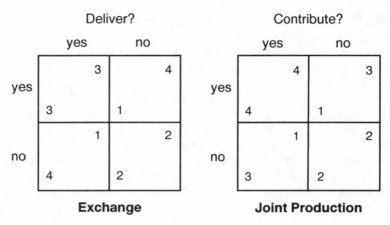

FIGURE 6.1    Two implementation games

would deliver the goods. This constellation has the character of a Prisoner's Dilemma game. Examples that come to mind are the implementation of General Agreement on Tariffs and Trade (GATT) rules on trade liberalization or the sluggish transformation into national law of agreed-upon directives of the European Union. The second constellation is characteristic of joint production—say, a joint research venture or the commitment to form and maintain a coalition government. Here the contribution of both is necessary for reaching the desired outcome, but if one party should fail to contribute, the costs incurred by the other one would be wasted. This is an Assurance constellation.

Among rational and purely self-interested parties dealing with one another in a single-shot encounter, agreements of the second type would be self-executing, whereas the implementation of contracts of exchange would remain problematical even if exogenous enforcement were, in principle, available (which is not the case in many political interactions). The expected difficulties of implementation would therefore need to be dealt with by the parties in concluding the contract, and they would add to the difficulties of reaching agreement in the first place. With this in mind, the emphasis in the remainder of this chapter will not be on implementation but on the difficulties that must be overcome in reaching agreement through negotiations.

### The Problem of Reaching Agreement

In discussing negotiations I will generally refer to the graphical representation of a minisociety consisting of two actors, X and Y, that was first introduced at the end of Chapter 4. Its relationship to the game-theoretic representation of actor constellations used thus far is straightforward, except that now it is no longer sufficient to use rank-ordered payoffs (Figure 6.2).

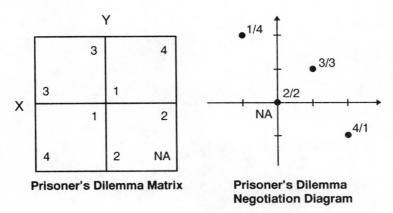

FIGURE 6.2    Matrix and negotiation diagram of Prisoner's Dilemma

The nonagreement point (NA) in the negotiation figure corresponds to the game-theoretic outcome obtained at the *intersection of the maximin strategies* of all players—that is, it represents the outcome that each player can at least obtain by unilateral action. Negotiations can then be understood as an attempt to capture (and divide) the potential gains from cooperation that can be achieved relative to the NA point. Figure 6.2 illustrates the translation from one to the other form of representation for the two-person Prisoner's Dilemma constellation.[2]

Clearly, if the NA point represents the best *unilateral* option, no rational self-interested party will agree to an outcome that is less attractive to it than NA. Assuming that negotiations are limited to the discrete outcomes contained in the game matrix, it is clear that agreement could only be obtained for the "cooperative" outcome at 3/3. But what if there were two or more discrete solutions above and to the right of the NA point, as would be true in Battle of the Sexes or in Chicken constellations? Or what if the welfare-improving outcome should lie outside of the northeastern quadrant of the negotiation figure? And, finally, what if feasible solutions are initially known only to one but not all parties or if they must be developed or discovered in the process of coming to an agreement? These are among the difficulties of reaching agreement.

For an illustration, consider the constellations represented in Figure 6.3. Assuming that the NA point is equivalent to the status quo and that the utility of party X is measured on the horizontal axis and that of party Y on the vertical axis, it is clear that for X only outcomes to the right of the vertical axis are attractive, whereas Y would accept only outcomes located above the horizontal axis. Thus, the northeast quadrant of the negotiation space represents a "zone of common attraction," the southwest quadrant a "zone of common aversion," and the remaining two quadrants define zones of conflicting preferences. In the figure, negotiators are confronted with three possible outcomes—A, B, and C—which

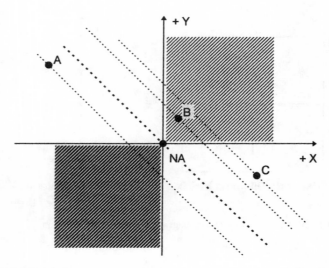

FIGURE 6.3    Negotiation space

might be thought of, for example, as three discrete locations of waste-treatment projects within the territories of two adjacent states. If agreement is necessary, only outcome B might be initially acceptable to both.

The Coase Theorem, however, represents a different partitioning of the negotiation space. Its orientation is to the northwest-southeast diagonal intersecting NA. The diagonal represents the "welfare boundary" where $X + Y = 0$. Outcomes located below and to the left of it represent welfare losses that should be avoided, and negotiators should be able to agree on the outcome located on the highest welfare isoquant—that is, on the parallel that is farthest above and to the right of the boundary. According to the Coase Theorem, therefore, negotiators should reject outcome A, and they ought to prefer outcome C over outcome B, even though only B is located in the zone of common attraction and C is located in the zone of conflicting interests where X would gain at the expense of Y.

In discussing the difficulties associated with welfare-maximizing negotiations it is thus useful to distinguish two dimensions, which may be variously described as production and distribution or as the "creation and sharing of value" (Lax/Sebenius 1986). Along the first dimension the parties should be jointly interested in pushing the welfare frontier as far out as possible in the northeast direction; in the second dimension they will fight over the location of a negotiated outcome on any given welfare isoquant, with X preferring locations as far southeast as possible and Y pulling in the opposite, northwestern, direction.

*The Production Dimension.*    The Coase Theorem postulates that negotiators will adopt the solution located on the highest welfare isoquant. But that solution will often not be given initially but must be searched for or created by the joint efforts of the parties involved. However, as Figure 6.3 demonstrates, searching for the welfare maximum also implies that the parties must not limit their search to the northeastern quadrant of "mutual attraction" but need to explore outcomes in the "zones of conflict" as well, where one party will gain at the expense of the other. For self-interested actors these are not auspicious conditions for learning, and we have every reason to think that the potentially disadvantaged party (Y in this case) will not participate in good faith in that search unless it is fully assured that it will not be hurt by the outcome (Sabel 1994). In practical terms, this will generally require an acceptable solution to the problem of how costs and benefits will ultimately be distributed. In other words, the analytical distinction between production and distribution highlights the *empirical connectedness* between them: The creation of value will be impeded unless the acceptable sharing of value is assured.

*The Distributive Dimension.*    But what would be an acceptable sharing of value? Let us begin with Figure 6.4 and assume that negotiations are about a given object that is located, in the production dimension, on a given welfare isoquant. In that case, negotiations will solely have to deal with the distribution of costs and benefits among the parties. Assume, moreover, that side payments are possible but that there exists no market price to which both parties could refer. For an example, think of negotiations over the price of a unique work of art or over the size of the German financial contribution to the U.S. effort in the Gulf War.

Since the agreement of both parties is necessary, the outcome in the figure can only be found on that segment of the welfare isoquant that intersects the northeastern quadrant. Y would never accept an outcome located below point A, and X would equally reject anything to the left of point B. Thus negotiations would serve no purpose unless an outcome between A and B is in fact feasible, and the sole object of negotiation seems to be the determination of the exact location of the outcome within that interval. At first sight this might appear as a zero-sum conflict in which one side must lose what the other gains (and in which therefore negotiations would serve no useful purpose).[3] But that would overlook the crucial importance of the nonagreement point (NA).[4] Since this point is less attractive to either side than any location between A and B, the constellation is not zero sum but positive sum (and resembles the Battle of the Sexes).[5]

But even though both parties would like to do better than NA, the question is which of the many outcomes located between A and B they would, or should, ultimately select. The phrasing of the question is deliberate, since it obviously has a positive as well as a normative side that should not be confused. Nevertheless, the analytical theory of cooperative games has developed algorithms that are meant to provide, at the same time, normatively plausible rules of fair distribution and empirically plausible rules that rational self-interested actors can be expected to follow in practice. In general terms, these rules reflect the relative starting positions, or outside options, of the parties, the maximal gains that they could possi-

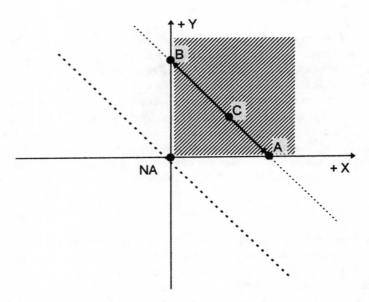

FIGURE 6.4    Conflict over distribution

bly obtain, and their respective valuations of the obtainable outcomes (Nash 1950; 1953; Kalai/Smorodinsky 1975; Osborne/Rubinstein 1990).[6] Within this frame of reference they amount to a form of "splitting the difference," which, in the figure, would lead to an agreed-upon outcome located near C.

In terms of normative theory, this outcome can be considered a fair solution if the location of the nonagreement point is not itself put in question (Barry 1989). That, however, is a very big if. In fact, there are two levels of distribution that are being ignored: The first is the distribution of original endowments, which, compared to a zero point of absolute equality,[7] defines the status-quo position of the parties. It may be highly unequal in ways for which none of the normative justifications discussed at the end of Chapter 4 may be available. Second, even if the status-quo position were somehow accepted, the nonagreement point may significantly differ from it, depending on the attractiveness of outside options and the availability of credible threats. Both possibilities are illustrated in Figure 6.5.

For an interpretation, think of trade negotiations between the European Union and, say, Hungary. Clearly, the EU (in the position of player X) is already favored in the status quo (SQ)—that is, its relative dependence on gains from trade is smaller than that of Hungary. Moreover, if negotiations should fail, the EU might threaten to reduce Hungarian imports even below the present level, whereas Hungary could not retaliate in kind. Thus the nonagreement point would be located not at SQ but at NA. Under these assumptions the outcome specified by the theory of cooperative games would be located at A. That solution

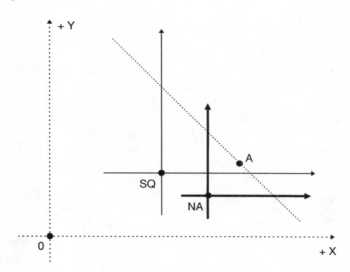

FIGURE 6.5   Reference points of distributive justice: Zero, status quo, or nonagreement

is "fair" relative to NA, but it may seem grossly unfair relative to SQ or to the zero point. In other words, negotiated solutions will reproduce the existing distribution of advantages and disadvantages;[8] they are not a tool for realizing concepts of distributive justice that depend on redistribution.

But even if the nonagreement outcome at NA is accepted as the reference point of a "fair" distribution, the distribution problems ignored by the Coase Theorem will undercut its plausibility as positive, as distinguished from normative, theory. At the analytical level, it is true, the move from normative to positive theory has been successful: It can be shown that the normatively specified outcome (in the version defined by John Nash) will also be reached through an iteration of offers and counteroffers in which, at each step, the next concession is made by the party that, at the point reached, would have more to lose if negotiations were now broken off (Harsanyi 1977, chap. 8; Rubinstein 1982).

In spite of its pragmatic plausibility, however, the experimental support for these analytical solutions to the bargaining problem is not particularly strong (Bartos 1978; Willer/Patton 1987; Bazerman/Neale 1991). The difficulties seem to be related to the strong common-knowledge assumptions (Aumann 1976) of these algorithms. When all parties are in fact fully informed of all aspects of the negotiation situation, including one another's true valuation of all options, agreement on an outcome that is identical with or very close to the solutions generated by the normative or analytical algorithms is indeed likely to be obtained (Zintl 1992; Thompson 1992). But when these postulated conditions are not fulfilled, the distributive outcome is likely to be affected by "competitive" stratagems in which parties try to influence one another's perceptions of the relative attractiveness of their available outside options or of their own valuation of the outcomes obtainable (Lax/Sebenius 1985; Young 1991).

For an illustration, take Figure 6.6, which describes the same objective situation as Figure 6.4. But now assume that X (as a consequence of an asymmetric information advantage) succeeds in persuading its opponent that Y's alternative options are worth much less and that its own are somewhat better than they are in reality, so that the fictitious nonagreement point would now seem to be located at NA' instead of at NA. By implication, the "fair" solution would then be shifted from C to A (located close to Y's former lower threshold, and X's maximal aspiration)—which is of course much more advantageous to X and much less attractive to Y than the original solution at C. Under conditions of incomplete or asymmetric information, in other words, misrepresentation and other forms of "opportunism" may indeed pay—which implies that the other side will have reason to distrust and discount even true claims in the "market for lemons" (Akerlof 1970).

*The Negotiator's Dilemma.*  The consequence of this vulnerability to information asymmetries, dissimulation, deception, and similar opportunistic stratagems has been appropriately described, by David A. Lax and James K. Sebenius (1986), as the "Negotiator's Dilemma." This description deserves to be taken literally. In having to solve simultaneously the problems of production and of distribution, the parties are confronted with another Prisoner's Dilemma: The successful joint search for better overall solutions requires creativity, effective communication, and mutual trust, whereas success in the distributive battle depends on the strategic, and even opportunistic, communication and withholding of available information—and a good deal of distrust against potential misinformation. This means not only that the "cooperative" interaction orientation that is conducive to joint learning in the production dimension is psychologically incompatible with the "competitive" orientation that facilitates success in distribution but also that the party that contributes most to the search for better solutions lays itself open to exploitation by a party that concentrates its efforts on the distributive dimension.

It is thus the distributive dimension that is ignored in the Coase Theorem, which may interfere fundamentally with the interactions that are empirically necessary for the realization of the theorem's welfare-theoretic claims. It is also clear, however, that not all constellations will involve problems of production and distribution to the same degree. It is thus useful to distinguish among four modes of negotiations that differ in this regard and hence in the difficulties that must be overcome in reaching negotiated solutions to policy problems.

## FOUR MODES OF NEGOTIATION

If the Negotiator's Dilemma is constituted by the simultaneous need to resolve problems of production and of distribution, and if individual negotiations will

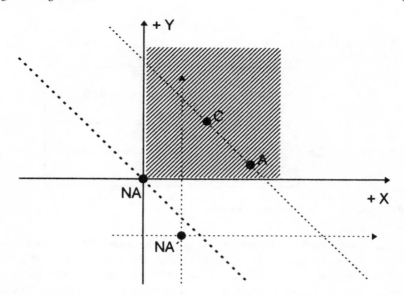

FIGURE 6.6    Effects of misrepresentation

differ in the relative salience of either one of these dimensions, it is possible to distinguish among four different modes of negotiations for which I will use the labels "Spot Contracts,"[9] "Distributive Bargaining," "Problem Solving," and "Positive Coordination." In this classification Spot Contracts are characterized by low salience in either dimension, Positive Coordination by high salience in both dimensions, and the other categories are defined as being high in one and low in the other dimension (Figure 6.7).

### Spot Contracts

In Chapter 5 I distinguished Negative Coordination from pure unilateral action by the fact that property rights and other types of veto positions must be respected. That is also true, of course, of many market exchanges in which the seller cannot be forced to sell and the buyer cannot be forced to buy, except under conditions that each finds more attractive than the status quo. Thus the difference that Negative Coordination can be achieved without negotiation, whereas market exchanges depend on explicit agreement, is less important than the fact that in both cases the outcome is treated as a take-it-or-leave-it proposition.

In transaction-cost economics, transactions in which neither the production of value nor distribution is a highly salient issue are described as "Spot Contracts" (Williamson 1985) in which the object of an exchange is assumed to be well-defined, in which distributional issues are settled by reference to market

**Salience of Distribution**

| Salience of Production | low | high |
|---|---|---|
| low | Spot Contracts | Distributive Bargaining |
| high | Problem Solving | Positive Coordination |

FIGURE 6.7    Four types of negotiation processes

prices, and in which commitment and execution are simultaneous or close in time. Examples in the political sphere might be the take-it-or-leave-it propositions of conference committees in a bicameral legislature or of international or intergovernmental agreements submitted for parliamentary ratification. In all of these cases, further negotiations serve no useful purpose: Acceptance or the veto is the final word. When that is all, transaction costs are at a minimum, and they rise only in linear fashion if the number of parties that must be consulted increases. However, as is also pointed out in transaction-cost economics, only a very limited range of standardized economic exchanges can be carried out through Spot Contracts; and in the discussion of Negative Coordination earlier, I showed that in the absence of market prices the welfare efficiency of pure veto systems is severely limited. Potential welfare gains will be "left on the table" if the parties are only willing to consider projects located within the "zone of common attraction" in the northeastern quadrant of our negotiation figures.

### Distributive Bargaining

The parties could avoid these welfare losses if those that gain from a given project could compensate those that lose by it through side payments or by other means. When the project itself is not put into question but only the distribution of costs and benefits, I will use "Distributive Bargaining" as a technical term to describe this mode of interaction.[10]

*Bargaining in Compulsory Negotiation Systems.*    I begin with a discussion of Distributive Bargaining under conditions in which both parties have a veto over projects proposed by either side—which may simply reflect the fact that projects depend physically on contributions by both parties or that both have protected property rights. For an illustration, consider Figure 6.8.

Here it is assumed that actor X is proposing a project located at A that is highly attractive to itself but would imply a loss to actor Y—which therefore would have

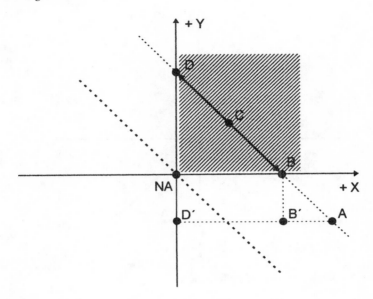

FIGURE 6.8   Side payments in a compulsory negotiation system

good reason to block its adoption by the exercise of its own veto. However, since A is located above and to the right of the "welfare boundary," X might avoid the veto by offering to Y side payments that would then move the effective outcome from A to a new location that lies within the area of common attraction. The exact amount of compensation would of course be the central object of bargaining. In order to obtain Y's agreement, the amount must be at least large enough to equalize the loss that Y would suffer from the completion of project A (which, in the figure, is equal to the distance AB' = B'B), and it could not be larger than the net gain that X can expect from the completion of the project (represented by the distance AD' = D'D). Under the rules of distribution proposed by the normative theory of cooperative games discussed earlier, the most likely outcome would be located at C. It is also clear that no project located below and to the left of the welfare boundary would have a chance of being realized in a system of compulsory negotiations.

***Bargaining in Voluntary Negotiation Systems.***   However, in interactions among private parties that do not involve protected property rights, and in most intergovernmental interactions, unilateral action is not ruled out. In that case, X could just go ahead with project A without offering any compensation to Y, and there is nothing that Y could do to avert the loss imposed on it. From the distribution-blind perspective of the Coase Theorem, that is fully acceptable since project A, by stipulation, increases aggregate welfare in comparison to the status quo.

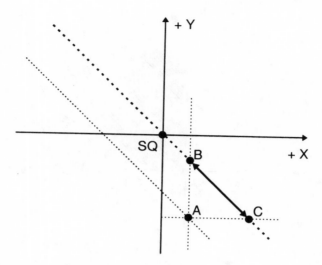

FIGURE 6.9   Bargaining to avoid welfare losses

But what about projects that, though benefiting one party, would actually reduce aggregate welfare?

In Figure 6.9, that is true of project A, which is located below the diagonal welfare boundary and which X now could carry out unilaterally. Here total welfare would be increased if X could be induced to abandon the project[11]—and since Y's losses exceed X's gains, it would be in Y's interest to pay X for not carrying out the project. How much it would have to pay is then, again, the subject of Distributive Bargaining. At the minimum, the side payment would have to compensate X for the potential gain it is asked to forgo; and at the maximum it could not be larger than Y's loss. Thus the solution will have to lie in the range between B and C, indicated by the thick arrow in the figure. Of course any such solution will place Y at a disadvantage in comparison with the status quo, but from the perspective of the Coase Theorem, the only thing that matters is that negotiations are indeed able to prevent an overall welfare loss.

*Bargaining Through Issue Linkage or Package Deals.*   As I have discussed it thus far, bargaining can only succeed if (monetary) side payments are permissible and acceptable to the veto player. But in practice such side payments may not be feasible or normatively acceptable,[12] and many policy problems will have discrete solutions that cannot be quantitatively reduced or enlarged to achieve a mutually acceptable compromise. Even then, however, the practices of "issue linkage," "package deals," or "logrolling" (Tollison/Willet 1979; Stein 1980; McGinnis 1986) may still facilitate mutually acceptable and welfare-increasing solutions. In an example of issue linkage in Figure 6.10, both of the original proj-

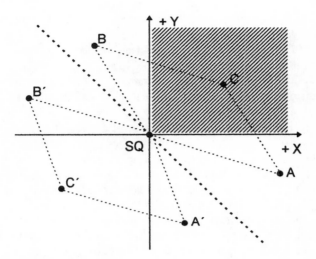

FIGURE 6.10    Issue linkage

ects, A and B, have positive welfare balances but neither would, by itself, be acceptable to the party that is disadvantaged. If both can be combined, however, their joint outcome C (obtained through vector addition) will be located in the northeast quadrant and hence is more attractive to both parties than the status quo (which would continue if negotiations fail). Thus when appropriate combinations of projects with a positive welfare balance are available, even veto systems may approximate the welfare optimum.[13] This is how the European Union has time and again been able to overcome deadlocks through package deals involving unrelated issues that were worked out in the "summits" of the European Council.

In practice, however, the political feasibility of issue linkage is limited by a serious difficulty. As a consequence of the "pluralistic" specialization of policy processes, actors involved in a particular policy area are generally not interested in benefits accruing outside of their own field. Within any particular policy area, however, the constellation of interests will often be characteristically asymmetric across all interactions: In the field of waste disposal, for instance, the city-state of Hamburg will always depend on its rural neighbors to provide locations for waste-treatment plants, whereas in transportation the city is always pressed to provide better transit facilities and better access to the center from the outlying regions (Scharpf/Benz 1991). Similarly, there are few projects within the confines of European environmental policy that Denmark and Germany could offer as compensation to overcome British resistance. When that is so, there will be few opportunities for reciprocal package deals within a given policy area—and hence negotiations in specialized arenas (e.g., in a conference of environmental ministers) will be of little use. If package deals can be reached at all, they will typically have to involve two or more distinct policy areas with complementary asymmetries in their interest constellations.

Hence the first requirement for package deals to succeed is that there must be actors at a "summit" level who are authorized to engage in negotiations spanning several policy areas—as is true of the conference of heads of governments in German federalism or of the European Council of heads of state. Often, however, such summit agreements must be ratified at home, and even if the outcomes, considered in combination, would be quite favorable to the country as a whole, the chances of success in these two-level games (Putnam 1988) depend very much on the degree of specialization and decentralization in domestic policy processes (Mayer 1992). If ratification in plenary parliament is sufficient, package deals may survive intact. However, if functionally specialized committees have the last say, the package may well get unpacked. That is even more likely if some elements of the package must be implemented by lower levels of government over which "summit" actors have no direct hierarchical control.[14]

Hence Distributive Bargaining will not always succeed. But where it does, it will prevent the welfare losses that otherwise could be expected in pure veto constellations. Moreover, this welfare-preserving effect is not affected by the Negotiator's Dilemma discussed earlier. Since, by stipulation, the creation of value is not a salient issue in this mode, the haggling over the distribution of the costs and benefits of a given, well-defined project will affect distribution but will not reduce the level of aggregate welfare.

### Problem Solving

Whereas our definition of Distributive Bargaining focuses exclusively on the distribution of costs and benefits, "Problem Solving" focuses on value creation. Thus, in the figures presented here, the parties would be exclusively interested in searching for new solutions located as far in the northeast direction as possible. Whereas in Distributive Bargaining the objects of negotiation, or the possibility frontier, are assumed to be given, the joint creation of better projects or objects is the central purpose of Problem Solving.

The power of Problem Solving is the power of joint action. To illustrate it, let us assume a constellation of actors, each of which has individual control over a number of separate action resources (including skills and access to specialized information) that interact with one another to produce a joint outcome. Such constellations are typical of coalitions, of joint ventures, or of policymaking in the ministerial bureaucracy. Under such conditions the action space—and hence the chances of finding effective solutions to given problems—is significantly increased if the separate options can be pooled instead of being used by each actor separately. To give an abstract example: If three actors, A, B, and C, each have two policy options, 1 and 2, and if the overall status quo is defined by their use of options a1, b1, and c1, each party acting unilaterally can only contemplate one new overall outcome as long as the other parties do not move:

A could reach a2, b1, c1;
B could reach a1, b2, c1;
C could reach a1, b1, c2.

If none of these outcomes would be superior to the status quo from the point of view of the individual actor contemplating it, then no one would make a move, and the overall status quo would be maintained.[15] However, if the three actors, under the same conditions, are able to pool their options, then their combined action space now includes seven outcomes that are different from the status quo, namely:

a1, b2, c1;
a1, b2, c2;
a1, b1, c2;
a2, b1, c1;
a2, b2, c1;
a2, b2, c2;
a2, b1, c2.

In general terms, a group of N members that have S policy options each can reach a set of $S^N - 1$ outcomes that are different from the status quo, whereas the same number of actors acting unilaterally could attain only $(S - 1)N$ new outcomes. Obviously the chances of discovering solutions that are superior to the status quo would increase accordingly. In order to utilize this enlarged action space, however, all of the actors involved must not only explore their own options but also communicate these to one another accurately, and they must then jointly explore the interaction effects among these choices. The mode of communication, in other words, is quite different from what is characteristic of Distributive Bargaining. Instead, Problem Solving is most likely to succeed if the participants are able to engage one another in truth-oriented "arguing" about the best possible solution and the best way of achieving it (Elster 1986; Majone 1989; Saretzki 1996).

At the interpersonal level, the common search for better solutions benefits from, and in fact depends upon, maximum openness, good communications skills, and mutual trust. These are difficult preconditions to achieve, but under the definition of Problem Solving, the task is greatly facilitated by the assumption that distribution problems are somehow taken care of and that the parties are focusing exclusively on finding, or designing, the solution that best advances their common interest. Thus, though the decision rule may still be unanimity, veto positions are not needed to block decisions that are thought to damage a particular party's interests—they merely assure that the outcome is in fact convincing to all of the parties involved in the search.

In the light of the economic and game-theoretic literature on negotiations, these may appear as highly idealistic and hence unrealistic stipulations.[16] Thus it may be useful to point out that their realization does not depend exclusively on the subjective frame of "cooperative" or "solidaristic" interaction orientations that I discussed at the end of Chapter 4—even though these are obviously helpful where they exist. But apart from these subjective conditions, it is often true that actors are engaged in negotiations in which distributional issues are objectively quite irrelevant.

This is trivially true if the underlying actor constellation can be characterized as a game of pure coordination or as an Assurance game in which the parties involved are exclusively motivated by convergent or compatible interests. Such constellations do exist, but the more likely conditions in policy processes would be mixed-motive constellations in which at least the distribution of the costs and benefits of cooperation remains an issue. Even then, however, distributional conflict may be eliminated through prior explicit agreements on how the costs and benefits of a joint venture are to be allocated. Thus, in the Swiss federal government, distributional conflict among the semipermanent coalition parties is reduced through a long-standing agreement on the number of ministerial positions that each of them will have. By the same token, Problem Solving within organizations is generally facilitated by the employment contract that largely disengages private self-interest from the performance of organizational roles (Simon 1957; 1991)—or from the policymaking roles of civil servants (Egeberg 1995). In the Japanese ministerial bureaucracy even career interests are neutralized through the practice of promoting all members of a cohort at the same pace and providing attractive external options for those who cannot make it to the very top. But though such career patterns greatly facilitate Problem Solving in negotiations *within* a ministry, distributional conflicts arising from organizational self-interest are still endemic in *interministerial* bargaining (Lehmbruch 1995).[17] Nevertheless, the logic is clear. Whenever the willingness to cooperate in a joint search for good solutions is more important than individual effort, there are possibilities of constructing institutional arrangements and incentive systems that disengage individual, and even organizational,[18] self-interest from the choice of outcomes. When that is the case, negotiations may indeed proceed in a Problem-Solving mode.

### Positive Coordination

Nevertheless, Problem Solving depends on special psychological conditions, or on institutional arrangements, that neutralize issues of distribution, and in that sense it remains exceptional. In the general case, parties to a negotiation have to deal with problems of production and problems of distribution at the same time. Hence we might also say that they are simultaneously engaged in Distributive Bargaining and in Problem Solving. If they succeed, this mode of interaction is being described here as "Positive Coordination." Like its companion, Negative Coordination, it was first named in our studies of interministerial coordination (Mayntz/Scharpf 1975). We used the term to describe the work of successful interministerial project groups set up by the cabinet to deal with problems affecting the jurisdictions of, or requiring policy instruments controlled by, several departments. Typically, the members of such task forces were, for a limited period, excused from their ordinary duties and free from hierarchical directives within their home departments. But they were chosen with a view to their personal and professional standing in their respective home departments. It was expected that such task forces would be able to develop innovative approaches that departed from the established policy routines of the ministries involved but that the solutions proposed would, in the end, also be acceptable to these ministries (and their respective clienteles).

These elaborate arrangements were thought necessary to overcome the conservative bias inherent in the usual patterns of Negative Coordination and interministerial bargaining, in which each department developed project ideas only with a view to its own responsibilities and capabilities and opposed other initiatives that would have encroached on its own routines. From the point of view of the government as a whole, represented by the Chancellor's Office, too many potential gains in terms of effective Problem Solving were "left on the table" in this fashion. It was also realized, however, that there were legitimate policy interests represented by the specialized departments, which the government could not ignore. Thus, though innovative solutions were sought from the integrative perspective of the government as a whole, they also had to be acceptable to the departments severally. These were tough conditions to meet, and it is hardly surprising that many of the task forces set up in the heyday of "reform politics" were in the end unsuccessful. The difficulties they had to cope with were precisely those that were discussed earlier as being characteristic of the Negotiator's Dilemma. As a consequence, the transaction costs associated with successful Positive Coordination are likely to be very high—and they will increase exponentially as the number of independent negotiating parties increases (see Appendix 2). Often they will be too high to permit the successful resolution of collective-action problems. But what could be done to overcome the dilemma?

Speaking generally, a first requirement for successful Positive Coordination is the recognition of the simultaneous existence and legitimacy of problems of distribution as well as of production problems and the willingness to deal with both of them explicitly. This is by no means generally assured. Often the "official" commitment to Problem Solving is so strong that considerations of individual or institutional self-interest are delegitimated and, as it were, driven underground— where they become a "hidden agenda" that distorts and corrupts arguments that are explicitly presented as contributions to Problem Solving. In the culture of international standardization committees in telecommunications, for instance, only "technical" arguments about the efficiency and quality of competing proposals are considered legitimate. Hence the "economic" interests that would be furthered or frustrated if one or another standard were accepted cannot be explicitly resolved or even talked about. Yet everyone knows, or at least suspects,

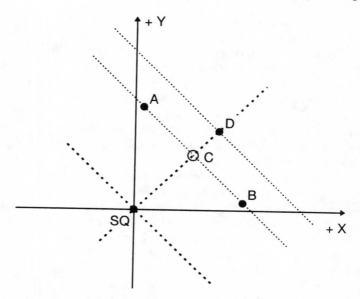

FIGURE 6.11    Dependence of production on distribution

that they are very much on the minds of representatives of firms or national governments even when they present their purely technical arguments. Since standards must be adopted by consent, solutions are in fact often impeded or even prevented by these undiscussed and unresolved distributive issues (Schmidt/ Werle 1993). Indeed, an even stronger claim can be made: Unless it is explicitly recognized that any acceptable solution must also include a fair distribution of the costs and benefits, negotiations will not be able to approach the welfare maximum. For an illustration, consider Figure 6.11.

Here X will unconditionally prefer outcome B not only over outcome A but also over outcome D; and Y will similarly prefer outcome B over all others. As long as both are not forced to understand that no outcome is feasible that does not also constitute a fair distribution (represented by the dotted line SQ-D), they will fight over A and B without realizing that the best outcome that they could get in that fashion would be located near C and that *compared to this compromise solution* the welfare-superior outcome D will also be more attractive from their individual points of view. In other words, only if it is realized that the battle over distribution cannot be won by one side or the other, and that it can at best end in a settlement that is fair to both, will rational self-interested actors engage in earnest in the search for welfare-superior solutions.[19]

If the explicit treatment of both issues of production and issues of distribution is a necessary condition of successful Positive Coordination, and if the battle over distribution is likely to interfere with the mindset that is conducive to joint learning, then a *procedural separation of both types of interaction* seems to be useful on theoretical grounds. On the one hand, an explicit focus on the distributive dimension may help the parties to discover, or to define, standards of distributive fairness that will serve as general guidelines in future interactions as well. On the other hand, if separate agreement on the allocation of costs and benefits can in fact be reached, this will create a framework for the common search for productive solutions that may approximate the conditions that were described earlier as being conducive to Problem Solving. In short, separation may facilitate the coexistence of "arguing" and "bargaining," which generally are thought to be mutually incompatible modes of communication and interaction.[20]

However, procedural separation may not be feasible when distributive implications are inseparable from the specific design features of a solution—just think of negotiations between "pro-life" and "pro-choice" advocates over the details of a compromise statute on abortion. When that is so, successful Positive Coordination depends on the mutual commitment to approach distributive issues, if and when they arise, with a view to finding a "fair" solution rather than a solution that maximizes the advantage of one's own side. The difficulty of maintaining this commitment, in the face of ubiquitous temptations to exploit the advantages of asymmetric information, should be obvious. It is here, therefore, that the institutional setting within which negotiations take place will make the greatest difference.

## THE IMPORTANCE OF INSTITUTIONAL SETTINGS

Negotiations can take place in all types of institutional settings, and all types of settings will affect the outcomes that can be reached—but not all will alleviate the difficulties of the Negotiator's Dilemma. In the present chapter I will only deal with those settings in which negotiations are the typical mode of interaction. I will not say much, therefore, about negotiations under conditions of anarchic fields and minimal institutions, and I will discuss negotiations taking place in majoritarian and hierarchical institutions in later chapters. The major focus here will be on negotiations in self-organizing "networks," in normative "regimes," and in "joint-decision systems." Nevertheless, a few remarks on anarchic fields and minimal institutions are also necessary.

### Negotiations in Anarchic Fields and Minimal Institutions

Under conditions of anarchic fields, negotiations can only succeed in constellations, discussed at the beginning of this chapter, in which implementation is not a problem. But even when agreements would be self-executing, they may be difficult to reach, and anarchic fields will certainly not alleviate these difficulties. The same is essentially true of the minimal institutional setting that was described at the beginning of the preceding chapter. It requires a legal system that defines property rights and binding contracts as well as the machinery for their protection and enforcement. These are also the minimal institutional preconditions of a market economy recognized by otherwise "institution-free" neoclassical economics. They are sufficient to assure the binding force of contracts. But if no more is assured, and if everyone is free to pursue any unilateral action that he or she can legally "get away with," then the writing of watertight contracts that would regulate all eventualities would entail prohibitive transaction costs in all but the simplest cases. It is plausible, therefore, that transaction-cost economics has emphasized the limited domain of the "classical contracts" that may be efficiently concluded under minimal institutional conditions (Williamson 1975; 1985).

Using the distinction between self-executing and non-self-executing agreements introduced earlier, one would have to conclude that under such conditions even mutually advantageous agreements about "joint production" would be affected by uncertainty and that "exchange" agreements would be restricted to Spot Contracts for standardized or otherwise well-defined goods and services in situations in which promise and delivery are not separated in time or space. Any commitment beyond that would be confronted with the problem that the true intentions of other actors cannot be known and that in the face of fundamental uncertainty a maxim of generalized caution would prevent the parties from agreeing to potentially profitable but risky common undertakings. Hence more profitable agreements depend on more effective, and more demanding, institutional arrangements to cope with the problems of an uncertain future and the risks of opportunism. In the following sections I will consider three such arrangements—"networks," "regimes" and "joint-decision systems."

## Networks

The *network* concept is made to serve quite diverse purposes in the policy-related literature. The term "policy networks," for instance, is meant to describe semipermanent relations of resource exchange and mutual support within the wider set of organizational actors that are trying to influence the primary policy actors or the "collective decider" within a given policy domain (Knoke et al. 1996). Similar connotations are implied by the literature on cooperative interactions in "implementation networks" (Hjern/Porter 1981; Sabatier 1986; Agranoff 1990; Gage/Mandell 1990), or in "industrial networks" among suppliers and producers (Johanson/Mattson 1987), or among firms engaged in research collaboration (Häusler/Hohn/Lütz 1993), or, finally, in "regional networks" among firms, banks, training and research institutions, associations, and public authorities that jointly contribute to the economic vitality of certain regions (Hull/Hjern 1987; Sabel 1989). Though all of these literatures emphasize specific empirical aspects, they also share an emphasis on the longer-term or "structural" characteristics of network relationships.

What is generally less clear is whether in addition to stability over time the "cooperative" quality of the relationship should also be included among the defining features of the "network" concept. As I have suggested in a previous article (Scharpf 1994), the ambiguity will disappear if one distinguishes between relationships from which low-cost exit is possible and relationships among actors that cannot avoid dealing with each other. In the first case, the existence of a semipermanent relationship is also likely to imply cooperative interactions. In the second instance, however, permanent relations among actors that cannot avoid each other may or may not be cooperative, and they are likely to sort themselves into opposing coalitions (Knoke et al. 1996, 21–24).

Within the present context, the network concept is defined abstractly and without reference to any particular empirical domain. At the same time, however, it is employed for the specific purpose of explicating one type of general conditions that are capable of reducing the transaction costs of negotiated agreement. What matters here is that network relationships will reduce the risk of opportunism by two mechanisms, the longer "shadow of the future" and the higher visibility of transactions to relevant others. As a consequence, the existence of a "network" influences the interactions that take place among its members—making some more likely than others, enabling some that would not otherwise have been possible, and changing the outcomes of some in favor of one or another of the actors.

*Network Relationships as Social Capital.* Beginning with the dyadic relationship, it is crucial that it be understood as a semipermanent structure within which individual interactions are embedded. The fact that two actors have a memory of past encounters as well as an expectation of future dealings with each other is assumed to have an effect on the individual interaction. It is also important that continuation is voluntary in the sense that exit, though costly, is still a feasible option.[21] Such relationships arise and are maintained because of the benefits that they provide in comparison to "single-shot" interactions. As I argued earlier, the inherent difficulty of knowing other actors' true intentions, and the resultant need for generalized caution, limits the opportunity for productive and mutually profitable interaction among strangers. There is a premium, therefore, on relationships that allow actors to accept higher degrees of vulnerability because they are able to trust each other. This, in my interpretation, is the central meaning of "social capital" (Coleman 1990, chap. 12; Putnam 1993) in the present context. In a previous article (Scharpf 1994), I have argued that trust may operate at two levels—weakly at the level of communication and strongly at the level of strategy choices. Even though conceptualized for different purposes, the two levels of trust may be equated with Mark Granovetter's (1973) distinction of "weak ties" and "strong ties."

*Weak trust* implies at least the *expectation that information communicated about alter's own options and preferences will be truthful,* rather than purposefully misleading, and that *commitments explicitly entered will be honored* as long as the circumstances under which they were entered do not change significantly;[22] and it may also imply a willingness to do small favors and to forgo small advantages that would entail large losses for alter. Weak trust, in other words, would suffice to render cooperation in constellations resembling the Assurance game completely unproblematic. At the second, more demanding level, *strong trust* implies the *expectation that alter will avoid strategy options attractive to itself that would seriously hurt ego's interests* and that in case of need help can be counted on even if it entails considerable cost to the helper. In terms of the mixed-motive games discussed earlier, the implication is that exploitative strategies will not be used, and hence need not be guarded against, in the Prisoner's Dilemma and in Chicken games. In other words, strong trust can be equated with some degree of a solidaristic interaction orientation.[23]

At the level of the dyadic relationship, therefore, weak trust, and even more so strong trust, will alleviate or eliminate the difficulties associated with the Negotiator's Dilemma. But while *being able to trust is advantageous,* the investment necessary to achieve *trustworthiness is costly* in the sense that some potential advantages in individual interactions must be forgone. Moreover, since trust tends to be "studied" rather than unconditional (Sabel 1992; 1993), it is difficult to build up and is easily destroyed when disappointed. Hence it may be necessary for the trustee to avoid even the appearance of being untrustworthy in situations that are nontransparent to others.

Thus among self-interested actors the stability of trustful relations depends largely on the anticipation of the costly investments necessary to rebuild them if they were to be destroyed. Moreover, the existence of a larger network of connected actors adds greatly to the incentives for maintaining trustworthiness. On the one hand, membership in a network allows access to a larger number of potential partners of trustworthy interactions and thus increases the value of social capital. On the other hand, close relationships among network members create conditions under which reliable information about the performance of other members will spread throughout the network (Milgrom/North/Weingast 1990). This increases not only the visibility of potential violations of trust but also the severity of sanctions, since self-interested actors are likely to distrust partners that are known to have been untrustworthy in other instances.

At any rate, however, the maintenance of strong ties implies that certain individual interactions will be carried out at a loss. For that reason alone the number of strong ties whose maintenance an actor can "afford" will be severely constrained, and the need for selectivity is further increased by the likelihood that different trustors may address incompatible expectations to the same actor. For an example, one may think of the difficulties of West German foreign policy in the 1960s, when it tried to maintain its "special relationships" with both de Gaulle's France and the United States. The implication is therefore that each actor is able to maintain only a limited number of strong ties and that networks constituted by strong trust linkages will not be able to connect all actors to all other actors. In other words, networks that are constituted by strong ties *at the level of the dyad* are likely to have a highly selective structure *at the level of the network.*

*Networks as Opportunity and Power Structures.* Though the quality of dyadic relationships in itself is of obvious importance for the transaction costs of the negotiated agreements that can be reached, it is not equally clear that the structure of the overall network that emerges from such dyadic relationships should be equally significant for policy research. Hence, though the topological characteristics of networks have become the object of a large body of research that has developed formal measures of the degree of connectedness of networks and of the centrality, reachability, and structural equivalence of individual positions within these networks (Burt 1976; 1980; 1982; Wellmann/Berkowitz 1988), not all of these characteristics are of relevance for the explanation of policy processes and outcomes. What seems to matter most is the implication of different network architectures for the opportunity structure and for the power structure of policy processes.

The notion of networks as an opportunity structure has become central to a line of research on "policy networks" (Atkinson/Coleman 1989; Knoke 1990; Marin/Mayntz 1991; Schneider 1992), which developed from a critique of James Coleman's (1986; 1990) model of a "political market." The Coleman model had assumed that all actors could equally deal with all others in order to trade their own influence on policy outcomes in which they were less interested for other actors' influence on outcomes for which they cared more. Network theorists, however, insist that the existence—or the nonexistence—of network linkages among specific actors creates highly selective opportunity structures within which political exchange must take place (Marsden 1983; 1987; König 1994). Not everyone, that is to say, can trade influence with everyone else; preexisting connections matter, and not all phone calls are returned.

In a sense such opportunity structures can also be interpreted as a kind of power structure, since some actors will have more connections through which they are able to reach other actors with whom they might negotiate mutually advantageous trades of influence opportunities.[24] However, a much more precise meaning of power structures has been developed in the network-exchange literature that goes back to Richard Emerson's (1962) power-dependence theory. There power is conceptualized as an asymmetrical exchange[25] relationship in which B's dependence on A is defined by both the importance of the resources (or services) provided by A and their nonavailability from alternative sources. Network structures are thus able to create asymmetrical dependence, and hence power, when one member of a dyadic exchange relationship but not the other has access to alternative sources. Power will be neutralized if either A also becomes dependent on the resources supplied by B or if B manages to find other partners from whom it is able to obtain the same resource (Figure 6.12).

The proper definition and measurement of structural power in more complex networks have generated a large and partly controversial literature (Cook et al. 1983; Willer/Patton 1987; Yamagishi/Gillmore/Cook 1988; Markovsky/Patton/Willer 1988; Cook/Yamagishi 1992). These methodological and conceptual controversies need not concern us here since the basic proposition, according to

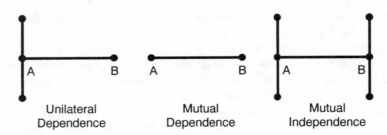

FIGURE 6.12    Forms of dependence in a relationship between A and B

which a unilateral monopoly position creates asymmetric power whereas competition destroys unilateral advantages, is not itself in question.[26]

Its importance is easily demonstrated if we translate the exchange relationship into a game-theoretic constellation (which, so far, has not been done in the network-exchange literature). Thus exchange under conditions of mutual dependence could be represented as a variant of the Battle of the Sexes in which both players have an interest in concluding the deal but differ in their preferences for one or the other coordinated outcome (Figure 6.13a). Under these circumstances, each player could obtain its second-best payoff by a "soft" bargaining strategy, and neither player could credibly threaten to break off negotiations in order to obtain the best payoff, since nonagreement (NA) would leave both of them with their worst-case result. Thus, if outcomes were divisible or side payments possible, one would expect a compromise solution that "splits the difference."

However, if one of the parties (Column in this example) should obtain an alternate source for the services performed by Row, the constellation will change. Even if the alternate game were identical to the one originally played between Column and Row, that game would now change into the asymmetrical constellation of Figure 6.13b. Since Column could count on getting at least its second-best payoff in the alternate game, its threat to break off negotiations unless it was offered its most preferred payoff would now be credible—and Row, being without any alternative option, would have no choice but to give in. In other words, by being in the position of a monopolist with two competing partners, Column will now be able to capture all potential gains from cooperation with either of them.

For the understanding of real-world policy situations, this difference between constellations of mutual and unilateral dependence is of crucial significance. Thus, in a coalition government, a small party that has the option of also forming a majority coalition with the major opposition party may have greater bargaining power than a much larger party that is prevented by high levels of ideological conflict from entering into a coalition with the opposition. This was the case in Germany in the 1970s (Scharpf 1991a). Similarly, this model is sufficient to explain the enormous impact that the completion of the Single European Market has had on the capacity of European nation-states to regulate business. To make a

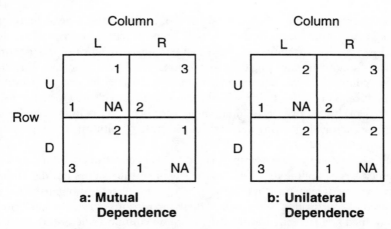

FIGURE 6.13    Battle of the Sexes under conditions of mutual and unilateral dependence
(NA = Nonagreement)

profit, firms depend on public infrastructure and public services, whereas governments depend on firms for tax revenue and for the creation of jobs. As long as access to the national market could be limited to firms producing within the national territory, the relationship was characterized by mutual dependence. After the completion of the single market, however, firms are free to move production to any location within the European Union without losing access to their home market. Thus European nation-states must now compete with each other for firms that are willing to invest and produce locally—with the consequence that the tax "price" that governments are able to exact has been reduced for all of them (Sinn 1993).

## Regimes

Negotiation networks have been defined as being informal and self-organizing structures that evolve from the frequency of voluntary dyadic interactions; negotiation regimes, by contrast, are purposefully created normative frameworks governing negotiations among a formally specified set of actors that have explicitly undertaken to respect certain interest positions of other parties, to pursue certain substantive goals, and to follow certain procedures in their future interactions. In a sense, therefore, the private law of contracts, torts, and civil procedure could be considered the most comprehensive model of a negotiation regime. However, the regime concept in political science has been developed in the context of international relations, and it is there set off against the "anarchy" of the international system in which property rights are not protected, and contractual commitments not enforced, by the authority of a state endowed with the monopoly of legitimate violence (Krasner 1983). But even if the absence of authoritative and external enforcement were accepted as a necessary element of its definition,[27] the regime concept would have domestic applications as well. Think of "coalition treaties" among political parties that are about to form a coalition government or of "framework agreements" among neighboring domestic regions or adjacent regions of different European countries to facilitate negotiated policy coordination and cooperation across political boundaries. Other salient examples are provided by the rules governing neocorporatist concertation among governments, trade unions, and employers' associations in the postwar decades (Schmitter/Lehmbruch 1979; Lehmbruch/Schmitter 1982).

What is common to these examples is the fact that effective outcomes are not determined by the regime itself (just as the law of contracts does not determine the substance of agreements) but by the subsequent interactions of parties committed to observe its rules. Nevertheless, these interactions will at the same time be constrained and facilitated by the orientation to common rules. More specifically, the constraining force of rules will mainly affect unilateral action, whereas negotiations will be facilitated by the knowledge that certain potentially damaging unilateral strategies are ruled out (so that they could no longer be used as credible threats) and that fair procedures are available for the settlement of future disputes over the interpretation of incomplete contracts.

The establishment of regimes may itself be due to freely entered contractual agreement, or it may be due to pressures exerted by a hegemonic leader (Young 1982). Once a regime is established, continuing adherence to it depends on the self-interest of the parties involved as well as on the willingness of other parties to sanction breaches of regime obligations. In that regard it is useful to distinguish between breaches of contractual obligations toward another party and "free riding" on the production of a collective good. In the first case, the injured party may have an interest in retaliating in kind, and it may be sufficient to provide rules governing such sanctions—as is true under the GATT, where the victim is entitled, after going through proper procedures, to exclude the transgressor from most-favored-nation benefits. In the second case, individual self-interest could not assure the application of costly sanctions (Hardin 1985; Heckathorn 1989). But if individual violations were left without sanctions, it is likely that other parties would also defect and that the whole regime would progressively unravel.

The theory of regimes in international relations therefore began by emphasizing the role of a hegemonic power whose interest in the benefits of general compliance was sufficiently large to allow it to assume the costs of sanctioning. Thus the establishment and maintenance of international economic regimes such as the Bretton Woods system of fixed exchange rates, the International Monetary Fund, or the GATT were ascribed to the economic self-interest and the hegemonic power of the United States (Stein 1984; Snidal 1985b; Yarbrough/Yarbrough 1985). When it was realized that most of these regimes (with the exception of Bretton Woods) not only survived the erosion of the relative economic strength of the United States but also continued to develop and intensify, atten-

tion shifted to the benefits derived by all participants from the institutionalization of "diffuse reciprocity" (Keohane 1984). In addition, the neorealist assumption according to which nation-states are the only relevant actors to be considered was challenged by two-level approaches (Putnam 1988) that emphasized the
need to examine the domestic political constellations that might undercut or stabilize national commitments to an international regime (Moravcsik 1992).

But when that is being done at all, there is no obvious reason why only domestic interests of an economic nature (say, of export industries) should be considered and why analysts should ignore the role played by influential segments of
political parties, the bureaucracy, the judiciary, the press, and academe, which are
normatively, or ideologically, committed to international law or to free trade or
to the reduction of worldwide environmental pollution. To the extent that such
influences will affect national positions, international regimes not only may operate as external constraints on the pursuit of national interest but also may come
to shape the definition of what is considered to be the national interest as well.

## *Joint-Decision Systems*

Networks can be characterized as voluntary negotiation systems in which parties
are free to choose between negotiations and unilateral action;[28] and though
regimes may impose obligations, they will not usually eliminate the capacity for
unilateral action. By contrast, I use the term "joint-decision system" to describe
constellations in which parties are either physically or legally unable to reach their
purposes through unilateral action and in which joint action depends on the
(nearly) unanimous agreement of all parties involved. Such constellations may
arise naturally from physical adjacency or functional interdependence, when goals
of a particular kind or beyond a certain order of magnitude cannot be attained
without collaboration. Examples that come to mind are common infrastructure
or environmental policy projects among neighboring states and large-scale scientific, technical, or industrial undertakings such as the European Organization for
Nuclear Research (CERN) or the European Space Program or Airbus Industries.

Of greater practical importance, for our purposes, are institutionalized joint-
decision systems requiring that certain actions be undertaken only on the basis of
negotiated agreement or unanimous vote. Examples range from private partner-
ships and joint business ventures to collective bargaining, to government coalitions in which the participating parties will not outvote each other with the help
of the opposition, to constellations of "divided government" in which decisions
can only be reached with the support of the opposition, and to constellations in
German federalism and in the European Union in which certain decisions are de
jure, and most are de facto, dependent on the unanimous agreement of member
governments (Scharpf 1988). In the latter two cases not only is there a legal *obligation* to abstain from contrary actions (which might be disregarded in fact), but
also the doctrines of legal "supremacy" and "direct effect" allow ordinary courts

to disregard national legislation and government decisions that are seen to violate the prohibition of unilateral action (Weiler 1981; 1994).

Joint-decision systems are thus instances of compulsory negotiation systems that, in the multiparty case, may also be characterized as collective-decision or voting systems operating under either unanimity or consensus rules. For that reason the outcomes so achieved also seem to require no additional legitimation beyond the Roman-law maxim of *volenti non fit iniuria* (meaning that consenting parties cannot claim to be injured)—which may explain the strong preference of public-choice theorists for the unanimity rule in collective-choice situations (Buchanan/Tullock 1962). However, such arguments also imply a strong bias against collective action. Though this may be normatively defensible when the "default rule" in case of disagreement is that everyone remains free to act individually, it is difficult to justify for collective-action systems that have exclusive jurisdiction over certain matters. And even if jurisdiction should be concurrent rather than exclusive, the argument remains persuasive only for the initial decision to resort to collective action.

But once a collective decision has been adopted, it becomes binding and can only be changed again with the agreement of all. Individual members will then have lost the freedom of unilateral action even when external circumstances or preferences should change in ways that will render a standing decision unacceptable to some (but not all) of its original supporters. Thus, if renegotiation should involve high transaction costs (as is likely to be true under large-numbers conditions), the unanimity rule turns into a "joint-decision trap" (Scharpf 1988) in which the beneficiaries of the status quo can block all reforms, or at least extract exorbitant side payments.

Transaction costs can be greatly reduced, however, if the decision rule is not unanimity but "consensus," defined as a mode of interaction in which discussion is continued until no one still insists on opposing a proposed solution—but in which, in the face of blatant obstruction, it is still possible to resort to nonunanimous decisions (Coleman 1990, 857–862). This rule is likely to evolve in committees and other constellations that formally operate under the majority rule but in which all participants would prefer to avoid overriding the interests of a minority. One reason for this may lie in norms of reciprocity based on the expectation that everyone will be in the minority position at one time or another. Such norms are as common in university faculties as they are in international committees defining technical standards (Genschel 1995). Similar rules seem to apply in the Council of Ministers of the European Union, in which most decisions are still taken by consensus even after the Single European Act had introduced the possibility of qualified majority voting. What has changed is that isolated opponents that cannot claim to be affected in their "essential national interest" can no longer extort excessive side payments, since if the search for consensus should fail, the majority is now able to have its way by resorting to a vote. As a consequence, the Single European Act has had the effect of greatly reducing the time needed to reach agreement in the Council of Ministers (Dehousse/Weiler 1990).

Transaction costs are further reduced if systems operating under near-unanimity rules can rely on an agenda setter that defines the propositions that will be voted upon. Under majority rule, as will be seen in Chapter 7, the agenda setter has the power to select quite different outcomes and, in the process, to pick and choose among alternative majorities (Riker 1980; 1982; Shepsle/Weingast 1987). Under unanimity or near-unanimity rules, that power is greatly reduced. What matters instead is the facilitating role that could help the principal actors to discover the solution on which they might all be able to agree.

One reason for this is purely quantitative: In the absence of an agenda setter, a voting body with N members would need to engage in multilateral negotiations involving $N(N-1)/2$ bilateral relationships in order to find a universally agreeable outcome, whereas a single agenda setter would need to contact only N members to explore the acceptability of a proposal. Even more important are the implications of the Negotiator's Dilemma discussed earlier. In multilateral negotiations, rational self-interested actors would begin by proposing solutions favoring their own interests, and any communication among them would also be suspected of being self-serving and disingenuous. To work out a mutually acceptable solution under these conditions would be extremely difficult indeed. By contrast, an external agenda setter, which has no stake of its own in the distributional conflict, may be trusted not to engage in the strategies and tactics of Distributive Bargaining. Hence it may be easier for an external agenda setter to assess the limits of acceptability for all participants and to propose a jointly acceptable solution—if one in fact exists. Such services are typically performed by the central staffs of associations or by the "secretariats" of international organizations. Precisely because they can neither offer favors of their own nor inflict punishment, they are likely to be accepted as an "honest broker" whose good offices may enable governments that are much more powerful than themselves to reach outcomes that they could not have reached on their own (Young 1995).

In short, the inherent limitations of systems that depend on unanimous or near-unanimous agreement can be extended by the institutionalization of an agenda-setting function. However, even in the best of circumstances, joint-decision systems are cumbersome, difficult to manage, and easily blocked. Nevertheless, they may sometimes be the best that can be obtained, considering the difficulties of installing a majoritarian system that would have democratic legitimacy. Under such conditions, which may now exist in the European Union, it seems more worthwhile to explore institutional solutions that would make the existing joint-decision system more effective, rather than to call for majoritarian reforms (Scharpf 1996). At any rate, as will be seen in the following chapter, the switch to the majority rule is certainly no panacea for all the difficulties associated with unanimity.

## CONCLUSION

In light of the Coase Theorem, negotiations in general, and Positive Coordination in particular, offer the attractive promise of reaching welfare-maximizing resolutions of collective-action problems through voluntary agreement. But that attractive promise is qualified by two limitations. The first limitation concerns distribution. Voluntary negotiations involve only those parties that have something to contribute that is of value to others. There is simply no room at the bargaining table for those who have neither valuable resources nor skills to offer. And even in compulsory negotiation systems (in which institutionalized veto positions are able to create "artificial" bargaining power), outcomes will reproduce rather than change the given distribution of physically controlled assets, legally protected property rights, and outside opportunities. Thus if redistribution is the central policy problem, negotiations (or any form of unanimous or consensual decisionmaking) would not be a good mode of interaction (Mueller 1989b).

By contrast, if the problem constellation resembles a positive-sum game like Assurance, Battle of the Sexes, or even Prisoner's Dilemma, negotiations are in principle capable of providing welfare-maximizing solutions. They are, however—and this is the second limitation—associated with high transaction costs when distributive conflict must be resolved in the same interactions in which better overall solutions are to be designed or discovered. Hence negotiations will often fail altogether or will merely produce unsatisfactory compromises in which potential welfare gains are "left on the table." Moreover, transaction costs will increase exponentially as the number of (independent) participants increases.

The large-numbers problem can be reduced somewhat if full-fledged negotiations in the sense of Positive Coordination can be concentrated upon a core group of actors that will solve the design problem among themselves but who will then have to obtain the agreement of others through Distributive Bargaining or through Negative Coordination. Since the transaction costs of Negative Coordination and of Bargaining are considerably lower than those of Positive Coordination, the size of negotiating groups and the range of interests that are effectively accommodated through negotiations can be considerably extended without incurring prohibitive transaction costs. Matthias Mohr and I have shown this to be true in a computer-simulation study that is reprinted in Appendix 2. Beyond that, there are two possible solutions to the large-numbers problem.

The first is favored by the way economists tend to think about society. In the context of transaction-cost theory it has been described as a "nexus of treaties" (Williamson 1990), suggesting that all relevant social outcomes could be produced by crisscrossing patterns of bilateral and small-numbers negotiations. This is a view that is particularly well fitted to market interactions but that also describes a large part of what is in fact going on outside of the market in modern societies. What it cannot deal with is collective-action problems involving numbers of participants that are too large to be accommodated by multilateral negotiations.

The second solution is "collective bargaining." If large-numbers problems are to be dealt with through negotiations, there is a need for the aggregation of individual and corporate actors into larger units that are capable of representing the aggregated preferences or interests of their members in negotiations with other such units. The implication is that such negotiations must be conducted by "clubs" or "associations," as defined in Chapter 3, and perhaps by associations of associations (or "peak-level" organizations). When that is the case, the theoretical focus shifts back from the interaction among large organizations to the internal interactions within associations in which the "logic of influence" in external negotiations is constrained and must be legitimated through the internal "logic of membership" (Streeck/Schmitter 1981). This will be the subject of the next two chapters.

## NOTES

1. The character of the implementation game may, and usually will, differ from the actor constellation that characterizes the substance of the agreement. Hence agreement may have to deal with a Battle of the Sexes constellation, but implementation could still be an Assurance game.

2. A three-person game would be represented by a three-dimensional cube figure; for larger numbers of players, neither form of representation would be useful. However, Appendix 2 contains a tabular representation that is relatively transparent even for larger games.

3. A pure zero-sum conflict would be located on the diagonal representing the welfare boundary.

4. Though it is often permissible to identify the NA point with the status quo, this is not correct if, for instance, one party could avail itself of an outside option (say, another contract offer) that would also represent an improvement over the status quo, or if one party can credibly threaten to reduce the other's payoff below the previous status quo if it should fail to agree to "an offer that you cannot afford to reject."

5. The difference between zero-sum and Battle of the Sexes constellations is illustrated by the history of competition and cooperation among firms in the Japanese auto industry: Within the closed Japanese market, there was fierce competition for market shares. It was only after they began to enter foreign markets in the 1970s, where market shares could be captured from foreign competitors, that cooperation among Japanese firms gained in significance (personal communication from Kjell Hausken and Thomas Pluemper).

6. The reader should be warned that my use of this literature is nonstandard. In the standard version the parties will negotiate *on a given possibility frontier,* and in order to be acceptable the outcome will only have to be "fair" but not welfare maximizing. Starting from the Coase Theorem, I assume instead that parties should be negotiating *on the welfare frontier* (i.e., the highest available welfare isoquant) and that *on that welfare level* the distribution should be fair. If side payments or package deals are possible, as must be assumed for the Coase Theorem to hold, there is in fact no reason that rational parties should negotiate on a given possibility frontier rather than on the welfare frontier.

7. For individuals that zero point could be defined by the income provided by public welfare.

8. That distribution will not always favor the bigger or more powerful party. When the constellation is not a Battle of the Sexes (as was assumed in the EU-Hungary example) but

a Prisoner's Dilemma (which is characteristic of military alliances), the "exploitation of the big by the small" (Olson/Zeckhauser 1966) may be the more likely outcome.

9. For reasons that will quickly become clear, we have previously used the term "Negative Coordination" for this mode of interaction (Appendix 2). But since the use of a single term for two different, though functionally equivalent, modes was found confusing by some readers, I have switched to "Spot Contracts," which parallels the terminology used in transaction-cost economics.

10. Richard Walton and Robert McKersie (1965) have used this label for the same purpose. In earlier articles, and in Appendix 2, I used simply "bargaining" to describe the same mode. Paul Sabatier has persuaded me that the wider connotations of the generic term could be misleading.

11. Another way to read Figure 6.9 is to consider A as the new nonagreement point and the restoration of the status quo at SQ as a project proposed by Y that could not be realized without X's agreement.

12. That is generally true of issues of high normative or ideological salience, such as abortion or nuclear energy or ethnic identity. However, even on policy issues involving monetary costs, there are interesting differences among countries. Thus, the idea that one local or state government might claim monetary compensation from another if its services are used by the other's inhabitants is thought to be incompatible with the "public" character of state services in Germany, whereas such arrangements are highly developed in Switzerland and in the United States (Scharpf/Benz 1991; Parks/Ostrom 1981).

13. Similarly, in voluntary negotiations the party whose interests are damaged by a project with a negative welfare balance might respond with a similarly damaging threat project of its own, which could then be used as a bargaining counter in negotiations. In Figure 6.10, this possibility is represented by projects A' and B', which would have a joint outcome at C' that is located in the quadrant of "mutual aversion" and hence is unacceptable to both. This is the logic of mutual deterrence and disarmament negotiations, but we also have found civilian threat projects developed for purely "defensive" purposes even in the relations among neighboring German states (Scharpf/Benz 1991). In neocorporatist interactions between governments and industrial or professional associations, governments may also introduce legislation that is merely intended as a threat to "encourage" negotiated agreement. In order to be credible, however, the defensive project must have some intrinsic value for the government that is using it as a threat—and it must seem politically feasible. This point will be discussed more fully in Chapter 9.

14. In our study of interstate coordination problems in German federalism, we found serious problems of implementation with regard to a widely acclaimed package deal between Hamburg and a neighboring state. The agreement, reached after years of negotiations at the level of heads of government, involved a trade between investments in the city to improve rail and road transit from the peripheral regions and investments in the hinterland to provide waste-disposal facilities for the city. However, when the agreement was to be implemented, the benefit that the state as a whole might derive from better access to interregional transport networks was insufficient to assure the cooperation of those local communes that were asked to accept waste-treatment plants on their premises. Hence the best that the state could do was to offer additional side payments to the local communes involved. Opportunities for package deals, in other words, are often frustrated by the complexities of multilevel policy systems (Scharpf/Benz 1991; Benz 1992; Mayer 1994).

15. In other words, the status quo would represent a noncooperative Nash equilibrium.

16. For Jürgen Habermas, by contrast, "rational discourse" is defined not only as being distinct from "negotiations" (which are equated with what here is called "Distributive Bargaining") but as being incompatible with communications in which actor-specific interests and differences in bargaining power play any role at all (Habermas 1992, 204–206). For that reason, Problem Solving as it is defined here (which is assumed to maximize the common *interests* of the actors involved) would not qualify as "rational discourse" (Elster 1986).

17. Conversely, it can be shown that external competition is a powerful facilitator of internal cooperation (Hausken 1995).

18. This point has been emphasized by Renate Mayntz (1994) in her case study of the role of West German science organizations in the reconstruction of East German research institutions after German unification. Once it was clear that the basic West German institutional structure would be maintained, distributive aspects lost their salience and the ensuing negotiations could be characterized as a joint search for appropriate solutions.

19. This, I take it, is also the message conveyed by the maxim that individual negotiators should "negotiate from principle" (Fisher/Ury 1981). It is to teach the other side the futility of battling for victory in the distributive dimension.

20. An alternative solution, "learning by monitoring," has been introduced by Charles Sabel (1994). Rather than separate production from distribution, he proposes that they should be associated as closely as possible, so that continuous monitoring of learning processes will eliminate the risk of opportunism in the distributive dimension. This approach was originally discovered in the organization and continuous improvement of work flows in the Japanese automobile industry under "just-in-time" conditions. The application of the concept to interactions between manufacturing firms and their suppliers seems straightforward, though its extension to government-industry interactions or to interactions in policymaking processes still needs to be worked out.

21. Exit can have two different meanings: Among actors that are free to choose or leave their partners, it means not dealing with one another. Among actors that cannot avoid dealing with one another, "exit" may still mean to switch to one of the noncooperative (i.e., "individualistic," "competitive," or even "hostile") interaction orientations discussed at the end of Chapter 4. Though transaction-cost economics and economic sociology are mainly interested in networks among firms that are constituted by voluntary relationships of the first type, the disciplines of industrial relations, political science, and International Relations primarily study compulsory relationships between capital and labor, among political parties and interest organizations, ministerial departments, and local, regional, and national units of government, or between territorial states that cannot avoid dealing with one another.

22. An ongoing network relationship can thus be equated with an iterated "trustworthiness game" in which, in each individual interaction (regardless of the substantive issues involved), the parties also must choose between maintaining or abandoning their own trustworthiness—and maintaining or abandoning their own trust in the other's trustworthiness (Scharpf 1990).

23. Nevertheless, trustful long-term relationships will rarely depend on subjectivities alone but rather are likely to arise in constellations in which individual interactions are *on average* objectively advantageous to both parties. In other words, it is likely that—at the level of the "given matrix"—a large portion of individual interactions will have the character of games of coordination and of dilemma games in which mutual cooperation is

more advantageous than mutual defection for all concerned. Because that is so, losses in the individual case will be offset against generalized expectations of future gain.

24. The notion of indirect linkages, and of reachability by a chain of linkages, plays a significant role in the topological literature that is interested in classifying the structural characteristics of different positions in complex networks. I have yet to be convinced, however, that indirect linkages play much of a role in real-world policy processes.

25. For our purposes, the propositions of power-dependence theory apply to interactions aiming at *joint production* just as much as they apply to interactions of *exchange*.

26. It is worth noting, however, that network-exchange theory is only concerned with the power resulting from the exchange of positively valued resources, not with negative sanctions, coercion, or "punishment power" (Molm 1989). In other words, the focus has been exclusively on interest constellations of the Battle of the Sexes variety but not on other types of mixed-motive constellations. Moreover, within the class of exchange relations, network-exchange theory has fully conceptualized only multiparty constellations that are "negatively connected" in the sense that an exchange between A and B reduces A's interest in an exchange with C. But of course there are also real-world constellations in which an exchange between A and B will not significantly affect the chances of a similar transaction between A and C or in which one transaction may even positively depend on the conclusion of another (Willer 1987).

27. The usefulness of that dividing line is not completely obvious given the largely automatic acceptance, by most countries, of international-law obligations pronounced by an established dispute-settling body on the one hand and the tendency of many parties involved in domestic-law disputes to prefer out-of-court settlements on the other.

28. Obviously, these are differences in degree. Even if a network relationship is entered freely, leaving it may be costly, and refusing to negotiate within an existing network relationship may amount to an exit decision. Conversely, even in joint-decision systems without legitimate exit options, a disaffected party may decide to resort to passive resistance or to reduce its own aspirations to a level that can be maintained without joint action.

# 7

## Decisions by Majority Vote

In comparison with the Nash equilibria that may be reached through unilateral action, the outcomes achieved through negotiated agreements are attractive in welfare-theoretic terms. However, negotiations run into prohibitive transaction costs when the number of independent parties increases. By contrast, the choices of very large numbers of actors may be coordinated at very moderate transaction costs if collectively binding decisions can be imposed by majority rule or by hierarchical fiat. In order to be considered "collectively binding," these must be decisions for which compliance can be expected from a given set of actors, even though they have not agreed to them, even though these decisions go against their interests, and even though these actors might have options of unilateral action that would improve the outcome for them individually (i.e., even though the outcomes are not Nash equilibria). But what could account for this binding force?

### COLLECTIVELY BINDING DECISIONS

Nash equilibria reached through unilateral action among independent actors will generate their binding force endogenously within the interaction itself—none of the parties has a better option that it could choose unilaterally. In the case of negotiations, as I pointed out at the beginning of Chapter 6, this is also true of contracts that can be classified as instances of "joint production," in which neither party has a motive to renege on its commitments. This is not so in contracts involving the "exchange" of goods or services, in which, if performance is not simultaneous with the agreement, implementation becomes a problem when purely self-interested rational actors are assumed. As long as alter is keeping its side of the contract, ego could benefit from defaulting on its own commitment. This is a Prisoner's Dilemma constellation that may have an endogenous solution under network conditions, in which actors will have to deal with one another repeatedly, will observe each other, and will invest in valuable reputations that would be lost in case of default (Milgrom/North/Weingast 1990; Scharpf 1994; de Jasay 1995). Where these conditions do not exist, even the implementation of negotiated agreements depends on enforcement mechanisms that are exogenous to the transaction itself. The same is true a fortiori for binding decisions adopted by majority vote or by hierarchical fiat.

## *The Need for Legitimation*

One element of such mechanisms is of course the expectation of positive rewards or of negative sanctions applied by superior power. But since reward-based power is expensive, it tends to exhaust itself if used successfully. Negative sanctions, that is, the infliction of severe deprivations (Lasswell/Kaplan 1950), may of course be even more expensive when actually applied.[1] Nevertheless, there is a fundamental advantage of negative over positive incentives that derives from their usefulness in threats. Threats and promises are highly asymmetric in one aspect: Promises that are successful in influencing alter's behavior must be kept, whereas successful threats do not have to be carried out. For that reason threats are highly cost-efficient: A single gun may suffice to scare off a crowd, but a single check will pay for only one successful bribe. Moreover, threat power that is based on a preponderant capacity for physical coercion is reinforced, rather than exhausted, through successful use, and it is thus less likely to erode over time.

In practice, however, the exercise of threat power is also fraught with risks. On the one hand, threats of severe deprivations, and even more so the actual infliction of losses, are likely to generate strong psychic reactions in target actors (Kahneman/Tversky 1984; Quattrone/Tversky 1988), which, rather than inducing obedience, may in fact provoke resistance (Molm 1989; 1990). Within the frame of reference introduced in Chapter 4, this psychic reaction may be interpreted as a switch from "individualistic" to "competitive" or even "hostile" interaction orientations. Even though it might be "objectively" better (from the perspective of purely rational self-interested action) to give in to the threat in order to avoid even greater damage, disobedience and even active resistance may subjectively appear as the only appropriate response once the orientation has switched.

The same reaction may also be derived from a less subjective interpretation: If the threat stands by itself, the apparent willingness of ego to inflict severe deprivations on alter may justify an interpretation of the constellation that is analogous to neorealist assumptions about the nature of international relations in the anarchic world system. That is, there is a possibility that ego is out to destroy alter. When that possibility is assumed and is combined with a healthy appreciation of the fortuitous turns and reversals that are possible in all-out conflict, it may indeed be rational for alter to act on the maxim that "those who fight may lose, but those who don't have already lost." At this point, either ego will have to carry out its threat, even at considerable cost to itself, or the credibility of future threats, and hence their effectiveness, will rapidly erode.[2]

If such counterproductive reactions are to be avoided, threats and the exercise of punishment power must be based on rules that are accepted as legitimate by the wider social and political community. From the point of view of the target actor, this has two important implications. On the one hand, rule-based power tends to be restricted in its domain (i.e., the factual conditions that give rise to its application) and in its scope (i.e., the types and magnitudes of sanctions that may be employed), so that there is less reason to fear that all-out victimization might follow if a threat is not forcefully resisted from the beginning.[3] On the other hand, acceptance by the wider community creates normative expectations, sanctioned at least by social disapproval, to the effect that the exercise of rule-based power should not be resisted but rather ought to be accepted by the target actors as well.[4] Thus, to be generally effective, the expectation of sanctions must be supported by generally shared legitimating beliefs that imply a duty to accept and to comply even with decisions that go against the actor's self-interest and even if it were possible to avoid them (Ayres/Braithwaite 1992).[5] Hence what ultimately matters for legitimacy is not the actual preference of the individual affected but the sense on the part of the wider community that the rule or order in question is one that ought to be generally obeyed.

### Two Types of Legitimacy

But what creates legitimacy? Analytically, it is useful to distinguish between two types of legitimating beliefs, which, in the context of democratic theory, I have described as being either "input-oriented" or "output-oriented" (Scharpf 1970). Input-oriented arguments must ultimately derive legitimacy from the agreement of those who are asked to comply, whereas output-oriented notions refer to substantive criteria of *buon governo,* in the sense that effective policies can claim legitimacy if they serve the common good and conform to criteria of distributive justice. For collectively binding decisions,[6] therefore, democratic procedures are essential in input-oriented arguments, whereas they have only instrumental value in the context of output-oriented arguments. They are valued if and to the extent that majoritarian decisions or democratically accountable hierarchical decisions are generally capable of producing public-interest-oriented policy outcomes.

Thus, from an output-oriented perspective, there is nothing anomalous in constitutional constraints on the exercise of majority power, and it is also possible to acknowledge that even in modern societies some types of binding decisions continue to rely on nondemocratic forms of legitimacy. This is most likely to be true in areas where value or goal consensus is high and where the effective resolution of specific problems is highly dependent on expert knowledge that is neither generally available nor easily acquired. When that is true, even modern constitutional democracies may be willing to empower expert bodies that are shielded from the influence of majorities of the day and to rely on formal and informal systems of professional discourse and peer review to assure the public-interest orientation of delegated powers (Majone 1989). Thus in some countries monetary policy is entrusted to a politically independent central bank that is closely monitored and publicly criticized by bankers and academic economists.

Similarly, the power of a politically independent judiciary is generally embedded in and disciplined by systems of professional discourse and criticism in which not only courts of appeal but also the legal profession in general and academic law play crucial roles. In either case, the exercise of hierarchical authority remains acceptable as long as policy choices and decisions in individual cases are broadly upheld by the mainstream of professional discourse. Similarly, the power of constitutional courts to review not only administrative acts but also the constitutionality of statutes adopted by a democratically elected legislature ultimately rests on its congruence with what Harlan Fiske Stone, one of the great justices of the U.S. Supreme Court, once defined as the "sober second thought of the community" (Bickel 1962, 26; Mason 1956). Beyond that, however, output-oriented legitimacy arguments in modern constitutional democracies must also depend on mechanisms of democratic accountability. I will return to this later in this chapter and in the next.

Input-oriented legitimacy arguments, by contrast, imply that authentic agreement, though not necessarily assuring effective implementation by itself, is nevertheless able to *create an obligation to comply*—and hence to legitimate the enforcement of compliance. This argument works well to justify the enforcement of contracts and of unanimous decisions in clubs or associations or in self-governing political constituencies operating in the mode of direct democracy. Without more, however, this justification would clearly be insufficient to legitimate the enforcement of majority decisions against the minority that did not agree.

But what could constitute a convincing input-oriented argument legitimating majority rule? In the history of political ideas the most influential line of reasoning was developed in the "social contract" of Jean-Jacques Rousseau ([1762] 1984). Distinguishing between the *volonté de tous* and the *volonté générale*, Rousseau claimed that the latter represents not only the objective public good of a given society but also the true self-interest of every citizen, who therefore, in being forced to obey the law, is only realizing his or her own enlightened self-interest. The totalitarian possibilities of this argument are obvious enough (Talmon 1955). Nevertheless, it has been shown that there is one interpretation according to which Rousseau makes perfectly good sense, analytically as well as normatively, even within the strict confines of normative individualism. That interpretation presupposes that Rousseau (like Hobbes) interpreted the basic constellation among individuals in a society without government as a Prisoner's Dilemma game and, more specifically, as a *symmetrical* Prisoner's Dilemma game. When that is assumed, everything falls into place (Runciman/Sen 1965; Sen 1969): The *volonté générale* can be equated with the pursuit of pure public good, and the *volonté de tous* corresponds to the myopic self-interest that compels individuals acting unilaterally to choose "defection" even though doing so will produce inferior outcomes for all concerned. Thus the *volonté générale*, in order to produce superior results for all, must depend on sanctions to counteract the continuing temptation to defect. However, being forced to comply does in fact serve everybody's true self-interest. But how does that argument legitimate majority rule? The link is disappointingly simple: Since the cooperative outcome is in everybody's interest, it ought to find unanimous support, but agreement by a majority of individuals may suffice as a signal that a solution approximating the *volonté générale* has been found (Grofman/Feld 1988)—and hence that the minority must have been in error.[7]

However, the game-theoretic reconstruction also reveals the fatal flaw not only of Rousseau's theory but also of all concepts of democratic legitimacy that are based on the postulated identity of individual self-interest and the collective interest. They depend on the assumption of a *symmetrical* Prisoner's Dilemma game, and they all must ignore the salience or deny the legitimacy of social conflict. Thus Rousseau's justification of majority rule would not work even for constellations resembling the Battle of the Sexes[8] or for *asymmetrical* Prisoner's Dilemma constellations with several "cooperative" outcomes that differ in their distributive characteristics (Heckathorn/Maser 1987), and it fails completely for constellations approaching zero-sum conflict.

Historically, it may be argued that Rousseauian democracy was normatively most plausible in small polities with a homogeneous population and under conditions of a minimal state that was almost exclusively concerned with issues of external and internal security (which may indeed be characterized as pure public goods). In modern, highly differentiated societies, however, whose political systems must perform a wide range of functions that necessarily will affect different groups differently, the identity-based equation of collective and individual interest turns into an ideology that can be, and indeed has been and is being, used to justify the oppression of dissenters.

But if the pursuit of individual self-interest is considered legitimate in political processes, we are again confronted with the question of why a minority should be morally obliged to respect the policy choices of self-interested majorities. The answer, clearly, can no longer be generally provided by input-oriented legitimating arguments alone. They would have to be supported and qualified by showing under which conditions the outcomes obtained by majority vote can also be justified in the light of output-oriented criteria. This implies that collective action should generally be employed to solve societal problems that could not otherwise be solved and that solving them through majoritarian decision would produce outcomes that increase general welfare and that are defensible on grounds of distributive justice.

## DECISION BY MAJORITY RULE

Under the majority rule the objections of a dissenting minority can be overruled. As a consequence the transaction costs associated with unanimous decisionmaking can be greatly reduced if the voting rule can be changed to majority. But precisely for that reason there is a much greater need for explicit legitimation if decisions, potentially involving matters of life and death, may be imposed on dissenters. The need for legitimation increases further if exit from the majoritarian system is impossible or, at any rate, associated with significant costs.[9] With this in mind, I will examine the plausibility of output-oriented legitimating arguments for *decisions that are in fact taken by majority vote* either among the population affected (as would be the case in a referendum) or in a representative assembly; the legitimacy of (hierarchical) *decisions by democratically accountable governments* will be discussed in the next chapter. I will begin with the standard assumption of rational-choice institutionalism, according to which voters should be seen as being self-interested and fully rational. The same assumption is applied to the members of representative assemblies, who are expected to pursue individual preferences rationally—which may reflect, to different degrees, the interests of their constituents and their own interests (Cain/Ferejohn/Fiorina 1987).

### Self-Interested Majorities

Rousseau as well as the authors of the Federalist Papers abhorred cohesive majorities and warned of the "evils of faction." The argument is analytically plausible: The existence of a cohesive majority transforms majority rule into a two-actor interaction in which one side has dictatorial powers. Since the majority faction is assumed to be self-interested, there is nothing to prevent it from pursuing policies that inflict damages on the minority that are greater than the benefits accruing to itself. If instead of a cohesive majority we assume a *population of individual voters* with independently varying preferences, the two-actor constellation will turn into the multiactor constellation that Rousseau as well as James Madison thought to be conducive to the realization of the public interest. Similarly, public-choice theory has shown that under certain conditions self-interested voters casting their votes in accordance with their *individual* preferences will produce outcomes corresponding to the position of the "median voter," which, under additional assumptions, will maximize the aggregate satisfaction of preferences (Mueller 1989b). Unfortunately, however, the assumptions under which this is true are so restrictive that, as a practical matter, the justification of majority rule cannot be based on them (Riker 1982).

At the logical center of these difficulties lies the famous Condorcet-Arrow paradox (Arrow 1951), which implies that it is not generally possible to aggregate consistent individual utility functions into a consistent social welfare function and which, with regard to the majority rule, more specifically implies the possibility of cyclically unstable majorities (Black 1948; 1958). For an illustration, assume that there are three policy options, x, y, and z, and three voters, A, B, and C, whose preferences for these options are distributed as in Table 7.1.

In this case, x is preferred over y by a majority consisting of A and B; y is preferred over z by a majority consisting of A and C; and z is preferred over x by a majority consisting of B and C. Thus, perfectly rational (i.e., transitive) prefer-

Table 7.1 The Voting Paradox

| | | Voters | |
|---|---|---|---|
| Options | A | B | C |
| x | 1 | 2 | 3 |
| y | 2 | 3 | 1 |
| z | 3 | 1 | 2 |

ence orderings of individual voters are translated by the majority rule into an irrational (i.e., circular) collective preference function of the population as a whole: x > y > z > x.

The practical importance of this analytical discovery is by no means negligible. It is true that the paradox will not appear when there are only two cohesive actors; and it will also not appear when there are only two options among which voters must choose. With three or more independent actors, or three or more options to choose from, however, the paradox can be avoided only under very restrictive assumptions. The most plausible one is that it should be possible to rank all options in a single issue dimension (e.g., on a "left-right" scale) and that in this dimension the preferences of all voters should be "single peaked" (Black 1948).

Thus in Figure 7.1 options x, y, and z have been ranked in a single issue dimension (say, for example, "more" or "less" public spending), and voter preferences are represented in the vertical dimension. In Figure 7.1a, representing the constellation introduced in Table 7.1, only voters A and C have single peaked preferences, whereas in Figure 7.1b, all preferences are single peaked. Only if that is the case will the outcome be stable. Moreover, the winning outcome will then be located at the most preferred position of the median voter (i.e., voter B in Figure 7.1b), which—assuming a unimodal and symmetrical "normal" distribution of voter preferences—has the attractive welfare-theoretic implication that the aggregate satisfaction of preferences is being maximized (Mueller 1989b).[10]

Unfortunately, however, these conditions are rarely approximated in practice, and when options are evaluated in two or more issue dimensions, the paradox is practically certain to preclude an equilibrium outcome (Plott 1967).

In Figure 7.2 this constellation is presented in the form of a spatial voting diagram for three voters, A, B, and C, who are evaluating policy options in a two-dimensional issue space ("left versus right" and "industrialism versus green," for instance) and who can adopt a policy by simple majority. The ideal positions of the three voters are marked A, B, and C, respectively, and the present status quo is marked SQ. If we further assume that the indifference curves have the form of concentric circles around the ideal points, it is easy to see that for any SQ located

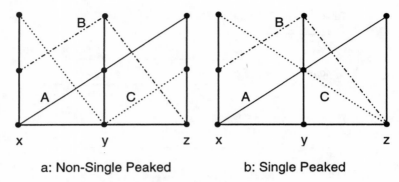

a: Non-Single Peaked                    b: Single Peaked

FIGURE 7.1    Preference distributions in a single issue dimension

*inside* the triangle ABC the indifference circles for any pair of voters (but not for all three voters)[11] will intersect. The space within this intersection includes locations of outcomes that are more attractive than the status quo for this pair of voters (say, an outcome located at AC for parties A and C). The implication is that any majority will always be able to agree on a new outcome that is more attractive than SQ to its own members. But by the same token, this new outcome will be less attractive than the status quo to the excluded third party (in this case B).

However, as soon as A and C have tentatively agreed on a new outcome (located at AC, for instance), new indifference curves through that point can be drawn. Assuming that A and C have already reached their Pareto frontier in the previous round of negotiations, they now have nothing more to offer to each other. But B, who was locked out in the previous round, is now able to offer agreements either to A (say, at AB) or to C (at BC), which for either of them would be more attractive than outcome AC. And so on: Every point that two of the actors can agree upon can be beaten by a possible agreement between either of these actors and the excluded third party. Thus all outcomes in two-dimensional issue space will be cyclically unstable—a result that can be generalized to more than three actors and more than two issue dimensions (McKelvey 1976).

But what is the empirical relevance of these theoretically devastating analytical conclusions? Cyclical instability is certainly not an empirically unknown phenomenon—the rapidly changing governing coalitions in the French Fourth Republic, in postwar Italy, and in some other multiparty political systems provide sufficient evidence for an existence hypothesis. Nevertheless, instability seems to be empirically far less ubiquitous than one would have reason to expect from Condorcet-Arrow analyses. The theoretical explanation can be summarized by the concept of "structure-induced equilibrium" (Shepsle 1979; Shepsle/Weingast 1981), that is, by the proposition that certain institutional arrangements shaping and constraining the voting process are able to prevent the manifestation of instability. There is in fact a considerable variety of institutional arrangements that have this capacity.

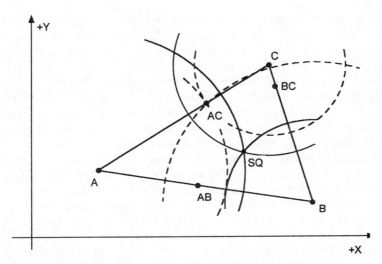

FIGURE 7.2    Cyclical instability in two-dimensional issue space

On the one hand, bicameral constitutions may require the concurrent agreement of both houses, which, when majorities differ, may amount to requiring unanimous agreement among all major factions in the party system. When this is so, the policy process again operates under the conditions of a pure negotiating system in which the problem of cyclical instability does not exist. On the other hand, certain types of election law tend to produce two-party legislatures (Sartori 1994), which, again, will prevent cyclical instability in parliament if party discipline can be imposed. The same result can be achieved even in multiparty systems if there is a stable split between a governing coalition and the opposition and if coalition discipline precludes the possibility of alternating majorities. From the point of view of democratic theory, however, both of these solutions have the disadvantage that the ultimate outcome may not represent the preferences of a majority of the electorate, and if party discipline is imposed it may not even represent the authentic preferences of a majority of the individual members of parliament.

But even when parliamentary votes are uncompelled by party discipline, procedural rules may prevent cyclical instability. The most important of these are related to the power of agenda control. Take again the situation represented by Figure 7.2. If one of the voters, or an outside party, has the right to define the option that is to be either accepted or rejected by majority vote, he or she could choose any point within the areas defined by the intersections of indifference curves through SQ. That is, if the default rule is continuation of the status quo, then any solution within the whole range of outcomes that is preferred to it by any majority of voters can become the final outcome. Under such conditions the quasi-dictatorial power of the agenda setter can in fact assure decisive and stable outcomes.[12]

There is also no reason to think that real-world constitutions are unlikely to install unilateral power of this magnitude: The European Commission enjoys exactly that power when it introduces initiatives that may be adopted by qualified majority but amended only by unanimous vote in the Council of Ministers (Pollack 1995)—a power that is now to some extent shared by the European Parliament (Tsebelis 1994). Similar powers are exercised by conference committees in bicameral legislatures that can formulate take-it-or-leave-it motions (Shepsle/ Weingast 1987). Moreover, minority governments—which are in fact quite frequent (Laver/Schofield 1990; Laver/Shepsle 1991; 1993)—generally have a unique chance to introduce legislation with a view to finding the support of an ad hoc majority in parliament.[13] And even if the agenda-setting party only has the power to determine the sequence in which given options must be voted upon, as is generally true of the presidency or a procedures committee in parliament, it will be able to determine the choice among these options if cyclical instability exists. This can easily be verified by another look at Table 7.1: Following ordinary parliamentary procedures of sequential pairwise voting, option z will win if the first vote pits x against y; option x will win if the first vote is on y against z; and option y will win if the first vote concerns x versus z.

It seems, therefore, that structure-induced equilibria in general, and the power of the agenda setter in particular, are sufficient to explain stable outcomes under conditions that should otherwise be plagued by cyclical instability. From the point of view of empirical research and positive theory as well as from the point of view of political practice, this advantage is certainly not to be underestimated. However, it also should be realized that structure-induced equilibria will only eliminate the problems of cyclical instability. They will not assure that the stable outcomes so achieved will have normatively attractive characteristics (Riker 1982). This is illustrated in Figure 7.3.

In this spatial-voting figure, the three vertices of the triangle ABC again represent the "ideal points" of three parties in two-dimensional issue space, and SQ represents the status quo. Since the utility of any actor decreases with the distance from its ideal point, the aggregate-welfare optimum will be located at the point that minimizes the sum-total of distances to the vertices of the triangle. In the figure, this welfare-optimal outcome is located at point O.[14]

Under the unanimity rule, and disregarding transaction costs, the parties could use negotiations and side payments to move the outcome from SQ to O. Under the majority rule, however, two of the three parties may simply vote for a proposal that for them is better than the status quo, even if it is located as far away from the welfare optimum as is point X in the figure. And even if negotiations within the majority should avoid outcomes that are not on the "contract curve" AC, the outcome that is most attractive for a given self-interested majority (e.g., a solution located at point AC) will systematically differ from the welfare optimum.[15]

That, of course, has been precisely the reason why public-choice theory has always favored the unanimity rule (Buchanan/Tullock 1962). The comparative ad-

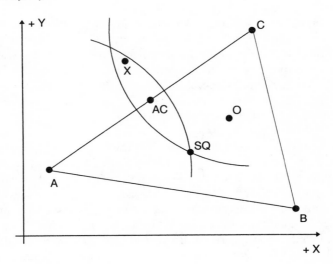

FIGURE 7.3    The suboptimality of majority decisions

vantage of the majority rule, by contrast, is seen in the capacity to decide distributive conflict (Mueller 1989b, 103–107). But, as the figure also demonstrates, this
implies that agreement among a majority of self-interested parties will always be
at the expense of the excluded minority. There is no suggestion here that majoritarian redistribution will systematically improve overall justice.[16] In fact, the political history of advanced capitalist democracies in the last two decades has driven home the message that democratic majorities are as likely to take from the
poor as from the rich. Thus the conclusion seems inevitable: If self-interested rational voters are assumed, majority rule cannot be justified by output-oriented
legitimation arguments (Riker 1980; 1982). There is no reason to think that majoritarian outcomes will systematically increase utilitarian welfare or improve
distributive justice. But what if voters could be assumed to be public-interest–
oriented rather than self-interested?

### Deliberative Democracy?

Things would change, or so it seems, if we could drop the assumption of self-
interested voting. If citizens could be assumed to appreciate the difference between their private interests and the public interest and to be concerned about
the *public good* when acting in their capacity as *citoyens* (rather than as *bourgeois*), most of the problems discussed thus far would disappear. That at least is
the hope of theories of "discursive" or "deliberative" or "reflexive" democracy,
which claim that the democratic process, properly understood, is not about individual interests and their aggregation to a "social utility function" but about the

construction of collective identity and the discovery of collective courses of action that can be justified in the light of the common good (March/Olsen 1989;
1995). Voting, in that perspective, is merely the last stage in an organized discourse in which preferences and perceptions about *collective* outcomes are to be
developed, communicated, elaborated, criticized, defended, and changed (Manin
1987; March/Olsen 1989; Habermas 1989; 1992; Cohen 1989; Dryzek 1990;
Bohman 1990; Schmalz-Bruns 1995; Prittwitz 1996).

*Collective Identity as a Precondition.* Logically, this line of argument either
presupposes the existence or implies the creation of a collective identity whose
collective interest could be the object of deliberation and could potentially override individual self-interest. Thus deliberative democracy presupposes boundaries
and the distinction between members and nonmembers of the relevant collectivity. Similar preconditions must exist to justify the expectation that policy outcomes will conform to criteria of distributive justice. But here the distinctions
among three aspects of justice—equity, equality, and need—discussed at the end
of Chapter 3 are important. *Equity,* defined by the equivalence of goods and services exchanged, or of rewards and contributions, appears as a universal norm that
is not compatible with negative discrimination between members and outsiders.
Formal *equality,* by contrast, is clearly tied to membership status. *Need,* finally,
seems to have two aspects: On the one hand, there is a universal claim to human
solidarity in the face of death, hunger, and natural or technical catastrophes that
finds its response in charity, disaster relief, and development aid. On the other
hand, there is the claim to solidaristic redistribution to reduce natural or economic inequalities among the members of the relevant communities, which has
found its modern expression in the welfare state. Such claims to redistributive justice do not seem to have a basis in universalistic norms (Breuer/Faist/Jordan
1995); they are claims to solidarity among the members of a given community.[17]

Logically, therefore, identity as well as solidarity presupposes boundary rules
that define whose welfare is to be counted in the aggregation and whose resource
position is to be equalized with regard to which reference group. Psychologically
and thus empirically, collective identity and solidarity can be treated as being
universally given only at the level of primary groups. Beyond that, it depends on
processes and strategies of identification and identity creation that construct
"we-identities" (Elias 1987) at various levels—which then can be used to circum-
scribe the "common" interest and the norms of solidarity for specific purposes. In
this "constructionist" rather than organismic view, collective identities above the
level of primary groups are not ontologically given (Weiler 1995; Habermas
1995). Nevertheless, their construction is facilitated by preexisting similarities or
commonalities that have a quality of "obviousness"—such as common kinship
and race or common locality, language, religion, culture, or history. Conversely,
however, the de facto membership in a common polity and even the mere subjec-
tion to a common government are also powerful creators of collective identities.[18]

Thus the modern nation-state has been uniquely successful in harnessing various preexisting commonalities for the creation of the most powerful collective identity and solidarity[19] above the level of primary groups.

But not all such efforts succeed, as is evidenced by the breakup of multinational "empires" such as Austria-Hungary or the Soviet Union or of artificially created nation-states such as the former Yugoslavia and Czechoslovakia. Belgium and Canada are other examples of the difficulty of constructing collective identities from ethnically or linguistically heterogeneous components. Moreover, as Gabriel Almond and Sidney Verba (1963) have shown, the identification of citizens with the political system varies greatly even among long-established and relatively homogeneous nation-states. Thus institution building by itself will not assure the political identity and solidarity on which legitimate government may be based—a conclusion that has obvious implications for the "democratic deficit" of the European Union (Grimm 1995). As of now it is still unclear whether such community-building efforts could succeed for entities above the level of nation-states (Howe 1995). For practical purposes, at any rate, they have not yet succeeded—which necessarily limits the legitimacy and hence the problem-solving capacity of transnational and supra-national governance systems. I will return to these issues in Chapter 9.

For the remainder of the present chapter, however, I will presume that the polity has indeed become the focus of political identity and solidarity to an extent that makes it at least meaningful to discuss outcomes by reference to criteria of public interest and distributive justice. That, however, is only the foundation on which democratic legitimacy could evolve. In addition, for deliberative democracy to work, we must assume that members or citizens will be public-interest–oriented rather than self-interest–oriented in forming their preferences, and we must assume that an institutional infrastructure exists that facilitates public-interest–oriented debate and its translation into effective public policy.

*Public-Interest–Oriented Citizens.* From an empirical point of view, it is indeed plausible to think that much or most *public debate* about public-policy issues is ostensibly oriented toward criteria of *common* interest and distributive *justice* rather than about individual or even group self-interest. As Jon Elster (1983, 35–36) has explained it, public discourse creates its own constraints: "Certain arguments simply cannot be stated publicly in a political setting. In a political discussion it is pragmatically impossible to assert that a given solution be chosen simply because it favors oneself or the group to which one belongs. By the very act of engaging in a public debate—by choosing to argue rather than to bargain—one has ruled out the possibility of such claims."

This appears intuitively plausible. But it also raises questions regarding the role of self-serving rhetoric in a "political setting." What Elster apparently has in mind is the Habermasian model of consensus-oriented scientific discourse in the ideal seminar, in which truth is the only acceptable frame of reference for all speakers and in which self-interest has no legitimate place (Habermas 1962; 1981). But since politics is about collective action that will affect, and may radically change, the lives of individuals and groups, there is no way in which the category of "interest" could be declared irrelevant. At the most, it is conceivable that private or group self-interest could be absorbed in the dual standards of the collective interest and of distributive justice.

As a logical consequence, "arguing" must always be defined in relation to the reference group whose collective interests would be affected by the policy options discussed. At a union meeting, appeals are likely to be made to the collective interest of union members or, perhaps, of the working class. But when the same union leader is speaking as a member of parliament, the reference would have to be either to the common interest of the nation or to shared notions of social justice. In either case, therefore, appeals to shared criteria would depend on the preconditions of shared identity or of solidarity discussed earlier.

As was assumed earlier for the Problem-Solving mode in negotiations, "arguing" in political debate must be about the search for solutions that will increase the common welfare rather than about the payoffs for any one individual or group. If the distributive dimension becomes salient at all, it must be discussed with a view to the distributive justice of outcomes rather than with a view to increasing the relative share of a group. But how could one expect these requirements to be met in political practice? I argued earlier, it is true, that Problem Solving is not unlikely to occur in real-world negotiations. But there I could point to specific institutional arrangements that would neutralize distributive conflict among the negotiating parties. None of these are generally available in the political process. Participants know that politics is about "who gets what, when, how" (Lasswell 1936) and that different policy choices will have different distributive consequences, and they know that there is no preexisting rule that would automatically neutralize unequal allocations of costs and benefits. So if there is nevertheless to be an appeal to *shared* criteria, the assumption must be that ego and alter have both internalized the criteria of common welfare and distributive justice. Only when this is the case is it possible to derive public-interest–oriented outcomes from the *uncompelled* preferences of individual citizens, and only then is there any chance at all that the political discourse might in practice approximate the ideals postulated in concepts of "deliberative" or "reflexive democracy."

At the level of individual citizens, the assumptions postulated here are in fact not entirely unrealistic. Rather, the standard assumption of rational self-interest not only fails to support a normatively acceptable theory of majority rule but also could not even explain why people should bother to vote at all—since they must be aware of the fact that their single ballot cannot have an appreciable impact on the outcome and hence on their own interest situation. If one must assume, therefore, that people should in fact vote out of a sense of civic duty, then it would be no more than consistent to think that they might also care about the public interest in deciding *how to vote* (Brennan 1989; Mueller 1989a). In a way, if voters cannot instrumentally relate their vote to their own situation, then the act of voting occurs, as it were, behind a "veil of ignorance" similar to the one that John Rawls (1971) thought to be conducive to justice-oriented choices. On that basis, theories assuming public-interest-oriented voters have in fact somewhat higher plausibility than theories postulating egotistically rational voters. But how much would be gained by this change of basic assumptions?

*Deliberation in Competitive Democracies.*   What could be the meaning of deliberative or discursive democracy in modern mass democracies for most of whose members the vote is the only practical form of participation? Policy debate, if it takes place at all, is vicarious—conducted by political parties, candidates, interest groups, experts, and publicists and communicated through the selective channels of the mass media and of highly specialized communications systems. Citizens at large will mainly find themselves in the role of passive spectators, listeners, and readers, and their attention to any one debate will be distracted by the claims of innumerable other policy issues that are publicly discussed at the same time—and by all other business and "infotainment" competing for places in their limited time budgets. It is most plausible, therefore, that the response of the average citizen to the average policy issue should be characterized by "rational ignorance" (Downs 1957), whereas specialized policy debates are primarily carried on among specialized politicians, bureaucrats, and representatives of interest groups (Zolo 1992).

But typically these more active participants in specialized policy discourses will have no difficulty in identifying the practical and distributive implications of policy choices within their specialized area of attention. Moreover, they will be obliged by role-specific norms to represent the interests of their clients, to fight for the interest of their party, and to stand by their own prior positions. All of these requirements are more conducive to self-interested bargaining than to the disinterested, truth-oriented deliberation that Habermas (1992), for one, wants to see clearly distinguished from bargaining. But this is not the most problematical aspect of real-world politics.

As we saw earlier, self-interested bargaining may also, even when it carries high transactions costs, approximate welfare-maximizing outcomes. What is truly incompatible with consensus-oriented discussion is *competitive interaction orientations*, which, as I have shown, will transform any interaction into a zero-sum conflict in which common interests have no chance of being realized. But precisely these orientations will come to dominate whenever competitive party politics plays a role in the resolution of policy issues—which is true whenever an issue is likely to gain electoral significance. For this involvement of political parties, there are good constitutional grounds. Historically, after all, democracy and majority rule were introduced not as arrangements for optimal policymaking but as *protection against the abuses of absolutist power.* This defensive rationale has survived the demise of absolutism, and it retains its salience in light of the potential harm that can still be done by the overwhelming power of the modern bureaucratic state. It has found its strongest manifestation in contemporary constitutional arrangements that bestow the exercise of governing power on political parties that can only gain the chance of governing through their success in the electoral competition.

Political competition among the suppliers of public policies, just like market competition among the suppliers of private goods, is supposed to reduce and control the power of these suppliers. On the whole this mechanism is effective enough (Bartolini 1996). If modern democracies have serious problems, it is probably not because their governments are too strong and autocratic. What is important here, however, is *the impact that electoral competition has on policy discourses.* For the political parties involved, elections are a zero-sum game in which the stakes are a limited number of seats in parliament and, ultimately, the participation in or exclusion from the exercise of governmental power and the perquisites of government office. At the limit, electoral losses will throw into doubt the very existence of a political party. In this respect, just as neorealist theory postulates for interactions among nation-states in international relations, political parties or coalitions involved in electoral competition have no common interests.[20]

Moreover, given the extremely high salience of the institutional self-interest that is at stake, electoral competition will not cease at the end of an election campaign. It is likely to color the relationship among these parties generally and to induce "competitive" interaction orientations even in parliamentary interactions that are far removed from election campaigns (Mayntz/Neidhardt 1989; 1992). What matters in this competition is not only the overwhelming need to present one's own side and any actions taken or proposed by it in the best possible light but also the equally overwhelming need to prevent or deny any success, real or argumentative, to the other side. Here, if anywhere, it is true that "if it is good for them, it must be bad for us." There is no question that this orientation is not conducive to an effective commitment to *common* problem solving.

What we seem to have, therefore, is a practical incompatibility between the consensual ideal of deliberative or discursive democracy on the one hand and the necessary implications of competitive democracy on the other. Under ordinary circumstances, at least, it is as unrealistic to expect the governing party and the opposition to agree on the policy that would be most conducive to the public interest as it would be to expect the prosecution and the defense in an Anglo-American criminal trial to agree on what would be a just sentence. The institutional roles that both have to perform, and the incentives associated with these roles, will usually rule out cooperative Problem Solving.

### Adversarial Democracy?

But should the comparison with the jury trial not open up an alternative approach to majoritarian legitimization? It suggests that Problem Solving may be achieved not only by approximating the consensus-oriented model of the ideal seminar discussion but also by approximating the conditions of an ideal adversarial process. There, it is not postulated that an exchange of disinterested arguments should lead to truth-oriented agreement among the interlocutors; rather it is assumed that judge and jury will be assisted, in arriving at their own judgment, by having the arguments on either side presented, and criticized, as forcefully as possible (and, by implication, with as much bias as necessary). For a theory of adversarial democracy, this would imply that the battle among the political parties is not meant to lead to agreement but rather to inform the electorate that will arrive at its own enlightened judgment.

Provided that we continue to assume a high level of public-interest orientation among voters, this seems indeed a plausible model for direct democracy under conditions in which a policy issue submitted to popular referendum is sufficiently salient to generate intense public discussion, sufficiently focused to justify a binary choice, and sufficiently controversial to stimulate competent advocacy for either side. Empirically, such conditions are not impossible, but they also cannot occur very often. Any attempt to use the referendum frequently would rapidly erode its effectiveness. Since the capacity of mass publics for focused attention is necessarily quite limited, it will be quickly overloaded by the simultaneous discussion of several or many issues. As a consequence, referenda are likely to lose voter interest and to generate random outcomes that have none of the characteristics of a considered judgment (Luthardt 1992; 1994).

Similarly, even under conditions of representative democracy there will be situations when elections are focused on a single, well-defined policy issue and might for that reason be as decisive for that issue as a formal plebiscite. For the overwhelming majority of highly diverse policy choices, however, it makes no sense to treat elections as substantive decisions according to the jury model. Even if all policy issues were clearly spelled out in party platforms, and even if voters took the trouble to become completely informed about them, and if they had perfect memories of actual policy choices, they would still have to aggregate their distinct responses to individual issues into a single vote that could only be interpreted as an expression, or a withdrawal, of generalized support for the government (Parsons 1967). And, of course, the conditions specified are highly implausible counterfactuals under ordinary conditions. Governments and political parties are unable or unwilling to spell out clearly their positions on all important policy issues in election platforms; voters are not very interested in party platforms and have short memories; and media attention is extremely selective, focusing on political scandals, symbolic politics, and personalities much more than on policy positions. It is in fact extremely difficult in modern mass democracies, especially for parties out of power, to gain sustained public attention for policy issues.

Thus to interpret elections as the majoritarian legitimation of specific policy choices is so rarely appropriate that the affirmative use of this argument in political discourse must indeed be considered ideological (Edelman 1964; Zolo 1992).

It might seem empirically more appropriate, in comparison, to interpret elections merely as allowing voters to exercise what William Riker (1982, 244) described as "the veto by which it is sometimes possible to restrain official tyranny." That is perhaps too pessimistic a view. Nevertheless, popular elections are generally not about the selection of policy choices but about the legitimation and control of the hierarchical authority of governments and other policymaking agencies. This function will be discussed in the following chapter.

## NOTES

1. Under certain conditions, it is true, the cost of negative sanctions may be lowered by the existence of asymmetrical exchange relationships in which alter depends on resources that ego may grant or withhold. Over time, however, asymmetrical exchange tends to develop toward more symmetrical relationships of mutual dependence in which unilateral boycott will gradually become more costly and hence less feasible (Emerson 1962).

2. The classical model of this problem is of course Reinhard Selten's (1978) famous "chain-store paradox."

3. Thus the Nazi regime in Germany relied very much on the pretense of rule-based power in order to disarm its victims.

4. Niklas Luhmann (1969, 32–37) adds the important argument that compliance, in order to be effective, requires that ego accept alter's decision premises even if these do not agree with ego's own perceptions and preferences—which would undercut the presentation of self-identities unless compliance is also morally supported by the relevant reference group.

5. David Held (1987, 182) distinguishes seven grounds for compliance: (1) coercion, (2) tradition, (3) apathy, (4) pragmatic acquiescence, (5) instrumental acceptance, (6) normative agreement, and (7) ideal normative agreement. He considers only the last two as being instances of legitimacy—and indeed, they are the only ones that assure compliance in cases in which decisions go against the self-interest of target actors and in which the risk of violations' being detected is low. An instructive example is provided by Margaret Levi's (1988) description of the extraordinary efforts that the Australian government needed to expend in order to reestablish tax compliance, which had been undercut by reports of large-scale tax evasion by high-income taxpayers. For exactly the same reasons the legitimacy of the tax system is now being challenged in Germany.

6. Where individual agreement is meaningful and possible, input-oriented legitimacy is better described as being contractual in character. The description becomes ideological, however, if it is applied to collective-choice constellations under conditions in which exit is costly or impossible.

7. Analytically the argument presupposes that there is a "correct" solution, that all voters will sincerely and independently vote for their own perception of the true solution, and that there is a positive probability that any individual voter is likely to perceive the true solution. When that is assumed, the likelihood that truth will be discovered increases with the number of votes cast for a solution according to the "Condorcet Jury Theorem" (Michaud 1988).

8. This seems to be the constellation that was assumed by the authors of the Federalist Papers (Cooke 1961), who were much impressed with the conflict of interest between the

uneducated and propertyless masses on the one hand and "the wise, the rich and the few" on the other (Beard [1913] 1965) and thus found it very important to develop institutional safeguards against the "tyranny of the majority." Though their system of constitutional checks and balances was not intended to short-circuit the search for mutually advantageous policy solutions, it was certainly meant to assure that the search would have to be conducted through negotiations between the majority and minority interests rather than through the straightforward exercise of majority power.

9. In popular discussions of political legitimacy it is often tacitly assumed that the agreement of a majority should per se have legitimating force. This is a historically plausible approximation in systems in which democratic accountability had to be wrested from regimes based on absolutist or dictatorial power. The limits of majoritarian legitimization are more obvious, by contrast, in polities with deep ethnic or religious or ideological cleavages—or in would-be polities such as the European Union that have not yet achieved a high level of political integration. I will return to this point later.

10. The same beneficial results can be expected in representative democracies under a two-party system, where the party platforms will also converge on the position of the median voter if parties are competing for the votes of an electorate in which all preferences are single peaked in a single dimension (Downs 1957).

11. If SQ is located *outside* the triangle ABC, all three indifference circles will overlap. Thus there will be policy changes that may find unanimous agreement—until the new status-quo point is located within triangle ABC.

12. In the literature, "agenda setting" is used in two senses. The first is the one discussed here, exemplified by the rules of procedure giving committees in the U.S. Congress or the European Commission sometimes exclusive power to introduce legislation and to prevent amendments. The second is the informal power of "policy entrepreneurs" to identify problems and potential solutions that may gain public attention and may be taken up by the political process (Kingdon 1984).

13. The same is true in disciplined two-party parliamentary systems, in which the government often has a de facto control over policy initiatives introduced by the majority (whereas minority bills are routinely voted down). There, even if majority bills must first find the support of a majority of the members of the parliamentary party, the government may have a wide range of agenda-setting discretion.

14. In general this minimum is located inside the triangle at the "Steiner point," from which the lines drawn to all three vertices form angles of 120 degrees. In triangles with an angle of 120 degrees or larger, the minimum is located at the vertex of that angle. I owe this information to Matthias Mohr, who obtained it via the Internet newsgroup sci.math from Bob Silverman, The MathWorks Inc., Natick, MA.

15. In any direction, an increase in the distance from the optimal point implies a reduction of total welfare. However, distances located on different vectors cannot be directly compared. I owe this insight to Kjell Hausken.

16. This is in contrast to what Anthony Downs (1957) showed for single issue two-party politics. For an explanation of the politics of reverse redistribution, see Appendix 1.

17. The empirical difference between these two aspects is striking: West Germany (along with most comparable countries) has never come close to the goal of spending 1 percent of gross domestic product (GDP) on development aid. In fact in the 1990s the German contribution has amounted to less than 0.35 percent and is still falling. During the same years, however, West Germany has in fact been spending more than 6 percent of

GDP in an effort to reduce economic and social inequality between West and East Germany after the fall of the Berlin Wall.

18. An interesting case in point is provided by postwar German federalism. In comparison with Bavaria or Hamburg, whose historical identity remained intact, the collective identity of those *Länder* that were created de novo after 1945 is generally weaker. But even artificial units whose boundaries were drawn by the occupation powers without any regard for historical continuity or religious or ethnic homogeneity have in the meantime "taken root"—with the result that all attempts at territorial reorganization have foundered on the political identification of voters with their new territorial states.

19. The point is well expressed by Howe (1995, 29): "One of the most striking features of modern liberal communities is the abundance of norms that require some measure of altruism on the part of citizens: witness, for example, the payment of taxes, often amounting to more than half of people's incomes, to support the welfare state and the provision of numerous public goods. Individual citizens, in complying voluntarily with such norms, demonstrate a willingness to sacrifice their own interests to the interests of others, many of whom are complete strangers. This, in the historical scheme of things, is unusual behavior. It seems as though citizens of modern liberal communities recognize some intrinsic value in their fellow citizens." Howe then points out, however, that "this generous disposition . . . does not extend to all of mankind" and goes on to discuss the conditions under which a "sense of community" might develop within the European Union.

20. They might, however, have a common interest in maintaining the institutions within which they are forced to compete.

# 8

## *Hierarchical Direction*

In modern political systems policy issues are rarely decided directly by the vote of citizens. As I argued at the end of the previous chapter, referenda, where they exist, are severely limited in the decision load that they can effectively deal with. General elections, by contrast, can rarely be interpreted as decisions on substantive policy; they should not primarily be considered as a mode of arriving at collectively binding decisions but rather as institutional arrangements for the legitimation and control of hierarchical government authority. From the citizen's point of view, therefore, modern constitutional democracies are not fundamentally different from their nondemocratic predecessors. Decisions can be imposed without the individual citizen's consent and are backed by the superior capacity of the state machinery to inflict severe deprivations. In comparison with absolutist and totalitarian systems, it is true, constitutional democracies are characterized by more, and much more effective, limitations on state power, defined by the constitutional protection of basic rights and by general laws that are binding upon the state as well and enforced through an independent judiciary. But within the domain so circumscribed, decisions of "the state" are still imposed on the citizen by hierarchical authority and enforced by superior force.

For the legitimacy of state authority it is of the utmost importance how these decisions are arrived at through interactions among the active participants in policymaking processes and how these interactions are connected to processes in which citizens are directly involved. But before I turn to these questions, which will continue the exploration begun in the previous chapter, it will be necessary to explicate the characteristics of the hierarchical authority relationship itself and of "hierarchical direction," which, in our understanding of actor-centered institutionalism, is one of the four basic modes of interaction—along with unilateral action, negotiated agreement, and the majority vote. The present chapter will therefore have to deal with two related but analytically distinct themes. I will first discuss the policy-relevant characteristics of hierarchical direction, and I will then return to the issue raised at the end of the previous chapter: the role of voting and elections in the legitimation and control of hierarchical authority.

## HIERARCHICAL DIRECTION

"Hierarchical direction" is defined as a mode of interaction in which ego is able to specify alter's choices or, more precisely, some of alter's decision premises (Simon 1957; March/Simon 1958). This possibility may merely arise from ego's superior capacity to offer rewards or to threaten severe deprivations, or it may rest on legitimate hierarchical authority. Such legitimacy may be based on a variety of foundations—religious belief, tradition, charisma, or formal legality (Weber 1947). Under modern conditions, however, negotiated agreement and democratic accountability are likely to be the most important sources of legitimacy, and I will turn to these later.

But even fully legitimated hierarchical authority must be experienced, and probably resented, by alter as an exercise of unilateral power that reduces or eliminates alter's freedom of choice. From the perspective of normative individualism, therefore, any form of hierarchical direction must appear highly suspect. In substantive policy analyses, by contrast, the hierarchical mode of interaction seems to be implicitly or explicitly considered most desirable since it reduces the transaction costs of concerted action and thus offers the potential of coordinating policy choices from an inclusive, welfare-maximizing perspective. With this normative ambivalence in mind, I will now consider the welfare-maximizing potential of "hierarchical coordination."

### *The Power of Hierarchical Coordination*

Hierarchical authority creates a capacity to override the preferences of other actors. Without more, of course, that capacity has nothing to recommend itself in normative terms. But if it were exercised from a policy perspective, it could eliminate the transaction costs of policy coordination. In the interest of consistency, hierarchical coordination is represented in Figure 8.1 in the form of our usual negotiation figure for the two-actor case (X and Y) with the status quo located at SQ and the welfare boundary represented by the diagonal through SQ. Assuming that a welfare-increasing project would be located at A, it is clear that according to its own preferences, Y would refuse to carry out this project. But if X should have hierarchical authority over Y, X could threaten to apply sanctions in case of noncompliance, which would move the nonagreement point from SQ to SA. As compared to *that* outcome, it would now be in the self-interest of Y to carry out project A.

As the figure suggests, the extent to which Y can be required to act against its own preferences depends on the severity of the sanctions that could be imposed. These sanctions could result from feelings of guilt if loyalty is a strongly internalized norm; they could result from the fear of shame, and perhaps of social ostracism, if conformity is required by social norms; in other circumstances, the same effect could be achieved by the threat of losing one's job if obedience is required by an employment contract, or of administrative and criminal penalties if

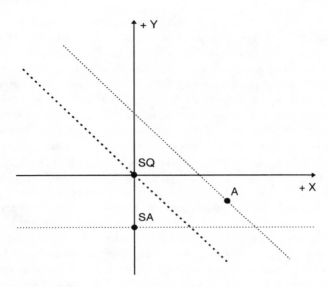

FIGURE 8.1   Hierarchical coordination

compliance is required by the law of the state. In assessing their severity, however, we should not forget that even though hierarchical authority facilitates *asymmetric* interaction, we are still considering variants of *strategic* interaction. That aspect is emphasized by principal-agent theory, which will be considered later, but it is also significant for the definition of the hierarchical relationship itself. It exists only to the extent that alter cannot avoid the sanctions associated with noncompliance.

Avoidance is least possible in the case of internalized norms, whereas violations of social norms, employment conditions, and legal rules may escape detection. In the absence of strongly internalized norms, moreover, the *reach of hierarchical authority is constrained by the exit options that are available to the target population.* In Figure 8.1, for instance, if Y is a skilled worker with attractive job opportunities elsewhere, his or her present employer would no longer be able to move the nonagreement point from SQ to SA—and thus the threat of sanctions would no longer induce Y to carry out project A, which violates his or her status-quo interests. Similarly, in the fall of 1989, once Hungary had opened its borders to the West, the government of East Germany was no longer able to maintain its extreme form of hierarchical control over its own citizens. In other words, hierarchical authority relationships are themselves embedded in a wider strategic constellation that determines the potential scope of unilateral direction.

These limitations are often ignored in substantive policy research, which, as was pointed out in the Introduction, is characterized by a strong elective affinity to hierarchical coordination. Policy recommendations are characteristically addressed to an idealized "policymaker" with the assumed capacity to overrule the preferences of other actors, regardless of any conflicting interests and perceptions. For the same reason, political theorists following Hobbes who were impressed with the social wastefulness of the *bellum omnium contra omnes* under conditions of anarchy have opted for the hierarchical authority of Leviathan to assure domestic peace; economic theorists following Pigou who were impressed with the inefficiency of market failures have opted for hierarchical state intervention in the economy to correct negative externalities; and transaction-cost economists following Coase who were impressed with the difficulties of negotiated agreements have opted for vertical integration in hierarchically organized firms to avoid the high costs of contracting under conditions of uncertainty and opportunism. From all of these perspectives, the focus is on the social benefits that can in principle be achieved through hierarchical coordination rather than on the contextual preconditions for the effective exercise of hierarchical authority.

But even if these preconditions were fulfilled, hierarchical coordination could only achieve the alleged beneficial welfare effects if it could also be assumed that the incumbents of authority positions approximate the ideal of the benevolent and omniscient dictator: They must be committed to using their power only for the purposes of maximizing welfare and securing justice rather than for furthering their own private interests;[1] and they must be able to obtain and have the capacity to process all the information that is necessary for that purpose. With a view to state intervention (but not with regard to hierarchically organized firms), both of these assumptions have been flatly denied in contemporary contributions to political economy—with public-choice theory focusing on the motivational and Hayekian economics focusing on the informational difficulties of hierarchical coordination. I will begin with the latter.

### The Information Problem

If decision premises are specified by superior authority, this implies not only that the preferences of lower-level actors are overruled but also that the information that they have available may be ignored. Thus the superior efficiency that transaction-cost theory claims for hierarchical coordination must be based on the assumption that the information available to superiors is as good as that available at lower levels. This corresponds well to the "wolf-pack" theory of leadership or to the assumptions underlying factory organization in high-quality industrial production, where the foreman is a master craftsman, the engineer a master craftsman with additional theoretical training, and the chief executive officer an engineer who has acquired managerial skills (Sorge/Warner 1986). But of course not all organizational hierarchies are of this character. In the ministerial bureaucracy, for instance, the specialized information that lower-level units have about the conditions, options, and constraints in particular policy areas cannot possibly be matched at the higher levels (Mayntz/Scharpf 1975)—and it is often difficult to assure the undistorted transmission of information from the lower to the higher levels of an organizational hierarchy or, if information is transferred, to assure that it will be properly processed at the center (Downs 1967).

At the analytical level, it is worth pointing out that the two lines of the new institutional economics that deal explicitly with hierarchical interactions differ primarily in their assumptions about the accessibility of local information. Transaction-cost theory is optimistic in this regard, whereas principal-agent theory starts from the assumption of basic information asymmetries that prevent the principal from observing either the agent's behavior or the external conditions that are relevant for the appropriate evaluation of the agent's performance. Finally, with regard to state intervention in the economy, Hayekian economics also emphasizes the importance of local information on production opportunities and consumer demand, and it asserts the impossibility of transferring this information to central decisionmakers or, if transfer were somehow achieved, of having it adequately processed at the central level (Hayek 1944; 1945; Streit 1993). Hence the result of centralizing economic decisions could only be information impoverishment or information overload at the center, producing either ill-informed and unresponsive decisions or interminable delay or both.

If we leave aside the either-or assumptions of economic theory, it seems clear that the informational feasibility of hierarchical coordination depends on two factors: first, on the range of the lower-level decision premises that are to be substituted by hierarchical direction, and second, on the variety and variability of local information that is relevant for the optimal specification of these decision premises. To begin with the former: There is, surely, a world of difference between, on the one hand, the Hayekian nightmare of central economic planners trying to coordinate the individual preferences of hundreds of millions of consumers for millions of different products with the production opportunities of hundreds of thousands of individual firms and, on the other hand, state interventions that merely try to fight inflation by raising the interest rate or to reduce energy consumption by taxing the use of oil, gas, and electricity. In denying the feasibility of the former, one is not logically compelled also to assert the futility of the latter.

More abstractly, transaction-cost theorists have responded to fears of information impoverishment or information overload at the center by pointing to the "principle of selective intervention," according to which superiors should strictly limit their directives to matters that must be handled at their own organizational level, leaving everything else to lower-level agents with better access to local information (Williamson 1985, 133–135; Milgrom/Roberts 1990). Classical organization theory, in turn, uses the "span-of-control" variable to adjust the number of agents supervised in response to the informational complexity of supervision (Gulick/Urwick 1937). But which matters must be handled at higher levels, and what are the tasks that must be performed by superiors? These requirements surely have different connotations for factory organization, for state interventions in the economy, and for hierarchical coordination in policymaking processes.

With regard to the latter, a precise meaning can be specified by reference to Herbert Simon's (1962) concept of "nearly decomposable" hierarchical structures. Its starting point is the assumption that real-world interdependence is selective rather than total. When that is the case, it may be possible to structure interactions in a multilevel hierarchy in such a way that at all levels internal interactions within organizational subunits are more frequent or more important than interactions cutting across the boundaries of such units or across the boundary between the organization and the outside world. What this implies can be specified more precisely by reference to James D. Thompson's (1967) important distinction of three types of interdependence—pooled, sequential, and reciprocal. In organizations the coordination requirements of pooled interdependence (in which several actors draw upon a common pool of resources) can be handled by common rules that, once established, can be followed individually by each target actor. Sequential interdependence (in which the output of one actor becomes the input of the next) requires planning, but once the plan is in place it will also reduce the need for direct interaction. Only reciprocal interdependence (which requires the simultaneous adjustment of choices) depends on direct interaction among the agents or units involved. It is this latter type of interdependence that is critical for the near decomposability of organizational interactions.

A structure is nearly decomposable if groups of agents whose tasks are characterized by reciprocal interdependence can be located within the same subunits at the lower levels of the organizational hierarchy. When that is assured, the inevitable conflicts arising from interdependent tasks need not be resolved, at high transaction costs, through bargaining among the agents involved but may be settled more efficiently by a common superior who is close enough to the action to have access to all relevant local information. The remaining instances of reciprocal interdependence among tasks located in different units should then be rare enough to be handled by the common superior of these units at the next higher level of the organizational pyramid, and so on. At the same time, reciprocal interactions with the outside world should be so infrequent that they can be handled by top leadership or a specialized "foreign relations" unit closely attached to the top. Under such conditions it is indeed conceivable that large multilevel hierarchies may be constructed that will not ignore pertinent local information and that also will not overtax the limited capacity of hierarchical superiors for information processing and conflict resolution.

But this presupposes, first, that the most important interactions should indeed be internal to the organization and that within the organization task-interdependencies should in fact be nearly decomposable. Moreover, it presupposes that these interdependencies should be sufficiently stable to be accommodated by organizational design. When that is not the case—that is, when external interdependencies increase in importance, or when reciprocal interdependencies become too extensive to be contained within the span of control of a single superior, or when interdependencies change too rapidly for organizational structures to catch up—hierarchical coordination ceases to be effective.

Then, if superiors insist on exercising their hierarchical prerogatives, too many conflicts will have to be settled at higher levels, and all the alleged evils of overcentralization—poorly informed decisions coming too late to be useful—are likely to appear. If, on the other hand, lower-level actors are left to work out policy conflicts among themselves and with the outside world, the system loses the advantages of hierarchical coordination and will fall back to the previously discussed modes of unilateral and negotiated interaction.

In the real world, well-functioning hierarchical coordination seems in fact to be quite rare, and the impression is that it is getting to be more difficult. Instead of increasing vertical integration, firms seek to spin off important functions to independent suppliers. In the race toward "lean production," flat hierarchies and radical decentralization have become the organizational fashions of the decade. Managers at higher levels are supposed to change their role from that of a hierarchical superior to that of a "coach," and the ideal configuration to strive for seems to be the small, independent, and extremely flexible unit that is able to exploit the opportunities of highly diverse and rapidly changing market niches—backed, of course, by the financial, technical, and informational resources of a large, globally operating corporation. In the public sector the equivalent managerial philosophy emphasizes privatization, deregulation, lean administration, and, again, the radical decentralization of services to flexible client-oriented units that are encouraged to respond to locally diverse conditions within "global" budgets that are freed from line-item constraints.

In the private sector it is hard to tell whether the net result is in fact a reduction of hierarchical coordination or merely a better utilization of new information and communication technologies, which now permit formally independent suppliers and semi-independent profit centers to be controlled even more precisely than was formerly possible with respect to fully integrated units and tightly supervised departments of the parent firm. In the public sector, by contrast, there is less reason to think that the privatization, deregulation, and decentralization of public services will be compensated by dramatic improvements in central management information systems. If they are carried out in fact, and not merely in rhetoric, they will mean greater local diversity in service levels and service mixes. Whether overall quality will be maintained, and whether efficiency will in fact be improved, seems uncertain but not impossible. On theoretical grounds one would expect the outcome to depend on whether the loosening of central controls is in fact compensated by more competition and more effective self-coordination among service providers and by their greater dependence on clients (Rhodes 1996). However, even if governments are able successfully to reduce their immediate involvement in the production and delivery of services, they cannot spin off their other essential functions, namely, regulation and redistribution, without seriously negative welfare consequences.

But these problems of service delivery are not our primary concern here. In the process of *policy formation*, at any rate, hierarchical coordination has always been a poorly fitting concept, even within the strictly hierarchical structures of the ministerial organization. What Renate Mayntz and I found instead in our empirical studies of policymaking in the ministerial bureaucracy was a "dialogue model" in which policy-area experts from lower-level units and "political" experts at the higher levels of the hierarchy jointly worked out the criteria by which acceptable policy initiatives should be judged (Mayntz/Scharpf 1975). However, this "vertical" dialogue within the hierarchy of a given ministry described only one dimension of the pattern of interactions. The second dimension is described by ubiquitous "horizontal" negotiations among the specialist units within and between ministries and, of course, with representatives of affected interest groups and firms, political parties, and members of parliament (and now, increasingly, with Brussels). Since other ministries have a de facto veto, interministerial negotiations tend toward the mode of Negative Coordination and will rise to the level of Positive Coordination only under exceptional circumstances. For external negotiations the pattern is less uniform and depends very much on the willingness of political leaders to risk, or even to seek, open political conflict. But since the capacity of political leaders for actively pursuing conflictful policy initiatives is, again, severely limited, Negative Coordination and, at best, Distributive Bargaining tend to be frequent in external interactions as well.

What matters here is that most of these negotiations must inevitably be conducted by the policy-area specialists at lower levels of the hierarchy. It is true that some spectacular conflicts will eventually be settled in "summit talks" among ministers and with the heads of important external organizations. But before these summits can be reached, the "sherpas" must have already done all the important work (Putnam/Bayne 1984), and most of the growing number of such negotiations will never make it to a summit—or will appear there only as one in a long list of items that are summarily disposed of. To the extent that this is true, hierarchical coordination will again be displaced by the complex networks of negotiated coordination, in comparison with which, in theory, it was meant to provide a far more efficient mode of interaction. I will return to this issue in Chapter 9.

### The Motivation Problem

Even if adequate information and information-processing capacity were assured, however, the welfare efficiency of hierarchical coordination would still depend on the "benevolent" motivation of the actors exercising it—which also cannot be taken for granted. In transaction-cost economics, it is true, the motivational problem is assumed to be resolved if hierarchical direction is exercised by a "residual claimant," typically the owner-manager of the firm, who will acquire all factors of production, including coworkers, at market prices, and who will keep all net profits and bear all losses (Coase 1937; Alchian/Demsetz 1972). Thus when external effects are ignored, it follows that the owner-manager must have an interest in maximizing the economic efficiency of the firm and, in that sense, overall welfare (while problems of distributive justice are assumed to be neutralized by reference to market prices and wages).

The motivational problem reappears, however, when the postulated identity of owner and manager is split into the roles of shareholders without managerial functions and of employed managers. If hierarchical direction is exercised by managers who are not residual claimants, their self-interest may diverge from either the interest of the firm as a going concern or from the profit-maximizing interest of shareholders. Theoretically, this problem has become the focus of principal-agent theory, another branch of the new institutional economics, which analyzes interactions in situations in which a self-interested agent is supposed to act in the interest of a principal in response to circumstances that are not transparent to the principal (Grossman/Hart 1983). If the relationship is characterized by severe information asymmetries, as is assumed to be true for shareholders and managers (Jensen/Meckling 1976), precise directives would be counterproductive: Managers need to be able to exercise discretion. But when they do so, what is to prevent them from maximizing their own interests at the expense of the owners? The theoretical answer consists in a search for "incentive-compatible mechanisms" that will assure Pareto-optimal Nash equilibria. Agency contracts, that is, should be specified in such a way that the agent, in pursuing his or her own self-interest, is also maximizing the overall product of the firm—and hence the interest of the principal. In practice this is generally interpreted to imply some element of profit sharing in the employment contracts of top managers.[2]

It seems fair to say, however, that the mathematical sophistication of principal-agent solutions is not matched by their realism and practicability (Jensen 1983). Moreover, the principal-agent problem, if it exists at all, will repeat itself in interactions within the firm among top management, middle management, and the lower echelons of multilevel hierarchies. Thus at every level some share of the firm's profits would have to be used for the purpose of motivating the firm's managers (presumably above and beyond their market-based salaries). The implication seems to be that all potential efficiency gains, and more,[3] would then be used for managerial incentives rather than for improving the profits paid out to shareholders. From a practical perspective, therefore, the main lesson taught by principal-agent theory seems to point in the opposite direction: It demonstrates that even profit-oriented firms could not be viable if managers, in the performance of their organizational roles, were exclusively guided by considerations of private self-interest. I will return to this point later.

In the public sector exactly the same type of principal-agent relationship is presumed to exist not only between voters and their elected representatives but also between Congress and executive agencies (Cook/Wood 1989) or between the

EU member states and the European Commission (Pollack 1995; Pierson 1996a). Again, there are multiple principals, with potentially diverse interests, that must delegate authority to agents that have privileged access to information on which the evaluation of their performance depends. Controls may be of two kinds: "police patrol," which involves direct monitoring by principals, and "fire alarm," which responds to complaints from parties actually affected by the decisions of the agency (Kiewiet/McCubbins 1991). In either case, however, even if monitoring information is available it is difficult to translate into effective sanctions if preferences vary among principals.

More generally speaking, the problem of containing and controlling the hierarchical power of the state has been the central issue of post-Hobbesian political philosophy. It also is the overriding concern of the positive and normative branches of public-choice theory, which apply the assumptions of self-interested rational action and the analytical tools of economic theory to public-sector interactions. Since it is difficult even in theory to construct profit-sharing arrangements that would solve the principal-agent problem in the relationship between citizens and their governors (modeled in analogy to the relationship between shareholders and managers), the predictable implication of public-choice theory is a deep distrust of all exercises of public authority—and a concomitant preference for maximizing constitutional restrictions on government action and, by default, for living with the uncorrected consequences of market failures (Brennan/Buchanan 1985).

From the perspective of actor-centered institutionalism, the public-choice approach appears theoretically deficient in its exclusive focus on the dangers of self-interest in the political process. As was explained in Chapter 3, Renate Mayntz and I suggest a more complex view of the preferences and perceptions that make up the action orientations of individual and corporate actors. Preferences, we argue, have at least three dimensions—individual and institutional self-interest, norms, and considerations of individual and corporate identity. In the performance of organizational or political roles, the private self-interest of individuals certainly cannot be ignored, as recurrent scandals and instances of corruption amply demonstrate. However, the very occurrence of a scandal testifies to the importance of norms. Thus when it was discovered in 1995 that managers of Opel, the German subsidiary of General Motors, had accepted large kickbacks from contractors and suppliers, not even the neoliberal business press was willing to praise this manifestation of the acquisitive spirit of free-enterprise capitalism. Instead the response was moral outrage, criminal prosecution, and the resignation of three top-level managers within whose spheres of responsibility the scandal had occurred. In other words, the norm is that private self-interest should have no place in negotiations between a firm and its suppliers, and the empirical expectation is that this rule will generally be observed. The same is even more clearly true of the exercise of public office, where the existence, and the force, of the norm is again manifested in numerous scandals resulting in resignations and criminal prosecutions in many countries, and culminating in quasi-revolutionary changes of the political system of Italy.

The implication is that a theory that assumes private self-interest to explain all interactions will be empirically wrong in most cases. In order to arrive at valid explanations and predictions, therefore, we need theories that acknowledge the empirical importance of norm-oriented behavior without denying the ever-present temptations of self-interested opportunism (Kirchgässner 1992). By the same token, it seems not only unrealistic but ultimately counterproductive to derive a normative "constitutional political economy" from the assumption of pervasive opportunism. If this assumption were true, then institutional safeguards could not possibly prevent determined and persistent wrongdoing in high places. If it is not true, however, then attempts to eliminate all opportunities for malfeasance by the construction of effective constitutional barriers to government action would be very costly in welfare terms. If the actions of public officials and politicians are on the whole norm-oriented, such prohibitions would fully succeed in crippling their capacity to deal effectively with the collective-action problems for which governments were instituted in the first place, and which—as we have seen—cannot be effectively dealt with by unilateral action and the various forms of negotiated coordination.

Given their theoretical premises, public-choice theorists can only warn of the pervasive dangers of rent seeking by self-interested bureaucrats, politicians, and interest groups (Niskanen 1971; Buchanan/Tollison/Tullock 1980; Olson 1982; Weede 1990), whereas principal-agent theory will mathematically demonstrate the impossibility, given the extreme degree of information asymmetry between governors and the governed, of equilibrium solutions that are, at the same time, welfare maximizing and incentive compatible. We know empirically, however, from anecdotal evidence as well as from comparative studies measuring the incidence of corruption in various countries, that there are in fact wide differences between countries where corruption is practically unknown and others where it is taken for granted (Lambsdorff 1995); and we also know from personal experience as well as from large bodies of empirical policy research that in many countries, and often for long periods, governments have effectively pursued public-interest objectives that were considered highly legitimate and important by their citizens.

What we need, then, are positive theories that do not force us to ignore these differences and prescriptive theories that will assist the design of constitutional arrangements that reinforce norm-oriented action and constrain opportunism without destroying the capacity for effective governmental action. For this reason, we find it necessary to modify the pretheoretical assumptions of economic institutionalism. If the coexistence of norm-oriented and self-interested preferences is recognized, it follows that explicit incentives and controls need not do all the work in bringing about a workable degree of public-interest orientation in the public sector—just as antitrust law need not do all the work in bringing about what economists call "workable competition" in the market. Legal rules and sanctions certainly remain necessary, but their function is less heroic than the one envisaged by public-choice theorists. Rather, they can be employed to perform what Andrew Dunsire (1993; 1996) has called "collibration"—an intervention to shift the preexisting balance between countervailing forces. Institutional arrangements that have the effect of strengthening one or weakening the other of these forces will require much less energy than institutions that would have to stop an unopposed force.

There is in fact a wide variety of institutional arrangements that are intended, on the one hand, to limit the damage that could be done by the abuse of public power and, on the other, to keep actors exercising hierarchical authority motivated to pursue the public interest rather than their private self-interest and to settle disputes with a view to criteria of distributive justice rather than to their own advantage. Among these are the mechanisms of professional self-control in areas of high value consensus that were discussed with regard to independent central banks and to judicial review at the beginning of the previous chapter. To these examples one might add the independent regulatory commissions in the United States and some regulatory functions of the European Commission (Majone 1994; 1995). But since they all depend on high degrees of value or goal consensus, the reach of these mechanisms is limited in principle. Beyond that, constitutional democracies depend primarily on majoritarian mechanisms to assure the accountability of officeholders. But since, as we saw in the previous chapter, majority-based power itself is also liable to be abused, it is first necessary to consider institutional safeguards that also work to limit the damage that could be done by self-interested majorities.

Foremost among these are institutions establishing the "rule of law," which essentially implies the realization of three principles. First is the principle of *legality,* according to which acts of public power must be based on a law of general application, which, because of its generality, will prevent discriminatory measures directed against individuals or groups. This principle has a central place in the constitutional thought of economic liberalism (Hayek 1944, chap. 6). In heterogeneous societies, however, it would not by itself provide much protection to ethnic, cultural, ideological, or economic minorities, whose interests could be violated precisely by general laws that fit the interests of the majority. Second, additional protection is generally provided by a *bill of rights* that not only protects life, liberty, and property against discriminatory invasions but also provides guarantees to the free practice of religion and to the freedoms of expression, assembly, and association. Third, both of these protections are effectuated by the institutionalization of an *independent judiciary,* to which recourse can be had against individual acts of government authority and, in an increasing number of constitutional democracies, against acts of the legislature. Moreover, these formal safeguards are complemented by the existence of free and investigative *media,* whose exposures cannot be legally suppressed by the government of the day.

It is clear, however, that the rule of law as well as the freedom of media communication will only provide safeguards at, as it were, the fringes of public power. If effective, they will prevent the abuse of power and arbitrary action in individual cases, but they cannot assure the commitment of policymakers to the public interest and distributive justice in the normal range of public policy making. This can only be achieved by mechanisms of political accountability, but it is important to keep in mind that these mechanisms must necessarily work within an institutional setting that assures the rule of law and free communication.

## POLITICAL ACCOUNTABILITY

Political accountability depends on institutional arrangements that create a circular relationship between governors and the governed. Being directly or indirectly dependent on the approval of the target population over whom hierarchical power is to be exercised, so it is assumed, will strengthen the motivation of policy actors to serve the collective interest of that population. In modern constitutional democracies this circular relationship is created through electoral mechanisms that require, as a minimum, periodic general elections with universal adult suffrage through which positions of hierarchical authority are filled for a limited period and from a set of candidates that allows voters an effective choice. Beyond that, however, institutional arrangements differ greatly in how they translate electoral choices into incentives for policy actors. The basic distinction is between models of competitive and consociational democracy. I begin with a discussion of the former.

### Competitive Democracy: The Westminster Model

The previous chapter ended with the conclusion that majority rule, by itself, was relatively ineffective in producing public-interest–oriented policies. In particular, I argued that the ideal of consensus-oriented deliberative democracy was bound to be undercut by the compulsions of party competition. But precisely because it creates strong incentives for exposing and exaggerating what is wrong with the other side, the competitive relationship between the government and the opposition is perfectly suited to controlling the exercise of hierarchical government power (Wittman 1989).

The control capacity of voters is maximized in the idealized "Westminster model" of a competitive two-party system, stabilized by first-past-the-post election rules and with highly centralized leadership within each of the two parties (Wilson 1994). The party that wins an election is invested with full control over the machinery of government; its capacity to act is not constrained either by the need to form coalition governments or by federal institutions, judicial review, or an independent central bank. It also has complete hierarchical authority over all members of the state machinery (except for the judiciary). By the same token, it also must assume undivided political responsibility for all policy outcomes. To that effect, the parliamentary party is invested with complete control over the political careers of its members, and that control is effectively exercised by the prime minister or by the leader of the opposition. It is further assumed that these leaders will be pursuing a variety of policy goals, some of them furthering the narrow self-interest of specific clientele groups, some of them defined by the ideology of their party, and some of them more personal. But since none of these goals can be obtained if the party is out of power, winning the next election must always be its paramount *instrumental* goal.

It is further assumed that the opposition will scrutinize government action for indications of policies violating either the public interest or the interests of specific groups and that it will try to publicize such violations. If these are taken up by the media, they may catch the attention of swing voters, whose negative reaction will damage, and may be fatal to, the political prospects of the government.[4] Finally, it is also assumed that the government must commit itself to policy choices at a time when it cannot yet know whether the opposition, the media, and ultimately the voters will in fact pay attention to this particular policy.

Within this model the control function does not make any unrealistic demands on voters who, as I argued earlier, are likely to be public interested but poorly informed and, at any rate, incapable of specifying in one vote their differing responses to the immense variety of policy issues that could play a role in elections. There is no way in which voters could rationally respond to *all* of these stimuli, nor can we assume that they should arrive at a well-informed and balanced *aggregate* judgment of the quality of public policy pursued by the acting government or proposed by the opposition. But neither is this required. It is sufficient that voters *sometimes* pay attention to public discussions of reported policy failures or scandals and that a substantial number of swing voters should *sometimes* change their vote in response to such information. Neither is it necessary that all swing voters *always* apply public-interest–oriented criteria to *all issues* to which they in fact respond. It is sufficient that a substantial part of them do so at least with regard to issues that do not obviously affect their immediate self-interest.

For accountability to function, it is then sufficient that in debates and political polemics about public policy, all arguments (regardless of the interest that is in fact pursued) necessarily be phrased in terms of claims to further, and of failures to realize, the public interest and distributive justice. If that is the case, then party competition and media investigation are likely to produce a steady stream of information on alleged violations of these normative criteria upon which interested voters may draw in arriving at their own electoral decisions. In addition, it is necessary that there be a nonzero probability that a decisive number of swing voters will vote against the government in response to some instance of policy failure that has caught the attention of the media or mobilized the protest of interest groups with mass membership or in reaction to some scandal that has incited public outrage.

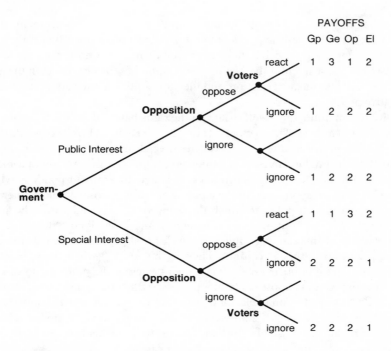

FIGURE 8.2    Government-opposition-voters sequential game

In highly stylized fashion, these assumptions may be modeled as an *asymmetrical zero-sum game between government and opposition* in which the stake is the all-or-nothing control of the machinery of government. In this game, only the government is capable of adopting and implementing effective policy choices, and the opposition must choose between challenging these choices or letting them pass. At the same time, both are playing a *connected positive-sum game with the swing voters,* in which the latter will either ignore an issue or respond to it by rewarding or punishing the government on election day. Since the swing voters, as a mere "actor aggregate," are incapable of strategic action, they can only have the last move. Though it is sometimes possible for the opposition to take the initiative, that is not the rule. Thus the government is modeled as having the first move in a three-player sequential game (Figure 8.2).

In this game the government must first choose between policy initiatives that serve either the public interest or the special interests of its own clientele. Given that choice, the opposition must then decide whether to ignore this particular policy or to oppose it by investing its limited resources in a massive effort to mobilize the public. The swing voters then will either ignore the issue or respond to the controversy generated by the opposition[5] by voting against the government if the policy in question violates the public interest or for the government if the policy seems to further the public interest. Finally, it is assumed that if the government adopts a policy that violates the public interest and if the opposition chooses to oppose it and if the swing voters respond to the dispute, then the government will lose the next election, and the opposition will then adopt its own alternative policy.

With this in mind, the payoffs listed on the right-hand side of the figure can be interpreted as follows: The electorate (El)[6] has two payoffs (1 or 2) depending on whether the policy in question serves the special interests of the government clientele or the public interest. The opposition (Op) has three different payoffs: a payoff of 3 if it opposes a special-interest–oriented government policy to which the swing voters respond negatively; a payoff of 1 if it opposes a public-interest–oriented government policy to which the swing voters respond positively; and a payoff of 2 if it does not oppose the issue or if the voters ignore the issue. The mirror image of this ranking applies to the electoral payoffs of the government, which are listed in the Ge column. They are highest (3) when the opposition chooses to fight a popular policy and is then beaten at the polls and lowest (1) when the opposition chooses to fight a policy to which the swing voters respond negatively. But in addition to electoral prospects, the government is also assumed to have specific policy-oriented preferences, the payoffs of which are listed in the Gp column, that are satisfied (2) when it is able to implement its special-interest policy choices and not satisfied (1) in all other cases.

An inspection of the figure leads to the conclusion that if the game structure is common knowledge, a rational opposition will always oppose government policies that serve special interests but will not oppose policies that are public-interest–oriented. Thus if the voters were to react every time the opposition chose to oppose, a rational government would never choose special-interest policies, since these would always lead to its worst-case outcome when the opposition chooses to fight and the voters react. By choosing public-interest–oriented policies, the government will assure itself a moderately good outcome, and it might gain its best outcome if the opposition chooses to fight and loses the battle.[7]

Of course, in the real world the opposition will not always oppose when it should, the media will not always be ready to amplify justified criticism, and swing voters will not always react to publicized policy failures and scandals. Hence governments may choose to gamble on the chance that self-serving policies will remain unsanctioned in order to achieve higher payoffs in the Gp column. But if the gamble should fail, the probability of a worst-case outcome for the government is far from zero. In order to avoid it, prudent political leaders have developed great sensitivity to early indications that this scenario might begin to unfold, and when things seem to go wrong in the eyes of the public, scapegoats are sought and severely punished—which, in turn, must impress officeholders within the government with the need to have good explanations ready whenever the searchlight of public attention should strike their own policy area.

Under these assumptions, the motivation of individual officeholders to pursue policies that can be publicly defended by reference to the public interest is reinforced by mechanisms that could be characterized as a combination of Carl Friedrich's (1937, 16) famous "doctrine of anticipated reactions" and the metaphor of a "fleet in being" that will affect enemy strategies merely because it *might* enter into the battle: Since it is impossible to know in advance which issues will become electorally decisive, it is prudent for officials and functionaries below the top levels to act on worst-case assumptions and to avoid decisions that, if they should be exposed and become politically salient, could alienate swing voters—which tends to place responsibility for policy choices favoring special interests precisely on those positions where political accountability is most directly effective. By the same token, redistributive policies that will visibly disadvantage important groups among the electorate will come under the most intense scrutiny; as a consequence, even single-party governments with a solid majority are likely to undertake them with great reluctance[8] and only if they can be defended by generally convincing public-interest and distributive-justice arguments.

Thus the idealized Westminster model seems to be normatively attractive. It must be remembered, however, that it presupposes the existence of a substantial share of swing voters who are oriented toward the *common interest*. As I argued in the preceding chapter, such orientations depend on the strength of a common identity (or on a single-peaked distribution of preferences). If the common identity is weak or lacking (or if the distribution of preferences is not single peaked), and if the constituency is divided into subpopulations with separate identities, even potentially public-interested voters will have difficulty in identifying a common interest. In that case, the orientation of policymakers toward the anticipated responses of swing voters could not assure output-oriented legitimacy.

The best that might then be hoped for under the conditions of the Westminster model would be "turn-taking" patterns in which each of the competing parties would, for a time, be able to govern and to pursue notions of the public interest prevailing in its own segment of the political spectrum. If the total electorate happened to be divided into two nearly equal "camps," the function of the swing vote could then be performed by voters "in the middle" who are likely to respond to ideological excesses on either side. As long as it can be assumed that the constellation of interests among the camps resembles a Battle of the Sexes game, turn taking among alternating partisan governments might then be sufficient to maintain legitimacy even in societies with clear-cut cleavages.

There is no assurance, however, that both of these conditions will be fulfilled in competitive two-party systems. Even if the constellation of interests is of the Battle of the Sexes type, the two camps may be of unequal size, and the asymmetrical outcomes produced by a "structural majority" may create so much resentment among the permanently disadvantaged minority that the legitimacy of the polity is undermined altogether. This may be the problem of Quebec in Canada. Moreover, even if the "camps" are of nearly equal size, the cleavages that divide them may be so deep and the constellations of interest so rent by conflict that no policy pursued by the majority of the day could be accepted as legitimate by the minority. Under either of these conditions, the Westminster model could not convey legitimacy—and in fact there are not many real-world political systems that can be characterized as being reasonable approximations of it (Lijphart 1984; 1991; Wilson 1994). Instead, the majority of constitutional democracies rely on variants of negotiation systems to assure the legitimacy of hierarchical governance.

### Negotiated Democracy: The Consociational Model

In order to discuss the capabilities and limitations of negotiated democracy, it is again useful to begin with the stylized presentation of the extreme model of "consociational" democracy that was constructed from the idealized characteristics of the Swiss, Austrian, and Dutch political systems in the early postwar decades (Lehmbruch 1967; 1974; Lijphart 1968). During that period these were societies divided by deep class-political (Austria), religious-ideological (Netherlands), or ethnic-linguistic (Switzerland) cleavages that weakened the foundations of political identity at the national level. As a consequence, straight majority rule would not have been able to generate legitimacy. The solution in Austria was the postwar Grand Coalition of the two large parties representing class interests, whereas in the Netherlands and in Switzerland all major parties in a multiparty system joined in a permanent governing coalition. In Switzerland, moreover, electoral competition was and still is further reduced by an equally permanent allocation of ministerial positions among the participating parties.

In its original form, the consociational model survives only in Switzerland. Here it is also important to note that regional (and hence ethnic) interests are specifically represented in the *Ständerat,* the federal chamber of a bicameral legislature, and that cross-cutting sectional interests are well organized and well integrated into the party system. Moreover, the referendum makes it easy for dissatisfied groups to challenge all government decisions (Linder 1994). Under these institutional conditions party competition is largely disabled as a mechanism of democratic accountability.[9] Instead, consociational democracy must depend on the negotiation logic of the Coase Theorem for the legitimation of collectively binding decisions. Assuming that all important societal interests are in fact represented and involved in multilateral negotiations, the final parliamentary vote is likely to register not simply the majority view but rather a "consensus" that is sensitive to the interests and the power resources of all major actors and groups involved (Coleman 1990, 857–862).

Consensus in this definition does not imply unanimous decisions in which everyone has a formal veto; it is more likely to represent the dominant view in an elite cartel. Nevertheless, the exploitative opportunities of this constellation are limited by the easy availability of the referendum, which provides "intense" minorities (Dahl 1956) with excellent opportunities to block even decisions supported by all major parties and interest associations (Hadley/Morass/Nick 1989; Luthardt 1992). The characteristic problems of consociational democracy are rather caused by the high transaction costs of multilateral bargaining and by the incapacity for involuntary redistribution that are typical of all negotiation systems. As a result, the Swiss welfare state is smaller than the welfare systems of other European countries,[10] and political reforms are more easily blocked there than elsewhere (Immergut 1992).

But in which sense can the consociational model be considered "democratic"? Agreements on policy choices are necessarily negotiated among the leaders of the respective "camps." From the perspective of rank-and-file members, therefore, they still constitute a form of hierarchical governance that must be internally legitimated through democratic accountability. But unlike the Westminster model, consociational democracy cannot assure that the policy choices of leaders will correspond to the preferences of their respective constituencies. The reason for this follows from the two-level character of interunit negotiations.

Let us first assume that *within* each of the negotiating units interests are homogeneous. Except for constellations resembling games of pure coordination, it follows from the discussion in Chapter 6 that a negotiated outcome could not satisfy the maximal original aspirations of all participating units. Thus if negotiators were bound to them, then negotiations would fail. In order to succeed in devising policies that increase *overall* welfare, negotiators must be free to search for innovative solutions and to accept "fair" distributions that must be acceptable to all other parties. Since constituents could not participate in the processes of common exploration and distributive haggling that must take place among negotiators, and since negotiations could not succeed if all communications at the bargaining table were publicized, we seem to be confronted with another dilemma: Negotiated democracy can only succeed in achieving welfare efficiency and distributive fairness *among* units by weakening democratic accountability *within* units. The dilemma seems even more severe if we drop the assumption of homogeneous preferences and allow for conflicting interests within units (Mayer 1992). This is a problem to which I will return in Chapter 9.

Here it suffices to remind ourselves that we are discussing criteria of *output-oriented legitimacy,* and that for negotiations the proper criterion, for all parties involved, cannot be that original aspirations should be maximized but that the outcome should be better than what would have been the case if negotiations had failed. If this is realized, then there will be legitimate political controversies about the true location of the nonagreement point and about whether better outcomes could have been achieved, but these will not differ fundamentally from disputes over internal policy choices under conditions of competitive democracy.

The critical issue, from a democratic-theory point of view, therefore shifts to the internal conditions of political accountability within the political parties and regional units involved in policy negotiations at the national level. These conditions vary considerably. But even there, the legitimacy problem is reduced by the fact that the negotiating camps are smaller than the polity as a whole and that their membership is to a larger degree self-selected. Hence policy preferences within each of the negotiating units are likely to be more homogeneous, or at least to be more often single peaked, than is the case in the constituency at large. Moreover, if these units have a collective identity, it will often be the case that in negotiations with "outsiders," outcomes can be unambiguously classified as being better or less good "for our side."[11] Thus there is less need for institutional safeguards to keep leaders committed to the median preferences of their constituents. In Switzerland, moreover, the referendum provides easily available correctives against negotiated outcomes that violate the intense preferences of a substantial minority of voters.

### *Competition and Negotiations Combined*

The conclusion is therefore that the stylized model of consociational democracy, though quite different from the Westminster model, also has normatively attractive characteristics. Most real-world democratic systems, however, are somewhere between the extremes discussed thus far. They have neither neutralized party competition to the extent that is true in Switzerland nor institutionalized single-party responsibility to the extent that is true in the Westminster model. As a consequence, policy processes involve competition as well as a good deal of negotiations among politically independent actors in most modern democracies (Lijphart 1984). But these negotiations vary significantly with regard to the sources of potential disagreement and the factors facilitating agreement. These differences may be classified as follows:

*Intraparty Negotiations.* Even in Westminster-type single-party governments there may be policy conflicts and competitive strategies within the governing party that cannot always be settled by the unilateral fiat of the prime minister. They may arise from bona fide disagreement over the substance of policy issues and potential solutions, or they may be fueled by the career aspirations and personal vanities of ambitious politicians. Such conflicts are ubiquitous in all political systems. However, they are dampened here by the fact that the institutional self-interest in maintaining, or in gaining, the power to govern the country and the perquisites of office can only be pursued at the level of the party as a whole. Even though factions may violently disagree with one another, they can only win or lose together against the opposition—and if internal feuds would jeopardize the chances of electoral success, there will be powerful pressures to reach some kind of agreement.

*Intracoalition Negotiations.* Matters are more difficult in negotiations among parties making up the coalition governments that are characteristic of multiparty systems. Here the interplay between the government coalition and the opposition continues to drive the mechanism of democratic accountability. But its effect on government policy is weaker than it is under the conditions of the Westminster model. Even if the coalition is committed to maintaining a united front against the opposition and to avoiding alternating majorities, the common strategy must be formulated in internal negotiations among coalition parties that, in the end, must face the electorate on their own account. Success or failure may determine the opportunity to participate again in government, and even if all members are committed to continue the coalition after the election, the number and importance of ministerial portfolios that a party can expect are likely to be affected by election outcomes.[12] Thus, though all parties in the coalition may have a common interest in the success of the government, each has a separate institutional interest in maintaining its political identity and in defending the interests of its clientele, even if that should endanger the electoral prospects of the government as a whole.[13] In this regard, small parties (like the religious parties in Israel or the Ulster loyalists in Britain) whose votes are essential for the continuation of the government may have a blackmail capacity that is quite out of proportion to their electoral support. As a result, coalition governments are not only less capable of decisive action than a single-party government would be under the same conditions, but they are also more likely to adopt policies that serve the narrow interests of the clienteles of particular parties.

*Divided Government.* In all cases discussed thus far negotiations occur "in the shadow" of the majority vote. Thus if agreement is entirely impossible, a determined majority could still have its way, even if at high political cost. As a background possibility, this majoritarian option greatly facilitates the achievement of "consensus" in the sense discussed earlier. This is not generally the case, however, under constitutional arrangements in which governing power is formally divided among several institutions whose members are *separately accountable* to the same constituency, or to parts of it. This is true in the United States of the House of Representatives, the Senate, and the presidency; in France it is true of the presidency and the government, with its parliamentary majority; and in Germany it is true of the federal government, with its parliamentary majority and the *Bundesrat* representing the governments of the *Länder*.

In purely formal terms, such constitutional arrangements could be described as "joint-decision systems," as discussed in Chapter 6. None of the participating units is able to act alone. In the United States, it is true, the formal veto of the president may be overcome through extraordinary majorities in both houses of Congress, and in Germany the veto of the *Bundesrat* may in some cases be overruled by extraordinary majorities in parliament (Wehling 1989). Normally, however, constitutionally protected vetoes can only be overcome through negotiated agreement. If that were all there is, the horizontal or vertical separation of governing powers would not differ analytically from other compulsory negotiation systems. Under the Coase Theorem we should still expect approximations of welfare-maximizing policy outcomes.[14]

Circumstances change, however, under conditions of "divided government" (Laver/Shepsle 1991; McKay 1994; Krehbiel 1996). When both houses of Congress are controlled by a majority opposed to the president (and when party discipline is high), when in France the president and the prime minister must practice *cohabitation,* or when in Germany a majority of seats in the *Bundesrat* is held by state governments that are controlled by the opposition parties in the *Bundestag,* policy outcomes come to depend on negotiations among actors who are in direct electoral competition *within the same constituency.*

For the definition of "divided government," the condition emphasized in the preceding sentence is in fact crucial. Among governments in the European Union party politics plays practically no role—the Franco-German alliance was equally close between Social-Democratic Helmut Schmidt and conservative Valéry Giscard d'Estaing and between Socialist François Mitterrand and Christian-Democratic Helmut Kohl. Even within Germany, *Länder* governments of different party-political hues will often cooperate very effectively (Hesse 1987). But under conditions of "divided government" interinstitutional or intergovernmental negotiations come to be dominated by the orientations of political parties and political leaders who find themselves in direct competition for the allegiance of the same voters. Under these conditions, their normal role is to oppose each other, and hence their perceptions and preferences are likely to be shaped by "competitive" interaction orientations, which, as I showed earlier, will transform all interactions into zero-sum conflicts.

When that is the case the cooperative search for mutually acceptable solutions will be blocked by the overriding interest of the opposition to demonstrate the impotence of the government and by the equally strong interest of the government to expose the irresponsibility and incompetence of the opposition. And even if negotiators may be close to a consensus on an issue of high political salience[15] they are likely to be tripped up by competitors on both sides who will try to stop them with the charge of having sold out to the "political enemy" (Ueberhorst 1991; Koenigs/Schaeffer 1993). The most likely outcome is then political immobilism. But there may also be constellations in which the competing parties will outbid one another in raising the level of popular spending programs (or in avoiding unpopular cuts)—with the result that the agreed-upon outcome will be more fiscally irresponsible than outcomes for which a single governing party would have to take full responsibility.[16]

In other words, under conditions of divided government political competition is likely to undercut the capacity of governments to deal effectively with societal problems. Conversely, the need to collaborate with the opposition in the interest of effective problem solving weakens the most important mechanism for controlling government power through democratic accountability. In the end, agreement may be thwarted by pressures to compete,[17] and competition is corrupted by surreptitious collusion. In short, negotiations under conditions of divided government are normatively unattractive from both a welfare-theoretic and a democratic-theory perspective.

## NOTES

1. It is true that a dictator who has an interest in exploiting "renewable" production possibilities must also have an interest in maintaining the factors of production and the motivation to produce (Olson 1993). Nevertheless, the revenue-maximizing tax rate of the "predatory ruler" will be higher than the tax rate that maximizes social production (Levi 1988).

2. However, when capital is highly mobile, incentive structures assuring the responsiveness of managers to the short-term profit orientation of shareholders may destroy the firm rather than maximize its social product.

3. It has been shown analytically that no budget-balancing incentive system (distributing only the additional revenues created by the agents' efforts) can create incentives such that Nash equilibrium outcomes are Pareto-optimal (Holmstrom 1982; G. Miller 1990, 330–331).

4. This is a crucial assumption: The Westminster model will not achieve democratic accountability if one of the two parties is structurally dominant, so that swing voters could not have a decisive effect on the outcome of elections. Also, though first-past-the-post elections favor the evolution and maintenance of two-party systems, they may also immunize the government against the swing vote if the opposition is nevertheless divided, as has been the case in Britain since the early 1980s.

5. If the opposition does not oppose a policy, it is assumed that the voters will always ignore it.

6. Payoffs do not go to the swing voters but to the electorate as a whole.

7. Under conditions of complete information a perfectly rational opposition would avoid that strategy. But information is rarely complete, and rationality rarely perfect. Historically, at any rate, opposition parties have often been unable to sidestep issues on which the government was doing the right thing in the eyes of the electorate. In Germany, for instance, this was true of the Social Democrats in the mid-1950s when they opposed Konrad Adenauer's pro-Western policy, of the Christian Democrats in the early 1970s, when they opposed Willy Brandt's *Ostpolitik,* and again of the Social Democrats in 1990, when they were seen to oppose Helmut Kohl's unification.

8. As Paul Pierson (1994; 1996b) has shown, even conservative governments with a strong ideological commitment to reducing the welfare "burden" on the economy have ultimately failed to pursue (visible) retrenchment policies, which could have alienated important segments of their electorates.

9. It is not completely disabled, since elections still determine the relative parliamentary strength of political parties, which continues to make a difference in legislative decisions.

10. In general, welfare expenditures increase with GDP per capita. Aside from Luxembourg, Switzerland is the richest country in Europe. Nevertheless, in 1992 social expenditures in Switzerland were at 20.8 percent of GDP, below the level of Ireland and Spain (21.6 and 22.5 percent, respectively) and much lower than that of Germany and Britain, each at 27 percent, let alone those of Denmark and the Netherlands, at 31 and 33 percent, respectively (Eurostat 1995, Table 3.31).

11. The same mechanism explains why in the United States and elsewhere a "bipartisan foreign policy" is more easily achieved than bipartisan consensus on domestic issues.

12. Coalition theory that tries to predict which coalitions will form and how the spoils will be allocated among the members has not yet reached a high degree of predictive power, since its analytical models tend to disregard the *political* dimensions of coalition formation. If all parties were equally likely to form coalitions with all other parties, then one could indeed expect minimum winning coalitions (Riker 1962), within which relative weights would correspond to a power index representing the probability that a given actor would be decisive for the formation of a randomly selected minimum winning coalition (Harsanyi 1981; 1991). In real-world politics, of course, ideology, personalities, and history rule out many potential coalitions. The crucial question, therefore, is which of the coalition parties could potentially switch to another *politically feasible* coalition. If only one party has an outside option, its relative weight will increase; if none has, even very large differences in numerical strength will be equalized.

13. This Prisoner's Dilemma game is mitigated if, as in Switzerland, electoral success has no influence on the assignment of ministerial portfolios, and it is exacerbated if, as was true in the French Fourth Republic and in Italy, coalitions are expected to be short-lived in any case.

14. From a democratic-theory point of view, it is often argued that accountability is weakened because none of the political actors involved may, in fairness, be held fully accountable for the outcome achieved. But voters are under no obligation to be fair, and they may not be much interested in who precisely is to blame when they are dissatisfied with the outcomes of government policy. This should generally increase the willingness of political actors to arrive at effective solutions to politically salient problems.

15. In this regard it is an advantage that public attention to political issues is a scarce good, and that parties therefore must be highly selective in deciding which issues to "politicize." In fact the overwhelming majority of items on the agenda of the *Bundesrat* are adopted without public controversy. If it were otherwise, a country like Germany could not be governed at all under conditions of divided government (Klatt 1989; Renzsch 1989).

16. Research on divided government has almost exclusively focused on the United States (but see Laver/Shepsle 1991) and on budgetary consequences. The empirical finding is that in periods of divided party control, governments run larger structural budget deficits and are less able to respond to negative revenue shocks (McKay 1994; Alt/Lowry 1994).

17. In German federalism it is important that the negotiators on the side of the opposition are acting from two identities—as representatives of their political parties and as representatives of their states. In this second identity (on which their bargaining position depends), they are also constrained not to sell out the institutional self-interest of their state to the ideological pressures of their party (Scharpf 1995). As a consequence, the federal government is sometimes able to buy off party-political opposition by offering concessions to some state interests.

# 9

## Varieties of the Negotiating State

### LOOKING BACK

It may be useful to begin this concluding chapter with a look back over the ground that we have covered. Substantive policy analysis, so I said at the beginning, is concerned with the relationship between conditions considered problematic by the individuals or groups affected and the means available for the collective resolution of such problems in ways that are thought to be superior in terms of the public interest. Interaction-oriented political science research, by contrast, would focus on the institutions and actors through which problems are converted into policy outputs and outcomes that—in the light of substantive policy analysis—may be considered more or less effective solutions. This book was to be about a set of conceptual tools that could facilitate the theoretically disciplined study of policy interactions.

Such tools, I suggested, could be located within the unifying framework of actor-centered institutionalism, which treats policy as the outcome of the interactions of resourceful and boundedly rational actors whose capabilities, preferences, and perceptions are largely, but not completely, shaped by the institutionalized norms within which they interact. I then discussed the reasons for using composite-actor concepts and for distinguishing among aggregate, collective, and corporate actors, and I suggested useful distinctions regarding the capabilities, perceptions, and preferences of composite and individual actors. Next I elaborated the potential of game-theoretic interpretations of constellations among policy actors, their relationship to the underlying substantive policy problems, and the welfare-theoretic and justice-oriented criteria by which solutions could be evaluated. In Chapters 5 through 8 I then presented in greater detail the four basic modes of strategic interaction—unilateral action, negotiations, voting, and hierarchy—and I discussed the conditions under which each of these is capable of generating policy outcomes that are likely to be welfare efficient and responsive to criteria of distributive justice.

That capacity varies with the type of actor constellations that a given policy process is supposed to deal with. Constellations resembling games of pure coordination or the Assurance game may be effectively dealt with in any one of the four modes of interaction, including unilateral action leading to Mutual Adjustment. For problems in the nature of the Battle of the Sexes game, the outcomes of unilateral action and of majority voting are also welfare efficient, but they will not conform to criteria of distributive justice. Under these circumstances negotiations could be easily blocked—but if agreement is reached, the outcome is likely to approximate welfare efficiency as well as distributive justice in the sense of "equity" (but not in the sense of "equality" or "need"). Problems in the nature of the (symmetrical) Prisoner's Dilemma game, by contrast, cannot be resolved on normatively satisfactory terms through unilateral action or through self-interested majority voting, whereas negotiations under the structural conditions of networks, regimes, and joint-decision systems can do so, but again at high transaction costs. Constellations with high levels of conflict, finally, are not resolvable in satisfactory fashion either by unilateral action or by self-interested voting. Self-interested negotiators are also likely to be blocked under these circumstances. At the most, they may be able to reach compromise solutions at the lowest common denominator that will not challenge status-quo distribution—and they will only be able to do so if the outcomes are divisible or if side payments or package deals are possible. That will not always be the case, and transaction costs will be very high under the best conditions (Underdal 1983).

Hierarchical coordination, by contrast, may in principle be able to produce outcomes that achieve both welfare efficiency and distributive justice for all types of societal problems and under all strategic constellations—which explains why this mode of interaction is typically presupposed in substantive policy analyses. It is equally obvious, however, that hierarchical interaction can reach these beneficial results only under very demanding conditions. I discussed these under the headings of an "information problem" and a "motivation problem," and I argued that the need to secure the *motivation* of incumbents in offices that dispose of hierarchical authority is reasonably well met by the institutionalization of democratic accountability under conditions that are, by and large, reasonably well approximated in a wide variety of real-world constitutional democracies. Though it is certainly possible in most political systems to point to instances of corruption and purposeful wrongdoing in high places, these are likely to be severely sanctioned when discovered, and in comparison with the expectations of pervasive opportunism postulated by public-choice theorists, it seems in fact to be relatively rare that democratically accountable governments will deliberately pursue policies that they assume to violate the public interest.

Theoretically there is also a plausible solution to the information problem, which presupposes that hierarchical superiors should limit their attention to just those matters that can only be decided at the higher level. But this solution depends on task structures that are "nearly decomposable" (Simon 1962), and I argued that this is becoming less and less feasible under real-world conditions, in which the number, variety, extent, and variability of causal interdependencies increase in practically all policy areas. Any attempt to practice effectively hierarchical coordination from the center is therefore likely to run into the combined problems of information impoverishment and information overload—which may explain the technical, economic, and social backwardness and ultimately the downfall of socialist regimes. But if the parties immediately affected by, or the subunits directly in charge of, particular aspects of interdependent problems are instead left to their own devices, problem solving must revert to the modes of unilateral action and negotiations, with all their deficiencies—which supposedly were to be overcome through hierarchical coordination.

Empirically, however, this appears to be an overly bleak conclusion, and thus the first puzzle that still must be discussed in this final chapter is how, within the framework presented here, one might account for policy success. Given the low problem-solving capacity of unilateral action, the excessive transaction costs of negotiations, and the narrow limits within which hierarchical coordination—the most potent and also the most dangerous mode—is likely to produce normatively acceptable outcomes, *how is it possible that public policy in most constitutional democracies has been able to produce reasonably satisfactory outcomes over quite long periods?* And while we consider this question we should also anticipate its empirically based sequel: *How is it possible that constitutional democracies, which have for so long produced reasonably satisfactory policy outcomes, seem to have lost much of that capacity since the mid-1970s?* In order to get a handle on both of these questions, we have to extend our perspective beyond our previous focus on interactions within the public policy making system itself. It will be seen, however, that this can be done with exactly the same conceptual tools that have been presented so far.

## THE SHADOW OF HIERARCHY

Empirically, the answer to the first question was already implicit in the account of coordination practices in the German ministerial bureaucracy (Mayntz/Scharpf 1975) to which I referred earlier. Conceptually this answer depends on the distinction introduced at the end of Chapter 2 between a certain type of institutional setting and the characteristic modes of interaction occurring within that setting. For the hierarchical mode this implies a distinction between a hierarchical *authority structure* and the actual use of *hierarchical direction* in order to override the decision preferences of other actors. I also suggested that any given institutional structure could be considered a "possibility frontier" in the sense that it cannot support institutionally more demanding modes of interaction—in a network structure one could not resort to majority voting or hierarchical coordination—but permits less demanding options to be practiced. Within a hierarchical authority structure, therefore, it is indeed possible that actual interactions will have the character of negotiations or of unilateral action.

### Negotiations in Bureaucratic Hierarchies

Negotiations that are *embedded in a hierarchical authority structure* are conducted under conditions that differ significantly from those of "freestanding" negotiations. In the same way in which democratic accountability, even if it is severely limited in its capacity to respond to policy failures, remains effective as a "fleet in being," hierarchical authority is still able to affect lower-level interactions that it could not effectively coordinate unilaterally. Thus the task structure of the German ministerial bureaucracy that we had studied was certainly not "nearly decomposable" in the sense defined by Herbert Simon (1962), and it was clear that policy production would come to a standstill if all internal disagreements would have to be settled through hierarchical coordination by the minister and all interministerial disputes by the cabinet. Nevertheless, the stream of policy choices that is continuously produced by the government is clearly shaped by the political preferences of the ministers responsible and of the chancellor.

In actual fact, policy proposals are usually produced through a "nexus" of horizontal negotiations among lower-level units within and across ministries and with outside actors in parliament, in political parties, as well as in interest organizations. Conflicts either are avoided unilaterally by the practices of Negative Coordination or are settled through Distributive Bargaining over compromise solutions that allow the units involved to present *common* proposals to the minister and to the cabinet, where, under the circumstances, they are likely to be accepted summarily. It is important, however, that in these processes of horizontal self-coordination each of the participating units is also involved in a "vertical dialogue" in which the political concerns of the minister or of the chancellor's office are communicated "downward" and issues regarding the technical feasibility and appropriateness of available options are communicated "upward."

Thus lower-level units will usually have a good idea about the positions on which they are likely to be backed by the political leadership if horizontal negotiations should fail. At the same time, however, all parties involved are aware of the fact that not many issues can be appealed to higher authority without overloading the center and producing arbitrary outcomes. Moreover, losing on an issue that is appealed upward, or even developing a reputation for bothering the minister with disputes that could have been settled below, is almost as unhelpful for a bureaucratic career as would be "selling out" on a position that is important from the minister's point of view. As a consequence, horizontal self-coordination proceeds under conditions in which the pressure to reach agreement is very great indeed but in which each side has the option of appealing to higher authority and, ultimately, to a common superior if it is being pushed too far or confronted with unfair bargaining strategies. In our usual negotiation figure, the constellation can be represented through the addition of a threat option for either party (Figure 9.1).

Let us assume that two sections, X and Y, within a ministerial department are favoring widely divergent solutions, A and B, for a particular policy problem—

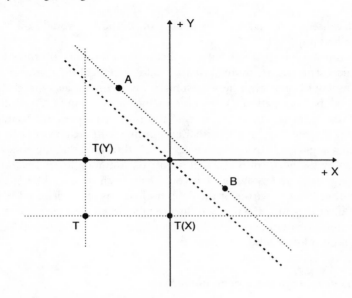

FIGURE 9.1    Negotiations in a hierarchy

perhaps because each has a special responsibility for the welfare of a particular clientele group. In comparison with the status quo, neither A nor B would be within the zone of common attraction. In freestanding negotiations, therefore, a compromise solution would be most difficult to reach, since its advantage over the status quo would be relatively insignificant in comparison with the concessions that each side would be required to make. In a ministerial organization, however, each party could threaten to take the dispute to the minister, trying to demonstrate that the position taken by the other side would violate important interests of the ministry as a whole. Yet if one side does that, the other would have to present its version as well—with the very real risk that a substantively inferior decision (or nondecision) may be imposed from above and with a loss of reputation for both parties to the dispute. From their point of view, therefore, the outcome obtained if both threats were realized might be located at point T. *In comparison with the threat outcome at T,* however, both of the original proposals, A as well as B, would now be preferred by either party, so that a compromise outcome should be relatively easy to reach.

It is important, moreover, that the threat mechanism can be credibly invoked only by parties that are able to argue that they are defending the best interest of the minister. If only one side, say Y, could plausibly do so, it would not incur a loss of reputation by appealing unilaterally to the minister—who would then be likely to support its position, and the other side would lose on policy grounds and in career prospects. In that case, the threat point might be located at T(Y)—

with the consequence that solution A, but not solution B, would now be within the negotiation space.

The implication is therefore not only that negotiations that are embedded in a hierarchical structure are more likely to lead to agreement than freestanding negotiations would be under otherwise similar conditions but also that these negotiations will be systematically influenced by the anticipation of a potential decision of the minister. In other words, the principal-agent problem largely disappears if agents can only act either by agreeing with each other or by appealing to the (single) principal. It is to be expected, therefore, that the policy output generated by the nexus of horizontal negotiations among lower-level units will tend to approximate the output that could have been produced by hierarchical coordination. Thus by virtue of the dual mechanisms of "anticipated reactions" and the "fleet in being," the policy influence of a hierarchical authority structure reaches much farther than hierarchical coordination, in the narrower sense of a specific mode of interaction, ever could.

### Self-Organization in the Shadow of the State

The mechanisms just described for the ministerial bureaucracy also apply to the relationship between the hierarchical authority of the state and certain types of negotiated policymaking among actors in civil society. This is most obvious in cases in which a negotiation regime or a joint-decision system, as defined in Chapter 6, is specifically set up by the state for the regulation of certain economic or societal problem areas. Thus in the corporatist welfare states of the European continent, health care, old-age pensions, and unemployment benefits are typically financed through self-governing insurance "corporations" in which employers and workers are represented (Esping-Andersen 1990). In health care, moreover, these insurance corporations are continuously engaged in collective bargaining with associations of service providers over types of services covered and their respective prices (Alber/Bernardi-Schenkluhn 1992; Immergut 1993).

In some cases it is the states that set up the associations themselves and that regulate the conditions of (compulsory) membership. But even when that is not the case, state law regulates the institutional settings within which such negotiations take place and assures the binding force of negotiated agreements. Among the pertinent examples are laws regulating collective bargaining over wages and working conditions and the "works constitution act" regulating the role of works councils in the hiring and firing decisions of German firms (Rogers/Streeck 1995). Another example is the statutory requirement that representatives of environmental public-interest groups must be included in the nongovernmental standard-setting organization (DIN) in which industrial norms are negotiated in Germany. Similar corporatist standard-setting institutions have been set up by the European Union and, again, their membership and hence the distribution of bargaining power is determined and could be changed by European law (Voelzkow 1996).

Moreover, the power to establish a negotiation regime also implies a power to manipulate its institutional parameters so as to affect the balance of relative bargaining power and hence expected outcomes. Thus to moderate the perceived militancy of labor unions both the Thatcher government in Britain and the Kohl government in Germany changed the institutional ground rules of collective bargaining in the 1980s in order to weaken the unions' relative bargaining power (Streeck 1992). Even more instructive is the response of German legislation to the continuing rise of health care costs after an initial round of cost containment reforms in the 1970s had turned out to be relatively ineffective. Since a plurality of sickness funds was negotiating with the (statutory) monopoly of physicians' associations, it was assumed that competition among funds was a major cause of escalating fee settlements (Ryll 1993).[1] In order to eliminate this competition the 1988 reforms required all sickness funds to negotiate centrally and jointly over a uniform fee schedule. As a consequence, cost pressures have been greatly reduced in the ambulatory health care sector (Döhler/Manow-Borgwardt 1992).

All of these examples share two characteristics: The interests contributing to or affected by a public-policy problem are highly organized (in some cases with the assistance of the state), and there is a reasonable chance that the underlying policy problems can be effectively dealt with through negotiated agreements among organized groups. When that is the case, the information about situational conditions, preferences, and potential solutions that is available among the groups concerned, but difficult to obtain for central government, can be fully utilized. Nevertheless, the state is able to influence the drift of negotiated settlements by shifting the balance of bargaining power from one side to the other through relatively minor changes in the institutional setting.[2]

### The Negotiating State

The constellation changes when the state is itself party to negotiations, rather than a third party setting the stage for and intervening in negotiations between societal groups. This, again, is quite frequent in corporatist countries with well-organized associations that have a capacity for decisions that either are binding upon their members or that at least are able to influence the courses of action the members take. That capacity may itself be derived from the state, as would be the case when state law and the courts enforce compulsory membership in professional associations or tolerate the "closed shop" or the "union shop." Beyond that, the capacity of associations to impose obligations on their members depends on the balance of benefits and costs of membership as compared to the exit option (Streeck 1992). These "private-interest governments" (Streeck/Schmitter 1985; Hollingsworth/Schmitter/Streeck 1994) are of course primarily concerned with maximizing the interest of their members; nevertheless, they may also perform functions that serve the interest of third parties or of the public, such as the delivery of welfare services, industrial training, technical standardization, consumer protection, or environmental protection (Mayntz 1992; Voelzkow 1996). The conditions under which this is possible can be systematically described in terms of the underlying actor constellations.

Thus voluntary associations should have little difficulty in adopting effective regulations that serve the individual self-interest of their members under conditions resembling games of coordination, as is true of technical compatibility standards (Genschel/Werle 1993). Moreover, voluntary associations may also be able to adopt and enforce quality standards that protect the interests of consumers—but typically only under conditions in which "certification" by the association is able to provide a competitive advantage in the market to its members individually. This has been true, for instance, of the accrediting associations of colleges and schools in the United States (Wiley/Zald 1968).

Greater difficulties are encountered by associations and cartels attempting to impose regulations that are in the collective self-interest of their members but burdensome individually (i.e., that would resolve an n-person Prisoner's Dilemma). Though such rules may be willingly adopted, they are generally threatened by the free-rider problem (Olson 1965) unless associations are also able to sanction offenders, which in the case of voluntary associations depends on the existence of other benefits of membership that are highly valued. Beyond that, one would expect that regulations serving primarily the interest of third parties (such as in the control of industrial emissions) could not be adopted and enforced by voluntary associations. The limits of self-regulation may be extended, however, if associations are operating "in the shadow of the state."

Thus in the early self-description of environmental policy in Germany the "principle of cooperation" played a large role alongside two or three other principles such as "polluter pays" or "prevention" (Hartkopf/Bohne 1983). What it meant was that the government was negotiating for voluntary commitments from industrial associations, whose self-regulation would then have priority over compulsory statutory regulations as long as effective "cooperation" was forthcoming. For a while, at any rate, this practice was reasonably effective, reducing pollution in ways that were more cost-efficient, in light of the specific conditions obtaining in particular industries, than standardized statutory rules would have been. Similarly, in the late 1970s, German industrial associations promised and were able to provide sufficient training places for a rising number of school leavers. But they did so "in the shadow" of a statute that would have allowed the government, if need be, to impose a levy on firms that did not train apprentices and to subsidize firms that did.

In both instances the outcome can be explained in the negotiation-theoretic terms presented earlier: The fact that these negotiations were embedded within the hierarchical authority structure of the state moved the location of the non-agreement point away from the status quo. If a negotiated agreement acceptable to the government was not found, industry could not expect to continue as before but would have to reckon with the unilateral imposition of (conceivably ill-informed and inefficient)[3] state regulations. For the association itself, this eventuality also changed the conditions under which it was able to influence the conduct of its members. If its commitment vis-à-vis the state was not generally honored, members could no longer expect to enjoy the benefits of free riding but would have to reckon with bureaucratic controls imposed by the state administration. Quite obviously, the effectiveness of self-regulation would vary with the perception of whether, in case cooperation should not be forthcoming, the government had the legal and political capacity to adopt and implement statutory regulations.[4] But when that is assured, even major problems of pollution control and other externalities may be effectively dealt with through negotiated agreements (Hoffmann-Riem 1990).[5]

These examples are taken mostly from Germany, a "semisovereign state" (Katzenstein 1987) in which corporatist associations are well organized and powerful and federal legislation is fettered by high consensus requirements among government coalitions and between federal majorities and *Länder* governments and where, moreover, the central government does not have its own administrative infrastructure in most policy areas but must rely on implementation by *Länder* administration, which it cannot directly control. From the point of view of "state actors" in a national ministry, therefore, "voluntary" agreements negotiated with industrial associations may appear quite attractive in comparison with the difficulties of getting the same policy adopted and implemented within the structures of the state itself.

That motive is lacking in unitary and "statist" countries such as France or Britain, where associations are weaker and state actors have much greater autonomy in policy formation and where statutes will then be implemented by administrative agencies under the direct control of the central government. Nevertheless, even in France negotiations between state actors and the affected groups or industries or individual firms do play a critical role at the implementation stage in facilitating the exercise of hierarchical authority. As Vivien Schmidt (1990; 1996) has emphasized, government-business relations in France, at least before the judicialization required by regulations of the European Union, were characterized by a combination of uniform and strict legislation and wide administrative discretion that could be and was used for negotiated settlements that could respond to atypical local conditions and thus were able to avoid the negative consequences of information-impoverished hierarchical direction.

A third variant of negotiated policymaking is characteristic of the pluralist political system of the United States—for which even the concept of "the state" is considered to be of doubtful theoretical value (Truman 1951; Dahl 1967; Evans/Rueschemeyer/Skocpol 1985; Skocpol 1987). There the weakness of political parties and the fragmented committee structure in Congress may make it seem more plausible to consider regulation by federal statute as being the outcome of agreements negotiated directly among the organized interests affected. Nevertheless, the existence of the state structure is of critical importance since it assures the binding character of the agreements reached and since it allows the associations involved to avoid any internal free-rider problems by making use of the authoritative implementation capacities of the state for purposes of self-regulation.

Neither is the logical place of "the state" as a guardian of the public interest left empty. The presidency must be conceptualized as a strategic actor that is responsive to the electorate as a whole, and policy implementation is generally left to "state actors" in the administrative service or in independent regulatory agencies whose role definition also requires an orientation to the public interest. At the same time, the electoral system assures the representation of a wide variety of societal interests, and the lobby also includes a proliferation of public-interest pressure groups that must be included in negotiated settlements. Moreover, the institutional control that the majorities in both houses of Congress may exercise over committee jurisdictions and assignments also creates possibilities for influencing the balance of bargaining powers and hence the outcomes of negotiated compromises (Shepsle/Weingast 1987; Shepsle 1988). Additional opportunities for majoritarian influences are provided by the choice among implementation agencies and by congressional control over the budgets of these agencies (Cook/Wood 1989; Quirk 1989; Campbell/Hollingsworth/Lindberg 1991). In short, even in the United States it is meaningful to consider pluralist policymaking as a form of negotiations in the shadow of the hierarchical authority of the state and of majoritarian accountability.

### Policymaking in the Shadow of the State

Under all of these variants of self-organization and the negotiating state, much effective policy is produced not in the standard constitutional mode of hierarchical state power, legitimated by majoritarian accountability, but rather in associations and through collective negotiations with or among organizations that are formally part of the self-organization of civil society rather than of the policy-making system of the state (Ostrom 1990). To the extent that these associations are solving the problems of their members, their capacity to do so may be legitimated by mechanisms of "associative democracy" (Cohen/Rogers 1992). Beyond that, however, the capacity of associations to contribute to the problem-solving capacity of society at large is mainly owed to the fact that they are performing these functions "in the shadow of the state": In corporatist countries they may be created or subsidized by the state; their membership, their organization, and their procedures may be determined by state law; and they are likely to operate under the more or less close supervision of state authorities and under the ever present possibility that their functions may be taken over by public agencies themselves or that their institutional structure might be modified to better suit policy purposes pursued by the state. In pluralist systems, by contrast, the directive capacity of the state is more limited. Nevertheless, the fact that negotiated compromises among economic and social interest groups can make use of the enforcement machinery of public administration creates a regulatory capacity that goes far beyond anything that could be achieved by purely self-organized private-interest governments.

None of this, to be sure, could be described as "hierarchical coordination" in the sense defined earlier (Teubner/Willke 1984). Policy choices are not preempted by the unilateral prerogatives of hierarchical authority but rather are largely shaped by negotiations among, and hence by constellations of preferences and perceptions of, the groups affected. Nevertheless, the fact that these negotiations are embedded in a hierarchical or majoritarian authority structure will have a powerful influence on the "drift" of interactions and on the outcomes that they are likely to produce. As a consequence, the problem-solving capacity of hierarchical authority structures reaches beyond the narrow limits of hierarchical coordination. By empowering and shaping associations in civil society and negotiation systems involving such associations, the welfare-theoretic advantages of self-organization and negotiated agreement can be harnessed to serve public purposes, and the fundamental limitations of negotiation systems can be corrected by the creation of "artificial" bargaining power in negotiation regimes and joint-decision systems.

## GOVERNANCE WITHOUT BOUNDARY CONTROL

It must be understood, however, that these beneficial effects of embedded negotiation systems depend, on the one hand, on the potential effectiveness of the hierarchical authority of the state and, on the other, on the capacity of self-regulating associations effectively to impose rules that in the individual case may not conform to the short-term self-interest of their members. The latter capacity, I have argued, does often depend on the former. Conceptually and historically, however, the hierarchical authority of the state is tightly linked to the concept of *sovereignty*—defined as the internally superior and externally independent authority over a (territorially) limited domain (Held 1991; Hindess 1991; Ruggie 1993). It depends, in other words, on the capacity of the state to control its own boundaries against the outside world. The reason for this follows directly from the discussion of Figure 8.1 at the beginning of the previous chapter: Hierarchical authority ceases to be effective if negative sanctions can easily be avoided through low-cost exit options, and the same is true of the self-governing capacity of associations (Streeck 1992).

### Transnational Interdependence

With this in mind, it is now possible to address the second question raised in the introduction to this chapter: What could account for the widespread impression that the problem-solving capacity of the nation-state is increasingly overwhelmed by the problems with which it is confronted? What has in fact changed significantly since the mid-1970s is the extent to which the territorially limited authority of the nation-state has itself become *embedded in ever tighter contexts of transnational interdependence.* This is true of transnational migration, of transnational terrorism and organized crime, of transnational environmental pollution, and of transnational communication, all of which have significantly increased since the early postwar decades, and all of which represent challenges to the capacity of nation-states to deal effectively with problems (and opportunities) that are of major concern to their citizens. The major constraint on national problem-solving capacity is, however, caused by the reintegration of global capital markets and transnational markets for goods and services.[6]

The relationship between the political system and the economic system is problematic in principle (Luhmann 1988b). Thus the collapse of the centrally planned economies of socialist states is widely interpreted as confirmation of the Hayekian doctrine according to which the hierarchical authority of the state could not possibly coordinate the myriad investment, employment, production, and consumption decisions in modern complex economies. In capitalist democracies, therefore, these are in fact left to coordination by the market. However, the capitalist economy, if left to itself, not only will produce wealth and employment opportunities but also is known to generate financial "bubbles" and crashes, recurrent cyclical and structural crises of the real economy, massive negative externalities, and highly unequal distributions of incomes and life chances. These are effects that must be of obvious concern for democratically accountable governments.

At the same time, the political viability of democratic polities has itself become crucially dependent on the performance of their economies, which directly determines the economic welfare of citizens and voters and which generates the tax revenues to finance government services and welfare spending. There is no question, therefore, that massive failures of economic performance, as in the Great Depression of the 1930s, not only will destroy political support for the government of the day but also may undercut the legitimacy of democratic government altogether. In short, *democratic governments cannot plan and control the operations of the economic system, but they also cannot live with the crises and distributive injustices generated by uncontrolled capitalism.* The dilemma is greatly exacerbated by the fact that the capitalist economy tends to ignore national boundaries and to evolve toward global integration, whereas political interventions are constrained by the boundaries of the territorial state.

### The Rise and Fall of National Boundary Control

Nevertheless, in the "Great Transformation" (Polanyi 1957) after the end of World War II the dilemma seemed to have lost its force. The Great Depression had unleashed the rampant protectionism of all industrial countries, which eventually destroyed the world market. Nation-states everywhere reasserted their boundary control, imposing strict regulations on capital exports and protecting national producers through import quotas and high tariff barriers. The result was a dramatic decline not only of world trade but also of world production (Kindleberger 1995). But behind these protectionist barriers, national policy makers finally learned to intervene without preempting microeconomic choices. Using the Keynesian techniques of macroeconomic demand management, they generally succeeded in maintaining full employment and steady economic growth, which then permitted the expansion of mass incomes, public services, and welfare transfers. Moreover, since imports could be controlled, national taxes and regulations as well as industry-wide collective bargaining would equally affect all firms in direct competition with one another—which meant that their cost could in fact be passed on to consumers without endangering the return on capital investments. In short, during the postwar decades democratic governments were able to approximate normative criteria of general welfare and distributive justice even in the economic sphere—and they were able to do so without endangering the vitality of their capitalist economies.

During the same period, world markets for goods, services, and capital were gradually liberalized and integrated again within the framework of U.S.-led international economic regimes (Keohane 1984) that respected the need of national governments to protect the welfare of their citizens against unmanageable disruptions (Ruggie 1982). Things changed radically, however, when the breakdown of the Bretton Woods regime of fixed but adjustable exchange rates, combined with the oil-price crises of the 1970s, unleashed the explosive growth of completely unregulated "offshore" financial markets while technological innovations undercut the effectiveness of any remaining national controls over capital transfers (Cerny 1994). At the same time, the liberalization of markets for goods and services was also pushed to new extremes by the further progress of GATT and World Trade Organization (WTO) negotiations and by the spread of deregulation and privatization policies from the United States and Britain to the rest of the OECD world. Within the European Community, finally, even the remaining legal barriers protecting national economies were abolished by the successful completion of the "internal market" at the end of 1992.

As a result, the territorial state has again lost control over its own economic boundaries. Financial assets are now completely mobile around the globe, and any national policy that would unilaterally raise taxes on capital incomes or reduce the expected rate of return on investments would be followed by massive capital flight (Sinn 1993). At the same time, the world market for goods and services is now more integrated, and domestic producers now face more competition from abroad than ever before. Within the European Union, moreover, firms are completely free to shop for the most attractive location of production without losing access to their home market, and national governments are legally (and effectively) constrained from adopting any policy that could be construed as a distortion of competition in favor of domestic producers (Kapteyn 1996; Scharpf 1996). And since domestic firms can no longer be protected from foreign competitors, there is also massive pressure to avoid regulations with purely national effect that might damage the international competitiveness of domestic firms.

In other words, in comparison with the early postwar decades, the hierarchical authority of national governments over economic actors is now reduced by two types of constraints: First, capital owners and mobile firms now have exit options that either they did not have at all before the 1970s or that are now significantly more attractive than they were before. Looking again at Figure 8.1, this implies that the capacity of governments (or unions for that matter) to induce capital owners and firms to comply with regulations or taxes (or wage settlements) that they consider to be burdensome has been greatly reduced. Second, even with regard to economic actors that are not themselves mobile across borders but that are exposed to international competition, governments must now respect the fact that higher costs cannot be passed on to consumers any longer and that burdensome regulations will destroy firms and workplaces, which, in periods of high unemployment, would be politically self-defeating.

Moreover, since the exit options of national firms, and the competitiveness of foreign suppliers, are affected by the regulatory and tax policies of other governments and by the strategies of unions in other countries, national governments and unions now must compete with other locations under conditions resembling a noncooperative Prisoner's Dilemma game. As a result, all national policy makers may find themselves making greater concessions to capital and business interests than any of them would have preferred.[7] The need to attract mobile capital and business and to maintain the international competitiveness of the national economy has obvious and significant consequences for distribution: Capital incomes have risen, and income from labor has fallen behind, while governments everywhere had to shift the tax burden from mobile to relatively immobile factors—that is, primarily onto wage incomes and consumer spending (Sinn 1993; Steinmo 1994). As a consequence, the welfare state is under siege even in countries like Sweden, where there existed a strong political commitment to its continuation (Canova 1994; Freeman 1995; Pierson 1996b).

There is not much point in speculating about what rising and long-term unemployment, increasing inequality, and the erosion of welfare-state protection will do to the legitimacy of democratic government. On the one hand, there have been theoretical analyses that even in the heyday of the welfare state in the early 1970s warned of the inevitable "legitimacy crisis of the state" under conditions of "late capitalism" (Offe 1972; 1984; Habermas 1973; 1976); and on the other hand we know that, unlike Weimar Germany, most democratic states did in fact survive the Great Depression, the war, and postwar poverty without lasting damage to their political legitimacy. There is no question, nevertheless, that political legitimacy would be easier to maintain if somehow the ruinous competition among national regulatory regimes could be brought under control.

## The Limits of Supranational Governance

That, above all, is the hope associated with the development of international co-operation, international regimes, and international and supranational organizations: Problems that can no longer be effectively dealt with at the level of the nation-state might again be brought under control if the political system could also expand its operations to a scale that is commensurate with that of economic interactions (or of ecological externalities and the worldwide web of communications, for that matter). The difficulties associated with this solution can be expressed in a nutshell: In the absence of (U.S.) hegemony, policy solutions at the transnational level must be obtained through one of two modes of interaction—either through unilateral action or through negotiations among national governments, international organizations, nongovernmental organizations, and firms. For the first case, I have shown in Chapter 5 that unilateral action, in the form either of noncooperative games or of Mutual Adjustment, is likely to lead to outcomes that are welfare deficient except under special circumstances. For the second case, I have shown in Chapter 6 that outcomes depending on negotiated agreement are potentially welfare efficient but will, even under favorable institutional conditions, be afflicted by high transaction costs. In any case, however, negotiation systems will not be able to deal effectively with issues involving high levels of distributive conflict among the parties to the negotiation.[8] Thus transnational governance is likely to lack the majoritarian or hierarchical capabilities that have assured the effectiveness of public-interest–oriented policymaking at the national level.

Empirically these analytical implications of transnational governance are best exemplified by the European Union, which has created an internal market in which the movement of goods, services, capital, firms, and persons across national boundaries is almost as unconstrained as are movements across provincial or state boundaries in long-established federal states such as the United States, Canada, Germany, and Switzerland. At the same time, the political and legal system of the EU is also more comprehensive, more authoritative, and more resourceful than are the institutional arrangements of any other international organization (Weiler 1981). Nevertheless, it is far from clear that the EU will be able to develop governance capacities that can assume the functions that its member states are no longer able to perform in the internal market. To appreciate the magnitude of the problem, it seems useful to take a look at the vertical division of governance functions in nation-states with a federal constitution.

In these federal states, subnational units of government—states, provinces, *Länder,* or *Kantone*—have long been confronted with the fact that their own territorial jurisdiction is more narrowly circumscribed than the (effectively national) boundaries of the market and that they are constitutionally constrained to respect the freedom of border-crossing movements and economic transactions. As a consequence, all federal systems have been confronted with the same choice of either moving responsibility for policies raising the production costs of mobile firms "upward" to the national level or avoiding such policies altogether (CEPR 1993). An instructive historical example is provided by the failure of child-labor legislation in the United States in the early decades of the twentieth century (Graebner 1977). Since regulation of the conditions of production was considered to be beyond the reach of the federal power over interstate commerce, and the states were prohibited from interfering with interstate commerce, those states that attempted to limit the employment of children in industrial production found that their industries were outcompeted by imports from states that still allowed child labor. In fact, therefore, child labor continued unabated even in "progressive" states until the New Deal "constitutional revolution" finally permitted regulation at the federal level after 1937.

The lesson seems clear: Within federal states the hierarchical power of local or regional governments (or unions) is limited by the exit options that capital owners and firms have in a nationally unified market. In effect they will be unable to raise the unit costs[9] of production above, or to reduce the rate of return on capital investments below, the terms prevailing in other regions of the same market. The implication, which was and is generally accepted in federal states, is that regulations and taxes that impose burdens on business or capital must be adopted at the national level, if they are to be adopted at all. The same is now becoming true for the European market.[10] Once the process of market integration and monetary union is completed, therefore, the conclusion seems inevitable that member states must either agree effectively to "Europeanize" all those competencies that had been "nationalized" for economic reasons in the past or else accept a significant reduction of their capacity to regulate the economy and to tax capital owners and businesses. Thus to insist on national "sovereignty" while promoting full market integration is a position that makes sense only from neoliberal or Hayekian premises, according to which the welfare state of the postwar decades was an aberration, and general welfare is best promoted by unregulated markets.

But even if the Europeanization of economy-related competencies were accepted as the necessary consequence of the completion of the internal market, it is important to realize that the institutional conditions under which these competencies will be exercised at the European level differ fundamentally from those prevailing in national political systems. There the hierarchical power of the state, exercised by democratically accountable governments and by majority vote in parliaments constituted by general elections, exists as a "fleet in being" even if actual policies are worked out in complex negotiations among the interests affected. In the European Union, by contrast, hierarchical imposition exists as a last resort only for one specific type of policies, labeled "negative integration." These are policies that abolish and prevent national regulations and government actions that interfere with the free movement of goods, services, capital, and persons in the European market. In other words, these policies are part of the *problem, rather than the solution* to the decline of national governance capacity. Since negative integration can be derived from the obligations undertaken by governments in the original treaties, it can indeed be imposed "hierarchically" by decisions and directives of the European Commission and by the judgments and preliminary rulings of the European Court of Justice (Weiler 1981; 1994; Burley/Mattli 1993). But by itself negative integration can only result in wholesale deregulation in many important policy areas (Scharpf 1996).

Measures of "positive integration," by contrast, cannot be hierarchically imposed by the Commission or the Court. They depend on the agreement of national governments in the Council of Ministers and thus on negotiations that are embedded not in a superarching framework of hierarchical authority but in an institutional context, which in our terminology would be characterized in part as a transnational regime and in part as a joint-decision system.[11] The involvement, in various modalities, of the European Parliament has thus far had only the effect of *adding one more veto position* to the negotiations among national governments. In contrast to the role of national elections, elections to the European Parliament do not have the effect of legitimating a European government and thus of strengthening its *political* weight in interactions with the governments of member states, nor will the anticipation of European elections (or of national elections embedded in a Europe-wide context of political attention and opinion formation) put pressure on national governments to reach agreement in the Council.[12] In comparison with the hierarchical power of democratically accountable national governments, therefore, the problem-solving capacity of the European Union, though surely much greater than the capacity of other international regimes, is still quite limited.

Negotiation regimes and joint-decision systems, as I showed earlier, work best in constellations resembling games of pure coordination where the interests of all member governments are convergent, and they work least well in policy areas characterized by high levels of conflict among member states. For the European Union, this explains the coexistence of areas—such as the harmonization of product-related health and safety standards—in which European regulations have been very successful indeed (Eichener 1995) and other areas—such as social policy and industrial relations policy—where progress at the European level has been extremely limited (Leibfried/Pierson 1995; Scharpf 1996). Given the fact that the European Union includes some of the economically most advanced countries and some member states that have barely risen above the level of threshold economies and that among the more developed countries deep institutional cleavages are standing in the way of harmonizing welfare-state provisions, that could hardly be otherwise (Scharpf 1997).[13] But as a consequence, the European policymaking system is blocked precisely in those areas in which national problem-solving capacity is most severely damaged by the market integration at the European level.

In theory, this obstacle could be overcome by a general move to majority voting in the Council of Ministers and by granting a more decisive political role to the European Parliament. As a consequence, the Council might be reduced to a role similar to that of the German *Bundesrat*, and the European Commission, elected by and responsible to the European Parliament, would become the democratically legitimated government of Europe.[14] However, since constitutional reforms in the EU depend on the unanimous agreement of national governments and parliaments, the evolution of European institutions is still caught in its "joint-decision trap" (Scharpf 1988), and it remains most unlikely that such recommendations will in fact be followed.

But even if they were adopted, the effectiveness of European policymaking would be restricted by the European "democratic deficit" (Williams 1991). Democratic legitimacy, I have tried to show, cannot be derived from majority rule by itself. Self-interested majorities would maximize their own advantage at the expense of the common interest and in violation of criteria of distributive justice. In other words, the mechanics of democratic accountability can only convey legitimacy if it is true, and generally understood, that voters are oriented not only to their immediate self-interest but also toward the common interest and that elected officials are exposed to mechanisms of accountability that are likely to be triggered by violations of the common interest.

These would depend on the existence of a competitive European party system, of European media, and of Europe-wide political controversies in which a democratically accountable European "government" would have to hold its own in order to survive the next elections. As of now this institutional infrastructure of democratic accountability is not yet in place, and even if it could be created, the most important precondition would still be lacking. As I pointed out earlier, democratic legitimacy presupposes a *collective identity* and public discourses about common interests and rules of fair distribution based on that common identity (March/Olsen 1995). Western Europe may be moving in that direction, but it is still far from having a collective identity that could legitimate majoritarian choices in the face of conflicts among intense national interests, even if these are not defined in purely ethnic terms (Howe 1995; Weiler 1995; Habermas 1995). As a consequence, even far-reaching constitutional changes, if they could be adopted, would not immediately create conditions under which a majority vote in the European Parliament would be accepted as legitimate by those whose deeply held preferences or vital interests are violated.[15] A fortiori that would be true of majority decisions in the Council of Ministers: By what mechanism could the governments of the new north-central European majority be held accountable to the citizens of the southern rim? Or why should Austrians have to accept the preferences of Denmark, Holland, Germany, and Italy on the issue of transalpine road haulage?

Since the democratic legitimacy of decisions reached above the national level is precarious even in the European Union—and not even claimed for other international organizations, such as the North Atlantic Treaty Organization or the International Monetary Fund or the World Trade Organization or the United Nations and its special organizations—we are left with an unresolved problem. And though the relationship of democratic governance at the national level to the growing transnational interdependence of policy choices has now become a major concern of normative democratic theory (Bobbio 1984; Dahl 1989; Held 1991; Hindess 1991; Böhret/Wewer 1993; Hirst/Thompson 1995), I think it is fair to say that normatively convincing and empirically plausible solutions have not been proposed thus far. For the time being, at any rate, it seems most appropriate to conceptualize the policies emerging from transnational interactions not as being democratically legitimate in their own right but either as being based on non-majoritarian concepts of legitimacy, such as technical expertise or the authority of the law (Majone 1989; 1994; 1995; Dehousse 1995), or as being indirectly derived from the legitimacy of national governments that are accountable to their own national electorates (Grimm 1995).

But these are weak forms of legitimation that cannot convey a capacity to act in the face of strongly divergent preferences based on intensely held values or vital interests. On the one hand, technical expertise will only suffice to justify the choice of efficient means in situations in which the goals are beyond dispute (Majone 1989), and the authority of, as it were, "freestanding" law is ultimately restricted to the explication of a preexisting normative consensus (Bickel 1962). On the other hand, to rely on the indirect democratic legitimacy conveyed by the assent of national governments has the unfortunate consequence of freezing the European Union in its present condition of an intergovernmental negotiation system in which even the move from unanimity to qualified-majority voting in the Council of Ministers is of doubtful legitimacy. This also implies that conflicts of interest among national governments will continue to constrain the problem-solving capacity of the EU to the level that can be attained through negotiations in transnational regimes and joint-decision systems.

It is not to be expected, therefore, that capabilities lost at the national level as a consequence of the creation of transnational or global markets could be regained at the European level (let alone at the level of the World Trade Organization or similar international bodies). There is a real danger, therefore, that the legitimacy of European nation-states will be undercut by the widespread perceptions of their growing impotence in the face of transnational and global market forces while the emergence of legitimate and effective governance at the European level is prevented by the lack of democratic accountability. Normatively convincing, practically effective, and politically feasible solutions are nowhere in sight. Thus European democracies may, for some time to come, have to cope with, rather than solve, the problems described. In the meantime, it would follow from the analysis suggested here that the best chance over the medium term might be associated with simultaneous moves in opposite directions: On the one hand, one should hope that *political integration* will go forward to strengthen the legitimacy and capacity of European governance by increasing the political accountability of the European Commission and the political visibility and salience of votes in the

European Parliament. On the other hand, it would seem desirable to slow the relentless progress of *economic integration* by relaxing some of the legal constraints of negative integration and by allowing member states to regain some degree of control over their economic boundaries (Scharpf 1996).

But these are questions beyond the scope of a book that is meant to be about the *tools of political analysis* rather than about the analysis of a specific political constellation. They have been raised here merely to show how the analytical tools presented in the preceding chapters can indeed be employed to advantage in order to clarify some of the most vexing problems of multilevel governance in an ever more interdependent world. Whether I have succeeded in this demonstration remains, of course, for the reader to judge.

## NOTES

1. The background assumptions of Andreas Ryll's game-theoretic model are a bit complicated: Sickness funds compete for members, and they differ in the risk composition of their membership. It is further assumed that patients think that doctors will pay more attention to the members of better-paying funds. With this in mind, physicians' associations will begin the annual round of fee negotiations by dealing with those funds that have the most favorable risk composition among their members (and hence the highest ability to pay without having to raise membership charges). In order to avoid a competitive disadvantage, however, other sickness funds will then find themselves compelled to accept these more favorable settlements as well (which then forces them to raise contributions).

2. These forms of "collibrating" intervention have been systematically analyzed by Andrew Dunsire (1993; 1996).

3. In this context, the objective weakness of hierarchical coordination is turned into a tactical strength. The fact that the government has a serious "Hayekian" information deficit and that, as a consequence, unilateral administrative action might be unnecessarily burdensome increases the incentive for industry to avoid this eventuality.

4. In the industrial training example, industry cooperation lapsed after the statute authorizing the training levy was struck down by the Constitutional Court on procedural grounds and when it became clear that the Social-Liberal government did not have the votes in the (opposition-dominated) *Bundesrat* to pass it again.

5. At the time of this writing, the "cooperation principle" is again employed in a major role: On March 27, 1996, the German government announced that its plans for an energy tax or a carbon dioxide tax were being shelved in exchange for a commitment by nineteen industrial associations to reduce aggregate carbon dioxide emissions by 20 percent in comparison to the 1990 level by the year 2005 (FAZ 1996). Other examples where self-regulation in the shadow of the state has been effective in Germany include regulations governing the security of bank deposits (Ronge 1979; Deeg 1993) and the control of stock exchanges.

6. I distinguish between capital markets and other markets because only the former have become truly global, whereas markets for goods and services, though surely transcending national boundaries, are still segmented by the importance of transportation costs and by significant differences in consumer tastes and consumption cultures.

7. It should be recognized that the effect of regulatory competition is not necessarily a "race to the bottom." As is true in the market, there may be quality competition as well as

cost competition. Thus regulations that protect the quality of goods and services that are important (and sufficiently visible) to consumers may be pushed to higher levels by regulatory competition. This was the case, for instance, for regulations prohibiting insider trading in the German stock market. Thus the race-to-the-bottom hypothesis applies only to regulations (or taxes and levies) raising the cost of production without improving the attractiveness of the product in the eyes of the consumer. This class, unfortunately, includes most environmental and all welfare-state regulations.

8. The qualification is important. What matters is the actor constellation among negotiators. Thus what at the societal level might appear as a zero-sum case of class conflict may at the level of transnational negotiations appear as a Battle of the Sexes or a Prisoner's Dilemma game among the national governments involved.

9. It is important to realize that what matters economically are not costs as such but *unit costs*—that is, factor costs corrected for differences in *factor productivity*—which, among other things, are affected by state-provided training, infrastructure, and services. For that reason, highly productive national economies can remain internationally competitive in spite of relatively high production costs. Productivity, in turn, is affected both by factor input per physical unit of production and by the price obtained for that unit. Thus highly innovative economies that can obtain above-average prices for novel or highly attractive goods may remain competitive even if their production processes are not the most efficient.

10. It is not yet quite true for two reasons: On the one hand, national differences in consumer tastes persist in Europe to a much larger degree than is the case for interregional differences in national markets, and linguistic barriers to mobility also remain significant, at least for small and middle-sized firms. On the other hand, since the European Monetary Union is not yet in place, nation-states still retain the power to devaluate the currency in order to neutralize above-average increases of production cost.

11. It is true that this "intergovernmentalist" view will not do justice to the de facto influence of supranational institutions such as the European Commission or the European Court of Justice (Weiler 1992; Schneider/Werle 1990; Burley/Mattli 1993)—but this influence is much more relevant for "negative integration" than for "positive integration."

12. In my article on the "joint-decision trap" (Scharpf 1988) I emphasized the institutional parallels between German federalism and the European Community without examining the differences caused by the presence or absence of electoral politics. In a nutshell, European negotiations are not encumbered by party-political conflicts and by the risks of "divided government" (Dehousse 1995), but neither are they expedited by the threat that governing parties *at both levels* could lose Europe-wide political support.

13. The argument was spelled out in Chapter 4.

14. This was the vision of the Spinelli draft (1985) of a European constitution adopted by the European Parliament—only to be completely ignored by the Commission and member states in their reform initiatives leading to the Single European Act and to Maastricht.

15. The point is well established by Joseph Weiler's (1995) thought experiment: If Denmark were somehow annexed to a democratic Germany, would a majority vote in the *Bundestag* create legitimacy for the Danes?

# Appendix 1

# A Game-Theoretical Interpretation of Inflation and Unemployment in Western Europe

## INTRODUCTION

Political scientists and economists with a comparative bent have for some time been fascinated by the opportunities for theory testing and theory building provided by the large-scale "natural experiment" of the worldwide economic crisis that began in the early 1970s. Compared to the preceding decade, the middle and late 1970s and the early 1980s were indeed a difficult period for all industrialized Western (OECD) countries. Economic growth and employment growth were reduced by half, while rates of unemployment and inflation levels were on the average twice as high.[1]

But even as the average economic and employment performance of OECD countries declined after 1973, the relative distance between more and less successful countries increased considerably for most indicators of economic performance. Equally interesting is the fact that cross-national differences do not seem to correspond to conventional economic hypotheses (Therborn 1986). Even the almost tautological link between economic growth and employment is weak ($r^2 = .32$); there is no statistical association between employment growth and levels of unemployment (which are affected not only by the course of the economy but also by changes of the supply of labor); and the relationships between economic and employment growth on the one hand and inflation on the other hand are also extremely weak.

Similarly, a glance at a scatterplot of the two indicators with the greatest political salience, inflation and unemployment, does not confirm expectations (associated with the once-popular Phillips curve) of a strongly negative correlation. The correlation is weakly positive, instead, and there have been countries with low and others with high rates of inflation at every level of unemployment (Figure A1.1). Confronted with the worldwide crisis, OECD countries apparently have achieved widely differing profiles of economic performance—some reaching a compromise among several goals, some doing poorly in most respects, and some doing well in one dimension and poorly in another.

Political scientists have been attracted by this body of economically unexplained variance. Cross-national quantitative studies, focusing on the party-political orientation of

First published in *Journal of Public Policy* 7 (1987):227–257.

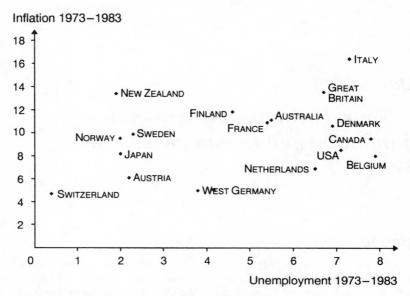

FIGURE A1.1    Inflation and unemployment in OECD countries, 1973–1983
$(r = .33; r^2 = .11)$

national governments, were initially able to show that left-of-center governments were associated with lower rates of unemployment and higher rates of inflation than conservative
governments (Hibbs 1977). When that relationship, which had been established for the
1960s, did not hold up in the 1970s, the focus shifted to "tripartite" institutional arrangements linking the state with the peak associations of capital and labor, whose relevance for
the general "governability" of countries had been postulated by Philippe Schmitter's
(1974; 1981) theory of "neocorporatism." In particular, it could be shown in a considerable number of studies using a variety of indicators that, by and large, countries with powerful, organizationally concentrated and centralized labor movements and left-of-center
governments had done relatively well in economic terms during the 1970s (Cameron
1978; 1984; Schmidt 1982; 1983; Paloheimo 1984; Lange/Garrett 1985).

But, once again, the explanations that were successful in one decade did not survive far
into the next. Some of the former model countries got into trouble in the 1980s, and other
countries that were clearly not dominated by parties of the left, and in which organized labor was weak and fragmented, were doing relatively well. In response, the "corporatist"
model was revised to emphasize the functional equivalence of labor-dominated concerta-
tions between organized economic interests and the state, and of Japanese- or Swiss-style
"corporatism without labor" (Schmidt 1986; Garrett/Lange 1986; Wilensky/Turner 1987).

On the whole, it seems fair to say that these cross-national political science studies have
not yet converged upon an explanatory model that is stable over time and theoretically
well grounded (Therborn 1986). It is also easy to identify the reasons for these deficiencies: Governments of differing political complexion may indeed have specific political
preferences—but their ability to translate these into effective public policy is institutionally constrained, and the outcomes of effective public policy are crucially dependent upon

changing economic circumstances. Thus the extension of explanatory models to include (neocorporatist) institutional arrangements was a step in the right direction that did not go far enough. However difficult, we must try to disentangle the interaction among changes in the economic environment, the economic strategy choices available to national policy makers, and the institutional conditions facilitating and constraining such choices if we hope to develop explanations of economic performance that are not so easily upset by the mere passage of time (Scharpf 1984; Hall 1986; Martin 1986a). In the present paper I will try to develop a more comprehensive, yet still relatively parsimonious explanatory model of the macroeconomic policy choices of Western European countries during the 1970s and early 1980s.

## THE PUZZLE

In the spirit of the "most similar case" approach (Przeworski/Teune 1970), the following analysis is based on comparative studies of the economic and employment policies pursued by four Western European countries, Austria, Great Britain, Sweden, and West Germany (Scharpf 1981; 1984; 1987). All of them were governed, in the first critical years after 1973, by Socialist, Social-Democratic, or Labour parties that had a clear political commitment to maintaining full employment. Furthermore, on the eve of the crisis, all four countries had found themselves in rather similar, and on the whole quite comfortable, economic circumstances. Britain, in particular, had not at all looked like the "sick man of Europe" in 1973, achieving the highest rate of economic growth (7.6%) and doing relatively well on inflation. By comparison, Austria and Sweden (with growth rates of 4.9% and 4.0% respectively) might have had more reason to be worried about their relative performance. Yet immediately after the onset of the crisis in the fall of 1973, the four countries began to move apart economically.

Between 1974 and 1979 (when the Labour party left office), Britain became clearly the worst case of the four, with the lowest rate of average economic growth (1.5%), by far the highest rate of inflation (16%), and the highest unemployment (5.0%) as well. By contrast, Austria now had the best all-around record, with the highest economic growth (2.9%), the second-lowest inflation (6.0%), and the lowest unemployment (1.8%). Even more interesting is the contrast between the two countries with intermediate performances: West Germany suffered the largest increase in unemployment compared to 1973 (from 0.8% to an average of 3.2%) and achieved the greatest degree of price stability (4.8%); Sweden was even able to reduce unemployment during the first five years of the crisis (from 3.0% to 1.9%) but suffered from two-digit inflation (10.6%) in the 1974–1979 period.

In order to explain this puzzle of widely diverging economic outcomes in the face of similar policy preferences and starting conditions, it is necessary to begin with a brief analysis of the economic environment and strategy choices of industrialized countries in the early 1970s. In a nutshell, the dominant economic problem of the 1970s was "stagflation"—i.e., the simultaneous occurrence of exceptionally high rates of inflation and of levels of mass unemployment unheard of in the postwar period. In order to understand its intractability, it is useful to distinguish between causes on the demand side and on the supply side of the markets for goods and services (Malinvaud 1977). Inflation could be either of the "demand-pull" or the "cost-push" variety, and unemployment could be either "Keynesian" (if firms were unable to sell as much as they would have liked to produce at current prices and costs) or "classical" (if firms did not find it profitable to produce more

**Source of Problem**

|  | Demand Side | Supply Side |
|---|---|---|
| **Nature of Problem** | | |
| Inflation | Demand-Pull Inflation | Cost-Push Inflation |
| Unemployment | Demand-Gap ("Keynesian") Unemployment | Profit-Gap ("Classical") Unemployment |

FIGURE A1.2    Typology of economic policy problems in the 1970s

at current prices and costs). It was also possible that more than one type of problem was manifest at a given time (Figure A1.2).

In the early 1970s the world economy had already suffered from a good deal of demand inflation, which had been initiated by the U.S. decision to finance the Vietnam War without raising taxes. Price rises accelerated significantly, however, when the powerful cost push of a raw-materials boom and of the first oil crisis was added in 1973–1974. At the same time, the twelvefold increase of the oil bill within a few months constituted a sudden transfer of purchasing power from the oil-consuming industrial countries to the oil-exporting countries. As these were not immediately able to spend their new wealth in the international markets for goods and services, OPEC surpluses jumped from US$8 billion in 1973 to $60 billion in 1974 (*OECD Economic Outlook* 28:125). The immediate consequence was a demand gap of corresponding magnitude in the industrialized countries, which, if it was not compensated, would generate "Keynesian" unemployment.

For this combination of cost-push inflation and demand-gap unemployment, national macroeconomic policy makers and the prevailing practice of Keynesian demand management were ill prepared. Their major policy instruments were government fiscal policy and central-bank monetary policy.[2] Both could be used to reflate aggregate demand, by increasing government expenditures or cutting taxes and by increasing the money supply and lowering interest rates. Alternatively, both instruments could be used restrictively, by reducing the fiscal deficit and the money supply. As both sets of instruments affect the same parameters of aggregate demand, they needed to be employed in parallel in order to be effective. Under the conditions of stagflation, that meant that governments were able to fight either inflation or unemployment, but not both at the same time. Worse yet, in trying to solve one problem they would aggravate the other (Figure A1.3).

The dilemma could be avoided only if economic policy makers were not limited to the use of fiscal and monetary policy but were also able to influence wage settlements, which, although they affect aggregate demand as well, have a larger and more direct impact upon the supply side of the economy (Figure A1.4). Thus the inclusion of wage policy in the macroeconomic tool kit greatly increased the range of problems that macroeconomic policy could deal with (Weintraub 1978).

| Fiscal and Monetary Policy | Demand-Gap Unemployment | Cost-Push Inflation |
|---|---|---|
| expansionary | helps a lot | hurts |
| restrictive | hurts a lot | helps |

FIGURE A1.3    Effects of fiscal and monetary policy under conditions of stagflation

| Wage Policy | Demand-Gap Unemployment | Cost-Push Inflation |
|---|---|---|
| moderate | hurts | helps a lot |
| aggressive | helps | hurts a lot |

FIGURE A1.4    Effects of wage policy under conditions of stagflation

Quite apart from the controversy about whether unions were actually responsible for the rise of inflation in the early 1970s, the direct impact of wages on the costs of production made wage restraint a highly plausible defense against the rising tide of cost-push inflation. In practical terms, that meant that the unions would need to refrain from exploiting their full bargaining power—which was considerable as long as the government was able to maintain full employment. In order to succeed, they would have to accept settlements that, when discounted by the increase of labor productivity, kept the rise of unit labor costs below the current rate of inflation.[3] In exchange, the government was then free to use its own policy instruments to reflate aggregate demand in order to maintain full employment (Figure A1.5).

If that "Keynesian concertation" of government and union strategies was practiced, it was possible to avoid both a steep rise of unemployment and runaway inflation, even under the crisis conditions of the mid-1970s (but not in the 1980s).[4] If, however, the unions were unwilling or unable to practice wage restraint, inflation would continue; and if the government would not reflate the economy, unemployment would increase. In actual practice, the four countries differed significantly in their ability to achieve, and to maintain, a pattern of Keynesian concertation between macroeconomic policy and union wage policy.

In 1974 the immediate response of government policy to the beginning crisis was expansionary in all countries except West Germany—and even there the fiscal deficit increased as much as it did in the other three countries. The overall deflationary effect was due to the tight-money policy of the central bank. At the same time, the unions in all four countries continued their more or less aggressive wage strategies.[5] As a consequence, employment was

**Wage Policy**

| Fiscal and Monetary Policy | moderate | aggressive |
|---|---|---|
| expansionary | Inflation: moderate<br>Unemployment: low | Inflation: very high<br>Unemployment: low |
| restrictive | Inflation: low<br>Unemployment: high | Inflation: high<br>Unemployment: very high |

FIGURE A1.5   Levels of inflation and unemployment as outcomes of government and union strategies under conditions of stagflation

stabilized in all countries except West Germany, which suffered very large job losses in the 1974–1976 period but had the lowest rate of inflation of all OECD countries.

By 1976, however, the severity of the crisis was realized, and unions had begun to moderate their wage claims in most countries—earliest in Germany and most dramatically in Britain, where inflation had exceeded 24 percent in 1975. As a consequence of the "social contract" of 1975 (which had limited wage and salary increases for 1976 to six pounds per week for everyone), unit labor cost increases were brought down from 32.6 percent in 1975 to 12.7 percent (and hence below the current level of price inflation) in 1976. Only in Sweden did the unions still pursue an aggressive wage policy, while the "bourgeois" coalition government, new in office after more than forty years of Social-Democratic rule, was doing everything in its power to defend full employment.

After another two years, in 1978, policy coordination had improved in West Germany and Sweden and deteriorated again in Great Britain. With inflation below 3 percent, and with the help of considerable U.S. pressure at the Bonn Summit of 1978 (Putnam/Bayne 1984), Chancellor Helmut Schmidt was finally able to persuade the *Bundesbank* of the wisdom and feasibility of a substantial fiscal and monetary reflation of domestic demand. As the unions continued on their course of wage moderation, employment in West Germany profited until 1980 from the country's assumption of the "locomotive" role. In Sweden, the unions now also accepted the need for wage moderation, even though unemployment was actually falling.

By contrast, the British Labour government, in an effort to defend the pound against devaluation and to push down inflation that was still above 15 percent, had switched to a strategy of (moderate) fiscal and monetary restraint in spite of comparatively high levels of unemployment. Inflation finally dipped below 9 percent in 1978, but now the unions were no longer able to uphold their part of the "social contract." The crippling strikes of the "Winter of Discontent" and the high wage settlements that ended it pushed inflation up again and prepared the ground for Margaret Thatcher's election victory in the spring of 1979.

By 1980, therefore, the new British government was practicing a brand of monetarist restraint that was not moderate at all, while the unions initially continued the aggressive wage drive that had led to the defeat of the Labour government. As a consequence, inflation returned to high levels while unemployment began to rise steeply. In the other three countries, Keynesian concertation continued as before, even as the international economic and monetary environment was again worsening under the double impact of the second oil crisis and of the U.S. conversion to monetarism.

But by 1982 the changes in the international environment had worked their way through the policymaking processes of all four countries. Monetary policy became restrictive everywhere, and even Austria and Sweden, which were still, or again, governed by Social Democrats, struggled to reduce fiscal deficits under the compulsion of escalating interest rates in the international financial markets. At the same time, the unions in all four countries, either out of insight or under the compulsion of rapidly rising unemployment, not only moderated their wage claims but also accepted significant real-wage losses. Thus the variance among the macroeconomic strategies of European countries had now all but disappeared.[6]

## THE PERSPECTIVES OF MACROECONOMIC ACTORS

In the 1970s, however, countries still had a choice among macroeconomic strategies with significantly different outcomes. So why were not all of them able to achieve, and maintain, the optimal concertation of fiscal and monetary reflation and union wage moderation that would have defended full employment and price stability at the same time?

The problem was not primarily a cognitive one: After some initial misjudgments of the nature of the crisis, the double threat of cost-push inflation and demand-gap unemployment as well as the characteristics of an economically optimal policy response were well understood in all four countries. Policymakers were also not yet inhibited by the notion that demand reflation might be entirely without effect upon the real economy or that wages ought to be settled entirely by the laws of supply and demand in the market. Collective bargaining was effective in all four countries, and wages were understood as a "political price" whose determination could also be influenced, within limits, by considerations of macroeconomic policy. But it was also understood, explicitly in Britain as part of a pre-election agreement between the Trade Union Congress (TUC) and the Labour Party (Crouch 1982; Bornstein/Gourevitch 1984), and implicitly in the other three countries, that cooperation could not be compelled. The record of statutory wage and price controls in the late 1960s and early 1970s in Britain and in the United States had been so negative (Frye/Gordon 1981) that voluntary wage restraint was the only option seriously considered in the four countries (Flanagan/Soskice/Ulman 1983).

But if the economics of the problem were so essentially simple and reasonably well understood by policymakers, why wasn't the optimal strategy practiced everywhere throughout the whole period? The reason, I suggest, lies in the inevitable discrepancy between the perspective of macroeconomic theory on the one hand and the action perspectives of those "corporate actors" (Coleman 1974) who are actually involved in macroeconomic policy choices on the other hand. They are, each of them, pursuing their own versions of the collective interest—and these are influenced not only by their differing politicoeconomic ideologies but also by the perceptions associated with their specific functional roles ("you stand where you sit") and by their self-interested concerns with organizational survival and growth, reelection, and career advancement. In heroic simplification, it may suffice to distinguish only three sets of such actors—elected governments, central banks, and labor unions[7]—in an attempt to explain macroeconomic outcomes in the 1970s.

Closest to the view implied by macroeconomic analysis is the perspective of *elected governments,* which are held politically accountable for both inflation and unemployment (as well as for tax increases, unbalanced budgets, balance-of-payments crises, and devaluations of the currency). Thus the government view of policy choices and outcomes is likely to correspond to the analysis presented earlier (Figure A1.5). *Labor unions,* however, upon whose cooperation the successful fight against stagflation critically depends, are likely to view the world from a different perspective (Figure A1.6). Although unemployment, or at least the threat of *rising* unemployment, must be of even greater importance to them than it is to governments, inflation is not one of their primary concerns. Instead, it is plausible to assume that they will be preoccupied with real wage increases whenever there is no threat of rising unemployment.[8]

Finally, it may be assumed that *central banks,* if they are sufficiently independent to have an orientation differing from that of the elected government, will tend toward a professional perspective that primarily emphasizes price stability (Figure A1.7). In addition, they are likely to be concerned with the level of capital incomes,[9] whose decline could trigger a sequence of capital outflows, devaluation, and domestic inflation.

## TWO GAMES OF MACROECONOMIC COORDINATION

To summarize: Macroeconomic policy outcomes are not produced by a single, unified actor but by a plurality of corporate actors whose strategies are not automatically coordinated by reference to a common goal or utility function. Furthermore, their choices are "strategically interdependent" in the sense that for all of them, the achievement of their own preferred bundles of outcomes is the joint product of the actions of all participants. If these conditions are granted, it is reasonable to expect that a game-theoretical form of presentation will help to simplify and clarify further analysis. The first task, then, is the construction of one or more payoff matrices that accurately represent both the (perceived) economic outcomes associated with any combination of strategic choices and the valuation of these outcomes by the respective "players."

On the basis of the economic analysis summarized in Figures A1.5, A1.6, and A1.7, the rank ordering of preferences is relatively easy to derive for unions and central banks. By and large, the goals of central banks are fully compatible with one another, so that they will consistently prefer less inflation and higher capital incomes. By comparison, union preferences are conditional, but still unambiguous: Under conditions of full employment, they will prefer higher real wage increases—but if unemployment is rising, their foremost concern must be to save the jobs of their members. Elected governments, however, are faced with a trade-off between inflation and unemployment. They would of course prefer to avoid both problems—but if they cannot do so, they have no obvious once-and-for-all ranking of the possible mixes of outcomes.

In order to simplify, the basic ambivalence of government preferences will be represented by two distinct games of macroeconomic coordination, labeled "Keynesian" and "monetarist." Both are played between the government and the unions;[10] the possible strategies of both sides (expansionary or restrictive fiscal and monetary policy, moderate or aggressive wage policy) are the same in both games; and so are the real-world consequences associated with these strategies. The two games differ only in the assumed valuation of these consequences by the (composite) player "Government."

In the *Keynesian game,* which was in fact played in almost all Western countries after 1973, the government considers unemployment as the most serious problem and treats in-

**Wage Policy**

| Fiscal and Monetary Policy | moderate | aggressive |
|---|---|---|
| expansionary | Real wages: low<br>Unemployment: low | Real wages: moderate<br>Unemployment: low |
| restrictive | Real wages: moderate<br>Unemployment: high | Real wages: high<br>Unemployment: very high |

FIGURE A1.6    Macroeconomic coordination: The union view

**Wage Policy**

| Fiscal and Monetary Policy | moderate | aggressive |
|---|---|---|
| expansionary | Inflation: moderate<br>Capital incomes: moderate | Inflation: very high<br>Capital incomes: low |
| restrictive | Inflation: low<br>Capital incomes: very high | Inflation: high<br>Capital incomes: moderate |

FIGURE A1.7    Macroeconomic coordination: The central-bank view

flation as a secondary (but still important) concern (Figure A1.8). Thus the government would clearly prefer to achieve the macroeconomically optimal "concerted" strategy of fiscal and monetary reflation and union wage restraint in cell 1 of the figure. The worst case for a Keynesian government is the combination of demand deflation and aggressive union wage policy (cell 4), which would lead to very high unemployment rates and still high inflation rates. The remaining two cases are of intermediate attractiveness. Their ordering depends on the relative importance of the concern about inflation.

From a union point of view, however, the government's optimum outcome (cell 1) would be only the second-best solution. As long as full employment is in fact maintained, it is in their immediate self-interest to shift to an aggressive wage policy in order to achieve the best outcome with low unemployment and higher real wages (cell 2). That this outcome is also associated with rising inflation may be an unfortunate side effect for the unions, while it must be a major political concern. Nevertheless, within the Keynesian game, the government could not now switch to a deflationary strategy unless it was willing to accept its own worst-case outcome with very high rates of unemployment (cell 4).

The Keynesian game, however, was not the only one that could be played. If either the central bank was able to impose its own preferences or the government was politically able

**Unions**

| Government | moderate | aggressive |
|---|---|---|
| expansionary | (1)   3<br>  4 | (2)   4<br>  3 |
| restrictive | (3)   2<br>  2 | (4)   1<br>  1 |

FIGURE A1.8    The Keynesian game of macroeconomic coordination. Preferences of both players rank-ordered 4 (best) to 1 (worst)

**Unions**

| Government | moderate | aggressive |
|---|---|---|
| expansionary | (1)   3<br>  3 | (2)   4<br>  1 |
| restrictive | (3)   2<br>  4 | (4)   1<br>  2 |

FIGURE A1.9    The monetarist game of macroeconomic coordination

and willing to treat inflation as the paramount problem and to tolerate high levels of unemployment, the character of the coordination game would change (Figure A1.9). Now the government would most prefer a combination of very low rates of inflation and moderately high unemployment (cell 3), while cell 2, with very high inflation and low unemployment, would become its worst-case outcome.

But if the government is willing to play the monetarist game, the options of the unions deteriorate dramatically. If they continue with an aggressive wage policy (as British unions did for a while after Margaret Thatcher's victory in 1979), they will end up in their own worst-case situation (cell 4), in which profit-gap unemployment caused by excessive wage increases is added on top of the demand-gap unemployment created by government policy. Thus it is now in their self-interest to shift to wage restraint in order to avoid, or at least reduce, further job losses and to improve their expected outcome from the worst case to second-worst (cell 3). For a monetarist government, however, this would be the best outcome, from which it would have no reason to depart.

As the government has a dominant strategy in both games—expansion in the Keynesian, deflation in the monetarist case—both have a game-theoretical equilibrium in which neither side can improve its outcome by a unilateral change of strategy (Rapoport/Guyer/ Gordon 1976, 18). It is in both cases defined by the unions' self-interested response to the government's strategy. Yet the underlying power relations are entirely different: In the Keynesian game, the unions are powerful because of the government's commitment to full employment—and they are entirely powerless when confronted with a monetarist strategy. By exploiting the former they may achieve their best short-term outcome, while they are forced to "collaborate" with the latter in order to avoid their worst-case outcome.[11] At least in the economic environment of the 1970s, union power was very much a function of government strategy.

## THE CHOICE OF COORDINATION GAMES

An explanation of economic outcomes in the 1970s thus needs to focus on the choice between the Keynesian and monetarist games that could have been played. In three of the four countries that choice was formally exercised by elected governments. In West Germany, by contrast, the government's fiscal response to the onset of the crisis (which was as expansionary as that of the other countries) was largely neutralized by the tight-money policy of the central bank. Thus the explanation for the de facto monetarism of West German economic policy in 1974–1975 is primarily to be found in the exceptional degree of institutional autonomy enjoyed by the *Bundesbank* (Woolley 1985; Kloten/Ketterer/ Vollmer 1985) and in the tactical brilliance with which it executed its shift to monetarism without risking an open political conflict with the government and the unions (Scharpf 1987, 165–177). When Keynesianism was practiced thereafter in West Germany, it was "on probation" and likely to be revoked at the first sign of rising inflation.

If we put the German case to one side, what factors can then explain the choice of games in the other three countries? In the literature there are essentially two competing strands of theory dealing with the issue: From a "class-politics" perspective, what game is being played depends essentially on the class orientation of the party in power (Hibbs 1977; Fiorina 1978; Tufte 1978) and on the "power resources" of the labor movement favoring the ascendancy of labor-oriented parties (Korpi 1983; Esping-Andersen 1985). The theory of "political business cycles," on the other hand (Nordhaus 1975; McRae 1977; Frey/Schneider 1978; 1979; Peel 1982; Lowery 1985), emphasizes the anticipation of voter reactions by all governments, regardless of their party affiliations.[12] Assuming that voters will respond more negatively to unemployment than to inflation, the theory predicts cyclical changes between Keynesian full-employment policy before, and monetarist anti-inflation policy after, general elections.

Applied in isolation, the power of both models to explain economic policy outcomes seems less than overwhelming[13]—which is not much of a surprise, as both theories tend to focus on the motives of economic policy makers and to ignore the conditions under which the preferences of governments can or cannot be translated into effective policy. Nevertheless it is promising to combine these hypotheses with the game-theoretical model of macroeconomic coordination developed earlier. The connection could be provided by the notion of a "linkage" between separate games played by one player against different opponents (Kelley 1984; Denzau/Riker/Shepsle 1985; Shepsle 1986; Putnam 1986). In the first "coordination" game, the outcomes of macroeconomic policy are jointly determined by the government and the unions, while in the second "politics" game the government responds to (its anticipation of) positive or negative voter reactions to these outcomes.[14]

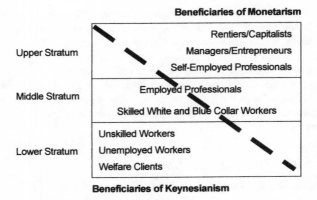

FIGURE A1.10    Class bases of Keynesian and monetarist strategies

Furthermore, it seems reasonable to assume that different groups of voters will respond differently to macroeconomic strategies. Simplifying again, one may lump these various groups into three socioeconomic strata (Figure A1.10). The first stratum is without property and depends for its livelihood on relatively insecure jobs in the secondary labor market (Piore 1979) and on government transfers. The second stratum of skilled blue- and white-collar workers and professionals derives its income from more secure jobs in the primary labor market but also from substantial property holdings (Miegel 1981). The third stratum of self-employed professionals, managers, entrepreneurs, and rentiers depends primarily on profits and the returns of real and financial assets and is not directly affected by the labor market.

If these assumptions are granted, it is plausible that voters in the lower stratum have most to fear from a monetarist strategy associated with high unemployment and cutbacks in welfare spending and that voters in the upper stratum would respond negatively to a Keynesian strategy associated with rising inflation, declining real interest rates, and aggressive union wage demands. By contrast, voters in the middle stratum would have reason to be more ambivalent in their preferences. Their jobs are more secure than those in the lower stratum, but if unemployment rises and companies fail, they may feel even more threatened because they are likely to fall so much farther. However, although these middle voters may even profit from inflation as home owners and debtors, they are likely to respond negatively to the disruption of established expectations associated with rapidly rising prices.

In addition, we need to introduce a set of assumptions about how governments might differ in their dependence on the electorate. Simplifying again, the model presupposes that the choices of the "government" are exercised by one of two competing parties, or coalitions of parties, with contrasting class bases of political support.[15] "Bourgeois" parties appeal primarily to voters in the upper socioeconomic stratum, while "labor" parties have their electoral stronghold in the lower stratum. Each government identifies ideologically with the interests of its core clientele and favors macroeconomic strategies that serve these interests. But it also will try to select policies that assure its reelection. If policies do not serve the interests of its core clientele, the model assumes that the government will lose some of their support but will not be able to attract votes from the core clientele of the opposition. If that were all there is to the politics game, labor governments would (under the economic conditions of the 1970s) always have pursued Keynesian strategies, and bourgeois governments would always have chosen to play the monetarist game.

But each government will also be defeated if it loses the volatile support of the middle stratum of voters. As they are potentially concerned with both unemployment and inflation, their choices depend not on a general preference for either Keynesian or monetarist strategies but rather on specific economic circumstances and perceived consequences for their own interests. In general, it is reasonable to assume that middle voters will respond positively to a situation in which both problems, inflation and unemployment, are avoided, and that they will respond negatively to a combination of high inflation plus high unemployment. When unemployment is low and inflation high, however, their response is likely to be asymmetrical: Whereas a shift from a labor government to the bourgeois opposition is plausible as a protest against high rates of inflation, the reverse shift is less probable if middle voters assume that under a labor government inflation could only get worse.

Even more difficult to predict is the response of middle voters to the combination of low inflation and high unemployment. If inflation and unemployment were perceived as symmetrical, one might now expect a negative response, with perhaps a somewhat greater tolerance for labor governments (on the hypothesis that they would be more motivated to work for a return to full employment). This response is indeed plausible when unemployment is a relatively new phenomenon. But once unemployment has persisted for some time, its political implications are likely to change.

While inflation is, by and large, perceived as a collective evil that irritates even those whose incomes keep up with prices, that is not generally true of unemployment. It is only the *threat* of mass joblessness, especially when it is experienced for the first time after almost two decades of full employment, that approximates a collective evil. But once unemployment has in fact risen, voters will realize that only a minority of the labor force is in fact affected—and it is also fairly obvious who is likely to be in that minority. For those who are not (and that is the overwhelming majority of the middle voters), unemployment is at best an "altruistic problem," whose salience depends entirely on the "moral climate" of the country[16] and of the times, but it is not a problem of their economic self-interest. Thus, if we continue to assume self-interested voting among the middle layer of the electorate, we would predict support for bourgeois as well as for labor governments under conditions of low inflation and long-term unemployment.

With this we are now able to return to the "linkage" between the macroeconomic "coordination" game and the "politics" game. One way to present it is in the form of "nested" games where the outer frame is provided by the coordination game, which effectively determines the various combinations of inflation and unemployment to which the different strata of the electorate may respond in the politics game. As these will respond differently to governments of different political persuasion, each cell of the coordination game will contain two variants of the politics game, one for labor and one for bourgeois governments (Figure A1.11).

Obviously, cell 1 of the coordination game (obtained through a combination of Keynesian reflation and union wage restraint) did provide the optimal economic environment for the politics game from the perspective of a *labor government*. The interests of its core clientele (and its own political preferences) were satisfied, and middle voters had no reason to defect. For a *bourgeois government*, however, the same situation was less attractive since its own ideological preferences as well as the interests of its core clientele could not be satisfied by a Keynesian strategy. But as upper-stratum voters could not benefit from

| Government | Unions | |
|---|---|---|
| | moderate ————→ aggressive | |
| **Keynesian** | Unemployment: low<br>Inflation: moderate | Unemployment: low<br>Inflation: very high |
| | Voter Stratum | Voter Stratum |
| | lower   middle   upper<br>\| + \| + \| – \|<br>Labor Government | lower   middle   upper<br>\| + \| – \| – \|<br>Labor Government |
| | lower   middle   upper<br>\| – \| + \| (+) \|<br>Bourgeois Government<br>(Cell 1) | lower   middle   upper<br>\| – \| ? \| (+) \|<br>Bourgeois Government<br>(Cell 2) |
| **Monetarist** | Unemployment:<br>high<br>Inflation: high | Unemployment:<br>very high<br>Inflation: high |
| | Voter Stratum | Voter Stratum |
| | lower   middle   upper<br>\| (+) \| ?/+ \| – \|<br>Labor Government | lower   middle   upper<br>\| (+) \| – \| – \|<br>Labor Government |
| | lower   middle   upper<br>\| – \| –/+ \| + \|<br>Bourgeois Government<br>(Cell 3) | lower   middle   upper<br>\| – \| – \| + \|<br>Bourgeois Government<br>(Cell 4) |
| | moderate ←———— aggressive | |

FIGURE A1.11    Voter responses to coordination game outcomes

defecting to the labor opposition, the government was still politically secure—and it could not improve its position by switching to a monetarist strategy as long as middle voters would still respond negatively to a rise of unemployment.

But if a union wage offensive shifted the Keynesian game into cell 2, as was likely under the assumptions introduced earlier, a *labor government* would become extremely vulnerable in the politics game. While its core clientele would be satisfied, middle voters would respond negatively to the rapid increase of inflation, and the bourgeois opposition would present a highly credible alternative. Thus, if the government could not persuade the unions to shift back to wage moderation (and thus to cell 1), it was faced with two equally unattractive political options: It could choose to stick to its Keynesian guns, even if that meant almost certain electoral defeat, or it could gamble on a switch to monetarism (whose short-run effect would be the worst-case outcome of cell 4) in the hope that the unions might then move toward wage restraint quickly enough to permit the government to reach the relatively safe haven of cell 3 before the next election.

If a *bourgeois government* found itself in the same economic situation (cell 2), its political survival would be less in danger, as middle voters could not expect a more vigorous anti-inflation strategy from the labor opposition. Given the political risks associated with a switch to monetarism and an initial massive increase of unemployment (cell 4),[17] a bourgeois government might well prefer to continue the Keynesian game even in the absence of union wage restraint, and in doing so its chances of political survival might be better than those of a labor government.

The economic environment of cell 4, with very high unemployment and still high rates of inflation, was politically viable for neither party. Perhaps a *labor government* might do marginally better if the middle voters had reason to fear that a shift to the bourgeois opposition could only make unemployment still worse. However, its own core clientele would suffer the most, while a *bourgeois government* would at least begin to satisfy the interests of its upper-class clientele and would profit from their improving morale. Nevertheless, it is plausible to assume that either government would lose if elections were held during a period in which the economy found itself in cell 4. But the coordination game was unlikely to remain there for long. If the monetarist game continued, the unions were forced by rising unemployment to moderate their wage claims. Thus, if governments managed to hang on long enough for this shift to become economically effective and politically salient, they would face more attractive prospects.

Cell 3, finally, was Janus-faced. Its political implications were entirely different, depending upon whether it was entered from cell 1 or from cell 4. In the first case, the political response would have been negative, as middle voters would be confronted for the first time with a significant rise of unemployment under conditions in which there was not even much concern about inflation to justify the switch to monetarism. Unlike independent central banks, therefore, rational governments, labor or bourgeois, would not shift to the monetarist game as long as they found themselves in cell 1.

When cell 3 was entered from cell 4, however, the politics game was of an entirely different character. Now the return to union wage restraint would help to reduce inflation visibly, and as business profits improved, unemployment would at least be stabilized and might even decline somewhat. As a consequence, joblessness would no longer appear as a personal threat to voters in the middle stratum. Under these conditions, cell 3 would become the political optimum for a *bourgeois government*. Its own core clientele was pleased by the economic effects of the monetarist strategy, and the support of middle voters was initially assured by favorable comparisons to the preceding period. If it was plausible to blame a predecessor labor government for its initial rise, the political salience of continuing unemployment would be greatly reduced,[18] and after a while dissonance-reducing psychological mechanisms would blunt its moral salience as well.

For a *labor government*, by contrast, the situation was less comfortable. Although the unconcern of middle voters might assure its short-term political survival, continuing unemployment would hurt and demoralize its own core clientele. Thus the government would be under strong political pressure to move back to a Keynesian full-employment strategy (cell 1). If it did so, however, it was now uncertain of the continuing support of the middle stratum, whose sensitivity to inflation must have increased as they lost their fear of unemployment. At the least, a labor government that returned to Keynesianism after a monetarist interlude would be vulnerable defeat as soon as inflation rose again.

## HOW AND WHEN DID CORPORATISM MATTER?

The model is now sufficiently complex and realistic to be plausibly applied to the historical experience of macroeconomic choices in the four countries between 1974 and 1982.

What we are now able to add to the economic analysis presented earlier in section 2 is an explanation of government choices between Keynesian and monetarist strategies. It is derived from the logic of the "politics" games that are played within each of the cells of the outer "coordination" game (Figure A1.12).

The linkage between these games is established by the fact that the government is a player in both and by the assumption that the government's moves in the coordination game are determined by its prospect of winning or losing in the politics game. Hence the model would predict that governments will try to reach, or remain in, coordination cells in which they are politically secure and that they will try to avoid, or escape from, cells in which they are politically vulnerable. Voters are assumed to respond nonstrategically to a given economic environment, and union moves in the coordination game are also assumed—for the time being—to be solely determined by their short-term economic self-interest.

If we now apply this radically simplified "rational-choice" model of macroeconomic policy making to the actual policy experiences of the four countries (during the period when they still had a choice between Keynesian and monetarist strategies, i.e., before the U.S. conversion to monetarism), the model appears to fit quite well in some, but not in all, instances.

At the beginning of the crisis, in 1974, all four countries were governed by labor parties, and all four governments found themselves in macroeconomic positions that were vulnerable in the politics game. In Austria, Britain, and Sweden the governments were able to assure full employment while the unions obtained inflationary wage settlements. In Germany, by contrast, the central bank enforced a tight-money policy that limited, but could not avoid, the rise of inflation and caused extremely high job losses. The model would predict that if these situations should continue until the next general elections,[19] all four governments would be politically vulnerable. Hence all had an interest in moving away from their uncomfortable positions. For this, however, they depended on the unions, as no government could have directly accessed a more secure political position by the exercise of its own economic policy options alone.

By 1976, nevertheless, only one country, Sweden, had not changed its position within the coordination game—and the Swedish Social Democrats were indeed defeated by a bourgeois coalition in the fall of 1976.[20] In the other three countries the unions had helped to improve the government's political prospects by a move to wage moderation. But only in one country, Germany, can this move be explained within the present model as a self-interested response to rising unemployment. In Austria and Britain, institutional factors not yet discussed must be drawn upon to explain the unions' willingness to shift to a pattern of Keynesian concertation, which, in terms of short-term economic payoffs, was only the second-best solution that they could obtain.

By 1978 Swedish unions had also shifted to wage moderation, while the bourgeois government remained firmly committed to full employment. The same was now true in Germany, where the federal government was able to shift toward a full-employment strategy after inflation was more or less under control. Thus Austria, Sweden, and West Germany were now (and until 1980) following a course of Keynesian concertation that was politically optimal for labor governments and at least politically viable for the Swedish bourgeois coalition but which depended upon union wage restraint not yet explained within the model.

In Britain, by contrast, both the government and the unions had departed from Keynesian concertation by 1978 for reasons that may be plausibly interpreted within our model. The government had responded to persistent inflation with a shift to monetarism, hoping to push down prices without a dramatic increase of unemployment, and thus to

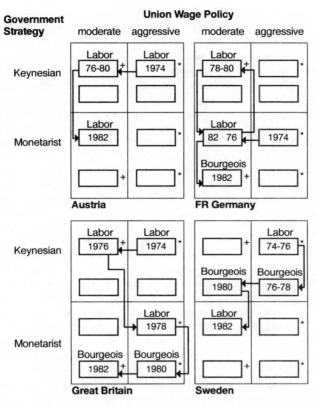

FIGURE A1.12 Historical sequences of coordination and politics games
(* = politically vulnerable position; + = politically secure position)

reach the relatively safe haven of cell 3. At the same time, the unions were aiming at cell 2 when they resumed their wage offensive in order to improve the real-wage position of their members after two years of extreme wage restraint. As a consequence of both moves, they found themselves in cell 4, which was economically least attractive for the unions and politically nonviable for the labor government in the 1979 general elections.

Later developments also seem to conform well to the model: After their victory in 1979, Margaret Thatcher's Conservatives had sufficient time to wait for the unions to return to wage moderation (shifting the game to cell 3) under the compulsion of very high unemployment. When that point had been reached by 1982, the bourgeois government was politically secure. The German Social Democrats were ousted in the fall of 1982 not by the voters but by their Liberal coalition partners. Yet their position had also become electorally vulnerable, as unemployment was rapidly increasing after another heavy dose of monetarism applied by the *Bundesbank*. As a consequence, the new Christian-Liberal government was able to win comfortable majorities in subsequent elections.

In Sweden, by contrast, the bourgeois government did not survive the externally imposed shift to monetarism (after which unemployment had begun to creep up by 1982), but the Social Democrats' subsequent hold on power remained tenuous, even though the devaluation of the kronor kept Swedish unemployment at comparatively very low levels. The same is by and large true of Austria, where the unions have been even more cooperative than in Sweden but where the commitment to fixed exchange rates against the deutsche mark precluded devaluation, so that the rise of unemployment did more to undercut labor support.

Thus the model seems to be reasonably successful in explaining the policy choices of elected governments in all four countries. It is also successful in explaining union responses to a monetarist government strategy that allowed unemployment to rise. If governments practiced Keynesian reflation, however, unions in all countries sometimes conformed to the model by adopting an aggressive wage policy, and sometimes they were able and willing to exercise wage restraint even though full employment was maintained. It was this choice of unions, as yet unexplained, that ultimately determined government preferences for Keynesian or monetarist strategies.

To summarize: There were in the 1970s and early 1980s two positions within the coordination game at which a government might be secure within the politics game (cell 1 for labor, and cell 3 for bourgeois governments), and there were a number of positions at which governments were politically vulnerable. But the chances of survival were unevenly distributed: While bourgeois governments, once they had reached their politically preferred position, could count on the self-interested collaboration of the unions in the coordination game, the same was not true of the optimal position of labor governments. It represented a political equilibrium but not a coordination equilibrium. If unions followed their own short-term preferences in the coordination game, labor governments would find themselves in a politically untenable position (cell 2). If the government then looked only to its own political survival, it would be tempted into a desperate shift to monetarism, which, even if it succeeded politically, would increase unemployment. If it failed, as it did in Britain, it would help to establish a bourgeois government that was politically secure in spite of continuing high unemployment.

Thus, if both labor governments and unions were to follow their short-term institutional self-interests, the result would have been a sequence of unstable game situations that could only come to an end in a bourgeois-monetarist constellation that represented a stable equilibrium in the politics game as well as in the coordination game. From the perspective of the labor movement, however, that sequence was a disaster for labor parties as well as for unions—and one that was easily anticipated. The question is, therefore, under which conditions the sequence could have been interrupted and reversed before the bourgeois-monetarist equilibrium was established. What was required is clear enough: The unions would have to be willing and able to forgo short-term wage gains in order to allow the government to reach cell 1 of the coordination game, where it was in its own political self-interest to defend full employment. That was the essence of the "neocorporatist-Keynesian concertation" achieved in Austria between 1976 and 1980, in Britain between 1976 and 1978, and in Sweden and West Germany between 1978 and 1980.

What was involved was not in the strict sense a question of "political exchange" (Pizzorno 1978; Marin 1985). To the extent that a labor government pursued full-employment strategies, it was acting out of self-interest—not to reward the unions. It had nothing else to offer them in return for wage moderation, and it could only warn them of its own impending political demise, not threaten it. What was in question, instead, was the unions' capacity of "self-management" (Elster 1979; Schelling 1984), that is, their ability to avoid both the "temporal trap" of favoring short-term over longer-term definitions of self-interest and the "social trap" of favoring competitive subgroup interests over the collective interest of the union movement (Messick/McClelland 1983).

In other words, an explanation of instances of successful Keynesian concertation must focus on departures from the action perspective of narrow and myopic self-interest that is presupposed in rational-choice models. With this we are now finally approaching the institutional explanations upon which political science studies of macroeconomic performance have focused primarily (and with insufficient justification). Certain institutional arrangements will permit and perhaps encourage (but not compel) actors to take a more inclusive and longer-term perspective—and other institutional conditions will make it more difficult (but not impossible) to take a wider view. It is in this respect that neocorporatist institutions in general, and centralized and concentrated union organizations in particular, seem to make a difference: Solidarity, as well as the ability to anticipate the future in present choices, is undercut by competition between individual unions, and it is facilitated (though not assured) by organizational concentration in the union movement and by the effective centralization of collective-bargaining decisions.

In Britain, to begin with the most obvious case, the extreme fragmentation of union organization (the TUC alone still had over 100 member unions in the 1970s), and the decentralization of collective bargaining to the level of individual firms, plants, or even the shop floor within plants must create enormous competitive pressures within the union movement (Barnes/Reid 1980). Negotiators in each of the small bargaining units tend to exploit fully the profitable firms' ability to pay and the bargaining strength of scarce skill groups—and they would suffer in interunion competition if their own settlements were more moderate than those achieved elsewhere. Under such conditions, voluntary wage restraint, even if its economic or political benefit to the union movement as a whole were obvious, is a collective good whose attainment is highly vulnerable to free riding.

By contrast, the free-rider problem is significantly reduced in the other three countries, whose institutions, though quite different, conformed to a greater degree to the neocorporatist model. In Austria and West Germany the national union movements consist of no more than sixteen or seventeen industrial unions that do not compete against each other. Collective bargaining is also quite centralized within each union, with effective decisions taken at the national level even if regional settlements may differ. Under such conditions, union negotiators must be concerned about job losses in weaker firms or regions, and they are less free to exploit pockets of local bargaining strength. They must, in other words, permanently work to achieve a collective or solidaristic definition of the self-interest of divergent groups of workers in order to assure their own organizational survival (Streeck 1981). An even more inclusive perspective is introduced by the formal role of the central union federation in collective bargaining in Sweden and Austria (Marin 1982), and by the de facto wage leadership of the largest industrial unions in West Germany (Streeck 1982; 1984). In one way or another, therefore, a collective definition of the self-interest of the union movement could be worked into the normal processes of collective bargaining by large, "encompassing" (Olson 1982) organizations on the union side. At the same time, organizational centralization assured union leaders some (limited) freedom to pursue longer-term strategies even in the face of rank-and-file discontent, and it provided them with opportunities to present and defend more "enlightened" and longer-term definitions of union self-interest in internal discussions.

Thus Austrian and German unions were able to practice wage restraint after 1975 in a spirit of "business as usual" that was hardly noticed by anyone outside of professional circles. In Britain, by contrast, the success of the "social contract" in 1976 and 1977 depended entirely on a most extraordinary exertion of political and moral pressure by government and top union leaders. Local bargaining units and shop stewards were browbeaten into compliance by a national campaign to "give a year to Britain," replete with appeals to the "spirit of Dunkirk" and to the solidarity of the labor movement with an embattled Labour government. The emphasis was on short-term sacrifices, and the six-pounds rule itself (which wreaked havoc with jealously defended wage differentials) was chosen for its maximal moral appeal and for its high visibility, which did discourage evasions.

The Swedish case is less clear-cut (Martin 1984; 1986b). The number of unions is larger than in Austria or West Germany (about twenty-five), and there is considerable wage competition between the blue-collar unions, organized by industry, and the white-collar unions, which are mainly organized by skill level. At the same time, however, the national federation of blue-collar unions and national cartels of white-collar unions have a larger role in collective bargaining than is the case in the other countries. Yet there is also a good deal of wage drift generated by local wage rounds in the more profitable (or state-owned) firms—which is then generalized to the whole economy by an ever denser network of "compensation" clauses in collective agreements. Nevertheless, whenever this was considered necessary, the Swedish labor movement was able to draw upon moral resources and an unspectacular but effective commitment to solidaristic values that were able to constrain self-interested competition between individual bargaining units.

Thus it seems more plausible to ascribe the aggressive and economically damaging Swedish wage rounds after 1975 not to a fundamental institutional incapacity but perhaps to a temporary lapse of judgment and, after 1976, to the fact the unions saw little need to assist the new bourgeois government in its macroeconomic management. After all, if that government had failed, the Social Democrats, rather than Thatcherite conservatives, would have returned to office. But when it became clear after 1978 that the Swedish economy was in fact suffering, union wage moderation was again forthcoming—and the same was true, in spite of considerable tensions within the union movement, in the period after 1982.

In short, if and when the union movement as a whole had reason to consider wage restraint as its own best strategy, neocorporatist institutional conditions facilitated that choice in Austria, West Germany, and Sweden. In Britain their absence could be compensated for a time by extreme exertions of ideological pressure and moral leadership. But it was always clear that the "social contract" was not institutionally viable as a longer-term strategy and that the inevitable return to "free collective bargaining" would again release the pent-up pressures of wage competition. The only question was whether the breakup had to occur under dramatic circumstances in 1978, or whether a more sensitive management of government-union relations and better timing could have facilitated a more orderly retreat that might have allowed Jim Callaghan to survive another general election.

Finally, it is perhaps worth pointing out that neocorporatist institutions are of relevance to macroeconomic policy only as long as the Keynesian game is being played. If the government shifts to a monetarist strategy, wage restraint (which is still required for its success) no longer depends on the organizational concentration of the union movement and on the centralization of collective-bargaining decisions.[21] The reason is analytically straightforward: Job losses, unlike inflation, are primarily experienced not as a collective evil but as an individual risk whose avoidance is in the immediate self-interest of individual workers and hence not vulnerable to free riding. As soon as unemployment is allowed to rise, therefore, the overriding interest in protecting existing jobs will motivate wage concessions not only at the level of the union movement as a whole but also at lower levels of collective bargaining.[22] Under such conditions, there is no reason to assume that decentralized and fragmented union movements (which are otherwise characterized by greater militancy— Cameron 1984) should be any less "docile" than highly centralized and disciplined corporatist unions are said to be (Panitch 1979). It is thus entirely plausible, within the model developed here, that neocorporatist institutions should explain a great deal of economic variance during the Keynesian 1970s—and much less during the monetarist 1980s.

## NOTES

1. The story is summarized in Table A1.1.

2. In this paper I concentrate on the explanation of *macroeconomic policy*, which affects unemployment through its impact on the number of jobs offered in the economy. This is of course not the whole "story" (which is presented more fully in my book, Scharpf 1987). Governments did resort to a variety of other strategies to prevent, reduce, or conceal the rise of *unemployment* (Wilensky/Turner 1987). Switzerland, for instance, relied almost entirely on the repatriation of foreign workers to compensate for very large job losses (Schmidt 1985). Sweden, on the other hand, reduced potential unemployment by almost four percentage points between 1974 and 1978 through "active labor market" retraining and subsidized employment. West Germany combined both strategies with the early retirement of older workers to achieve a similar reduction of the labor supply (Scharpf 1987, 279–293).

3. In the monetarist environment of the 1980s, by contrast, wage restraint came to mean falling real wages or, at the least, reductions of real unit labor costs in order to increase the profitability of capital.

4. After the onset of the second oil crisis in 1979, the United States, which before had facilitated worldwide expansionary strategies through its relatively loose fiscal and monetary policy, switched to a monetarist tight-money policy, which increased real long-term dollar interests from a low of −3 percent at the beginning of 1980 to an average of +6 percent in 1982 and a high of more than +8 percent in 1983. Given the paramount role of the U.S. dollar in the international capital markets, all other industrial countries were also forced to reduce their money supply and to raise their interest rates (Funke 1986). As a further consequence, national fiscal policy also became less effective as an instrument of expansion (and much more expensive). In effect, therefore, most Western European countries pursued restrictive fiscal and monetary policies after 1981—and those that did not do so at first (Mitterrand's France, for instance) were soon compelled to follow suit in order to avoid massive outflows of capital and a dramatic devaluation of their currencies.

5. Wages contributed to accelerating inflation whenever the rise of unit labor costs (nominal wage increases minus gains in labor productivity) exceeded the current rate of inflation (Table A1.2).

6. When the Social Democrats returned to power in Sweden in the fall of 1982, they achieved a limited degree of demand reflation through the competitive devaluation of the kronor—a strategy that not all countries could have adopted.

7. In their collective-bargaining role, one might include employers' associations as macroeconomic actors of marginal importance. Even though one may generally presume

TABLE A1.1  Changes in Gross Domestic Product, Employment, and
Consumer Prices, 1963–1973 and 1973–1983, Average Rates of
Unemployment, 1968–1973 and 1973–1983

| | GDP Growth | | Employment Growth | | Unemployment | | Inflation | |
|---|---|---|---|---|---|---|---|---|
| | 63–73 | 73–83 | 63–73 | 73–83 | 68–73 | 73–83 | 63–73 | 73–83 |
| Canada | 5.7 | 2.8 | 3.6 | 2.3 | 5.4 | 7.8 | 3.7 | 9.3 |
| USA | 4.1 | 2.2 | 2.6 | 1.9 | 4.6 | 7.1 | 3.6 | 8.3 |
| Japan | 9.8 | 4.2 | 1.5 | 0.9 | 1.2 | 2.0 | 6.2 | 8.2 |
| Australia | 5.6 | 2.5 | 3.3 | 0.9 | 2.0 | 5.5 | 4.0 | 11.2 |
| New Zealand | 4.0 | 2.0 | 2.4 | 1.1 | 0.3 | 1.9 | 5.4 | 13.4 |
| Austria | 5.1 | 2.6 | − 0.1 | 0.0 | 1.5 | 2.2 | 4.2 | 6.1 |
| Belgium | 4.9 | 2.1 | 0.8 | − 0.7 | 2.5 | 7.9 | 4.1 | 8.0 |
| Switzerland | 4.1 | 0.6 | 0.8 | − 0.7 | – | 0.4 | 4.5 | 4.7 |
| W. Germany | 4.4 | 1.9 | 0.0 | − 0.7 | 1.0 | 3.8 | 3.6 | 5.0 |
| Denmark | 4.0 | 1.7 | 1.4 | 0.0 | 1.0 | 6.9 | 6.3 | 10.4 |
| France | 5.5 | 2.6 | 0.9 | 0.1 | 2.5 | 5.4 | 4.7 | 10.9 |
| Finland | 4.9 | 3.2 | 0.2 | 1.1 | 2.6 | 4.6 | 6.2 | 11.8 |
| Great Britain | 3.3 | 1.6 | 0.2 | − 0.5 | 3.3 | 6.7 | 5.3 | 13.3 |
| Italy | 5.0 | 2.4 | − 0.5 | 0.7 | 5.7 | 7.3 | 4.9 | 16.2 |
| Norway | 4.3 | 3.9 | 1.7 | 1.8 | 1.7 | 2.0 | 5.3 | 9.4 |
| Netherlands | 5.1 | 1.9 | 0.7 | 0.6 | 1.5 | 6.5 | 5.5 | 6.7 |
| Sweden | 4.0 | 1.8 | 0.6 | 0.9 | 2.2 | 2.3 | 4.9 | 9.9 |
| Average | 4.9 | 2.4 | 1.2 | 0.6 | 2.4 | 4.7 | 4.8 | 9.6 |
| Range* | 1.4 | 0.9 | 1.2 | 0.9 | 2.2 | 1.6 | 0.9 | 3.1 |
| Coeff. Var.** | 0.3 | 0.4 | 1.0 | 1.6 | 0.7 | 0.5 | 0.2 | 0.3 |

*Relative Range = (Maximum minus Minimum) / Average
** Coefficient of Variability = Standard Deviation / Average

| | | |
|---|---|---|
| GDP Growth | 73–83 / Employment Growth | 73–83: $r^2$ = .32 |
| GDP Growth | 73–83 / Inflation | 73–83: $r^2$ = .02 |
| Employment Growth | 73–83 / Inflation | 73–83: $r^2$ = .07 |
| Employment Growth | 73–83 / Unemployment | 73–83: $r^2$ = .01 |
| Unemployment | 73–83 / Inflation | 73–83: $r^2$ = .11 |

*Source: OECD Historical Statistics, 1960–1984.*

that the degree of their resistance to wage increases is determined by economic self-interest, it is at least conceivable that the relative toughness of their position may also be influenced by considerations including the state of the macroeconomy. But it is not plausible to assume that business associations could be a player in a macroeconomic "inflation game," modeled after the Prisoner's Dilemma, in which they choose between high and low price increases while the unions choose high or low wage increases (Maital/Benjamini 1979; Neck 1985). Price-setting decisions (and investment decisions for that matter), although of critical importance for the performance of the economy, are not the subject of *collective* choices in capitalist economies. The recent concern of social scientists with the

Table A1.2   Consumer Price Inflation and Annual Increases of Unit
Labor Costs in Manufacturing, 1974–1980 (in percent)

|  | 1974 | 1975 | 1976 | 1977 | 1978 | 1979 | 1980 |
|---|---|---|---|---|---|---|---|
| *Austria* | | | | | | | |
| Inflation | 9.5 | 8.4 | 7.3 | 5.5 | 3.6 | 3.7 | 6.4 |
| Unit L.C. | 9.7 | 15.1 | 0.5 | 5.6 | 1.2 | − 1.8 | 5.9 |
| *Great Britain* | | | | | | | |
| Inflation | 16.0 | 24.2 | 16.5 | 15.8 | 8.3 | 13.4 | 18.0 |
| Unit L.C. | 24.0 | 32.6 | 12.7 | 11.7 | 14.9 | 17.2 | 21.0 |
| *Sweden* | | | | | | | |
| Inflation | 9.9 | 9.8 | 10.3 | 11.4 | 10.0 | 7.2 | 13.7 |
| Unit L.C. | 12.9 | 19.3 | 16.7 | 11.1 | 8.3 | − 0.1 | 9.3 |
| *West Germany* | | | | | | | |
| Inflation | 7.0 | 6.0 | 4.5 | 3.7 | 2.7 | 4.1 | 5.5 |
| Unit L.C. | 9.1 | 6.8 | 0.6 | 5.3 | 5.0 | 2.4 | 7.3 |

*Source: OECD Historical Statistics, 1960–1984.*

"organization of business interests" (Streeck/Schmitter 1985) should not obscure this important difference.

8. Rising rates of inflation may cut into the real value of nominal wage settlements, but from a union perspective that insight is more likely to justify aggressive wage bargaining than wage moderation.

9. Capital incomes are influenced by both policy variables: Wage moderation increases profits, and high interest rates increase income from monetary assets.

10. Even when the central bank is an autonomous player, it is not necessary to represent the constellation as a three-person game. As fiscal and monetary policy operate upon the same parameters of aggregate demand, any discrepancy between the two will affect the de facto choice of a single "government" player.

11. In my view it is thus not correct to argue, as Peter Lange and Geoffrey Garrett (1985, 799–800, 817) have done, that wage restraint is rational for unions only as long as the government will guarantee economic growth and full employment. On the contrary, that is precisely the government with whom self-interested unions will find it most difficult to cooperate. Only a government that is willing to tolerate high unemployment may count upon their self-interested moderation.

12. Bruno S. Frey and Friedrich Schneider (1978; 1979) combine both assumptions: In their model, governments will pursue their own ideological preferences until their popularity falls below a critical threshold at which their reelection is in danger.

13. The class orientation of political parties did indeed matter in the switch from Jim Callaghan to Margaret Thatcher in Britain, or from Valéry Giscard d'Estaing to François Mitterrand in France, but it does not explain the relative continuity of economic policy after changes of government in Sweden and in the United States in 1976, or in West Germany in 1982. Similarly, the theory of the "political business cycle" may perhaps explain German fiscal policy in 1980, but the Austrian and Swedish governments seem to have continued their chosen course with little regard for the timing of elections, and the Jimmy

Carter administration did switch to a monetarist anti-inflation strategy in 1979, which predictably increased U.S. unemployment before the 1980 elections.

14. It is perhaps necessary to emphasize that we are trying to explain not election outcomes but policy choices, and that we are dealing with the perceptions of policymakers. Elections are in fact won or lost over a multitude of issues, of which the course of the economy is not always the most salient one. Nevertheless, it is reasonable to assume that risk-averse economic policy makers will anticipate the response of self-interested voters.

15. The model could accommodate coalition governments with cross-cutting class orientations, but not the "new politics" of nonclass issues, movements, and parties (peace, ecology, gender, life styles, ethnic, regional, etc.).

16. It is here that the "power resource" theory is most persuasive: A powerful labor movement of the Scandinavian or Austrian type, with a strong presence in all societal institutions, including the mass media, may indeed exercise a degree of "ideological hegemony" that may at least postpone the shift to a neoconservative "lifeboat ethics" and the egoistic redefinition of middle-stratum interests.

17. Here, the length of the electoral cycle and the closeness of the next general election are obviously important. Quite apart from other differences, the British five-year electoral cycle enhanced, and the Swedish three-year cycle reduced, the political feasibility of a switch to monetarism.

18. A change of government thus changes the "framing" (Kahneman/Tversky 1984) of the baseline from which political success and failure are being measured.

19. As the seriousness of the economic crisis did not become obvious until the winter of 1974–1975, the British elections in the fall of 1974 would not count as a deviation from the model.

20. It is perhaps fair to add that Swedish Social Democrats attribute the change of government more to the dispute over nuclear energy than to a deep dissatisfaction with their management of the economy.

21. There might actually be a reverse relationship: Under conditions of high unemployment, it would require a highly solidaristic labor movement to design and implement an aggressive wage campaign that, by further increasing unemployment in the short run, might help to defeat a monetarist government at the next election. On that hypothesis, the union-busting thrust of recent industrial-relations legislation in Britain, while entirely counterproductive within a Keynesian frame of reference, may actually make partisan-political sense.

22. It is still true, however, that fragmented industrial-relations systems tend to generate more endogenous wage pressure than neocorporatist ones. Even under conditions of high general unemployment, there will be firms that are doing well and skill groups that are in high demand—and these pockets of labor power will be exploited in fragmented systems. Thus, even though unemployment was much higher, the real wages of those who still had jobs rose more in Britain after 1980 than they did in Austria, Sweden, and West Germany.

### REFERENCES

Barnes, Denis/Eileen Reid, 1980: *Governments and Trade Unions: The British Experience, 1964–1979.* London: Heinemann.

Bornstein, Stephen/Peter Gourevitch, 1984: Unions in a Declining Economy: The Case of the British TUC. In Peter Gourevitch/Andrew Martin/George Ross/Christopher

Allen/Stephen Bornstein/Andrew Markovits, eds., *Unions and Economic Crisis: Britain, West Germany, and Sweden,* 13–88. London: Allen & Unwin.

Cameron, David R., 1978: The Expansion of the Public Economy: A Comparative Analysis. *American Political Science Review* 72, 1243–1261.

———, 1984: Social Democracy, Corporatism, Labor Quiescence, and the Representation of Economic Interest in Advanced Capitalist Society. In John H. Goldthorpe, ed., *Order and Conflict in Contemporary Capitalism: Studies in the Political Economy of Western European Nations,* 143–178. Oxford: Clarendon Press.

Coleman, James S., 1974: *Power and the Structure of Society.* New York: W. W. Norton.

Crouch, Colin, 1982: *The Politics of Industrial Relations.* 2d edition. London: Fontana Paperbacks.

Denzau, Arthur/William Riker/Kenneth A. Shepsle, 1985: Farquharson and Fenno: Sophisticated Voting and the Home Style. *American Political Science Review* 79, 1117–1134.

Elster, Jon, 1979: *Ulysses and the Sirens: Studies in Rationality and Irrationality.* Cambridge: Cambridge University Press.

Esping-Andersen, Gösta, 1985: *Politics Against Markets: The Social-Democratic Road to Power.* Princeton: Princeton University Press.

Fiorina, Morris P., 1978: Economic Retrospective Voting in American National Elections: A Microanalysis. *American Journal of Political Science* 11, 426–473.

Flanagan, Robert J./David W. Soskice/Lloyd Ulman, 1983: *Unionism, Economic Stabilization, and Incomes Policies: The European Experience.* Washington, DC: Brookings Institution.

Frey, Bruno S./Friedrich Schneider, 1978: An Empirical Study of Politico-Economic Interaction in the United States. *Review of Economics and Statistics* 60, 174–183.

———, 1979: An Econometric Model with an Endogenous Government Sector. *Public Choice* 34, 29–43.

Frye, Jon/Robert J. Gordon, 1981: Government Intervention in the Inflation Process: The Econometrics of "Self-Inflicted Wounds." *American Economic Review* 71, 288–294.

Funke, Michael, 1986: Nominalzinsen, Realzinsen, und internationale Kapitalbewegungen. Discussion Paper IIM/LMP 86-11, Wissenschaftszentrum, Berlin.

Garrett, Geoffrey/Peter Lange, 1986: Performance in a Hostile World: Economic Growth in Capitalist Democracies, 1974–80. *World Politics* 38, 517–545.

Hall, Peter A., 1986: *Governing the Economy: The Politics of State Intervention in Britain and France.* Cambridge, MA: Polity Press.

Hibbs, Douglas A., 1977: Political Parties and Macroeconomic Policy. *American Political Science Review* 71, 1467–1487.

Kahneman, David/Amos Tversky, 1984: Choices, Values, and Frames. *American Psychologist* 39, 341–350.

Kelley, Harold H., 1984: The Theoretical Description of Interdependence by Means of Transition Lists. *Journal of Personality and Social Psychology* 47, 956–982.

Kloten, Norbert/Karl-Heinz Ketterer/Rainer Vollmer, 1985: West Germany's Stabilization Performance. In Leon N. Lindberg/Charles S. Maier, eds., *The Politics of Inflation and Economic Stagnation: Theoretical Approaches and International Case Studies,* 353–402. Washington, DC: Brookings Institution.

Korpi, Walter, 1983: *The Democratic Class Struggle.* London: Routledge & Kegan Paul.

Lange, Peter/Geoffrey Garrett, 1985: The Politics of Growth: Strategic Interaction and Economic Performance in the Advanced Industrial Democracies, 1974–1980. *Journal of Politics* 47, 792–827.

Lowery, David, 1985: The Keynesian and Political Determinants of Unbalanced Budgets: U.S. Fiscal Policy from Eisenhower to Reagan. *American Journal of Political Science* 29, 428–460.

Maital, Shlomo/Yael Benjamini, 1979: Inflation as a Prisoner's Dilemma. *Journal of Post-Keynesian Economics* 2, 459–481.

Malinvaud, Edmond, 1977: *The Theory of Unemployment Reconsidered.* Oxford: Basil Blackwell.

Marin, Bernd, 1982: *Die Paritätische Kommission: Aufgeklärter Technokorporatismus in Österreich.* Vienna: Internationale Publikationen.

_____, 1985: Generalized Political Exchange: Preliminary Considerations. Working Paper No. 85/190, European University Institute, Florence.

Martin, Andrew, 1984: Trade Unions in Sweden: Strategic Responses to Change and Crisis. In Peter Gourevitch/Andrew Martin/George Ross/Christopher Allen/Stephen Bornstein/Andrew Markovits, eds., *Unions and Economic Crisis: Britain, West Germany, and Sweden,* 189–359. London: Allen & Unwin.

_____, 1986a: The Politics of Employment and Welfare: National Policies and International Interdependence. In Keith Banting, ed., *The State and Economic Interests,* 157–240. Toronto: University of Toronto Press.

_____, 1986b: The End of the "Swedish Model"? Recent Developments in Swedish Industrial Relations. Unpublished manuscript, Center For European Studies, Harvard University, Cambridge, MA.

McRae, C. Duncan, 1977: A Political Model of the Business Cycle. *Journal of Political Economy* 85, 239–263.

Messick, David M./Carol L. McClelland, 1983: Social Traps and Temporal Traps. *Personality and Social Psychology Bulletin* 9, 105–110.

Miegel, Meinhard, 1981: *Sicherheit im Alter: Plädoyer für die Weiterentwicklung des Rentensystems.* Stuttgart: Bonn Aktuell.

Neck, Reinhard, 1985: Das österreichische System der Sozial- und Wirtschaftspartnerschaft aus politisch-ökonomischer Sicht. *Journal für Sozialforschung* 25, 375–403.

Nordhaus, William, 1975: The Political Business Cycle. *Review of Economic Studies* 42, 169–190.

Olson, Mancur, 1982: *The Rise and Decline of Nations: Economic Growth, Stagflation, and Social Rigidities.* New Haven: Yale University Press.

Paloheimo, Heikki, 1984: Distributive Struggle, Corporatist Power Structures, and Economic Policy of the 1970s in Developed Capitalist Countries. In Heikki Paloheimo, ed., *Politics in the Era of Corporatism and Planning,* 1–46. Tampere: The Finnish Political Science Association.

Panitch, Leo, 1979: The Development of Corporatism in Liberal Democracies. In Philippe C. Schmitter/Gerhard Lehmbruch, eds., *Trends Toward Corporatist Intermediation,* 119–146. London: Sage.

Peel, David A., 1982: The Political Business Cycle: Have We Seen the End of It? *Long Range Planning* 15, 30–33.

Piore, Michael J., ed., 1979: *Unemployment and Inflation: Institutionalist and Structuralist Views.* White Plains, NY: M. E. Sharpe.

Pizzorno, Alessandro, 1978: Political Exchange and Collective Identity in Industrial Conflict. In Colin Crouch/Alessandro Pizzorno, eds., *The Resurgence of Class Conflict in Western Europe Since 1978,* vol. 2, *Comparative Analyses,* 277–298. London: Macmillan.

Przeworski, Adam/Henry Teune, 1970: *The Logic of Comparative Social Inquiry.* New York: John Wiley.

Putnam, Robert D., 1986: The Logic of Two-Level Games: International Cooperation and Western Summitry, 1975–1986. Unpublished manuscript, Department of Government, Harvard University, Cambridge, MA. (Since published as "Diplomacy and Domestic Politics: The Logic of Two-Level Games," *International Organization* 42 [1988], 429–460.)

Putnam, Robert D./Nicholas Bayne, 1984: *Hanging Together: The Seven-Power Summits.* London: Heinemann.

Rapoport, Anatol/Melvin J. Guyer/David G. Gordon, 1976: *The 2 x 2 Game.* Ann Arbor: University of Michigan Press.

Scharpf, Fritz W., 1981: The Political Economy of Inflation and Unemployment in Western Europe: An Outline. Discussion Paper IIM/LMP 81–21, Wissenschaftszentrum, Berlin.

_____, 1984: Economic and Institutional Constraints of Full-Employment Strategies: Sweden, Austria, and West Germany. In John H. Goldthorpe, ed., *Order and Conflict in Contemporary Capitalism: Studies in the Political Economy of Western European Nations,* 257–290. Oxford: Clarendon.

_____, 1987: *Sozialdemokratische Krisenpolitik in Europa: Das "Modell Deutschland" im Vergleich.* Frankfurt am Main: Campus. (Since published as *Crisis and Choice in European Social Democracy.* Ithaca: Cornell University Press, 1991.)

Schelling, Thomas C., 1984: *Choice and Consequence.* Cambridge, MA: Harvard University Press.

Schmidt, Manfred G., 1982: Does Corporatism Matter? Economic Crisis, Politics, and Rates of Unemployment in Capitalist Democracies in the 1970s. In Gerhard Lehmbruch/ Philippe C. Schmitter, eds., *Patterns of Corporatist Policy-Making,* 237–258. London: Sage.

_____, 1983: The Welfare State and the Economy in Periods of Economic Crisis: A Comparative Study of Twenty-three OECD Nations. *European Journal of Political Research* 11, 1–26.

_____, 1985: *Der Schweizerische Weg zur Vollbeschäftigung: Eine Bilanz der Beschäftigung, der Arbeitslosigkeit und der Arbeitsmarktpolitik.* Frankfurt am Main: Campus.

_____, 1986: Politische Bedingungen erfolgreicher Wirtschaftspolitik: Eine vergleichende Analyse westlicher Industrieländer. *Journal für Sozialforschung* Heft 3.

Schmitter, Philippe C., 1974: Still the Century of Corporatism? *Review of Politics* 36, 85–131.

_____, 1981: Interest Intermediation and Regime Governability in Contemporary Western Europe and North America. In Suzanne Berger, ed., *Organizing Interests in Western Europe: Pluralism, Corporatism, and Transformation Politics,* 287–327. Cambridge, MA: Harvard University Press.

Shepsle, Kenneth A., 1986: Cooperation and Institutional Arrangements. Paper prepared for the Harvard Conference on International Regimes and Cooperation, February 13–15, 1986.

Streeck, Wolfgang, 1981: *Gewerkschaftliche Organisationsprobleme in der sozialstaatlichen Demokratie.* Königstein: Athenäum.

_____, 1982: Organizational Consequences of Neo-corporatist Cooperation in West German Labor Unions. In Gerhard Lehmbruch/Philippe C. Schmitter, eds., *Patterns of Corporatist Policy-Making,* 29–81. London: Sage.

_____, 1984: Neo-corporatist Industrial Relations and the Economic Crisis in West Germany. In John H. Goldthorpe, ed., *Order and Conflict in Contemporary Capitalism: Studies in the Political Economy of Western European Nations,* 291–314. Oxford: Clarendon.

Streeck, Wolfgang/Philippe C. Schmitter, 1985: *Private Interest Government: Beyond Market and State.* London: Sage.

Therborn, Göran, 1986: *Why Some Peoples Are More Unemployed Than Others: The Strange Paradox of Growth and Unemployment.* London: Verso.

Tufte, Edward R., 1978: *The Political Control of the Economy.* Princeton: Princeton University Press.

Weintraub, Sidney, 1978: *Capitalism's Inflation and Unemployment Crisis.* Reading, MA: Addison-Wesley.

Wilensky, Harold L./Lowell Turner, 1987: *Democratic Corporatism and Policy Linkages: The Interdependence of Industrial, Labor-Market, Incomes, and Social Policies in Eight Countries.* Berkeley: Institute of International Studies.

Woolley, John T., 1985: Central Banks and Inflation. In Leon N. Lindberg/Charles S. Maier, eds., *The Politics of Inflation and Economic Stagnation: Theoretical Approaches and International Case Studies,* 318–351. Washington, DC: Brookings Institution.

# Appendix 2
# Efficient Self-Coordination in Policy Networks—A Simulation Study

*Fritz W. Scharpf and Matthias Mohr*

## THE PROMISE OF SELF-COORDINATION

Normative theories of representative democracy generally presuppose hierarchical governance. Democratic accountability seems to require that policy choices should originate from a unitary government (or a presidency) that is legitimated through competitive general elections, that they should be ratified by majority decisions in parliament, and that they should then be implemented by a disciplined bureaucracy relying on the superior force of the state and using resources collected through general taxation. By holding the governing hierarchy accountable to the *general* electorate, and by minimizing the direct influence of special interests on any phase of the policy process, the democratic process is supposed to produce policy outcomes that will maximize the *general welfare* of the polity.

In the real world of Western democracies, of course, actual policy choices are often worked out through negotiations among the representatives of partial interests in a great variety of arenas—among ministerial departments, among coalition parties, among specialized legislative committees, between the federal government and the states, in transnational agreements, in neocorporatist concertation between the government and associations of capital and labor, or other representatives of sectoral self-organization, and in issue-specific policy networks involving interest organizations together with specialized subunits within the executive and legislative branches of government. Typically, parties to these negotiations not only represent particular interests but also are likely to control specific action resources—jurisdictional competencies or the loyalty of certain segments of the population—whose use may be essential for the achievement of policy goals.

All of these forms of negotiated policymaking present challenges to conventional democratic theory that are not yet well understood. During the 1970s and 1980s, the attention

---

Originally published as Discussion Paper 94/1, Max Planck Institute for the Study of Societies, Cologne, 1994.

of political scientists was mainly focused on the implications of neocorporatist concertation (Schmitter/Lehmbruch 1979; Lehmbruch/Schmitter 1982; Goldthorpe 1984). After
the apparent decline of this mode of governance, there now seems to be a renewed interest
in pluralist policy networks involving a larger number of governmental and nongovernmental corporate actors in more loosely coupled interactions (Laumann/Knoke 1987;
Schneider 1988; Marin 1990; Marin/Mayntz 1991).

Much of this recent work is empirical and explanatory, drawing on the powerful tools
of social network analysis (cluster analysis, block models, graph theory, etc.) for more accurate descriptions of highly complex structures of interaction. In general (but see Mayntz
1992; 1993b), less systematic attention is now paid to the normative, or evaluative, questions that were a central concern of the theorists of pluralist democracy in the 1950s and
1960s (e.g., Truman 1951; Dahl 1967) as well as of their critics (McConnell 1966; Lowi
1969). In the present paper, we will address these concerns in an analytical effort that takes
as its point of departure the intellectually most ambitious attempt to justify pluralist policymaking in welfare-theoretical terms.

Charles Lindblom (1959) described governance in pluralist democracies as a "science of
muddling through" that relies on *disjointed incrementalism* as its "strategy of decision"
(Braybrooke/Lindblom 1963) and whose "intelligence" is produced through *partisan mutual adjustment* (Lindblom 1965). Both of these practices are primarily justified *ex nega-
tivo*—by comparison, that is, to the counterfactual ideal of hierarchical governance based
on "synoptic" analyses of all pertinent issues and affected interests. While the synoptic
ideal is said to overtax the bounded rationality of real-world decisionmakers, the incrementalist strategy will disaggregate large and complex issues into series of small steps that
reduce the risks of misinformation and miscalculation, and that can use rapid feedback to
correct any errors. Similarly, instead of relying on the benevolence and omniscience of
central decisionmakers, partisan mutual adjustment will directly involve representatives of
affected groups and specialized officeholders that are able to utilize local information and
to fend for their own interests in pluralist bargaining processes. In short, compared to an
impossible ideal, muddling through is not only feasible but also likely to increase overall
welfare by producing policy choices that are, at the same time, better informed and more
sensitive to the affected interests.

It is fair to say that Lindblom's critique of the synoptic and centralized ideal found a
much more sympathetic audience than his welfare-theoretic defense of incrementalism
and pluralist bargaining. Incrementalism was equated with the "tyranny of small decisions" (Kahn 1966) that must systematically preclude large-scale policy changes. Its conservative implications were thus in conflict with the planning optimism and the reformist
spirit of the period (Dror 1964; Etzioni 1968). On the pluralist front, the egalitarian assumption that all societal interests were in fact effectively organized had been attacked on
empirical grounds by "elite theorists" in American sociology and political science (Hunter
1953; Mills 1956; Schattschneider 1960). An even more fundamental challenge was raised
by Mancur Olson's analytical demonstration that under rational-actor assumptions, the
most widely shared interests would be least capable of organization, or at least systematically disadvantaged in collective action (Olson 1965). Finally, the rise of public-choice theory with its emphasis on rent seeking in the public sector has dampened any remaining
enthusiasm for the welfare potential of pluralist bargaining—in fact, Mancur Olson has
since placed the blame for the economic "decline of nations" precisely on the effectiveness
of "distributive coalitions" in pluralist democracies (Olson 1982).

In his later work, Lindblom himself has conceded some of these points. That is particularly true of the egalitarian issue—where he now describes the "market as prison" (Lindblom 1982) to characterize the superior influence of capitalist interests in market economies. Since policymakers depend on profit-oriented private investment for economic growth and employment, capital interests must be respected through "deferential adaptation" and need not even be actively pursued through pluralist lobbying (Lindblom 1977). At the same time, Lindblom also had second thoughts on the virtues of incrementalism and mutual adjustment, suggesting that these practices might be most useful for a subclass of "secondary issues" while "grand issues" would benefit from "broad-ranging, often highly speculative, and sometimes utopian thinking about directions and possible futures, near and far in time" (Lindblom 1979, 522). In that regard, however, he may well have gone too far in his self-criticism. Some recent work suggests that the incrementalist strategy of decision may have greater reformist potential than it was given credit for by Lindblom's critics (Gregory 1989; Weiss/Woodhouse 1992). In our opinion, the same can also be demonstrated for partisan mutual adjustment. In order to do so, we will first reconstruct and systematize the variety of coordinating mechanisms that can be subsumed under the common label of partisan mutual adjustment, and we will then present the results of computer simulation experiments that were designed to explore the welfare effects as well as the transaction costs of these coordination mechanisms used separately and in combination.

## VARIETIES OF PARTISAN MUTUAL ADJUSTMENT

When the decisions of one actor have an impact on matters that are also the object of the decisions of another actor, welfare gains may be obtained through the coordination of these decisions. While coordination is generally considered desirable, it is also a poorly understood concept. Lindblom (1965, 154) provides at least a rudimentary definition: "A set of decisions is coordinated if adjustments have been made in it such that the adverse consequences of any one decision for other decisions in the set are to a degree and in some frequency avoided, reduced, counterbalanced, or outweighed."

Thus negative externalities should be avoided or compensated and, of course, positive externalities should be identified and exploited. Optimal coordination, in other words, is defined not merely by the Pareto criterion but also by the utilitarian Kaldor criterion, according to which public policy measures should be undertaken whenever their negative consequences are outweighed by their expected aggregate benefits (Kaldor 1939). But Lindblom is less concerned with definitions of welfare-theoretic optimality than with the demonstration that the welfare gains of coordination can be realized in the absence of a central, hierarchical coordinator and even in the absence of common goals and worldviews among the actors involved. In everyday life, "people can coordinate with each other without anyone's coordinating them, without a dominant common purpose, and without rules that fully prescribe their relations to each other" (1965, 3)—and the same is supposedly true of the multiple participants in pluralist policy processes. They should be able to achieve coordination through one of several methods of partisan mutual adjustment.

Lindblom provides an "exhaustive list" of twelve such methods altogether, subdivided into two classes, "adaptive adjustment" and "manipulated adjustment" (1965, 33–34). While the latter class describes variants of negotiations whose definitions are neither particularly original nor very systematic (and which we will try to redefine in the latter part of this section), the former includes two forms of nonnegotiated coordination, "parametric adjustment" and "deferential adjustment," whose existence is not generally recognized in the literature. They are important enough to merit a more thorough explication and discussion of their welfare-theoretic characteristics.

## Parametric Adjustment

We begin our examination with parametric adjustment, which Lindblom defines as follows (1965, 37): "In a decision situation, a decision maker X adjusts his decision to Y's decisions already made and to Y's expected decisions; but he does not seek, as a recognized condition of making his own decision effective, to induce a response from Y; nor does he allow the choice of his decision to be influenced by any consideration of the consequences of his decision for Y."

It is clear from this definition and the accompanying descriptive examples that Lindblom has in mind a form of interaction that, in game-theoretic terminology (which he never uses, however), could be described as a peculiar type of noncooperative sequential game. What makes it peculiar—in contrast to the superhuman assumptions of classical game theory—are the much more modest demands on the information available to, and the computational capacities possessed by, the players. In parametric adjustment, players depend on only two sets of information: the first describing the status quo, as it was brought about by the past moves of players, and the second describing their own potential moves and the outcomes that these will, ceteris paribus, be able to produce. In addition, players must of course be able to compare these outcomes to the status quo in the light of their own self-interest. But they are explicitly not required to have prior information on the payoffs and potential moves of other players, and they are not expected to be able to anticipate the future responses of other players to the moves that they themselves are considering. It is only when another player makes a move, or proposes a certain move, that they must be able to identify its impact on their own interest position. In other words, the need for omniscience and the infinite regress of conditional expectations, which are likely to overtax the capacities of real actors in the simultaneous or in the fully anticipated sequential games of noncooperative game theory (Scharpf 1990), are cut short by these assumptions of bounded rationality.

By itself, that is not remarkable. Bounded rationality is a flexible concept that can be defined to mean various things. The point that Lindblom needs to make is that the assumed constraints on rationality will not necessarily have negative effects, in welfare-theoretic terms, on the outcomes obtained. He achieves this purpose through a peculiar interpretation of the sequential nature of moves in parametric adjustment. In effect, the functions that classical game theory ascribes to mutual anticipation, based on the common knowledge of strategies and payoffs, are here supposed to be performed by hindsight in ongoing processes of interaction. In these processes, prior information and forward planning are replaced by sequences of responses, "creating in the 'present' a rapid succession of 'pasts' to which each rapidly succeeding decision can be adapted" (Lindblom 1965, 39).

But while it is surely true that in ongoing processes of interdependent choices, each move of a self-interested and myopic player may impose externalities on others, or create new opportunities for others, to which these will again respond, and so on—that does not assure the equivalence of outcomes to those that would be achieved under conditions of complete information and perfect foresight. If there is an equivalence, it must be owed to the concept of a noncooperative Nash equilibrium that—regardless of how it was reached—cannot be unilaterally left again by perfectly or boundedly rational players. It is this possibility of a Nash equilibrium that justifies Lindblom's optimism that, in parametric adjustment, "chaos is not the only possible consequence. What may ensue is a kind of process of successive approximation" (1965, 40).

So far, so good. We know from historical case studies that myopic actors, in noncooperative games played sequentially, may "lock in" on a path-dependent equilibrium in which none of the players is left with an option that could still improve its own situation (David 1985; Arthur 1990); and we have it from the best game-theoretic authority that a game of incomplete information, in which players are ignorant of one another's preferences, may be the equivalent of a (much more complicated) game of complete information (Brams/Doherty 1993).

But as Lindblom recognizes, equilibrium is not the most likely outcome. While mathematical game theory assures us that every noncooperative simultaneous game has at least one Nash equilibrium in mixed strategies, players in Lindblom's version of a sequential game are constrained to use only pure strategies, and the path-dependent nature of the process may also place some existing pure-strategy equilibria beyond the reach of players who must start from a particular status-quo position. As a consequence, the probability of reaching any equilibrium outcome at all diminishes rapidly as the number of players and the number of their available options increase. Interaction may then deteriorate into an unending sequence of meandering moves—with presumably negative welfare consequences.

But even when an equilibrium can be reached, there is no reason to think—as Lindblom seems to do—that it must be a good solution. In fact, any speculation about the welfare-theoretical qualities of noncooperative equilibria is meaningless unless the original game constellation is well defined. When that constellation resembles an n-person Prisoner's Dilemma, the outcome of a sequential noncooperative game—even when players are non-myopic and fully rational—will be the "Tragedy of the Commons" (Hardin 1968), in which all parties end up worse off than in the status quo from which they started. That this is by no means an unlikely outcome is demonstrated by the inflationary spirals produced by partisan mutual adjustment among fragmented and competing labor unions (Scharpf 1991). And even when constellations are more benign, mutual adjustment may well "lock in" on a local optimum that is inferior to better solutions that, however, cannot be reached through path-dependent sequential moves. A pertinent example is provided by Paul David's famous study of the evolution of the QWERTY typewriter keyboard (David 1985).

However, while there surely is no general reason to consider parametric adjustment or sequential noncooperative games as a promising method for achieving welfare-increasing coordination, there are certain specific types of game constellations in which precisely this method is superior to all others in achieving coordination at the lowest transaction costs. One obvious example are games of pure coordination in which interests coincide and in which even the problem of converging upon one among several equally acceptable coordination points (Schelling 1960) is eliminated by the sequential character of Lindblom's game. Once one party has moved, the other one has no problem in making an optimal choice. Of course, under such benign circumstances, all other methods of coordination would also work equally well.

But parametric adjustment also turns out to be the optimal approach to certain types of mixed-motive game constellations in which other coordination mechanisms would run into difficulties. The prime example is constellations resembling the Battle of the Sexes game, in which all parties prefer a coordinated outcome over the consequences of noncoordination but in which there is conflict over the choice among several coordinated solutions that differ in their distributive consequences. Under such conditions coordination may not be achieved at all in noncooperative games with simultaneous moves, and even when binding agreements are possible, they may fail to be reached because of high transaction costs. By contrast, coordination is quite easily achieved in a noncooperative game that is being played sequentially. Here, whichever player moves first is able to select its most preferred solution, while later players (assuming perfect information on others' past moves) will find it in their interest to converge on the coordinated solution so defined, even though it is by no means their most preferred outcome.[1] Given the fact that they still prefer coordination to noncoordination, they have no rational alternative. Similar conditions are likely to prevail in constellations resembling the Chicken game.

### Deferential Adjustment

Nevertheless, these are narrowly circumscribed constellations that will not justify a positive evaluation of the welfare consequences of parametric adjustment in the general case. To a somewhat lesser degree, this verdict also applies to deferential adjustment, Lindblom's second type of noncooperative coordination mechanism, which he defines as follows (1965, 45): "In a decision situation, a decision maker X does not seek, as a condition of making his own decision, to induce a response from another decision maker Y. He either deliberately avoids impinging adversely on Y's values or he takes care not knowingly to impinge adversely, except trivially, on Y's values as Y perceives them at the time of X's decision; nor does he tailor his decision to create a gain for Y."

In other words, deferential adjustment requires that decisionmakers unilaterally avoid negative externalities for other actors or their jurisdictional domains. This resembles the "Negative Coordination" that Renate Mayntz and Fritz Scharpf found to prevail in the German federal bureaucracy, where departmental policy initiatives must, as a rule, be designed so as to avoid potential objections from other departments since the cabinet is generally unwilling to act in the face of unresolved interdepartmental conflict (Mayntz/Scharpf 1975, 145–150). More generally, the pattern is likely to arise in all constellations in which jurisdictional domains, property rights, or vested interests are protected by substantive law, by procedural veto positions, by the anticipation of retaliation, or by mutual sympathy (Scharpf 1993). While the existence of these conditions surely cannot be universally assumed, deferential adjustment or Negative Coordination still occurs frequently enough to merit systematic attention.

In their study of interdepartmental policymaking, Mayntz and Scharpf emphasized the dangers of political immobilism when innovative options were blocked by interdepartmental vetoes. Lindblom, on the other hand, had focused on the welfare-theoretic advantages of deferential over parametric adjustment: Excluding moves that would violate another party's interests would prevent players from locking into Nash equilibria that are inferior to the status quo. Moreover, since the status quo cannot be left at all[2] if any party has reason to object, the danger of endlessly meandering moves and countermoves in situations without a Nash equilibrium is also eliminated. Unlike parametric adjustment in noncooperative games, therefore, Negative Coordination will only permit policy changes that are Pareto-superior to the status quo.

At the same time, however, this form of coordination can hardly exploit the potential welfare gains inherent in a particular constellation of interests. Lindblom, it is true, hopes that the self-blocking tendencies of veto systems will also stimulate the search for innovative solutions that are acceptable all around (1965, 47–51). But when all is considered, it is still analytically true that the space for innovative solutions must rapidly shrink as the number and variety of veto positions increase.[3] With three actors, the probability of agreement is reduced to $p = 1/4$, and with n actors it shrinks to $p = 1/2(n - 1)$. Deferential adjustment is able to avoid disturbances and losses, but it is not, by itself, able to approximate the welfare optimum.

## Varieties of Negotiated Coordination

Thus Lindblom's welfare-theoretic claims appear questionable for both[4] of the "adaptive" variants of partisan mutual adjustment. But that may not be equally true of manipulated adjustment, or at least not of those variants that in one way or another involve negotiations and binding agreements. Lindblom distinguishes among "negotiation," "bargaining," "partisan discussion," "compensation," and "reciprocity."[5] All of these modes provide for coordination through voluntary agreement, which can only be expected when all parties can expect to be better off than they would be without the agreement. Under such conditions coordination is indeed likely to produce positive welfare effects for participants—and according to the Coase Theorem (which Lindblom does not mention), outcomes may systematically approximate the utilitarian welfare optimum (Coase 1960), provided that they are divisible and transferable, or that side payments or package deals are possible (Scharpf 1992). Depending on the allocation of property rights, either winners could compensate losers if aggregate gains are higher than aggregate costs, or potential victims could pay for the avoidance of initiatives whose aggregate costs exceed aggregate benefits. Of course distributional consequences would differ—but in both cases all initiatives that increase net aggregate welfare, and only those initiatives, would be realized through negotiated coordination.

However, the Coase Theorem not only is insensitive to distributional issues, but it also presupposes complete information and negligible transaction costs—and its welfare-theoretic conclusions are highly sensitive to real-world departures from these idealized conditions.[6] Moreover, the different variants of Negotiated Coordination seem to be affected in different ways and to different degrees by the obstacles to agreement encountered in real-world decision processes. In order to discuss these differences, however, Lindblom's phenomenological categories appear to be less useful than a theoretically derived classification that is based on the two crucial dimensions of the negotiation problem: Negotiated Coordination enables actors to create value (or to avoid losses), either through cooperating on the production of new goods or through the (utility-increasing) exchange of existing goods (the dimension of *value creation*). At the same time, parties must also agree on how to divide the value so created and how to allocate the costs of joint action among themselves—either by choosing among several coordinated solutions available or by defining appropriate side payments (the dimension of *distribution*).

Logically, all negotiations can be characterized in both of these dimensions (Walton/McKersie 1965; Lax/Sebenius 1986). But both dimensions will not be equally salient in all negotiations—which also means that different types of disagreement will have to be overcome in the individual case. This will in turn determine the procedures that must, at a minimum, be employed to reach successful coordination through negotiations.[7] When value creation is at issue, new solutions must be invented and comparatively evaluated in terms of their effectiveness and costs; when distribution is in dispute, the justification of competing claims must be discussed in the light of accepted standards of distributive justice. It thus seems promising to use the salience of potential disagreement over value creation and over distribution for a systematic classification of types of negotiations. They will here be labeled "Negative Coordination," "Bargaining," "Problem Solving," and "Positive Coordination" (Figure A2.1).

*Negative Coordination.* The first field is meant to describe minimal negotiations in which neither issues of joint production nor issues of distribution are of high salience but in which agreement is nevertheless necessary. This is true in market exchanges when a well-defined product is offered at a fixed price, leaving the buyer only the choice of accepting or rejecting it. It is also true, however, in a form of deferential adjustment, discussed earlier, in which the occupant of a veto position must explicitly agree to let a policy initiative pass. As in market exchanges, negotiations may be quite rudimentary, since they will be about a well-defined object (e.g., a policy initiative pursued by one of the parties, in which others are not expected to take an intrinsic interest). Since the exercise of a veto will simply end this particular transaction, there is also no incentive to dissimulate circumstances or motives. As a consequence, the transaction costs of pure Negative Coordination may be minimal—all that is needed is to check for agreement or vetoes, which, in either case, will bring the interaction to an end. But, for the reasons discussed earlier, if transaction costs are minimal, so are the welfare gains that can be expected if this form of coordination is practiced exclusively.

*Bargaining.*[8] The second field is the location of negotiations dominated by distributional issues, in which problems of value creation play little or no role. In market exchanges this would apply to the purchase of an existing object that is unique—a house or a work of art—so that its price must be determined through bargaining among the parties. Other examples may be collective bargaining over wages but also many political compromises in which it is expected that the outcome will be an "intermediate" solution between the extreme positions championed by the parties. Similarly, the Nash bargaining solution and its variants (Nash 1953; Kalai/Smorodinsky 1975; Rubinstein 1982) presuppose the existence of a given production possibility frontier that is not itself the object of negotiations. In any case, Bargaining is focused entirely on the distributional issue (Figure A2.2).

From a welfare-theoretical point of view, the great advantage that Bargaining has over Negative Coordination arises from the possibility of compensation. Solutions are not automatically ruled out when they seem to violate the status-quo interests of one of the parties. Thus, in Figure A2.2, if actor Y proposes solution A (which, by itself, would be completely unacceptable to actor X), an agreement can still be reached through side payments from Y to B, which will in effect transform solution A into solution B, to which X would have no reason to object. As a consequence, bargaining processes can potentially reach any solution that lies on the utility isoquant of a given proposal—provided that the parties are able to reach agreement on the distributional issue. This may be difficult, since both sides will have incentives to dissimulate factors affecting their valuation of the outcome—but when it is simply a case of buying off a potential veto through the compensation of expected damages, transaction costs may nevertheless remain within manageable bounds.

*Problem Solving.*[9] The third field of Figure A2.1 represents "cooperation" in its pure form. Here actors are somehow able to concentrate on issues of joint production and to

**Salience of Distribution**

|  | | low | high |
|---|---|---|---|
| | low | (1)<br>Neg. Coordination | (2)<br>Bargaining |
| **Salience of**<br>**Value-Creation** | high | (3)<br>Problem Solving | (4)<br>Pos. Coordination |

FIGURE A2.1    Ideal types of negotiations

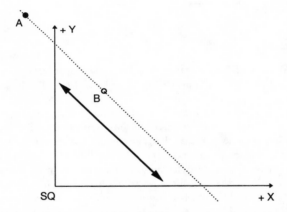

FIGURE A2.2    Bargaining over divisible outcomes (SQ = Status Quo)

put distributive issues aside at least temporarily. If the focus is on the comparative evaluation of available solutions, the criterion is their contribution to the common or aggregate
interest of all participants; but even more important will be the common search for new
solutions that will extend the possibility frontier—without regard to their distributional
consequences. In Figure A2.3 therefore, both parties would join in the search for the welfare-maximizing solution B, even though its realization would leave X worse off than
would have solution A.

These may appear to be highly idealistic stipulations—which is why the possibility of
Problem Solving is often dismissed as practically irrelevant by social scientists committed
to a rational-actor perspective. But that conclusion appears too simple-minded. Actors are
in fact often involved in negotiations in which distributional issues are quite irrelevant.
Sometimes these are effectively neutralized by prior agreement on explicit rules for the allocation of costs and benefits. This is the typical case in joint ventures, which are based on
elaborate contracts settling all sorts of distributive issues in advance in order to facilitate
uninhibited cooperation within the common undertaking. Similarly, in the Swiss federal
government a fixed allocation of ministerial positions to a set of political parties tends to

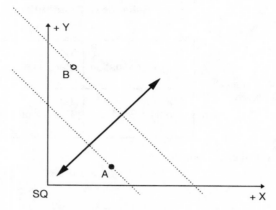

FIGURE A2.3    Problem Solving (SQ = Status Quo)

immunize "consociational" cooperation even against the distributional conflicts arising from electoral competition (Lehmbruch 1967; Bogdanor 1988). Examples in other areas are easy to find.

Another condition facilitating Problem Solving is the "veil of ignorance." It is well illustrated in a case study of successful research collaboration among firms that became feasible only after it had become clear that all of the competitors were as yet very far from the point at which they might have marketable products to introduce (Lütz 1993; Häusler/Hohn/Lütz 1993). Similarly, technical standardization by committees in telecommunications is relatively easy to achieve for technologies that have not yet been introduced, but it is extremely difficult when competing solutions are already on the market, so that their producers would benefit or suffer when one or another was adopted as a common standard (Schmidt/Werle 1992).

Problem Solving also occurs within organizations, in which the personal self-interest of staff members is largely neutralized when the actions required occur within the "area of acceptance" or "zone of indifference" specified by the employment relation (Simon 1957; 1991; March/Simon 1958). Similarly, corporate actors involved in policy networks may also engage in processes of Problem Solving governed by notions of public interest or "systemic rationality" as long as their own institutional self-interest is not challenged in the process. As Mayntz has shown, this was true of the role of the large West German research organizations in the transformation of the East German Academy of Sciences (Mayntz 1994).

In short, therefore, Problem Solving is by no means a rare and exotic mode of coordination that could be safely dismissed in realistic analyses of real-world negotiations. True, its practice does depend on specific preconditions that are neither ubiquitous nor easily created where they do not exist. But they do occur quite frequently, and where they do exist, the search for welfare-maximizing solutions can be immensely facilitated by negotiations in which distributive conflict is not a major obstacle to agreement.[10]

*Positive Coordination.*    The fourth field in Figure A2.1, finally, describes negotiations in which participants must simultaneously solve production problems and resolve conflicts over distribution. Mayntz and Scharpf identified this mode in their study of interdepart-

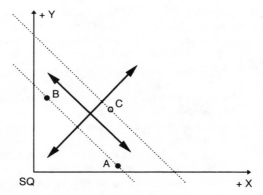

FIGURE A2.4     Positive Coordination (SQ = Status Quo)

mental task forces in the German federal bureaucracy, whose members were supposed to develop innovative policy solutions for problems cutting across several ministerial portfolios
but were expected at the same time to protect the domain interests of their respective home
departments (Mayntz/Scharpf 1975). In their view, this was the most desirable and, at the
same time, the most difficult form of coordination actually practiced in policy processes.

The difficulties result from the contradictory nature of the functions that must be simultaneously performed. In Figure A2.4, they are represented by moves in orthogonal directions. If attention is focused on distributional issues, parties concentrating on their most
preferred solutions, A or B, may not even perceive the overall superior solution C. This solution will not come into view unless participants realize that the pursuit of maximal advantage is ultimately pointless, since an equitable division will be the precondition of agreement in any case. Once this is accepted, it will be obvious that solution C may be better even
from a self-interested point of view than the inevitable compromise between A and B.

What stands in the way of agreement is not only a cognitive problem, however. As long
as negotiations are dominated by attention to distributive issues, success will in fact be facilitated by "playing one's cards close to one's chest," by understating one's own interest in
an agreed-upon solution, and by manipulating information about the likely consequences
of different solutions. Such stratagems, however, are objectively incompatible with the
joint search for superior solutions, which can only succeed if communication is open and
information freely exchanged. Worse yet, parties who are actively engaged in the search for
common advantage are most likely to be exploited by partners who are primarily trying to
maximize their own shares. This is the core of the "Negotiator's Dilemma" (Lax/Sebenius
1986), which often leads to the failure of Positive Coordination. If it is to be overcome, not
only must the parties develop mutual trust in the face of ubiquitous opportunities for deception, but also they must agree on fair rules of distribution and their application to the
case at hand (Scharpf 1992).

Thus it may seem that we have finally discovered a general mechanism that would permit pluralist polities to maximize their common welfare even when all parties involved are
pursuing their own self-interested goals rather than the public interest. Unfortunately,
however, the welfare-theoretic argument holds only for those corporate actors that in fact
participate in policy negotiations and for the interests represented by them. Because of the

difficulties of reaching agreement in the first place, external effects are even more likely to be ignored by negotiating groups of self-interested actors than by self-interested individual actors. Thus, unless all affected interests are in fact represented, there is again no assurance that Positive Coordination by itself will increase rather than reduce general welfare. And even if we restrict attention to only those interests that are in fact represented in pluralist policy networks, relegating those that are excluded to other representational mechanisms,[11] the welfare-theoretic attractiveness of the solution is undercut by the escalating transactions costs as the number of participants increases.

Positive Coordination depends on trust, and mutual trust among rational egoists requires costly investments in trustworthiness; it takes time to develop, and it is easily destroyed (Sabel 1993; Scharpf 1993). And even if all parties were to refrain from deception, they would still find it difficult to achieve simultaneous agreement on the solution that is best for all and on the fair distribution of benefits and costs. Moreover, these transaction costs will increase exponentially, not proportionately, with the number of parties participating in negotiations. If each of $N$ participants has $S$ options to choose from, the search for the optimal solution requires the comparison of $S^N$ outcomes, and agreement on a fair distribution involves the examination of $N(N-1)/2$ bilateral relationships. By comparison, the transaction costs of Negative Coordination are much lower: Each party needs to be concerned only with its own options and with its own benefits and costs, and whoever takes the initiative to change the status quo needs only to check with $(N-1)$ other parties to see whether a veto will be exercised. The implication is that Negative Coordination may indeed be practical among relatively large numbers of participants, whereas Positive Coordination is not feasible beyond limits that, though difficult to define with any precision, are bound to be very narrow.[12]

Thus we seem not to have come very far in our search for the welfare potential of pluralist policy networks. Parametric adjustment in sequential noncooperative games is likely to lead to unstable constellations and may end in social traps (but see note 1). And Negative Coordination, while protecting status-quo interests, is hostile to welfare gains that can only be realized through policy innovation. Bargaining has a somewhat greater welfare potential when negotiations are merely about the costs and benefits of predefined solutions. Problem Solving, by contrast, is highly effective in defining innovative welfare-maximizing solutions, but it depends crucially on the neutralization of distributive issues. Finally, both of these constraints are relaxed in Positive Coordination, which, like Problem Solving, would allow participants to pursue their common interest to the fullest degree. However, the number of possible participants is constrained by escalating transaction costs. Hence Positive Coordination is likely to be practiced among small numbers of active participants. As a consequence, there may be significant external effects, and welfare gains obtained by participants may under certain conditions be more than offset by the damage done to the interests of outsiders.

In reaching these skeptical conclusions we have considered each of these coordination mechanisms separately. In doing so, however, we may not have done justice to the spirit of Lindblom's work, in which the welfare effects of partisan mutual adjustment are discussed without actually distinguishing among its different variants. That may be criticized as a lack of analytical precision, but it may also be interpreted as an implicit[13] suggestion that, in combination, the several coordinating mechanisms might have more attractive welfare consequences than each of them has when applied in isolation. In the remainder of this paper we will pursue this suggestion for constellations in which Positive Coordination,

Negative Coordination, and Bargaining are jointly applied to solve a given coordination problem. In order to do so, one of us (Mohr) has developed a computer simulation program that allows us to determine the welfare effects (defined by the influence on the *joint payoffs* of all participants) of different types of negotiation procedures. In the following section, we will provide a brief description of the characteristic features and results of the simulation.

## THE SIMULATION PROGRAM

We use computer simulation not in order to model particular processes of interdependent policy choices under conditions approaching real-world constellations but in order to clarify the general characteristics of the methods of coordination discussed earlier and of their combinations. Conceivably this clarification could also be achieved more elegantly by analytical means, and we certainly hope that some of our results will eventually be confirmed analytically. But we know of no analytical procedures that would permit us, at this stage of our work, to vary assumptions as flexibly, and to explore such a variety of stipulated conditions, as is possible with simulation methods. Thus, without further excuses, we proceed to present our basic simulation model.[14]

In one sense our model is deliberately unrealistic: It represents the horror world of total interdependence—a world that Herbert Simon (1962) promised we would never have to face. Each of N actors is able to choose among S policy options,[15] and each choice will affect the payoffs of all actors at the same time. If a method of coordination succeeds here, it will succeed more easily under the more benign conditions of selective interdependence. Moreover, the interdependence among policy choices is unstructured, since our model uses random payoff matrices of size $S^N$ rather than matrices representing certain types of well-known game constellations.[16] Payoffs are assumed to be interpersonally comparable, measurable in a general medium of exchange, such as money, and transferable if required.[17] Games are played sequentially,[18] and players are assumed to be myopic in the sense defined earlier in the exposition of Lindblom's parametric adjustment. They will respond to other players' moves but cannot anticipate them; and in selecting their own moves, they will always pick the one that would give them the highest payoff if no other player should move again.[19]

Table A2.1 illustrates these assumptions in a form of presentation that allows the direct inspection and analysis of fairly large n-person games in normal form. It represents a game with four players, each of which has two options, labeled 1 or 2. Each row stands for a cell of the payoff matrix, which is defined by a combination of options producing an outcome consisting of a set of individual payoffs (varying between 0 and 100). Players' choices are driven by the (myopic) maximization of individual payoffs, but since we are exploring *welfare effects* of various types of negotiations, our attention is focused on the aggregate or *joint payoffs* represented in the last column. Thus the relative success of a coordination method is judged by the location of the outcome in the solution space between the joint-payoff minimum (cell 8) and the joint-payoff maximum (cell 4). In order to achieve comparability, joint payoffs are normalized to a range between 0 and 1 in all later presentations.

Another characteristic that departs from the usual game-theoretic conventions is the fact that all our simulation runs must start from a specific "status quo" cell and that outcomes must be reached through sequential moves from this point of departure. In the

TABLE A2.1  Random Payoffs, 4 Players, 2 Options

| Cell | Option of Player A | B | C | D | Payoff for Player A | B | C | D | Joint Payoffs | Normalized Joint Payoffs |
|---|---|---|---|---|---|---|---|---|---|---|
| 1 | 1 | 1 | 1 | 1 | 20 | 69 | 46 | 18 | 153 | 0.20 |
| 2 | 2 | 1 | 1 | 1 | 97 | 29 | 52 | 00 | 178 | 0.35 |
| 3 | 1 | 2 | 1 | 1 | 73 | 25 | 37 | 00 | 135 | 0.10 |
| 4 | 2 | 2 | 1 | 1 | 73 | 76 | 99 | 38 | 286 | 1.00 |
| 5 | 1 | 1 | 2 | 1 | 48 | 23 | 79 | 98 | 248 | 0.77 |
| 6 | 2 | 1 | 2 | 1 | 42 | 60 | 60 | 31 | 193 | 0.44 |
| 7 | 1 | 2 | 2 | 1 | 97 | 69 | 33 | 26 | 225 | 0.63 |
| 8 | 2 | 2 | 2 | 1 | 22 | 10 | 50 | 37 | 119 | 0.00 |
| 9 | 1 | 1 | 1 | 2 | 94 | 08 | 05 | 37 | 144 | 0.15 |
| 10 | 2 | 1 | 1 | 2 | 24 | 71 | 31 | 34 | 160 | 0.25 |
| 11 | 1 | 2 | 1 | 2 | 94 | 99 | 03 | 05 | 201 | 0.49 |
| 12 | 2 | 2 | 1 | 2 | 51 | 81 | 11 | 20 | 163 | 0.26 |
| 13 | 1 | 1 | 2 | 2 | 18 | 25 | 29 | 60 | 132 | 0.08 |
| 14 | 2 | 1 | 2 | 2 | 88 | 87 | 07 | 16 | 198 | 0.47 |
| 15 | 1 | 2 | 2 | 2 | 35 | 26 | 63 | 12 | 136 | 0.10 |
| 16 | 2 | 2 | 2 | 2 | 96 | 80 | 47 | 04 | 227 | 0.65 |

present article, simulations will either start from the cell representing the joint-payoff minimum or from a cell selected at random.

## Parametric Adjustment

In order to simulate Lindblom's version of a noncooperative sequential game, the first move is assigned to the player that could achieve the largest individual gain through a unilateral switch from its status-quo policy position on the assumption that all other players would meanwhile stick to their own status-quo positions. This move then defines a new point of departure to which other players will now respond. Again, the player that can now expect the greatest individual gain will move, and again other players will respond to the new situation, and so on. The sequential noncooperative game will stop under one of two conditions: On the one hand, it is possible that a cell will be reached that represents a Nash equilibrium, that is, an outcome in which no player could still improve its own payoff by a unilateral change of policy. On the other hand, if no equilibrium is reached, moves will continue until a cell is reached that was touched before with the same player being in the position to move—at which point the game moves into an infinite cycle and the simulation breaks off. In this case, we arbitrarily assign status-quo payoffs to the outcome.[20]

In our example, player A would initially move the game from cell 1 to cell 2. Thereafter, player B would have most to gain by moving the game to cell 4—which would also benefit players C and D but would reduce the payoff of player A. However, neither A nor any other player could still improve the payoff by *unilaterally* changing its own option. Thus, a Nash equilibrium is reached that, incidentally, also represents the welfare maximum. But, of course, this is a not a representative example.

## Negative Coordination

Negative Coordination (or deferential adjustment in Lindblom's terminology) also begins with a first move by the player that has the most to gain. But that move can only be completed if it is not vetoed by another player that would be made worse off in comparison to the status quo. In other words, whoever has the right of initiative cannot impose negative externalities on others. If no veto is exercised, the game moves to the new cell and continues from there. Otherwise the leading player will try its next best move, and so on, until the game comes to a stop. Thus, in Table A2.1, player A would have the most to gain by moving the game from cell 1 to cell 2. But this move would be blocked by players B and D, whose status-quo interests would be violated.

Again, however, our example is not representative. When there are relatively few players with relatively many options, chances are good that the leading player will find ways to improve its own situation without damaging the status-quo interests of any other player. This would be even more likely if the initiative were not restricted to a single player but would shift to others when the first one could not succeed. If the number of options per player stays constant or is reduced, however, while the number of players (and thus the number of veto positions) increases, there is a much greater possibility that all initiatives will be blocked and that the status quo cannot be left under conditions of Negative Coordination. In any case, however, Negative Coordination will not produce payoffs that are worse than the status quo, and any initiative that is not blocked will lead to welfare improvements.

## Bargaining

The Bargaining process begins like Negative Coordination: The player with the most to gain makes the first move. But if this player encounters one or more vetoes, the move is not immediately withdrawn. Instead, the player determines whether the expected gain would be sufficient to (just barely) compensate those players that are objecting, so that their status-quo payoffs ("reservation payoffs") would be maintained while the first player would still make a profit. When that is true, the move is carried out, and the game continues from the new cell—whose payoffs are adjusted according to the outcome of the bargain. In Table A2.1, for instance, if the game starts in cell 1, player A would gain 77 points from a move to cell 2. This would also improve the payoff of player C, but player B would lose 40 points and player D would lose 18. Since the gains of player A are sufficient to compensate these losses, the move can be completed. The new reservation payoffs in cell 2 would now be 39, 69, 52, and 18 for players A, B, C, and D, respectively. Next, player D could gain 16 points by moving to cell 10—but that would not be enough to compensate player A for a loss of 15 points and player C for a loss of 21 points. Player C could move to cell 6 for a gain of 8 points— which would not be enough to pay for player B's loss of 9 points. Finally, player B would gain only 7 points from a move to cell 4, but since this move would entail large windfall profits for all others, it would be carried out. Beyond that, no player could make a profit by moving away from cell 4, which, incidentally, is also the welfare optimum.

## *Problem Solving and Positive Coordination*

Both Problem Solving and Positive Coordination are here defined as methods for maximizing the collective payoff of coalitions of self-interested players.[21] They differ only in the distributive dimension—which is treated as being irrelevant for Problem Solving and highly relevant for Positive Coordination. In the simulation program, coalitions are formed incrementally. The nucleus is again the individual player that has the most to gain. This player will then join forces with a second player, who, when options are pooled, will allow the pair to achieve the largest additional gain,[22] and so on.

Two points are important to note. First, by pooling their policy options[23] the members of a coalition can significantly increase the action space available to themselves. Thus, starting from cell 1 in Table A2.1, player C would only have the option of moving to cell 5, and player D could only reach cell 9. A coalition of players C and D, however, could use these options of their individual members and, in addition, could also reach cell 13 by combining both of these moves. More generally, from any given status quo, a coalition of N members with S policy options each can reach a set of $SN - 1$ different outcomes, whereas a population of uncoordinated individual actors of the same size could only reach $(S - 1)N$ outcomes.

Second, in Problem Solving, the coalition's only criterion of choice is the aggregate net gain of the group. Individual losses are not compensated. Thus, in Table A2.1, the coalition of players C and D could obtain the maximum total gain of 113 points by moving to cell 5. Player C would collect 33 points, and 80 points would fall to player D. In Positive Coordination, by contrast, additional distributive negotiations are needed to allocate gains and losses among the members of the coalition. These are more demanding than the distributive negotiations involved in the Bargaining simulation. There, the player that proposes a solution is also the "residual claimant" that will keep the remaining profit after having paid minimal compensation to those other players that would otherwise suffer losses compared to their reservation payoffs. Within the coalition, however, a "fair" distribution is required for which a number of factors will be relevant. Of course, actors will not join a coalition if it will not at least allow them to maintain their reservation payoff. Beyond this, the Nash Bargaining solution would distribute profits in proportion to the status-quo payoffs of the players involved. This is also the rule applied in our simulation model.[24] However, our definitions of Problem Solving and Positive Coordination do not yet specify a complete coordination mechanism for all cases in which the coalition is smaller than the total population of players (i.e., is not a grand coalition). What is needed in addition is a specification of the rules governing the interaction between the coalition and players outside of it. This relationship could be dictatorial in the sense that the coalition is able to prevent all other players from responding to the coalition's preferred move, or it could be defined by one of the coordination mechanisms discussed thus far—Parametric Adjustment, Negative Coordination, or Bargaining. It is here that Lindblom's and our hunch, according to which combinations of coordination methods might produce particularly attractive welfare effects, would have to be tested.

## COMPARATIVE WELFARE EFFECTS

We have already discussed the potential welfare effects of simple coordination mechanisms—Parametric Adjustment, Negative Coordination, and Bargaining—and we will

TABLE A2.2 Nash Equilibria in Sequential Games

| Number of Players | Number of Nash Equilibria Reached |
|---|---|
| 2 | 90/100 |
| 3 | 70/100 |
| 4 | 55/100 |
| 5 | 34/100 |
| 6 | 30/100 |
| 7 | 22/100 |
| 8 | 11/100 |
| 9 | 10/100 |
| 10 | 8/100 |
| 11 | 4/100 |
| 12 | 6/100 |

here merely add some more precise observations derived from our simulation experiments. We will then present simulation results of the welfare effects of partial coalitions and from there will proceed to the main theme of this section, which is the examination of combination effects of partial coalitions and simple coordination methods. The section will conclude with an examination of the rise of transaction costs associated with coalitions of increasing size.

## *Simple Coordination Methods*

As discussed earlier, Parametric Adjustment may in fact be the most efficient coordination method available for certain constellations resembling games of pure coordination or the Battle of the Sexes. In the general case, however, the probability that a Nash equilibrium can be reached at all through sequential moves is greatly reduced as the number of options and/or the number of players increases. In order to test this intuition,[25] we have conducted series[26] of 100 simulation runs for games in which the number of players varied from 2 to 12, while the number of options available to each player was held constant at 2. The outcome is presented in Table A2.2. Similarly, when we held the number of players constant at 6 while varying the number of options available to each from 2 to 5, an equilibrium was reached in 24/100 plays when the players had 2 options but only in 4/100 cases when the number of options was increased to 5.

When a Nash equilibrium is in fact reached, however, the outcome usually constitutes a welfare improvement over the status quo[27]—but not invariably so. In a series of 60 simulation runs of a 3-players-by-3-options game, Nash equilibria were reached in 28 cases. Of these, 23 could be classified as welfare improvements, but in 5 cases aggregate payoffs were in fact lower than in the status quo. This is a reminder that even in nonstructured (randomized) game constellations players may encounter situations resembling a social trap— and that sequential noncooperative games among 3 or more players do not provide protection against the "lock in" on inferior solutions.

TABLE A2.3  Average Normalized Joint-Payoff Gains Through Negative Coordination

| Status Quo | Number of Players | | |
|---|---|---|---|
| | 4 | 8 | 12 |
| Joint payoff minimum | 0.51 | 0.35 | 0.02 |
| Random selection | 0.13 | 0.02 | 0.00 |

TABLE A2.4  Average Normalized Joint-Payoff Gains Through Bargaining

| Status Quo | Number of Players | | |
|---|---|---|---|
| | 4 | 8 | 12 |
| Joint payoff minimum | 0.68 | 0.53 | 0.03 |
| Random selection | 0.28 | 0.07 | 0.00 |

Our simulations have also confirmed the expectation that the welfare efficiency of Negative Coordination will decline as the number of independent players in veto positions increases. Table A2.3 summarizes the normalized joint-payoff gains of 30 simulation runs in which Negative Coordination is applied among 4, 8, and 12 players, respectively, each of which is provided with a choice between 2 options.

The table also shows that gains are higher if the simulation departs from a status-quo situation in which joint payoffs are at a minimum than if the status quo is selected by random choice. In the first case, when most players will also start from low individual payoffs, moves that will improve the outcome for the leading player are less likely to be blocked by vetoes. When the initial status quo is selected at random, however, it is more likely that any move that would improve one player's payoff will violate the vested interests of others.

Since Bargaining is in all respects similar to Negative Coordination, except that vetoes may be bought off, the outcomes show a similar tendency (Table A2.4). However, the level of gains that can be achieved is generally higher, since some profitable moves can be carried out here, whereas they would have been blocked under Negative Coordination.

## Partial (Dictatorial) Coalitions

When a coalition that is practicing Positive Coordination (or Problem Solving, for that matter) internally can impose its preferred outcome on all other players, there is of course no question that the collective welfare of coalition members will be maximized. And there

## Joint Payoffs

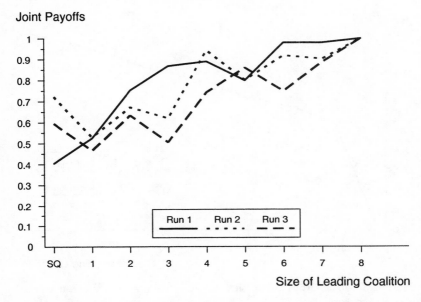

FIGURE A2.5    Welfare effects of dictatorial coalitions (individual simulation runs, 8 players, 3 options)

is also no question that a grand coalition that includes all affected parties would maximize aggregate welfare. But, as will be shown later, transaction costs of coalitions rise steeply as the number of members increases. As a consequence, coalitions are likely to be quite small, and the welfare consequences of small coalitions may be quite problematic. This is illustrated in Figure A2.5.

The figure shows the normalized joint payoffs of three individual simulation runs of a game with 8 players and 3 options. The status-quo cells were selected at random for each run. The lines represent the joint payoffs (aggregated over all players) achieved by self-interested coalitions from size 1 (K1) to size 8 (K8). Players that are not members of the coalition are here assumed to make no moves of their own—in other words, the coalition is "dictatorial" in the sense that it alone can exercise policy options.

Even under these unrealistic conditions the unrestricted pursuit of self-interest by a dictatorial individual (K1) will often reduce general welfare in comparison to the status quo. It is also interesting to note that in the individual case general welfare will not necessarily increase if the size of the coalition increases. Thus, in two of the three runs shown here, the move from a 2-member to a 3-member coalition, and from a 4-member coalition to a majority coalition including 5 of 8 players, would in fact have reduced general welfare. Since the members of the coalition are of course increasing their per capita payoff at each step, these reversals are an indication of negative externalities that are imposed on players outside of the coalition.

The selected results of individual simulation are of course not representative. In our randomized payoff matrices, positive and negative externalities will cancel out on the av-

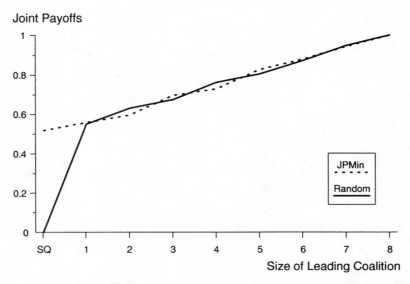

FIGURE A2.6    Joint payoffs from Positive Coordination (averages of 100 simulation runs, 8 players, 3 options)

erage, so that the aggregate result of large numbers of simulation runs will show a steady increase of average joint payoffs (Figure A2.6). It is interesting to note that the choice of the status quo from which the simulation starts (from the joint-payoff minimum or from a randomized point of departure) does not seem to make much of a difference. Even when starting from the minimum, the first move of the leading player brings the welfare level of the whole population up to a medium range, from which progress tends to be quite slow.

### Positive Coordination and Parametric Adjustment

When policy options are evenly distributed, as we have assumed, dictatorial coalitions are of course not a realistic proposition. We have included them for purposes of exposition but will in the remainder of the paper explore constellations in which the players outside of the coalition also have a role. At a minimum they should be able to exercise their own individual policy options in response to the new situation created by the initial move of the coalition. When that is so, we have in fact a noncooperative sequential game played between the coalition and all other players. In our simulations the coalition has the first move and will choose its most preferred cell. Starting from there, the outside player that has the most to gain will have the next move, to which the coalition or another player may again respond, and so on. Given its greater range of options, the coalition will be at an advantage, but it will not be able to determine the outcome unilaterally.

In comparison with the pure model of Parametric Adjustment discussed earlier, the number of players is reduced when some of them combine to form a coalition. Thus in a constant population of players the probability that a Nash equilibrium can be reached will increase as the size of the coalition increases. When it is reached, the welfare effect is likely

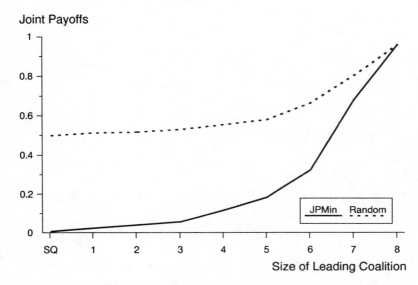

FIGURE A2.7 Positive Coordination plus Parametric Adjustment (averages of 100 simulation runs, 8 players, 3 options)

to be positive. But as long as the number of independent players is larger than four or five, a Nash equilibrium will not be reached in the majority of simulation runs. The probability that an equilibrium will be reached decreases further when players can choose from more than two policy options, as is the case in the example presented here. Since in the absence of an equilibrium outcome the status quo will be maintained by definition in our simulations, the average welfare gains achieved by a combination of Positive Coordination and Parametric Adjustment will be quite modest unless relatively large coalitions (implying very high transaction costs) are formed (Figure A2.7).

### *Positive and Negative Coordination*

In the next variant we explore the combination of Positive Coordination and Negative Coordination. As before, there is a coalition-building process that begins with the player that has the most to gain. But now the status-quo payoffs of all players that are not members of the leading coalition are protected (say, by institutionalized property rights). Thus the coalition is only able to complete its most preferred move if it leaves no other player worse off than in the status quo. If its initiative is blocked, the coalition will try its second-best move. When it is successful, or when its options are exhausted, the coalition is enlarged by co-opting the outside player whose addition promises the greatest joint gain for the larger coalition, and so on (Figure A2.8).

As is to be expected, single actors are not doing well against a large number of veto players. But here, having larger numbers of options is an advantage for the leading coalition. Thus if the game starts from the joint-payoff minimum, and if all players can choose from among three policy options, it takes only a two- or three-member coalition to bring

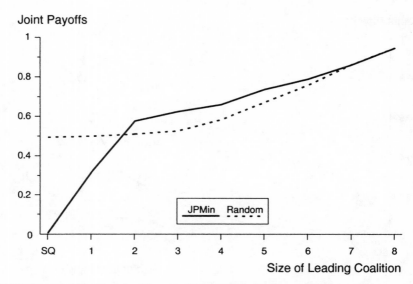

FIGURE A2.8    Positive plus Negative Coordination (averages of 100 simulation runs, 8 players, 3 options)

joint payoffs up to a medium level. However, the outcome is much less encouraging when the game starts from a random (on the average, medium) status-quo position. Here it takes a five- or six-member coalition before overall welfare increases noticeably. This suggests that veto systems are least constraining when things are really bad for everyone, while under more average conditions most proposals for change will have negative effects on some vested interests and hence are likely to be blocked.

### Positive and Negative Coordination and Bargaining

The last coordination method to be looked at builds upon the previous one by adding a Bargaining element to the combination of Positive Coordination and Negative Coordination. Again, the leading coalition cannot impose negative externalities on outsiders. But when an initiative encounters one or more vetoes, the simulation program determines whether the potential net gains of the coalition exceed the loss that would be suffered by the veto players. If not, the move must be withdrawn, as would be the case under Negative Coordination. If the gain is large enough, however, the proposed move is carried out, the reservation payoffs of the veto players are maintained through transfer payments, and an equal amount is deducted from the aggregate payoff of the coalition members.

As a result, coalition initiatives are more frequently successful, and joint payoffs will rise more rapidly than they would under the combination of Positive and Negative Coordination alone. The impact on joint payoffs is quite dramatic (Figure A2.9). Starting from the joint-payoff minimum, even a single actor can raise aggregate welfare to a medium level when it is willing to engage in Bargaining. Beyond that, both curves are close enough to be practically indistinguishable, and as the size of the leading coalition increases, joint payoffs move fairly rapidly toward the welfare maximum. Since vetoes can be bought off, the location of the status quo (minimum or random) loses its determining power.

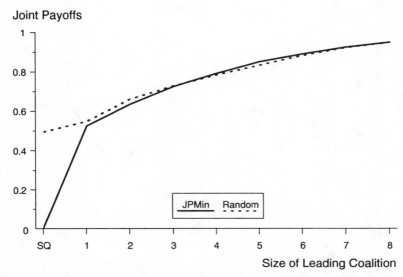

FIGURE A2.9 Positive plus Negative Coordination plus Bargaining (averages of 100 simulation runs, 8 players, 3 options)

## Comparative Discussion

When we now compare the welfare effects of combinations of coordination mechanism, our previous interpretations are confirmed. Leaving aside pure (dictatorial) Positive Coordination as being unrealistic under most circumstances, it appears that the most complex combination, Positive Coordination with Negative Coordination and Bargaining, is generally the most welfare-efficient method. It produces consistently superior welfare effects for all sizes of leading coalitions short of the grand coalition. This is true not only for constellations in which the actors start from the worst possible situation, the joint-payoff minimum (Figure A2.10), but also when the process starts from a randomly selected point of departure (Figure A2.11). In both cases, even two- or three-member coalitions will be able to reach two-thirds or three-quarters of the maximum welfare level that can be obtained by the grand coalition.

For Positive Coordination plus Negative Coordination, however, the point of departure does make an important difference. When the actors start from a worst-case position, this method is almost as welfare efficient as the combination that includes Bargaining. But when everyone is reasonably well off on the average, the veto system of Negative Coordination prevents improvements beyond the status quo. Even under those conditions, however, Positive Coordination plus Negative Coordination is more effective than the laissez-faire combination of Positive Coordination and Parametric Adjustment, in which small coalitions can pursue their own interests without exogenous constraints but cannot prevent the unilateral readjustment of excluded players.

These comparative results will also hold for simulation runs with larger numbers of options and larger numbers of players, whereas the combination of Positive Coordination and Parametric Adjustment will do relatively better if the number of players and options is

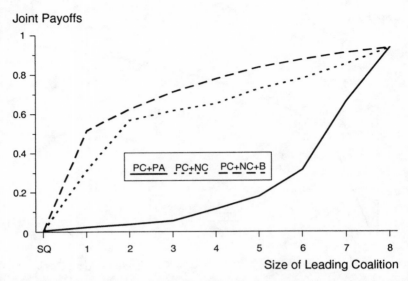

FIGURE A2.10   Comparison of welfare effects when the status quo is at the joint-payoff minimum (SQ = joint-payoff minimum; 8 players, 3 options)

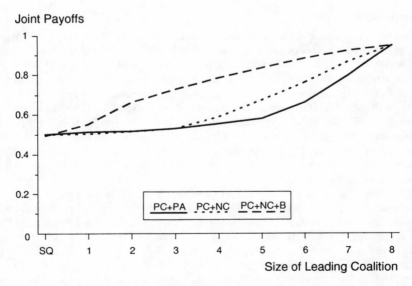

FIGURE A2.11   Welfare effects with random status quo (SQ = random; 8 players, 3 options)

reduced. What is less clear is how much these conclusions will actually mean in practice. In order to approach this question, we must now turn to the problem of transaction costs.

## Transaction Costs

Transaction costs arise when actors must search for an optimal outcome and when the members of the leading coalition must agree on the distribution of their net gains. We begin with a discussion of search costs. Given the conditions of bounded rationality introduced earlier, players are assumed to have prior information of their own status-quo payoffs and of their own options. They are also able to identify and compare the payoffs they receive, or would receive, if other players or they themselves make, or propose, a move away from the status quo—but they must do so at a cost. In addition, they must bargain over the allocation of aggregate gains within a coalition.

More specifically, when a leading coalition is enlarged, it is first necessary to identify and evaluate all outcomes that can be reached by combining the options of the members of the previous coalition with those of potential candidates for co-optation. The best of these outcomes determines both the membership of the new leading coalition and its most preferred move. If Parametric Adjustment is combined with Positive Coordination, all players outside of the coalition must then respond to this move by examining their own options to see if it is profitable for them to change their position; other players, including the leading coalition, must then again evaluate their new options, and so on. In combinations of Positive Coordination, Negative Coordination, and Bargaining, by contrast, the best outcome obtainable by the leading coalition must be compared to the reservation payoffs of all outsiders in order to determine whether one or more of them will have reason to veto the proposal. If it is vetoed, the leading coalition will have to determine whether its aggregate gains are sufficient to compensate all losers. If not, the same procedure must be repeated for the second-best outcome obtainable by the leading coalition (provided that it exceeds the aggregate reservation payoffs of its members), and so on. If a profitable proposal is not blocked by a veto, the coalition must then distribute its net gains (i.e., the gains remaining after all reservation payoffs have been maintained through side payments) among its members through processes of converging offers and counteroffers.

The simulation program includes an algorithm that keeps track of each step in this series of operations. On the heroic assumption that each of these steps represents the same degree of difficulty, or the same time delay, the number of transactions is aggregated over the whole history of a coalition-building and coordination process. In other words, the search costs associated with Positive-plus-Negative Coordination for a leading coalition of three members represent the cumulative costs incurred in a process that started with a single player that then co-opted a second one, and so on. These costs are significantly higher than they would have been if the process had started with a given three-member coalition. As a consequence, for larger leading coalitions the costs so defined will exceed those that would be incurred by negotiations in a grand coalition. Since we have generally characterized the transaction costs of (relatively large) grand coalitions as prohibitive, we have set these to unity and used them as an upper limit in Figure A2.12, which also represents the welfare effects of the relatively most efficient combination of Positive Coordination, Negative Coordination, and Bargaining.

In interpreting this figure, two things must be kept in mind: First, transaction costs are interpreted as opportunity costs of the time that must be spent in negotiations. Since we can make no assumptions about the opportunities that are forgone, it is even problematic

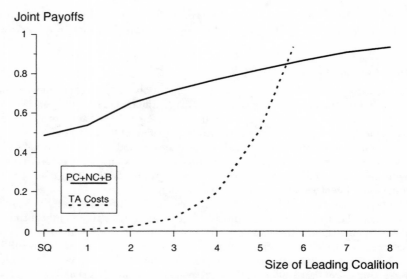

FIGURE A2.12    Search costs and welfare effects (SQ = random; 8 players, 3 options)

to assume (as we do) that costs should somehow be a linear function of time. Second, even though the maximum is set to unity for both curves, it should be clear that the scale of transaction costs is not comparable to the scale of joint payoffs. We also cannot tell at which point the relative differences in the transaction costs of different combinations of coordination methods will make a substantial difference in practice. All that we can say is that the number of operations required for arriving at a coordinated solution increases exponentially as the size of leading coalitions increases but that it stays well below the level associated with the grand coalition when leading coalitions remain relatively small.

In addition to search costs, the members of the leading coalition also incur distribution costs when they must divide the net gains obtained at a particular stage of the game. In our model, fair distributions are achieved through the Zeuthen-Harsanyi process of "multilateral bargaining based on restricted bilateral bargaining" (Harsanyi 1977, 201). This means that each pair of coalition members will, through converging offers and counteroffers, move toward a (preliminary) Nash distribution and that the overall Nash solution is obtained when all bilateral distributions are in balance. Again, the program will record the number of offers needed and compute an aggregate measure representing the transaction costs of distribution. These costs also increase exponentially with the size of the leading coalition. Unfortunately, however, search costs and distribution costs are not directly comparable and hence cannot be aggregated to a single overall measure of transaction costs.

## CONCLUSIONS

If we now return to the questions from which we departed, it is clear that computer simulations of games defined by randomized payoff matrices are far removed from the actual practices of real-world policy networks. For this we make no excuses, since it has been our aim to clarify analytically some underlying tendencies, opportunities, and difficulties rather than to develop a realistic model of a specific negotiation situation. Within these limitations, however, our simulation analyses have confirmed the intuition that combinations of simple coordination mechanisms may have more attractive welfare effects than each of these mechanisms does when applied alone.[28] More specifically, we can now make the following assertions with greater confidence than before:

1. The Coase Theorem shows that in the absence of transaction costs, negotiations (i.e., Positive Coordination) within a grand coalition that includes all members of a given population would reach the same welfare maximum as a benevolent and omniscient dictator could. But if, as Coase has pointed out, grand coalitions must, beyond a relatively small group size, run into prohibitive transaction costs, there is a premium on coordination mechanisms that will achieve relatively high welfare gains without coalitions or with partial coalitions of relatively small size.

2. We have shown that two simple coordination mechanisms that altogether avoid coalitions, and on which Lindblom had placed high hopes—namely Parametric Adjustment and Negative Coordination (deferential adjustment)—will not, by themselves, be able to attain high welfare levels for the population as a whole in the general case. Coalitions thus seem to be a necessary element, under most conditions, of efficient solutions to the coordination problem.

3. However, when relatively small leading coalitions are interacting with the rest of the population in a noncooperative game (i.e., Positive Coordination plus Parametric Adjustment), the welfare consequences are also unattractive. Welfare gains that could be achieved by Positive Coordination within the coalition are partly wiped out through the countermoves of outsiders except when the leading coalition is fairly large relative to the total population (implying high transaction costs). Thus the most laissez-faire form of coordination, in which both small coalitions and individual actors are pursuing self-interested goals in the absence of formal constraints, is also not an efficient solution.

4. It therefore seems that the need to achieve agreement with outsiders, through Negative Coordination and Bargaining, is an essential element of any efficient solution. When individual actors and coalitions are constrained to avoid negative externalities on outsiders, their search for self-interest-maximizing solutions will necessarily increase general welfare at the same time—and the same is true to an even greater extent when transfer payments permit welfare-improving solutions to be realized even when negative externalities (which are smaller than the potential gains) are present.

The conclusion is therefore that even though the welfare maximum could only be obtained by the all-inclusive grand coalition, the combination of Positive Coordination, practiced within relatively small leading coalitions, and Negative Coordination or Bargaining with the remaining members of the population is able to achieve intermediate levels of general welfare relatively efficiently. In that sense, therefore, our simulation study supports Lindblom's optimistic expectation that in the absence of a well-informed and public-spirited central coordinator, and even in the absence of individual and corporate actors who are primarily motivated by the public interest or by considerations of "system rationality," negotiated self-coordination in policy networks may improve the level of general welfare.

It is necessary, however, to emphasize three structural preconditions on which this optimistic expectation depends: First, we have modeled constellations in which action resources are not collectivized or centralized but rather distributed among individual actors. Second, unless the total population of actors is very small, successful self-coordination presupposes a division between a leading coalition whose members are willing and able to practice Positive Coordination internally, and the remaining population of interdependent actors. Third, there must be an exogenous[29] rule according to which the status-quo interests of any actor cannot be invaded without the latter's consent. These institutional preconditions are by no means ubiquitous (thus we are far from asserting the benevolence of an institution-free "invisible hand"), but they are not infrequently approximated, not only in the private-law world of contracts and torts but also in public-sector policy processes.

One example is provided by the institutional circumstances in which Mayntz and Scharpf (1975) first discovered the coexistence of Positive and Negative Coordination: bureaucratic policymaking in a government where policy responsibilities are distributed among ministries and where the cabinet will not ratify policy initiatives in the face of unresolved interdepartmental conflict. Another example is the system of policymaking within the European Union, where the European Commission is free to develop its policy initiatives in intense negotiations with a small set of interested member states but must ultimately respect the veto positions of practically all other member states when ratification in the Council of Ministers is required (Héritier 1993; Tsebelis 1994). Structurally similar conditions exist within the committee system of the United States Congress, which Lindblom had in mind when he discussed the virtues of partisan mutual adjustment. Many similar examples can easily be found.

However, one further caveat is in order. Our analysis throughout was based on the assumption that all actors are maximizing their own self-interest. This seems like a pessimistic assumption when contrasted to postulates of solidaristic or public-spirited action orientations. But it is also an extremely optimistic assumption when the real possibility of competitive ("relative-gains") or even hostile orientations is considered (Scharpf 1989; 1990; Grieco/Powell/Snidal 1993; Keck 1993). That such orientations can prevent negotiated self-coordination is illustrated not only by the conflicts in Northern Ireland or in the former Yugoslavia but also in the German political system under conditions of divided control, where one of the two major parties is in control of the *Bundestag* while the other controls a majority of *Länder* votes in the *Bundesrat*. When that is the case, the relative-gains logic of party-political competition interferes with the self-interested give-and-take that ordinarily characterizes federal-state and state-state bargaining (Scharpf 1995). Under such conditions the welfare benefits of negotiated self-coordination are hard to realize.

Finally, we should also point out that our simulation only provides a model of coordination in situations in which welfare improvements over the status quo are possible. We cannot draw any conclusions for constellations in which inevitable welfare losses must be accommodated (which may increasingly be the situation facing highly industrialized Western democracies). Our hunch is that in these situations veto systems, regardless of whether vetoes can be bought off or not, will be less able to minimize the overall loss than systems in which unilateral action is unconstrained (Positive Coordination plus Parametric Adjustment). But since we have not yet modeled such constellations, we are unable to test this hunch.

## NOTES

1. This form of coordination was identified by Philipp Genschel (1993) in an empirical study of coordination within and among specialized standard-setting committees in international telecommunications. Even though there is a high degree of overlap between the jurisdictional domains of these committees, and even though their membership is also overlapping (so that all actors are fully aware of the interdependence among separate standardization processes), there is no attempt to achieve overall coordination either through merging adjacent committees or through establishing liaison committees that would work out common solutions. Instead, whichever committee is further advanced in its own work will define its own standard, while the other committees will take that standard into account in their own subsequent work. As a result, the overall patchwork of standards tends to be highly coordinated and, in that sense, efficient.

2. That is only true if changes must be brought about by new decision initiatives. If the status quo should deteriorate as a consequence of external changes, a pure system of Negative Coordination would prevent the adjustment of standing decisions as long as there are still parties who are better off without the adjustment.

3. With two actors, orthogonal preference vectors, and policy options randomly distributed in Euclidean space, the probability that a proposal that is attractive to one side will be rejected by the other side is $p = 1/2$.

4. We do not discuss here the theoretically less interesting mixed form of "calculated adaptive adjustment."

5. In addition, the rubric of manipulated adjustment is to include "authoritarian prescription" and "unconditional manipulation" (i.e., direct and indirect forms of hierarchical control), as well as "prior decision" (i.e., exploiting the advantage of the first move in a sequential, noncooperative game) and "indirect manipulation" (i.e., prevailing on a third party to use its influence on the target actors). Analytically, this is an extremely heterogeneous list whose diverse welfare implications cannot be fully explored here. If Lindblom had thought that hierarchical control were generally efficient, he would have written a different book (Miller 1992). "Prior decision" seems to be a less myopic variant of parametric adjustment, discussed earlier. Its implications are highly contingent on the nature of the game, however. Having the first move in a sequential game is an advantage if the game has multiple Nash equilibria; it is irrelevant if the game has precisely one Nash equilibrium in pure strategies; and it is a disadvantage in mixed-motive games without a Nash equilibrium or in zero-sum games without a saddle point. "Indirect manipulation," finally, does not seem to have any specific consequences of welfare-theoretic interest.

6. In the absence of transaction costs, for instance, there would be no reason to consider external effects as a problem, since all parties affected could participate in negotiations leading to an agreed decision. By contrast, if transaction costs matter, the inevitable nonidentity between those who are able to participate in a decision and those who are affected by it must become the core problem of normative political theory. By the same token, the problems associated with the "logic of collective action" (Olson 1965) and empirical differences in the capacity of interests to achieve collective organization derive their political salience entirely from the real-world importance of transaction costs.

7. There is of course no suggestion here that negotiations should be the only means available for achieving coordination in the face of distribution and value-creation prob-

lems. Hierarchical fiat, majority vote, or noncooperative games may do as well or even better in some situations.

8. In the terminology of Walton and McKersie (1965), this would be "distributive bargaining."

9. "Integrative bargaining" is the term used by Walton and McKersie (1965), whereas Lindblom (1965, 28) describes this mode as "cooperative discussion"—whose practical relevance he considers to be marginal at best.

10. None of this should imply, however, that Problem Solving will necessarily be harmonious. Cognitive disagreement over cause-and-effect hypotheses or normative disagreement over the appropriate definition of organizational goals or the public interest may be as severe as, or more severe than, distributional conflict over personal or institutional self-interest could be.

11. Regardless of all normative advantages of pluralist and corporatist interest intermediation, universal suffrage remains the only truly egalitarian representational mechanism—and the political process will approximate egalitarian outcomes only to the extent that the relative weight of general elections remains high in comparison to other forms of political influence (Scharpf 1970).

12. The problem of prohibitive transaction costs seems to be acknowledged by Lindblom when he points out that the number of participants in negotiations must necessarily be very limited. In his view, therefore, the main burden of coordination has to be borne by parametric adjustment and deferential adjustment (1965, 68). But that throws us back to the welfare deficits discussed earlier.

13. In his discussion of parametric adjustment Lindblom explicitly suggests that when one form of coordination fails, actors might switch to another: "The coordinating potential of the various mutual adjustment processes may be greater than is at first supposed, since in these processes themselves are opportunities for participants to choose one or another of quite different methods, as circumstances require" (1965, 41). This seems plausible but is different from the combination effects discussed here.

14. A more complete description and a copy of the program, written in Turbo Pascal and running on IBM-compatible 386 PCs, can be obtained from Matthias Mohr.

15. These "options" are not "strategies" in the game-theoretic sense of a complete specification of moves in a sequential game. Rather, they are meant to represent specific policy stances among which a particular actor in a policy network may choose—such as among cutting the budget, raising taxes, or increased borrowing.

16. We have also experimented with matrices structured so as to represent specific types of game constellations but have chosen to present here only the general case.

17. For all examples presented here the random payoffs are distributed identically in the interval $[0 \ldots 100]$.

18. Since switching back to an earlier option in later stages of the game is not precluded, it is necessary, for each method of coordination, to define the point at which a particular sequence of moves will come to an end. Choices of options become final only at this point.

19. "Maximax," rather than "maximin," makes sense as a rule for myopic players who must choose one move at a time (rather than complete strategies) and who are ignorant of the options as well as of the preferences of other players. The risks are minimized in a sequential game in which a player may respond again to other players' responses.

20. Alternatively, players with perfect recall (and a capacity to commit themselves) might then backtrack to a nonequilibrium but Pareto-superior cell touched earlier during the sequence of moves. This is a possibility that we have not modeled.

21. Mayntz (1993; 1994) equates Problem Solving with "system rationality." Translated into our simulation model, this would mean that the members of a coalition are always aspiring to maximize the joint payoffs of the whole population of players, regardless of payoffs achieved by themselves (or, alternatively, provided that their own status-quo interests are not violated). In doing so, they could still use only the moves available to coalition members—and they might need to play a noncooperative game against players not included in the coalition. In the present paper we do not explore this variant of coordination mechanisms.

22. It should be clear that these are assumptions rather than deductions from a rational-choice theory of coalition formation. According to these assumptions, coalition partners will be selected by the criterion of maximally convergent or harmonious interests (i.e., coalitions should co-opt their closest friends, which corresponds to Fritz Heider's theory of "structural balance" [Cartwright/Harary 1956]). This is not the only plausible assumption, however. When outsiders can interfere with a given coalition's strategies (or have a veto), the coalition might do better by co-opting potential opponents rather than close friends. In a well-researched historical example, that was the logic of Otto von Bismarck's system of crisscrossing alliances. But since it was a very difficult system to manage, his successors in the 1890s regressed to the more harmonious "Triple Alliance" of Germany, Austria, and Italy—whose confrontation with the "Triple Entente" of England, France, and Russia then defined the lineup of World War I (McDonald/Rosecrance 1985). In our simulations the co-optation of opponents would increase the welfare effectiveness of combinations of Positive and Negative Coordination. But in the interest of comparability, the co-optation of friends was used as the coalition-building rule in all examples presented.

23. Coalitions are modeled here as a set of actors with distributed, rather than centralized, action resources—which is generally true in policy processes among corporate actors controlling certain policy instruments.

24. Alternatively, and perhaps more plausibly, distribution could be proportional to the highest potential gain that a coalition member could have achieved (Kalai/Smorodinsky 1975). However, if utility functions are linear, as in our case, or if they are identical, then both concepts lead to the same solution. We have chosen the Nash solution for pragmatic reasons since the Zeuthen-Harsanyi bargaining procedure, which easily lends itself to simulation, produces Nash distributions (Harsanyi 1977, 149–162, 198–203). However, both rules are likely to underestimate the difficulties of agreeing on the relevance of criteria for distribution. In Table A2.1, for instance, players C and D may agree to move to cell 5, which provides them with a common surplus of 113 points. But player C, who must produce this outcome through a change of strategy (while player D remains inactive), is unlikely to forget that it could have done even better by sitting still and letting the game move to its noncooperative equilibrium in cell 4—a prediction that player D might challenge by pointing to its own threat potential, whose credibility might again be disputed, and so on.

25. A mathematical proof is difficult because of the path-dependent character of our sequential games.

26. These series of simulation runs are not to be mistaken for "iterated games." We do not assume that players anticipate future interactions or react to past experiences. Thus

each run is a one-shot game, and the number of runs is increased simply to average out the variance of individual outcomes resulting from our use of random payoff matrices.

27. That is so because we use a random payoff matrix. While players' moves will improve their own payoffs, the external effects on the outcomes of other players may be positive or negative.

28. It may be useful to point out the difference between this proposition and the claim of Joseph Farrell and Garth Saloner (1988) that technical standardization may be best achieved by a combination of coordination through committees and coordination through the market. In our terminology, the "committee" would be a grand coalition, and the "market" would be the equivalent of Parametric Adjustment. Thus Farrell and Saloner suggest that members of a potential grand coalition might exit the coalition and play a noncooperative game against the remaining members—and they expect that this threat may facilitate agreement within the grand coalition. This is a constellation that we have not modeled.

29. The rule may emerge endogenously in a history of interactions among interdependent and self-interested actors (Scharpf 1993), but it is exogenous to the specific interaction at hand.

## REFERENCES

Arthur, W. Brian, 1990: Competing Technologies, Increasing Returns, and Lock-in by Historical Events. In Christopher Freeman, ed., *The Economics of Innovation*, 374–389. Aldershot: Elgar.

Bogdanor, Vernon, 1988: Federalism in Switzerland. *Government and Opposition* 23, 69–90.

Brams, Steven J./Ann E. Doherty, 1993: Intransigence in Negotiations: The Dynamics of Disagreement. *Journal of Conflict Resolution* 37, 692–708.

Braybrooke, David/Charles E. Lindblom, 1963: *A Strategy of Decision: Policy Evaluation as a Social Process*. New York: Free Press.

Cartwright, Dorwin/Frank Harary, 1956: Structural Balance: A Generalization of Heider's Theory. *Psychological Review* 63, 277–293.

Coase, Ronald, 1960: The Problem of Social Cost. *Journal of Law and Economics* 3, 1–44.

Dahl, Robert A., 1967: *Pluralist Democracy in the United States: Conflict and Consent*. Chicago: Rand McNally.

David, Paul A., 1985: Clio and the Economics of QWERTY. *American Economic History* 75, 332–337.

Dror, Yehezkel, 1964: Muddling Through: "Science" or Inertia? *Public Administration Review* 24, 153–165.

Etzioni, Amitai, 1968: *The Active Society: A Theory of Societal and Political Processes*. New York: Free Press.

Farrell, Joseph/Garth Saloner, 1988: Coordination Through Committees and Markets. *Rand Journal of Economics* 19, 235–252.

Genschel, Philipp, 1993: Institutioneller Wandel in der Standardisierung von Informationstechnik. Unpublished manuscript, Max Planck Institute for the Study of Societies, Cologne.

Goldthorpe, John H., ed., 1984: *Order and Conflict in Contemporary Capitalism*. Oxford: Clarendon Press.

Gregory, Robert, 1989: Political Rationality or Incrementalism? Charles E. Lindblom's Enduring Contribution to Public Policy Making Theory. *Policy and Politics* 17, 139–153.

Grieco, Joseph M./Robert Powell/Duncan Snidal, 1993: The Relative Gains Problem for International Cooperation. *American Political Science Review* 87, 729–743.

Hardin, Garrett, 1968: The Tragedy of the Commons. *Science* 162, 1243–1268.

Harsanyi, John C., 1977: *Rational Behavior and Bargaining Equilibrium in Games and Social Situations.* Cambridge: Cambridge University Press.

Häusler, Jürgen/Hans-Willy Hohn/Susanne Lütz, 1993: The Architecture of a Research and Development Collaboration. In Fritz W. Scharpf, ed., *Games in Hierarchies and Networks: Analytical and Empirical Approaches to the Study of Governance Institutions,* 211–250. Boulder: Westview Press.

Héritier, Adrienne, 1993: Policy-Netzwerkanalyse als Untersuchungsinstrument im europäischen Kontext: Folgerungen aus einer empirischen Studie regulativer Politik. In Adrienne Héritier, ed., *Policy-Analyse: Kritik und Neuorientierung,* 432–450. Opladen: Westdeutscher Verlag.

Hunter, Floyd, 1953: *Community Power Structure: A Study of Decision Makers.* Chapel Hill: University of North Carolina Press.

Kahn, Alfred E., 1966: The Tyranny of Small Decisions: Market Failures, Imperfections, Limits of Economics. *Kyklos* 19, 23–46.

Kalai, Ehud/Meir Smorodinsky, 1975: Other Solutions to Nash's Bargaining Problem. *Econometrica* 43, 513–518.

Kaldor, Nicholas, 1939: Welfare Propositions of Economics and Inter-personal Comparisons of Utility. *Economic Journal* 49, 549–552.

Keck, Otto, 1993: The New Institutionalism and the Relative-Gains Debate. In Frank R. Pfetsch, ed., *International Relations and Pan-Europe: Theoretical Approaches and Empirical Findings,* 35–62. Münster: Lit Verlag.

Laumann, Edward O./David Knoke, 1987: *The Organizational State: Social Choice in National Policy Domains.* Madison: University of Wisconsin Press.

Lax, David A./James K. Sebenius, 1986: *The Manager as Negotiator: Bargaining for Cooperation and Competitive Gain.* New York: Free Press.

Lehmbruch, Gerhard, 1967: *Proporzdemokratie: Politisches System und politische Kultur in der Schweiz und in Österreich.* Tübingen: Mohr.

Lehmbruch, Gerhard/Philippe C. Schmitter, eds., 1982: *Patterns of Corporatist Policy-Making.* London: Sage.

Lindblom, Charles E., 1959: The Science of Muddling Through. *Public Administration Review* 19, 79–99.

_____, 1965: *The Intelligence of Democracy: Decision Making Through Mutual Adjustment.* New York: Free Press.

_____, 1977: *Politics and Markets.* New York: Basic Books.

_____, 1979: Still Muddling, Not Yet Through. *Public Administration Review* 39, 517–526.

_____, 1982: The Market as Prison. *Journal of Politics* 44, 324–336.

Lowi, Theodore J., 1969: *The End of Liberalism.* New York: W. W. Norton.

Lütz, Susanne, 1993: *Steuerung industrieller Forschungskooperation: Funktionsweise und Erfolgsbedingungen des staatlichen Förderinstruments Verbundforschung.* Frankfurt am Main: Campus.

March, James G./Herbert A. Simon, 1958: *Organizations.* New York: John Wiley.

Marin, Bernd, ed., 1990: *Governance and Generalized Exchange: Self-Organizing Policy Networks in Action.* Frankfurt am Main: Campus.

Marin, Bernd/Renate Mayntz, eds., 1991: *Policy Networks: Empirical Evidence and Theoretical Considerations.* Frankfurt am Main: Campus.

Mayntz, Renate, 1992: Interessenverbände und Gemeinwohl: Die Verbändestudie der Bertelsmann Stiftung. In Renate Mayntz, ed., *Verbände zwischen Mitgliederinteressen und Gemeinwohl,* 11–35. Gütersloh: Bertelsmann.

———, 1993a: Networks, Issues, and Games: Multiorganizational Interactions in the Restructuring of a National Research System. In Fritz W. Scharpf, ed., *Games in Hierarchies and Networks: Analytical and Empirical Approaches to the Study of Governance Institutions,* 189–210. Frankfurt am Main: Campus.

———, 1993b: Modernization and the Logic of Interorganizational Networks. In John Child/Michel Crozier/Renate Mayntz, et al., *Societal Change Between Market and Organization,* 3–18. Aldershot: Avebury.

———, 1994: *Deutsche Forschung im Einigungsprozeß: Die Transformation der Akademie der Wissenschaften der DDR 1989 bis 1992.* Frankfurt am Main: Campus.

Mayntz, Renate/Fritz W. Scharpf, 1975: *Policy-Making in the German Federal Bureaucracy.* Amsterdam: Elsevier.

McConnell, Grant, 1966: *Private Power and American Democracy.* New York: Knopf.

McDonald, H. Brooke/Richard Rosecrance, 1985: Alliance and Structural Balance in the International System. *Journal of Conflict Resolution* 29, 57–82.

Miller, Gary, 1992: *Managerial Dilemmas: The Political Economy of Hierarchy.* Cambridge: Cambridge University Press.

Mills, C. Wright, 1956: *The Power Elite.* New York: Oxford University Press.

Nash, John, 1953: Two-Person Cooperative Games. *Econometrica* 21, 128–140.

Olson, Mancur, 1965: *The Logic of Collective Action.* Cambridge, MA: Harvard University Press.

———, 1982: *The Rise and Decline of Nations: Economic Growth, Stagflation, and Social Rigidities.* New Haven: Yale University Press.

Rubinstein, Ariel, 1982: Perfect Equilibrium in a Bargaining Model. *Econometrica* 50, 97–109.

Sabel, Charles F., 1993: Constitutional Ordering in Historical Context. In Fritz W. Scharpf, ed., *Games in Hierarchies and Networks: Analytical and Empirical Approaches to the Study of Governance Institutions,* 65–124. Frankfurt am Main: Campus.

Scharpf, Fritz W., 1970: *Demokratietheorie zwischen Utopie und Anpassung.* Konstanz: Universitätsverlag.

———, 1989: Decision Rules, Decision Styles, and Policy Choices. *Journal of Theoretical Politics* 1, 149–176.

———, 1990: Games Real Actors Could Play: The Problem of Mutual Predictability. *Rationality and Society* 2, 471–494.

———, 1991: *Social Democracy in Crisis.* Ithaca: Cornell University Press.

———, 1992: Koordination durch Verhandlungssysteme: Analytische Konzepte und institutionelle Lösungen. In Arthur Benz/Fritz W. Scharpf/Reinhard Zintl, *Horizontale Politikverflechtung: Zur Theorie von Verhandlungssystemen,* 51–96. Frankfurt am Main: Campus.

———, 1993: Coordination in Hierarchies and Networks. In Fritz W. Scharpf, ed., *Games in Hierarchies and Networks: Analytical and Empirical Approaches to the Study of Governance Institutions,* 125–165. Frankfurt am Main: Campus.

_____, 1995: Federal Arrangements and Multi-party Systems. *Australian Journal of Political Science* 30, 27–39.

Schattschneider, E. E., 1960: *The Semisovereign People: A Realist's View of Democracy in America.* Hinsdale, IL: Dryden.

Schelling, Thomas C., 1960: *The Strategy of Conflict.* Cambridge, MA: Harvard University Press.

Schmidt, Susanne K./Raymund Werle, 1992: The Development of Compatibility Standards in Telecommunications: Conceptual Framework and Theoretical Perspective. In Meinolf Dierkes/Ute Hoffmann, eds., *New Technology at the Outset: Social Forces in the Shaping of Technological Innovations,* 301–326. Frankfurt am Main: Campus.

Schmitter, Philippe C./Gerhard Lehmbruch, eds., 1979: *Trends Towards Corporatist Intermediation.* London: Sage.

Schneider, Volker, 1988: *Politiknetzwerke der Chemikalienkontrolle: Eine Analyse einer transnationalen Politikentwicklung.* Berlin: de Gruyter.

Simon, Herbert A., 1957: A Formal Theory of the Employment Relation. In Herbert A. Simon, *Models of Man: Social and Rational,* 183–195. New York: John Wiley.

_____, 1962: The Architecture of Complexity. *Proceedings of the American Philosophical Society* 106: 467–482.

_____, 1991: Organizations and Markets. *Journal of Econometric Perspectives* 5, 25–44.

Truman, David, 1951: *The Governmental Process: Political Interests and Public Opinion.* New York: Knopf.

Tsebelis, George, 1994: The Power of the European Parliament as a Conditional Agenda Setter. *American Political Science Review* 88, 128–142.

Walton, Richard E./Robert B. McKersie, 1965: *A Behavioral Theory of Labor Negotiations: An Analysis of a Social Interaction System.* New York: McGraw-Hill.

Weiss, Andrew/Edward Woodhouse, 1992: Reframing Incrementalism: A Constructive Response to the Critics. *Policy Sciences* 25, 255–274.

# References

Agranoff, Robert, 1990: Responding to Human Crises: Intergovernmental Policy Networks. In Robert W. Gage/Myrna Mandell, eds., *Strategies for Managing Intergovernmental Policies and Networks,* 57–80. New York: Praeger.

Akerlof, George A., 1970: The Market for "Lemons": Quality Uncertainty and the Market Mechanism. *Quarterly Journal of Economics* 84, 488–500.

Alber, Jens/Brigitte Bernardi-Schenkluhn, 1992: *Westeuropäische Gesundheitssysteme im Vergleich: Bundesrepublik Deutschland, Schweiz, Frankreich, Italien, Großbritannien.* Frankfurt am Main: Campus.

Alchian, Armen A., 1950: Uncertainty, Evolution, and Economic Theory. *Journal of Political Economy* 58, 211–221.

Alchian, Armen A./Harold Demsetz, 1972: Production, Information Costs, and Economic Organization. *American Economic Review* 62, 777–795.

Allison, Graham T., 1971: *Essence of Decision: Explaining the Cuban Missile Crisis.* Boston: Little, Brown.

Almond, Gabriel A./Sidney Verba, 1963: *The Civic Culture: Political Attitudes and Democracy in Five Nations.* Princeton: Princeton University Press.

Alt, James E./Robert C. Lowry, 1994: Divided Government, Fiscal Institutions, and Budget Deficits: Evidence from the States. *American Political Science Review* 88, 811–828.

Argyris, Chris/Donald Schoen, 1978: *Organizational Learning: A Theory of Action Perspective.* Reading, MA: Addison-Wesley.

Arrow, Kenneth J., 1951: *Social Choice and Individual Values.* New York: John Wiley.

Arthur, W. Brian, 1988: Competing Technologies: An Overview. In Giovanni Dosi et al., eds., *Technical Change and Economic Theory,* 590–607. New York: Pinter.

Atkinson, Michael M./William D. Coleman, 1989: Strong States and Weak States: Sectoral Policy Networks in Advanced Capitalist Economies. *British Journal of Political Science* 19, 47–67.

Aumann, Robert J., 1976: Agreeing to Disagree. *Annals of Statistics* 4, 1236–1239.

Axelrod, Robert, 1970: *Conflict of Interest.* Chicago: Markham.

_____, 1984: *The Evolution of Cooperation.* New York: Basic Books.

_____, ed., 1976: *Structure of Decision: The Cognitive Maps of Political Elites.* Princeton: Princeton University Press.

Ayres, Ian/John Braithwaite, 1992: *Responsive Regulation: Transcending the Deregulation Debate.* New York: Oxford University Press.

"Bagehot," 1994: Games People Play. *The Economist,* December 10, 51.

Barry, Brian, 1989: *A Treatise on Social Justice.* Vol. 1, *Theories of Justice.* London: Harvester-Wheatsheaf.

_____, 1995: *A Treatise on Social Justice.* Vol. 2, *Justice as Impartiality.* Oxford: Clarendon Press.

Barry, Brian/Douglas W. Rae, 1975: Political Evaluation. In Fred I. Greenstein/Nelson W. Polsby, eds., *Handbook of Political Science*, vol. 1, *Political Science: Scope and Theory,* 337–401. Reading, MA: Addison-Wesley.

Bartolini, Stefano, 1996: Collusion, Competition, and Democracy. Unpublished manuscript, European University Institute, Florence, Italy.

Bartos, Otimar, 1978: Negotiation and Justice. In Heinz Sauermann, ed., *Bargaining Behavior,* 103–126. Tübingen: Mohr.

Bazerman, Max H./Margaret A. Neale, 1991: Negotiator Rationality and Negotiator Cognition: The Interactive Role of Prescriptive and Descriptive Research. In H. Peyton Young, ed., *Negotiation Analysis,* 109–130. Ann Arbor: University of Michigan Press.

Beard, Charles A., [1913] 1965: *An Economic Interpretation of the Constitution of the United States.* New York: Free Press.

Benz, Arthur, 1992: Mehrebenen-Verflechtung: Verhandlungsprozesse in verbundenen Entscheidungsarenen. In Arthur Benz/Fritz W. Scharpf/Reinhard Zintl, *Horizontale Politikverflechtung: Zur Theorie von Verhandlungssystemen,* 147–205. Frankfurt am Main: Campus.

Berger, Peter L./Thomas Luckmann, 1966: *The Social Construction of Reality.* New York: Doubleday.

Bickel, Alexander M., 1962: *The Least Dangerous Branch: The Supreme Court at the Bar of Politics.* Indianapolis: Bobbs-Merrill.

Binmore, Ken, 1987: Why Game Theory Doesn't Work. In Peter G. Bennett, ed., *Analysing Conflict and Its Resolution,* 23–42. Oxford: Clarendon Press.

———, 1994: *Playing Fair: Game Theory and the Social Contract.* Vol. 1. Cambridge, MA: MIT Press.

Black, Duncan, 1948: On the Rationale of Group Decision Making. *Journal of Political Economy* 56, 23–34.

———, 1958: *The Theory of Committees and Elections.* Cambridge: Cambridge University Press.

Bobbio, Norberto, 1984: The Future of Democracy. *Telos* 61, 3–16.

Bohman, James F., 1990: Communication, Ideology, and Democratic Practice. *American Political Science Review* 84, 93–110.

Böhret, Carl/Göttrik Wewer, eds., 1993: *Regieren im 21. Jahrhundert—zwischen Globalisierung und Regionalisierung: Festgabe für Hans-Hermann Hartwich zum 65. Geburtstag.* Opladen: Leske & Budrich.

Boudon, Raymond, 1984: *La place du désordre: Critique des théories du changement sociale.* Paris: Presses Universitaires de France.

Brennan, Geoffrey, 1989: Politics with Romance: Towards a Theory of Democratic Socialism. In Alan Hamlin/Philip Pettit, eds., *The Good Polity: Normative Analysis of the State,* 49–66. Oxford: Basil Blackwell.

Brennan, Geoffrey/James M. Buchanan, 1985: *The Reason of Rules: Constitutional Political Economy.* Cambridge: Cambridge University Press.

Breuer, Michael/Thomas Faist/Bill Jordan, 1995: Collective Action, Migration, and Welfare States. *International Sociology* 10, 369–386.

Brittain, Samuel, 1977: *The Economic Consequences of Democracy.* London: Temple Smith.

Buchanan, James M./Robert D. Tollison/Gordon Tullock, eds., 1980: *Toward a Theory of the Rent-Seeking Society.* College Station: Texas A & M University Press.

Buchanan, James M./Gordon Tullock, 1962: *The Calculus of Consent: Logical Foundations of Constitutional Democracy.* Ann Arbor: University of Michigan Press.

Budge, Ian, 1973: Consensus Hypotheses and Conflict of Interest: An Attempt at Theory Integration. *British Journal of Political Science* 3, 73–98.

Burley, Anne-Marie/Walter Mattli, 1993: Europe Before the Court: A Political Theory of Legal Intervention. *International Organization* 47, 41–76.

Burns, Tom R./Thomas Baumgartner/Philippe Deville, 1985: *Man, Decisions, Society: The Theory of Actor-System Dynamics for Social Scientists.* New York: Gordon and Breach.

Burt, Ronald S., 1976: Positions in Networks. *Social Forces* 55, 93–122.

_____, 1980: Models of Network Structure. *Annual Review of Sociology* 6, 79–141.

_____, 1982: *Toward a Structural Theory of Action: Network Models of Social Structure, Perception, and Action.* New York: Academic Press.

Cain, Bruce/John Ferejohn/Morris Fiorina, 1987: *The Personal Vote: Constituency Service and Electoral Independence.* Cambridge, MA: Harvard University Press.

Campbell, Donald T., 1986: Rationality and Utility from the Standpoint of Evolutionary Biology. *Journal of Business* 59, 355–369.

Campbell, John L./J. Rogers Hollingsworth/Leon N. Lindberg eds., 1991: *Governance of the American Economy.* Cambridge: Cambridge University Press.

Canova, Timothy A., 1994: The Swedish Model Betrayed. *Challenge* 37(3), 36–40.

Casella, Alessandra/Barry R. Weingast, 1995: Elements of a Theory of Jurisdictional Change. In Barry Eichengreen/Jeffry Frieden/Jürgen von Hagen, eds., *Politics and Institutions in an Integrated Europe,* 11–41. Berlin: Springer.

CEPR, 1993: *Making Sense of Subsidiarity: How Much Centralisation for Europe.* London: Centre for Economic Policy Research.

Cerny, Philip G., 1994: The Dynamics of Financial Globalization: Technology, Market Structure, and Policy Response. *Policy Sciences* 27, 319–342.

Coase, Ronald H., 1937: The Nature of the Firm. *Economica* 4, 386–405.

_____, 1960: The Problem of Social Cost. *Journal of Law and Economics* 3, 1–44.

Cohen, Joshua, 1989: Deliberation and Democratic Legitimacy. In Alan Hamlin/Philip Pettit, eds., *The Good Polity: Normative Analysis of the State,* 17–34. Oxford: Basil Blackwell.

Cohen, Joshua/Joel Rogers, 1992: Secondary Associations and Democratic Governance. *Politics and Society* 20, 393–472.

Coleman, James S., 1964: *Introduction to Mathematical Sociology.* New York: Free Press.

_____, 1974: *Power and the Structure of Society.* New York: W. W. Norton.

_____, 1986: *Individual Interests and Collective Action.* Cambridge: Cambridge University Press.

_____, 1990: *Foundations of Social Theory.* Cambridge, MA: Belknap Press of Harvard University Press.

Collier, David/Steven Levitsky, 1994: Democracy "with Adjectives": Finding Conceptual Order in Recent Comparative Research. Unpublished manuscript, Department of Political Science, University of California, Berkeley.

Collier, David/James E. Mahon, Jr., 1993: Conceptual "Stretching" Revisited: Adapting Categories in Comparative Analysis. *American Political Science Review* 87, 845–855.

Colman, Andrew M., 1982: *Game Theory and Experimental Games: The Study of Strategic Interaction.* Oxford: Pergamon Press.

Cook, Brian J./B. Dan Wood, 1989: Principal-Agent Models of Political Control of Bureaucracy. *American Political Science Review* 83, 965–978.

Cook, Karen S./Richard M. Emerson/Mary R. Gillmore/Toshio Yamagishi, 1983: The Distribution of Power in Exchange Networks Theory and Experimental Results. *American Journal of Sociology* 89, 275–305.

Cook, Karen S./Toshio Yamagishi, 1992: Power in Exchange Networks: A Power-Dependence Formulation. *Social Networks* 14, 245–267.

Cooke, Jacob E., ed., 1961: *The Federalist.* Cleveland: Meridian Books.

Crouch, Colin, 1993: *Industrial Relations and European State Traditions.* Oxford: Clarendon Press.

Crouch, Colin/Alessandro Pizzorno, eds., 1978: *The Resurgence of Class Conflict in Western Europe Since 1968.* Vol. 2, *Comparative Analyses.* London: Macmillan.

Dahl, Robert A., 1956: *A Preface to Democratic Theory.* Chicago: University of Chicago Press.

_____, 1967: *Pluralist Democracy in the United States: Conflict and Consent.* Chicago: Rand McNally.

_____, 1989: *Democracy and Its Critics.* New Haven: Yale University Press.

Dahl, Robert A./Charles E. Lindblom, 1953: *Politics, Economics, and Welfare: Planning and Politico-Economic Systems Resolved into Basic Social Processes.* New York: Harper & Row.

Danto, Arthur, 1985: *Narration and Knowledge.* New York: Columbia University Press.

Dasgupta, Partha/Eric Maskin, 1986: The Existence of Equilibrium in Discontinuous Economic Games. *Review of Economic Studies* 53, 1–41.

David, Paul A., 1985: Clio and the Economics of QWERTY. *American Economic History* 75, 332–337.

Dawkins, Richard, 1976: *The Selfish Gene.* Oxford: Oxford University Press.

Dearborn, DeWitt C./Herbert A. Simon, 1958: Selective Perception: A Note on the Departmental Identification of Executives. *Sociometry* 21, 140–144.

Deeg, Richard, 1993: The State, Banks, and Economic Governance in Germany. *German Politics* 1, 149–176.

Dehousse, Renaud, 1995: Constitutional Reform in the European Community: Are There Alternatives to the Majoritarian Avenue? *West European Politics* 18(3), 118–136.

Dehousse, Renaud/Joseph H.H. Weiler, 1990: The Legal Dimension. In William Wallace, ed., *The Dynamics of European Integration,* 242–260. London: Pinter.

Dennett, Daniel C., 1981: Intentional Systems. In Daniel C. Dennett, *Brainstorms: Philosophical Essays on Mind and Psychology,* 3–22. Cambridge, MA: MIT Press.

Deutsch, Morton, 1975: Equity, Equality, and Need: What Determines Which Value Will Be Used as the Basis of Distributive Justice? *Journal of Social Issues* 31, 137–149.

_____, 1985: *Distributive Justice: A Social Psychological Perspective.* New Haven: Yale University Press.

Döhler, Marian/Philip Manow-Borgwardt, 1992: Gesundheitspolitische Steuerung zwischen Hierarchie und Verhandlung. *Politische Vierteljahresschrift* 33, 571–596.

Downs, Anthony, 1957: *An Economic Theory of Democracy.* New York: Harper & Row.

_____, 1967: *Inside Bureaucracy.* Boston: Little, Brown.

Dryzek, John S., 1990: *Discursive Democracy: Politics, Policy, and Political Science.* Cambridge: Cambridge University Press.

Dunsire, Andrew, 1993: Manipulating Social Tensions: Collibration as an Alternative Mode of Government Intervention. Discussion Paper 93/7, Max Planck Institute for the Study of Societies, Cologne.

_____, 1996: Tipping the Balance: Autopoiesis and Governance. *Administration and Society* 28, 299–334.

Easton, David, 1965: *A Systems Analysis of Political Life.* New York: John Wiley.

Eckstein, Harry, 1975: Case Study and Theory in Political Science. In Fred I. Greenstein/Nelson W. Polsby, eds., *Handbook of Political Science.* Vol. 7, *Strategies of Inquiry,* 79–137. Reading, MA: Addison-Wesley.

Edelman, Murray, 1964: *The Symbolic Uses of Politics.* Urbana: University of Illinois Press.

Egeberg, Morten, 1995: Bureaucrats as Public Policy-Makers and Their Self-Interests. *Journal of Theoretical Politics* 7, 157–167.

Eichener, Volker, 1995: European Health and Safety Regulation: No Race to the Bottom. In Brigitte Unger/Frans van Waarden, eds., *Convergence or Diversity? Internationalization and Economic Policy Response,* 229–251. Aldershot: Avebury.

Elias, Norbert, 1987: Wandlungen der Wir-Ich-Balance. In Norbert Elias, *Die Gesellschaft der Individuen,* 207–315. Frankfurt am Main: Suhrkamp.

Elster, Jon, 1983: *Sour Grapes: Studies in the Subversion of Rationality.* Cambridge: Cambridge University Press.

———, 1986: The Market and the Forum: Three Varieties of Political Theory. In Jon Elster/Aanund Hylland, eds., *Foundations of Social Choice Theory,* 103–132. Cambridge: Cambridge University Press.

———, 1989: *The Cement of Society: A Study of Social Order.* Cambridge: Cambridge University Press.

———, 1991: Rationality and Social Norms. *Archives Européennes de Sociologie* 32, 109–129.

———, 1992: *Local Justice: How Institutions Allocate Scarce Goods and Necessary Burdens.* Cambridge: Cambridge University Press.

Emerson, Richard M., 1962: Power-Dependence Relations. *American Sociological Review* 27, 31–41.

Esping-Andersen, Gösta, 1990: *The Three Worlds of Welfare Capitalism.* Cambridge: Polity Press.

Etzioni, Amitai, 1988: *The Moral Dimension: Toward a New Economics.* New York: Free Press.

Eurostat, 1995: *Statistische Grundzahlen der Europäischen Union. 32. Ausgabe.* Luxembourg: Amt für amtliche Veröffentlichungen der Europäischen Gemeinschaften.

Evans, Peter/Dietrich Rueschemeyer/Theda Skocpol, eds., 1985: *Bringing the State Back In.* Cambridge: Cambridge University Press.

Farrell, Joseph/Garth Saloner, 1988: Coordination Through Committees and Markets. *Rand Journal of Economics* 19, 235–252.

FAZ, 1996: Pläne für eine deutsche Ökosteuer sind vom Tisch: Regierung verzichtet auf fiskalische Maßnahmen zur Klimavorsorge: Industrie erweitert Selbstverpflichtung. *Frankfurter Allgemeine Zeitung,* March 28, 13.

Finifter, Ada W., ed., 1993: *Political Science: The State of the Discipline.* Washington, DC: American Political Science Association.

Fishburn, Peter C./D. Marc Kilgour, 1990: Binary 2 x 2 Games. *Theory and Decision* 29, 165–182.

Fisher, Roger/William Ury, 1981: *Getting to Yes: Negotiating Agreement Without Giving In.* Boston: Houghton Mifflin.

Freeman, Richard B., 1995: The Large Welfare State as a System. *AEA Papers and Proceedings* 85(2), 16–21.

Freud, Sigmund, 1915: Zeitgemäßes über Krieg und Tod. In Sigmund Freud, *Das Unbewußte: Schriften zur Psychoanalyse,* 185–213. Frankfurt am Main: S. Fischer.

Friedman, Milton, 1953: *Essays in Positive Economics.* Chicago: University of Chicago Press.

Friedrich, Carl J., 1937: *Constitutional Government and Politics*. New York: Harper & Brothers.

Fudenberg, Drew/Eric Maskin, 1986: The Folk Theorem in Repeated Games with Discounting or with Incomplete Information. *Econometrica* 54, 533–554.

Gage, Robert W./Myrna P. Mandell, eds., 1990: *Strategies for Managing Intergovernmental Policies and Networks*. New York: Praeger.

Garrett, Geoffrey, 1995: Capital Mobility, Trade, and the Domestic Politics of Economic Policy. *International Organization* 49, 657–687.

Genschel, Philipp, 1995: *Institutioneller Wandel in der internationalen Standardisierung von Informationstechnik*. Frankfurt am Main: Campus.

Genschel, Philipp/Thomas Pluemper, 1996: Wenn Reden Silber und Handeln Gold ist: Kommunikation und Kooperation in der internationalen Bankenregulierung. Discussion Paper 96/4, Max Planck Institute for the Study of Societies, Cologne.

Genschel, Philipp/Raymund Werle, 1993: From National Hierarchies to International Standardization: Historical and Modal Changes in the Coordination of Telecommunications. *Journal of Public Policy* 13, 203–225.

Gintis, Herbert, 1992: New Economic Rules of the Game. *Challenge* 35(5), 47–53.

Goldstein, Judith/Robert O. Keohane, 1993: Ideas and Foreign Policy: An Analytical Framework. In Judith Goldstein/Robert O. Keohane, eds., *Ideas and Foreign Policy: Beliefs, Institutions, and Political Change*, 3–30. Ithaca: Cornell University Press.

Graebner, William, 1977: Federalism in the Progressive Era: A Structural Interpretation of Reform. *Journal of American History* 64, 331–357.

Granovetter, Mark, 1973: The Strength of Weak Ties. *American Journal of Sociology* 78, 1360–1380.

––––––, 1978: Threshold Models of Collective Behavior. *American Journal of Sociology* 83, 1420–1443.

Greenstein, Fred I./Nelson W. Polsby, eds., 1975: *Handbook of Political Science*. Vol. 1, *Political Science: Scope and Theory*. Reading, MA: Addison-Wesley.

Grieco, Joseph M./Robert Powell/Duncan Snidal, 1993: The Relative Gains Problem for International Cooperation. *American Political Science Review* 87, 729–743.

Grimm, Dieter, 1995: Does Europe Need a Constitution? *European Law Journal* 1, 282–302.

Grofman, Bernard/Scott L. Feld, 1988: Rousseau's General Will: A Condorcetian Perspective. *American Political Science Review* 82, 567–576.

Grossman, Sanford J./Oliver D. Hart, 1983: An Analysis of the Principal-Agent Problem. *Econometrica* 51, 7–45.

Gulick, Luther/L. Urwick, eds., 1937: *Papers on the Science of Administration*. New York: Institute of Public Administration.

Haas, Peter M., 1992: Introduction: Epistemic Communities and International Policy Coordination. *International Organization* 46 (Special issue), 1–35.

Habermas, Jürgen, 1962: *Strukturwandel der Öffentlichkeit: Untersuchungen zu einer Kategorie der bürgerlichen Gesellschaft*. Neuwied: Luchterhand.

––––––, 1973: *Legitimationsprobleme im Spätkapitalismus*. Frankfurt am Main: Suhrkamp.

––––––, 1976: *Legitimation Crisis*. London: Heinemann.

––––––, 1981: *Theorie des kommunikativen Handelns*. Vol. 1, *Handlungsrationalität und gesellschaftliche Rationalisierung*. Frankfurt am Main: Suhrkamp.

––––––, 1989: Towards a Communication Concept of Rational Collective Will–Formation: A Thought Experiment. *Ratio Juris* 2, 144–154.

_____, 1992: *Faktizität und Geltung: Beiträge zur Diskurstheorie des Rechts und des demokratischen Rechtsstaats.* Frankfurt am Main: Suhrkamp.

_____, 1995: Comment on the Paper by Dieter Grimm: "Does Europe Need a Constitution?" *European Law Journal* 1, 303–307.

Hadley, Charles D./Michael Morass/Rainer Nick, 1989: Federalism and Party Interaction in West Germany, Switzerland, and Austria. *Publius: The Journal of Federalism* 19, 81–97.

Haffner, Sebastian, 1987: Die Pariser Kommune. In Sebastian Haffner, *Im Schatten der Geschichte: Historisch-politische Variationen aus zwanzig Jahren,* 61–103. Munich: Deutscher Taschenbuch Verlag.

Hall, Peter A., 1992: The Movement from Keynesianism to Monetarism: Institutional Analysis and British Economic Policy in the 1970s. In Sven Steinmo/Kathleen Thelen/Frank Longstreth, eds., *Structuring Politics: Historical Institutionalism in Comparative Analysis,* 90–113. Cambridge: Cambridge University Press.

_____, 1993: Policy Paradigms, Social Learning, and the State: The Case of Economic Policymaking in Britain. *Comparative Politics* 25, 275–296.

_____, ed., 1989: *The Political Power of Economic Ideas: Keynesianism Across Nations.* Princeton: Princeton University Press.

Hall, Peter A./Rosemary C.R. Taylor, 1996: Political Science and the Three New Institutionalisms. Discussion Paper 96/6, Max Planck Institute for the Study of Societies, Cologne.

Hannan, Michael T./John Freeman, 1977: The Population Ecology of Organizations. *American Journal of Sociology* 82, 929–964.

_____, 1984: Structural Inertia and Organizational Change. *American Sociological Review* 49, 149–164.

Hardin, Garrett, 1968: The Tragedy of the Commons. *Science* 162, 1243–1268.

Hardin, Russell, 1971: Collective Action as an Agreeable n-Prisoners' Dilemma. *Behavioral Science* 16, 472–481.

_____, 1985: Individual Sanctions, Collective Benefits. In Richmond Campbell/Lanning Snowden, eds., *Paradoxes of Rationality and Cooperation: Prisoner's Dilemma and Newcomb's Problem,* 339–354. Vancouver: University of British Columbia Press.

Harsanyi, John C., 1967–1968: Games with Incomplete Information Played by Bayesian Players. *Management Science* 14, 159–182, 320–334, 486–502.

_____, 1977: *Rational Behavior and Bargaining Equilibrium in Games and Social Situations.* Cambridge: Cambridge University Press.

_____, 1981: The Shapley Value and the Risk-Dominance Solutions of Two Bargaining Models for Characteristic-Function Games. In Robert J. Aumann et al., *Essays in Game Theory and Mathematical Economics in Honor of Oskar Morgenstern,* 43–68. Mannheim: Bibliographisches Institut.

_____, 1991: Measurement of Social Power in n-Person Reciprocal Power Situations. In Peter Abell, ed., *Rational Choice Theory,* 25–35. Cambridge: Cambridge University Press.

_____, 1995: A New Theory of Equilibrium Selection for Games with Complete Information. *Games and Economic Behavior* 8, 91–122.

Harsanyi, John C./Reinhard Selten, 1988: *A General Theory of Equilibrium Selection in Games.* Cambridge, MA: MIT Press.

Hartkopf, Günter/Eberhard Bohne, 1983: *Umweltpolitik I: Grundlagen, Analysen und Perspektiven.* Opladen: Westdeutscher Verlag.

Hausken, Kjell, 1995: Intra-level and Inter-level Interaction. *Rationality and Society* 7, 465–488.

Häusler, Jürgen/Hans-Willy Hohn/Susanne Lütz, 1993: The Architecture of an R&D Collaboration. In Fritz W. Scharpf, ed., *Games in Hierarchies and Networks: Analytical and Empirical Approaches to the Study of Governance Institutions*, 211–250. Boulder: Westview Press.

Hayek, Friedrich A., 1944: *The Road to Serfdom*. Chicago: University of Chicago Press.

———, 1945: The Use of Knowledge in Society. *American Economic Review* 35, 519–530.

Hechter, Michael, 1987: *Principles of Group Solidarity*. Berkeley: University of California Press.

Heckathorn, Douglas D., 1989: Collective Action and the Second-Order Free-Rider Problem. *Rationality and Society* 1, 78–100.

Heckathorn, Douglas D./Steven M. Maser, 1987: Bargaining and Constitutional Contracts. *American Journal of Political Science* 31, 142–168.

———, 1990: The Contractual Architecture of Public Policy: A Critical Reconstruction of Lowi's Typology. *Journal of Politics* 52, 1101–1123.

Held, David, 1987: *Models of Democracy*. Cambridge: Polity Press.

———, 1991: Democracy, the Nation-State, and the Global System. *Economy and Society* 20, 139–172.

Héritier, Adrienne, 1996: The Accommodation of Diversity in European Policy-Making and Its Outcomes: Regulatory Policy as a Patchwork. *Journal of European Public Policy* 3, 149–167.

Héritier, Adrienne/Christoph Knill/Susanne Mingers, 1996: *Ringing the Changes in Europe: Regulatory Competition and Redefinition of the State: Britain, France, Germany*. Berlin: de Gruyter.

Héritier, Adrienne/Susanne Mingers/Christoph Knill/Martina Becka, 1994: *Die Veränderung von Staatlichkeit in Europa: Ein regulativer Wettbewerb: Deutschland, Großbritannien, und Frankreich in der Europäischen Union*. Opladen: Leske & Budrich.

Hesse, Joachim Jens, 1987: The Federal Republic of Germany: From Co-operative Federalism to Joint Policy-Making. *West European Politics* 10(4), 70–87.

Hindess, Barry, 1991: Imaginary Presuppositions of Democracy. *Economy and Society* 20, 173–195.

Hirschman, Albert O., 1970: *Exit, Voice, and Loyalty: Responses to Decline in Firms, Organizations, and States*. Cambridge, MA: Harvard University Press.

Hirst, Paul/Grahame Thompson, 1995: Globalization and the Future of the Nation State. *Economy and Society* 24, 408–442.

Hjern, Benny/David Porter, 1981: Implementation Structures: A New Unit of Administrative Analysis. *Organizational Studies* 2, 211–227.

Höffe, Otfried, 1987: *Politische Gerechtigkeit: Grundlegung einer kritischen Philosophie von Recht und Staat*. Frankfurt am Main: Suhrkamp.

Hoffmann-Riem, Wolfgang, 1990: Verhandlungslösungen und Mittlereinsatz im Bereich der Verwaltung: Eine vergleichende Einführung. In Wolfgang Hoffmann-Riem/Eberhard Schmidt-Aßmann, eds., *Konfliktbewältigung durch Verhandlungen*, 13–41. Baden-Baden: Nomos.

Holler, Manfred J./Gerhard Illing, 1993: *Einführung in die Spieltheorie*. 2d edition. Berlin: Springer.

Hollingsworth, J. Rogers/Philippe C. Schmitter/Wolfgang Streeck, eds., 1994: *Governing Capitalist Economies: Performance and Control of Economic Sectors*. New York: Oxford University Press.

Holmstrom, Bengt, 1982: Moral Hazard in Teams. *Bell Journal of Economics* 13, 324–340.

Howe, Paul, 1995: A Community of Europeans: The Requisite Underpinnings. *Journal of Common Market Studies* 33, 27–46.

Hull, Christopher J./Benny Hjern, 1987: *Helping Small Firms Grow: An Implementation Approach.* London: Croom Helm.

Hurwicz, Leonid, 1972: On Informationally Decentralized Systems. In C. B. McGuire/Roy Radner, eds., *Decision and Organization: A Volume in Honor of Jacob Marschak,* 297–336. Amsterdam: North-Holland.

Immergut, Ellen M., 1990: Institutions, Veto Points, and Policy Results: A Comparative Analysis of Health Care. *Journal of Public Policy* 10, 391–416.

———, 1992: *Health Politics: Interests and Institutions in Western Europe.* Cambridge: Cambridge University Press.

———, 1993: The German Health System in International Comparison. In Fritz W. Scharpf, ed., *Games in Hierarchies and Networks: Analytical and Empirical Approaches to the Study of Governance Institutions,* 339–347. Boulder: Westview Press.

Janis, Irving, 1972: *Victims of Groupthink.* Boston: Houghton-Mifflin.

Jasay, Anthony de, 1995: Conventions: Some Thoughts on the Economics of Ordered Anarchy. Lectiones Jenenses 3, Max Planck Institute for Research into Economic Systems, Jena.

Jenkins-Smith, Hank C./Paul A. Sabatier, 1993: The Dynamics of Policy-Oriented Learning. In Paul A. Sabatier/Hank C. Jenkins-Smith, eds., *Policy Change and Learning: An Advocacy Coalition Approach,* 41–56. Boulder: Westview Press.

Jensen, Michael C., 1983: Organization Theory and Methodology. *Accounting Review* 58, 319–339.

Jensen, Michael C./William H. Meckling, 1976: Theory of the Firm, Managerial Behavior, Agency Costs, and Ownership Structure. *Journal of Financial Economics* 3, 305–360.

Johanson, Jan/Lars-Gunnar Mattson, 1987: Interorganizational Relations in Industrial Systems: A Network Approach Compared with the Transaction Cost Approach. *International Studies of Management and Organization* 17, 34–48.

John, Robert, 1980: Theory Construction in Sociology: The Competing Approaches. *Mid-American Review of Sociology* 5, 15–36.

Kahneman, Daniel/Amos Tversky, 1984: Choices, Values, and Frames. *American Psychologist* 39, 341–350.

Kalai, Ehud/Meir Smorodinsky, 1975: Other Solutions to Nash's Bargaining Problem. *Econometrica* 43, 513–518.

Kaldor, Nicholas, 1939: Welfare Propositions of Economics and Inter-personal Comparisons of Utility. *Economic Journal* 49, 549–552.

Kalecki, Michael, [1943] 1971: Political Aspects of Full Employment. In Michael Kalecki, *Selected Essays on the Dynamics of the Capitalist Economy,* 138–145. London: Cambridge University Press.

Kapteyn, Paul, 1996: *The Stateless Market: The European Dilemma of Integration and Civilization.* London: Routledge.

Katzenstein, Peter J., 1987: *Policy and Politics in West Germany: The Growth of a Semisovereign State.* Philadelphia: Temple University Press.

Keck, Otto, 1987: The Information Dilemma: Private Information as a Cause of Transaction Failure in Markets, Regulation, Hierarchy, and Politics. *Journal of Conflict Resolution* 31, 139–163.

_____, 1988: A Theory of White Elephants: Asymmetric Information in Government Support for Technology. *Research Policy* 17, 187–201.

_____, 1994: Die Bedeutung der rationalen Institutionentheorie für die Politikwissenschaft. In Gerhard Göhler, ed., *Die Eigenart der Institutionen: Zum Profil politischer Institutionentheorie,* 187–220. Baden-Baden: Nomos.

Kelley, Harold H./John W. Thibaut, 1978: *Interpersonal Relations: A Theory of Interdependence.* New York: John Wiley.

Kellow, Aynsley, 1988: Promoting Elegance in Policy Theory: Simplifying Lowi's Arenas of Power. *Policy Studies Journal* 16, 713–724.

Keohane, Robert O., 1984: *After Hegemony: Cooperation and Discord in the World Political Economy.* Princeton: Princeton University Press.

Kiewiet, Roderick/Mathew D. McCubbins, 1991: *The Logic of Delegation: Congressional Parties and the Appropriations Process.* Chicago: University of Chicago Press.

Kindleberger, Charles P., 1995: *The World Economy and National Finance in Historical Perspective.* Ann Arbor: University of Michigan Press.

King, Gary/Robert O. Keohane/Sidney Verba, 1994: *Designing Social Inquiry: Scientific Inference in Qualitative Research.* Princeton: Princeton University Press.

Kingdon, John W., 1984: *Agendas, Alternatives, and Public Policies.* Boston: Little, Brown.

Kirchgässner, Gebhard, 1992: Towards a Theory of Low-Cost Decisions. *European Journal of Political Economy* 8, 305–320.

_____, 1996: Ideologie und Information in der Politikberatung: Einige Bemerkungen und ein Fallbeispiel. Discussion Paper 9605, Department of Economics, University of Saint Gall, Switzerland.

Klatt, Hartmut, 1989: Forty Years of German Federalism: Past Trends and New Developments. *Publius: The Journal of Federalism* 19, 185–202.

Knoke, David, 1990: Networks of Political Action: Towards Theory Construction. *Social Forces* 68, 1041–1063.

Knoke, David/Franz Urban Pappi/Jeffrey Broadbent/Yukata Tsujinaka, 1996: *Comparing Policy Networks: Labor Policies in the U.S., Germany, and Japan.* Cambridge: Cambridge University Press.

Koenigs, Tom/Roland Schaeffer, eds., 1993: *Energiekonsens? Der Streit um die zukünftige Energiepolitik.* Munich: Raben.

König, Thomas, 1994: Die Bedeutung von Politik-Netzen in einem Modell politischer Entscheidung und politisch-privater Einflußnahme. *Journal für Sozialforschung* 33, 343–368.

Korpi, Walter, 1983: *The Democratic Class Struggle.* London: Routledge & Kegan Paul.

Krasner, Stephen D., ed., 1983: *International Regimes.* Ithaca: Cornell University Press.

Krehbiel, Keith, 1996: Institutional and Partisan Sources of Gridlock: A Theory of Divided and Unified Government. *Journal of Theoretical Politics* 8, 7–40.

Kreps, David M., 1995: Corporate Culture and Economic Theory. In Oliver E. Williamson/Scott E. Masten, eds., *Transaction Cost Economics: Theory and Concepts,* 497–552. Aldershot: Elgar.

Kreps, David M./Robert Wilson, 1982: Reputation and Imperfect Information. *Journal of Economic Theory* 27, 253–279.

Lambsdorff, Johann Graf, 1995: Korruption ist überall. *Die Zeit,* July 28, 16.

Lasswell, Harold D., 1936: *Politics: Who Gets What, When, How.* New York: McGraw Hill.

Lasswell, Harold D./Abraham Kaplan, 1950: *Power and Society: A Framework for Political Inquiry.* New Haven: Yale University Press.

Latsis, Spiros, 1972: Situational Determinism in Economics. *British Journal for the Philosophy of Science* 23, 207–245.

Lave, Charles A./James G. March, 1975: *An Introduction to Models in the Social Sciences.* New York: Harper & Row.

Laver, Michael/Norman Schofield, 1990: *Coalitions and Cabinet Government.* Oxford: Oxford University Press.

Laver, Michael/Kenneth A. Shepsle, 1991: Divided Government: America Is Not "Exceptional." *Governance* 4, 250–269.

_____, 1993: A Theory of Minority Government in Parliamentary Democracy. In Fritz W. Scharpf, ed., *Games in Hierarchies and Networks: Analytical and Empirical Approaches to the Study of Governance Institutions,* 429–446. Boulder: Westview Press.

Lax, David A./James K. Sebenius, 1985: The Power of Alternatives or the Limits to Negotiation. *Negotiation Journal* 1, 163–179.

_____, 1986: *The Manager as Negotiator: Bargaining for Cooperation and Competitive Gain.* New York: Free Press.

Lehmbruch, Gerhard, 1967: *Proporzdemokratie: Politisches System und politische Kultur in der Schweiz und in Österreich.* Tübingen: Mohr.

_____, 1974: A Non-competitive Pattern of Conflict Management in Liberal Democracies. In Kenneth D. McRae, ed., *Consociational Democracy: Political Accommodation in Segmented Societies,* 90–97. Toronto: McLelland & Stewart.

_____, 1995: Ressortautonomie und die Konstitution sektoraler Politiknetzwerke: Administrative Interessenvermittlung in Japan. In Karlheinz Bentele/Bernd Reissert/ Ronald Schettkat, eds., *Die Reformfähigkeit von Industriegesellschaften: Fritz W. Scharpf, Festschrift zu seinem 60. Geburtstag,* 64–100. Frankfurt am Main: Campus.

Lehmbruch, Gerhard/Philippe C. Schmitter, eds., 1982: *Patterns of Corporatist Policy-Making.* London: Sage.

Leibfried, Stephan/Paul Pierson, eds., 1995: *European Social Policy: Between Fragmentation and Integration.* Washington, DC: Brookings Institution.

Levi, Margaret, 1988: *Of Rule and Revenue.* Berkeley: University of California Press.

Liebowitz, S. J./Stephen E. Margolis, 1994: Network Externality: An Uncommon Tragedy. *Journal of Economic Perspectives* 8, 133–150.

Lijphart, Arend, 1968: *The Politics of Accommodation: Pluralism and Democracy in the Netherlands.* Berkeley: University of California Press.

_____, 1984: *Democracies: Patterns of Majoritarian and Consensus Government in Twenty-One Countries.* New Haven: Yale University Press.

_____, 1991: Majority Rule in Theory and Practice: The Tenacity of a Flawed Paradigm. *International Social Science Journal* 129, 483–493.

Lindblom, Charles E., 1965: *The Intelligence of Democracy: Decision Making Through Mutual Adjustment.* New York: Free Press.

_____, 1977: *Politics and Markets.* New York: Basic Books.

Lindenberg, Siegwart, 1989: Choice and Culture: The Behavioral Basis of Cultural Impact on Transactions. In Hans Haferkamp, ed., *Social Structure and Culture,* 175–200. Berlin: de Gruyter.

_____, 1991: Die Methode der abnehmenden Abstraktion: Theoriegesteuerte Analyse und empirischer Gehalt. In Hartmut Esser/Klaus G. Troitzsch, eds., *Modellierung sozialer Prozesse,* 29–78. Bonn: Informationszentrum Sozialwissenschaften.

Linder, Wolf, 1994: *Swiss Democracy: Possible Solutions to Conflict in Multicultural Societies.* New York: St. Martin's Press.

Little, Daniel, 1991: *Varieties of Social Explanation: An Introduction to the Philosophy of Social Science.* Boulder: Westview Press.

Lowi, Theodore, 1964: American Business, Public Policy, Case Studies, and Political Theory. *World Politics* 16, 676–715.

———, 1988: An Assessment of Kellow's "Promoting Elegance in Policy Theory." *Policy Studies Journal* 16, 725–728.

Lübbe, Hermann, 1975: Was heißt "Das kann man nur historisch erklären"? Zur Analyse der Struktur historischer Prozesse. In Hermann Lübbe, *Fortschritt als Orientierungsproblem: Aufklärung in der Gegenwart,* 154–168. Freiburg: Rombach.

Luhmann, Niklas, 1966: *Recht und Automation in der öffentlichen Verwaltung: Eine verwaltungswissenschaftliche Untersuchung.* Berlin: Duncker & Humblot.

———, 1969: *Legitimation durch Verfahren.* Neuwied: Luchterhand.

———, 1984: *Soziale Systeme: Grundriß einer allgemeinen Theorie.* Frankfurt am Main: Suhrkamp.

———, 1986: *Ökologische Kommunikation: Kann die moderne Gesellschaft sich auf ökologische Gefährdungen einstellen?* Opladen: Westdeutscher Verlag.

———, 1988a: Warum AGIL? *Kölner Zeitschrift für Soziologie und Sozialpsychologie* 40, 127–139.

———, 1988b: *Die Wirtschaft der Gesellschaft.* Frankfurt am Main: Suhrkamp.

———, 1995: Kausalität im Süden. *Soziale Systeme* 1, 7–28.

Lustick, Ian S., 1996: History, Historiography, and Political Science: Multiple Historical Records and the Problem of Selection Bias. *American Political Science Review* 90, 605–618.

Luthardt, Wolfgang, 1992: Direct Democracy in Western Europe: The Case of Switzerland. *Telos* 90, 101–112.

———, 1994: *Direkte Demokratie: Ein Vergleich in Westeuropa.* Baden-Baden: Nomos.

Macy, Michael W., 1989: Walking out of Social Traps. *Rationality and Society* 1, 197–219.

Majone, Giandomenico, 1989: *Evidence, Argument, and Persuasion in the Policy Process.* New Haven: Yale University Press.

———, 1994: The European Community: An "Independent Fourth Branch of Government"? In Gert Brüggemeier, ed., *Verfassungen für ein ziviles Europa,* 23–43. Baden-Baden: Nomos.

———, 1995: Independence Versus Accountability? Non-majoritarian Institutions and Democratic Government in Europe. In Joachim Jens Hesse/Theo A.J. Toonen, eds., *The European Yearbook of Comparative Government and Public Administration.* Vol. 1, 117–140. Oxford: Oxford University Press.

Manin, Bernard, 1987: On Legitimacy and Political Deliberation. *Political Theory* 15, 338–368.

March, James G./Johan P. Olsen, 1989: *Rediscovering Institutions: The Organizational Basis of Politics.* New York: Free Press.

———, 1995: *Democratic Governance.* New York: Free Press.

March, James G./Herbert A. Simon, 1958: *Organizations.* New York: John Wiley.

Marin, Bernd, ed., 1990: *Generalized Political Exchange: Antagonistic Cooperation and Integrated Policy Circuits.* Frankfurt am Main: Campus.

Marin, Bernd/Renate Mayntz, eds., 1991: *Policy Networks: Empirical Evidence and Theoretical Considerations.* Frankfurt am Main: Campus.

Markovsky, Barry/Travis Patton/David Willer, 1988: Power Relations in Exchange Networks. *American Sociological Review* 53, 220–236.

Marsden, Peter V., 1983: Restricted Access in Networks and Models of Power. *American Journal of Sociology* 88, 686–717.

———, 1987: Elements of Interactor Dependence. In Karen S. Cook, ed., *Social Exchange Theory*, 130–148. Newbury Park, CA: Sage.

Maruyama, Magoroh, 1963: The Second Cybernetics: Deviation-Amplifying Mutual Causal Processes. *American Scientist* 51, 164–179.

Mason, Alpheus Thomas, 1956: *Harlan Fiske Stone: Pillar of the Law.* New York: Viking Press.

Masuch, Michael, 1985: Vicious Cycles in Organizations. *Administrative Science Quarterly* 30, 14–33.

Mayer, Frederick W., 1992: Managing Domestic Differences in International Negotiations: The Strategic Use of Internal Side Payments. *International Organization* 46, 793–818.

Mayer, Jörg M., 1994: "Wann sind Paketlösungen machbar?" Eine konstruktive Kritik an F. W. Scharpfs Konzept. *Politische Vierteljahresschrift* 35, 448–471.

Maynard Smith, John, 1982: *Evolution and the Theory of Games.* Cambridge: Cambridge University Press.

Mayntz, Renate, 1986: Corporate Actors in Public Policy: Changing Perspectives in Political Analysis. *Norsk Statsvitenskapelig Tidsskrift* 3/1986, 7–25.

———, 1988: Funktionelle Teilsysteme in der Theorie sozialer Differenzierung. In Renate Mayntz/Bernd Rosewitz/Uwe Schimank/Rudolf Stichweh, *Differenzierung und Verselbständigung: Zur Entwicklung gesellschaftlicher Teilsysteme*, 11–44. Frankfurt am Main: Campus.

———, 1993: Große technische Systeme und ihre gesellschaftstheoretische Bedeutung. *Kölner Zeitschrift für Soziologie und Sozialpsychologie* 45, 97–108.

———, 1994: *Deutsche Forschung im Einigungsprozeß: Die Transformation der Akademie der Wissenschaften der DDR, 1989–1992.* Frankfurt am Main: Campus.

———, 1995: *Historische Überraschungen und das Erklärungspotential der Sozialwissenschaft.* Heidelberg: C. F. Müller.

———, ed., 1980: *Implementation politischer Programme: Empirische Forschungsberichte.* Meisenheim am Glan: Anton Hain.

———, ed., 1983: *Implementation politischer Programme II: Ansätze zur Theoriebildung.* Opladen: Westdeutscher Verlag.

———, ed., 1992: *Verbände zwischen Mitgliederinteressen und Gemeinwohl.* Gütersloh: Bertelsmann.

Mayntz, Renate/Birgitta Nedelmann, 1987: Eigendynamische soziale Prozesse: Anmerkungen zu einem analytischen Paradigma. *Kölner Zeitschrift für Soziologie und Sozialpsychologie* 39, 648–668.

Mayntz, Renate/Friedhelm Neidhardt, 1989: Parlamentskultur: Handlungsorientierungen von Bundestagsabgeordneten—eine empirisch-explorative Studie. *Zeitschrift für Parlamentsfragen* 20, 370–387.

———, 1992: Social Norms in the Institutional Culture of the German Federal Parliament. In Richard Münch/Neil Smelser, eds., *Theory of Culture*, 219–240. Berkeley: University of California Press.

Mayntz, Renate/Fritz W. Scharpf, 1975: *Policy-Making in the German Federal Bureaucracy.* Amsterdam: Elsevier.

_____, 1995a: Der Ansatz des akteurzentrierten Institutionalismus. In Renate Mayntz/Fritz W. Scharpf, eds., *Steuerung und Selbstorganisation in staatsnahen Sektoren,* 39–72. Frankfurt am Main: Campus.

_____, eds., 1995b: *Steuerung und Selbstorganisation in staatsnahen Sektoren.* Frankfurt am Main: Campus.

Mayntz, Renate/Volker Schneider, 1988: The Dynamics of System Development in a Comparative Perspective: Interactive Videotex in Germany, France, and Britain. In Renate Mayntz/Thomas P. Hughes, eds., *The Development of Large Technical Systems,* 263–298. Boulder: Westview Press.

McClintock, Charles G., 1972: Social Motivation: A Set of Propositions. *Behavioral Science* 17, 438–454.

McGinnis, Michael D., 1986: Issue Linkage and the Evolution of International Cooperation. *Journal of Conflict Resolution* 30, 141–170.

McKay, David, 1994: Divided and Governed? Recent Research on Divided Government in the United States. *British Journal of Political Science* 24, 517–534.

McKelvey, Richard D., 1976: Intransitivities in Multidimensional Voting Models and Some Implications for Agenda Control. *Journal of Economic Theory* 12, 472–482.

Meek, Lynn, 1988: Organizational Culture: Origins and Weaknesses. *Organizational Studies* 9, 453–473.

Messick, David M./Carol L. McClelland, 1983: Social Traps and Temporal Traps. *Personality and Social Psychology Bulletin* 9, 105–110.

Michaud, Pierre, 1988: The True Rule of the Marquis de Condorcet. In Bertrand R. Munier/Melvin F. Shakun, eds., *Compromise, Negotiation, and Group Decision,* 83–100. Dordrecht: Reidel.

Milgrom, Paul R./Douglass C. North/Barry R. Weingast, 1990: The Role of Institutions in the Revival of Trade: The Law Merchant, Private Judges, and the Champagne Fairs. *Economics and Politics* 2, 1–23.

Milgrom, Paul R./John Roberts, 1990: Bargaining Costs, Influence Costs, and the Organization of Economic Activity. In James E. Alt/Kenneth A. Shepsle, eds., *Perspectives on Positive Political Economy,* 57–89. Cambridge: Cambridge University Press.

Miller, Gary J., 1990: Managerial Dilemmas: Political Leadership in Hierarchies. In Karen Schweers Cook/Margaret Levi, eds., *The Limits of Rationality,* 324–348. Chicago: University of Chicago Press.

Miller, Hugh, 1990: Weber's Action Theory and Lowi's Policy Types in Formulation, Enactment, and Implementation. *Policy Studies Journal* 18, 887–906.

Mohr, Matthias/Kjell Hausken, 1996: Conflict, Interest, and Strategy: A Risk-Limit Approach to Conflict. Discussion Paper 96/9, Max Planck Institute for the Study of Societies, Cologne.

Molm, Linda D., 1989: Punishment Power: A Balancing Process in Power-Dependence Relations. *American Journal of Sociology* 94, 1392–1418.

_____, 1990: Structure, Action, and Outcomes: The Dynamics of Power in Social Exchange. *American Sociological Review* 55, 427–447.

Moravcsik, Andrew, 1992: Liberalism and International Relations Theory. Working Paper 92-6, Center for International Affairs, Harvard University, Cambridge, MA.

Moses, Jonathon W., 1995: The Social Democratic Predicament in the Emerging European Union: A Capital Dilemma. *Journal of European Public Policy* 2, 407–426.

Mueller, Dennis C., 1989a: Democracy: The Public Choice Approach. In Geoffrey Brennan/Loren E. Lomasky, eds., *Politics and Process: New Essays in Democratic Thought*, 78–96. Cambridge: Cambridge University Press.

———, 1989b: *Public Choice II*. Cambridge: Cambridge University Press.

Nash, John F., 1950: The Bargaining Problem. *Econometrica* 18, 155–162.

———, 1951: Non-cooperative Games. *Annals of Mathematics* 54, 286–295.

———, 1953: Two-Person Cooperative Games. *Econometrica* 21, 128–140.

Niskanen, William A., 1971: *Bureaucracy and Representative Government*. Chicago: Rand McNally.

North, Douglass C., 1990: *Institutions, Institutional Change, and Economic Performance*. Cambridge: Cambridge University Press.

Offe, Claus, 1972: *Strukturprobleme des kapitalistischen Staates*. Frankfurt am Main: Suhrkamp.

———, 1984: *Contradictions of the Welfare State*. London: Hutchinson.

Olson, Mancur, 1965: *The Logic of Collective Action: Public Goods and the Theory of Groups*. Cambridge, MA: Harvard University Press.

———, 1982: *The Rise and Decline of Nations: Economic Growth, Stagflation, and Social Rigidities*. New Haven: Yale University Press.

———, 1993: Dictatorship, Democracy, and Development. *American Political Science Review* 87, 567–576.

Olson, Mancur/Richard Zeckhauser, 1966: An Economic Theory of Alliances. *Review of Economics and Statistics* 48, 266–279.

Osborne, Martin J./Ariel Rubinstein, 1990: *Bargaining and Markets*. San Diego: Academic Press.

———, 1994: *A Course in Game Theory*. Cambridge, MA: MIT Press.

Ostrom, Elinor, 1986: A Method of Institutional Analysis. In Franz-Xaver Kaufmann/Giandomenico Majone/Vincent Ostrom, eds., *Guidance and Control in the Public Sector: The Bielefeld Interdisciplinary Project*, 459–475. Berlin: de Gruyter.

———, 1990: *Governing the Commons: The Evolution of Institutions for Collective Action*. Cambridge: Cambridge University Press.

———, 1996: Institutional Rational Choice: An Assessment of the IAD Framework. Paper prepared for the 1996 annual meetings of the American Political Science Association. Indiana University: Workshop in Political Theory and Policy Analysis.

Ostrom, Elinor/Roy Gardner/James Walker, 1994: *Rules, Games, and Common-Pool Resources*. Ann Arbor: University of Michigan Press.

Panitch, Leo, 1980: Recent Theoretizations of Corporatism: Reflections on a Growth Industry. *British Journal of Sociology* 31, 159–187.

Parks, R. B./Elinor Ostrom, 1981: Complex Models of Urban Service Systems. *Urban Affairs Annual Reviews* 21, 171–199.

Parsons, Talcott, 1967: Voting and the Equilibrium of the American Political System. In Talcott Parsons, *Sociological Theory and Modern Society*, 223–263. New York: Free Press.

Pierson, Paul, 1994: *Dismantling the Welfare State? Reagan, Thatcher, and the Politics of Retrenchment*. Cambridge: Cambridge University Press.

———, 1996a: The Path to European Integration: A Historical Institutionalist Analysis. *Comparative Politics* 29, 123–163.

———, 1996b: The New Politics of the Welfare State. *World Politics* 48, 143–197.

Pizzorno, Alessandro, 1978: Political Exchange and Collective Identity in Industrial Conflict. In Colin Crouch/Alessandro Pizzorno, eds., *The Resurgence of Class Conflict in Western Europe Since 1968*. Vol. 2, *Comparative Analyses*, 277–298. London: Macmillan.

Platt, John, 1973: Social Traps. *American Psychologist* 28, 641–651.

Plott, Charles R., 1967: A Notion of Equilibrium and Its Possibility Under Majority Rule. *American Economic Review* 67, 787–806.

Polanyi, Karl, 1957: *The Great Transformation: The Political and Economic Origins of Our Time.* Boston: Beacon Press.

Pollack, Mark A., 1995: Obedient Servant or Runaway Eurocracy? Delegation, Agency, and Agenda Setting in the European Community. Unpublished manuscript, Department of Political Science, University of Wisconsin, Madison.

Powell, Robert, 1991: Absolute and Relative Gains in International Relations Theory. *American Political Science Review* 85, 1303–1320.

Prittwitz, Volker von, ed., 1996: *Verhandeln und Argumentieren: Dialog, Interessen und Macht in der Umweltpolitik.* Opladen: Leske & Budrich.

Pruitt, Dean G., 1981: *Negotiation Behavior.* New York: Academic Press.

Przeworski, Adam/Henry Teune, 1970: *The Logic of Comparative Social Inquiry.* New York: John Wiley.

Putnam, Robert D., 1988: Diplomacy and Domestic Politics: The Logic of Two-Level Games. *International Organization* 42, 429–460.

———, 1993: The Prosperous Community: Social Capital and Public Affairs. *The American Prospect,* Spring, 1–8.

Putnam, Robert D./Nicholas Bayne, 1984: *Hanging Together: The Seven-Power Summits.* London: Heinemann.

Quattrone, George A./Amos Tversky, 1988: Contrasting Rational and Psychological Analyses of Political Choice. *American Political Science Review* 82, 719–735.

Quirk, Paul, 1989: The Cooperative Resolution of Policy Conflict. *American Political Science Review* 83, 905–921.

Ragin, Charles, 1987: *The Comparative Method: Moving Beyond Qualitative and Quantitative Strategies.* Berkeley: University of California Press.

Rapoport, Anatol/Melvin J. Guyer/David G. Gordon, 1976: *The 2 x 2 Game.* Ann Arbor: University of Michigan Press.

Raub, Werner/Gideon Keren, 1993: Hostages as a Commitment Device: A Game-Theoretic Model and an Empirical Test of Some Scenarios. *Journal of Economic Behavior and Organization* 21, 43–67.

Rawls, John, 1971: *A Theory of Justice.* Cambridge, MA: Belknap Press of Harvard University Press.

Renzsch, Wolfgang, 1989: German Federalism in Historical Perspective: Federalism as a Substitute for a National State. *Publius: The Journal of Federalism* 19, 17–33.

———, 1994: Föderative Problembewältigung: Zur Einbeziehung der neuen Länder in einen gesamtdeutschen Finanzausgleich ab 1995. *Zeitschrift für Parlamentsfragen* 25, 116–138.

Rhodes, R.A.W., 1996: The New Governance: Governing Without Government. *Political Studies* 44, 652–677.

Riker, William H., 1962: *The Theory of Political Coalitions.* New Haven: Yale University Press.

———, 1980: Implications from the Disequilibrium of Majority Rule for the Study of Institutions. *American Political Science Review* 74, 432–446.

———, 1982: *Liberalism Against Populism: A Confrontation Between the Theory of Democracy and the Theory of Social Choice.* San Francisco: W. H. Freeman.

Rogers, Joel/Wolfgang Streeck, eds., 1995: *Works Councils: Consultation, Representation, and Cooperation in Industrial Relations.* Chicago: University of Chicago Press.

Ronge, Volker, 1979: *Bankpolitik im Spätkapitalismus: Politische Selbstverwaltung des Kapitals?* Frankfurt am Main: Suhrkamp.

Rosenberg, Alexander, 1988: *Philosophy of Social Science.* Boulder: Westview Press.

Rosewitz, Bernd/Douglas Webber, 1990: *Reformversuche und Reformblockaden im deutschen Gesundheitswesen.* Frankfurt am Main: Campus.

Rothstein, Bo, 1992: Social Justice and State Capacity. *Politics and Society* 20, 101–126.

Rousseau, Jean-Jacques, [1762] 1984: *Of the Social Contract, or Principles of Political Right and Discourse on Political Economy.* Translated with an introduction and notes by Charles M. Sherover. New York: Harper & Row.

Rubinstein, Ariel, 1982: Perfect Equilibrium in a Bargaining Model. *Econometrica* 50, 97–109.

Ruggie, John Gerard, 1982: International Regimes, Transactions, and Change: Embedded Liberalism in the Postwar Economic Order. *International Organization* 36, 379–415.

———, ed., 1993: *Multilateralism Matters: The Theory and Praxis of an Institutional Form.* New York: Columbia University Press.

Runciman, Walter G./Amartya Sen, 1965: Games, Justice, and the General Will. *Mind* 74, 554–562.

Ryll, Andreas, 1993: Bargaining in the German Ambulatory Health Care System. In Fritz W. Scharpf, ed., *Games in Hierarchies and Networks: Analytical and Empirical Approaches to the Study of Governance Institutions,* 315–337. Boulder: Westview Press.

Sabatier, Paul A., 1986: Top-Down and Bottom-Up Approaches to Implementation Research: A Critical Analysis and Suggested Synthesis. *Journal of Public Policy* 6, 21–48.

———, 1987: Knowledge, Policy-Oriented Learning, and Policy Change: An Advocacy Coalition Framework. *Knowledge: Creation, Diffusion, Utilization* 8, 649–692.

Sabatier, Paul A./Hank C. Jenkins-Smith, eds., 1993: *Policy Change and Learning: An Advocacy Coalition Approach.* Boulder: Westview Press.

Sabel, Charles F., 1989: Flexible Specialization and the Re-emergence of Regional Economies. In Paul Hirst/Jonathan Zeitlin, eds., *Reversing Industrial Decline? Industrial Structure and Policy in Britain and Her Competitors,* 17–70. Oxford: Berg.

———, 1992: Studied Trust: Building New Forms of Co-operation in a Volatile Economy. In Frank Pyke/Werner Sengenberger, eds., *Industrial Districts and Local Economic Regeneration,* 215–250. Geneva: International Institute of Labour Studies.

———, 1993: Constitutional Ordering in Historical Context. In Fritz W. Scharpf, ed., *Games in Hierarchies and Networks: Analytical and Empirical Approaches to the Study of Governance Institutions,* 65–123. Boulder: Westview Press.

———, 1994: Learning by Monitoring: The Institutions of Economic Development. In Neil J. Smelser/Richard Swedberg, eds., *The Handbook of Economic Sociology,* 137–165. Princeton: Princeton University Press.

Saretzki, Thomas, 1996: Wie unterscheiden sich Argumentieren und Verhandeln? Definitionsprobleme, funktionale Bezüge, und strukturelle Differenzen von zwei verschiedenen Kommunikationsmodi. In Volker von Prittwitz, ed., *Verhandeln und Argumentieren: Dialog, Interessen und Macht in der Umweltpolitik,* 19–40. Opladen: Leske & Budrich.

Sartori, Giovanni, 1991: Comparing and Miscomparing. *Journal of Theoretical Politics* 3, 243–257.

———, 1994: *Comparative Constitutional Engineering: An Inquiry into Structures, Incentives, and Outcomes.* New York: New York University Press.

Scharpf, Fritz W., 1970: *Demokratietheorie zwischen Utopie und Anpassung.* Konstanz: Universitätsverlag.

_____, 1986: Policy Failure and Institutional Reform: Why Should Form Follow Function? *International Social Science Journal* 108, 179–191.

_____, 1988: The Joint Decision Trap: Lessons from German Federalism and European Integration. *Public Administration* 66, 239–278.

_____, 1989: Decision Rules, Decision Styles, and Policy Choices. *Journal of Theoretical Politics* 1, 149–176.

_____, 1990: Games Real Actors Could Play: The Problem of Mutual Predictability. *Rationality and Society* 2, 471–494.

_____, 1991a: *Crisis and Choice in European Social Democracy.* Ithaca: Cornell University Press.

_____, 1991b: Games Real Actors Could Play: The Challenge of Complexity. *Journal of Theoretical Politics* 3, 277–304.

_____, 1994: Games Real Actors Could Play: Positive and Negative Coordination in Embedded Negotiations. *Journal of Theoretical Politics* 6, 27–53.

_____, 1995: Federal Arrangements and Multi-party Systems. *Australian Journal of Political Science* 30, 27–39.

_____, 1996: Negative and Positive Integration in the Political Economy of European Welfare States. In Gary Marks/Fritz W. Scharpf/Philippe C. Schmitter/Wolfgang Streeck, *Governance in the European Union,* 15–39. London: Sage.

_____, 1997: Economic Integration, Democracy, and the Welfare State. *Journal of European Public Policy* 4, 18–36.

Scharpf, Fritz W./Arthur Benz, 1991: *Kooperation als Alternative zur Neugliederung? Zusammenarbeit zwischen den norddeutschen Ländern.* Baden-Baden: Nomos.

Scharpf, Fritz W./Bernd Reissert/Fritz Schnabel, 1976: *Politikverflechtung: Theorie und Empirie des kooperativen Föderalismus in der Bundesrepublik.* Kronberg: Scriptor.

Schimank, Uwe, 1995: Teilsystemevolutionen und Akteurstrategien: Die zwei Seiten struktureller Dynamiken moderner Gesellschaften. *Soziale Systeme* 1, 73–100.

Schmalz-Bruns, Rainer, 1995: *Reflexive Demokratie: Die demokratische Transformation moderner Politik.* Baden-Baden: Nomos.

Schmidt, Susanne K., 1995: The Integration of the European Telecommunications and Electricity Sectors in the Light of International Relations Theories and Comparative Politics. Max Planck Institute for the Study of Societies, Cologne. Now published in *Journal of Public Policy* 16, 233–271 (1997).

Schmidt, Susanne K./Raymund Werle, 1993: Technical Controversy in International Standardization. Discussion Paper 93/5, Max Planck Institute for the Study of Societies, Cologne.

Schmidt, Vivien A., 1990: *Democratizing France: The Political and Administrative History of Decentralization.* Cambridge: Cambridge University Press.

_____, 1996: *From State to Market? The Transformation of French Business and Government.* Cambridge: Cambridge University Press.

Schmitter, Philippe C./Gerhard Lehmbruch, eds., 1979: *Trends Toward Corporatist Intermediation.* London: Sage.

Schneider, Volker, 1992: The Structure of Policy Networks: A Comparison of the "Chemical Control" and "Telecommunications" Policy Domains in Germany. *European Journal of Political Research* 21, 109–129.

_____, 1995: Institutionelle Evolution als politischer Prozeß: Die Entwicklung der Telekommunikation im historischen und internationalen Vergleich. Unpublished manuscript, Max Planck Institute for the Study of Societies, Cologne.

Schneider, Volker/Raymund Werle, 1990: International Regime or Corporate Actor? The European Community in Telecommunications Policy. In Kenneth Dyson/Peter Humphreys, eds., *The Political Economy of Communications: International and European Dimensions,* 77–106. London: Routledge.

Schotter, Andrew, 1981: *The Economic Theory of Social Institutions.* Cambridge: Cambridge University Press.

Schulz, Ulrich/Theo May, 1989: The Recording of Social Orientations with Ranking and Pair Comparison Procedures. *European Journal of Social Psychology* 19, 41–59.

Selten, Reinhard, 1965: Spieltheoretische Behandlung eines Oligopolmodells mit Nachfrageträgheit. *Zeitschrift für die gesamte Staatswissenschaft* 121, 301–324 and 667–689.

_____, 1978: The Chain Store Paradox. *Theory and Decision* 9, 127–159.

_____, 1985: Comment. In Kenneth J. Arrow/Seppo Honkapohja, eds., *Frontiers of Economics,* 77–87. Oxford: Basil Blackwell.

_____, 1991: Evolution, Learning, and Economic Behavior. *Games and Economic Behavior* 3, 3–24.

Sen, Amartya, 1969: A Game-Theoretic Analysis of Theories of Collectivism in Allocation. In Tapas Majumdar, ed., *Growth and Choice: Essays in Honour of U. N. Ghosal,* 1–17. Oxford: Oxford University Press.

_____, 1970: *Collective Choice and Social Welfare.* San Francisco: Holden-Day.

_____, 1977: Rational Fools: A Critique of the Behavioral Foundations of Economic Theory. *Philosophy and Public Affairs* 6, 317–344.

_____, 1986: Behavior and the Concept of Preference. In Jon Elster, ed., *Rational Choice,* 60–81. Oxford: Basil Blackwell. (First published in 1973 in *Economica* 40, 241–259.)

Shepsle, Kenneth A., 1979: Institutional Arrangements and Equilibrium in Multidimensional Voting Models. *American Journal of Political Science* 23, 27–59.

_____, 1988: Representation and Governance: The Great Legislative Trade-off. *Political Science Quarterly* 103, 461–484.

Shepsle, Kenneth A./Barry R. Weingast, 1981: Structure-Induced Equilibrium and Legislative Choice. *Quarterly Review of Economics and Business* 21, 503–519.

_____, 1987: The Institutional Foundations of Committee Power. *American Political Science Review* 81, 85–104.

Simon, Herbert A., 1957: A Formal Theory of the Employment Relation. In Herbert A. Simon, *Models of Man: Social and Rational,* 183–195. New York: John Wiley.

_____, 1962: The Architecture of Complexity. *Proceedings of the American Philosophical Society* 106, 467–482.

_____, 1991: Organizations and Markets. *Journal of Economic Perspectives* 5, 25–44.

Sinn, Stefan, 1993: The Taming of Leviathan: Competition Among Governments. *Constitutional Political Economy* 3, 177–221.

Skocpol, Theda, 1987: A Society Without a "State"? Political Organization, Social Conflict, and Welfare Provision in the United States. *Journal of Public Policy* 7, 349–371.

Snidal, Duncan, 1985a: The Game Theory of International Politics. *World Politics* 38, 25–57.

_____, 1985b: The Limits of Hegemonic Stability Theory. *International Organization* 39, 579–614.

_____, 1991: Relative Gains and the Pattern of International Cooperation. *American Political Science Review* 85, 701–726.

Snyder, Glenn H./Paul Diesing, 1977: *Conflict Among Nations: Bargaining, Decision Making, and System Structure in International Crises.* Princeton: Princeton University Press.

Sorge, Arndt/Malcolm Warner, 1986: *Comparative Factory Organisation: An Anglo-German Comparison of Management and Manpower in Manufacturing.* Aldershot: Gower.

Spinelli draft, 1985: Entwurf eines Vertrages zur Gründung der Europäischen Union, vom Europäischen Parlament verabschiedet am 14. Februar 1984. In Werner Weidenfeld/ Wolfgang Wessels, eds., *Jahrbuch der Europäischen Integration 1984,* 404–425. Bonn: Europa-Union Verlag.

Stein, Arthur A., 1980: The Politics of Linkage. *World Politics* 32, 62–81.

_____, 1984: The Hegemon's Dilemma: Great Britain, the United States, and the International Economic Order. *International Organization* 38, 355–386.

Steinmo, Sven, 1994: The End of Redistribution? International Pressures and Domestic Policy Choices. *Challenge* 37(6), 9–17.

Stinchcombe, Arthur L., 1968: *Constructing Social Theories.* New York: Harcourt, Brace & World.

Streeck, Wolfgang, 1982: Organizational Consequences of Neo-corporatist Co-operation in West German Labour Unions. In Gerhard Lehmbruch/Philippe C. Schmitter, eds., *Patterns of Corporatist Policy-Making,* 29–81. London: Sage.

_____, 1992: Inclusion and Secession: Questions on the Boundaries of Associative Democracy. *Politics and Society* 20, 513–520.

Streeck, Wolfgang/Philippe C. Schmitter, 1981: The Organization of Business Interests: A Research Design to Study the Associative Action of Business in the Advanced Industrial Societies of Western Europe. Discussion Paper IIM/LMP 81-13, Wissenschaftszentrum, Berlin.

_____, 1985: Community, Market, State—and Associations? *European Sociological Review* 1, 119–138.

Streit, Manfred, 1993: Cognition, Competition, and Catallaxy: In Memory of Friedrich August von Hayek. *Constitutional Political Economy* 4, 223–262.

Talmon, Jacob L., 1955: *The Origins of Totalitarian Democracy.* London: Secker & Warburg.

Tetlock, Philip E./Aaron Belkin, eds., 1996: *Counterfactual Thought Experiments in World Politics: Logical, Methodological, and Psychological Perspectives.* Princeton: Princeton University Press.

Teubner, Gunther, 1989: *Recht als autopoietisches System.* Frankfurt am Main: Suhrkamp.

Teubner, Gunther/Alberto Febbrajo, eds., 1992: *State, Law, and Economy as Autopoietic Systems: Regulation and Autonomy in a New Perspective.* Milan: Giuffre.

Teubner, Gunther/Helmut Willke, 1984: Kontext und Autonomie: Gesellschaftliche Selbststeuerung durch reflexives Recht. *Zeitschrift für Rechtssoziologie* 5, 4–35.

Thompson, James D., 1967: *Organizations in Action: Social-Science Bases of Administrative Theory.* New York: McGraw-Hill.

Thompson, Leigh L., 1992: A Method for Examining Learning in Negotiation. *Group Decision and Negotiation* 1, 71–85.

Tollison, Robert D./Thomas D. Willet, 1979: An Economic Theory of Mutually Advantageous Issue Linkages in International Negotiations. *International Organization* 33, 425–449.

Truman, David B., 1951: *The Governmental Process: Political Interests and Public Opinion.* New York: Knopf.

Tsebelis, George, 1990: *Nested Games: Rational Choice in Comparative Politics.* Berkeley: University of California Press.

———, 1994: The Power of the European Parliament as a Conditional Agenda Setter. *American Political Science Review* 88, 128–142.

Tsebelis, George/John Sprague, 1989: Coercion and Revolution: Variations on a Predator-Prey Model. *Mathematical Computer Modelling* 12, 547–559.

Ueberhorst, Reinhard, 1991: Technologiepolitische Verständigungsprozesse als Herausforderung für neue parlamentarische Arbeitsformen. In Jörg Schneider, ed., *Risiko und Sicherheit technischer Systeme: Auf der Suche nach neuen Ansätzen,* 177–181. Basel: Birkhäuser.

Underdal, Arild, 1983: Causes of Negotiation Failure. *European Journal of Political Research* 11, 183–195.

Voelzkow, Helmut, 1996: *Private Regierungen in der Techniksteuerung: Eine sozialwissenschaftliche Analyse der technischen Normung.* Frankfurt am Main: Campus.

Vowe, Gerhard, 1993: Qualitative Inhaltsanalyse—Cognitive Mapping—Policy Arguer: Demonstration systematischer Vorgehensweise zur Analyse politischer Kognition. Unpublished manuscript, Max Planck Institute for the Study of Societies, Cologne.

Walton, Richard E./Robert B. McKersie, 1965: *A Behavioral Theory of Labor Negotiations: An Analysis of a Social Interaction System.* New York: McGraw-Hill.

Waltz, Kenneth N., 1954: *Man, the State, and War: A Theoretical Analysis.* New York: Columbia University Press.

———, 1979: *Theory of International Politics.* New York: McGraw-Hill.

Walzer, Michael, 1983: *Spheres of Justice: A Defense of Pluralism and Equality.* New York: Basic Books.

Wasem, Jürgen, 1992: Niederlassung oder Poliklinik: Zur Entscheidungssituation der ambulant tätigen Ärzte im Beitrittsgebiet. In Peter Oberender, ed., *Steuerungsprobleme im Gesundheitswesen,* 81–134. Baden-Baden: Nomos.

Weber, Max, 1947: *The Theory of Social and Economic Organization.* Translated by A. M. Henderson and Talcott Parsons. New York: Free Press.

Weede, Erich, 1990: Democracy, Party Government, and Rent-Seeking as Determinants of Distributional Inequality in Industrial Societies. *European Journal of Political Research* 18, 515–533.

Wehling, Hans-Georg, 1989: The Bundesrat. *Publius: The Journal of Federalism* 19, 53–64.

Weiler, Joseph H.H., 1981: The Community System: The Dual Character of Supranationalism. *Yearbook of European Law* 1, 257–306.

———, 1992: After Maastricht: Community Legitimacy in Post-1992 Europe. In William James Adams, ed., *Singular Europe: Economy and Polity of the European Community After 1992,* 11–41. Ann Arbor: University of Michigan Press.

———, 1994: A Quiet Revolution: The European Court of Justice and Its Interlocutors. *Comparative Political Studies* 26, 510–534.

———, 1995: Does Europe Need a Constitution? Reflections on Demos, Telos, and the German Maastricht Decision. *European Law Journal* 1, 219–258.

Wellmann, Barry/S. D. Berkowitz, eds., 1988: *Social Structures: A Network Approach.* Cambridge: Cambridge University Press.

White, Hayden, 1973: *Metahistory: The Historical Imagination in Nineteenth-Century Europe.* Baltimore: Johns Hopkins University Press.

Wildavsky, Aaron, 1992: Indispensable Framework, or Just Another Ideology? Prisoner's Dilemma as an Antihierarchical Game. *Rationality and Society* 4, 8–23.

Wiley, Mary Glenn/Mayer N. Zald, 1968: The Growth and Transformation of Educational Accrediting Agencies: An Exploratory Study in Social Control of Institutions. *Sociology of Education* 41, 36–56.

Willer, David, 1987: *Theory and the Experimental Investigation of Social Structures.* New York: Gordon & Breach.

Willer, David/Travis Patton, 1987: The Development of Network Exchange Theory. In Edward J. Lawler/Barry Markovsky, eds., *Advances in Group Processes,* Vol. 4, 199–242. Greenwich, CT: JAI Press.

Willer, David/Judith Willer, 1973: *Systematic Empiricism: Critique of a Pseudoscience.* Englewood Cliffs, NJ: Prentice-Hall.

Williams, Shirley, 1991: Sovereignty and Accountability in the European Community. In Robert O. Keohane/Stanley Hoffmann, eds., *The New European Community: Decision Making and Institutional Change,* 155–176. Boulder: Westview Press.

Williamson, Oliver E., 1975: *Markets and Hierarchies: Analysis and Antitrust Implications.* New York: Free Press.

———, 1985: *The Economic Institutions of Capitalism: Firms, Markets, Relational Contracting.* New York: Free Press.

———, 1990: The Firm as a Nexus of Treaties: An Introduction. In Masahiko Aoki/Bo Gustavson/Oliver E. Williamson, eds., *The Firm as a Nexus of Treaties,* 1–25. London: Sage.

Wilson, Graham, 1994: The Westminster Model in Comparative Perspective. In Ian Budge/David McKay, eds., *Developing Democracy: Comparative Research in Honour of J.F.P. Blondel,* 189–201. London: Sage.

Wittman, Donald, 1989: Why Democracies Produce Efficient Results. *Journal of Political Economy* 97, 1395–1424.

Yamagishi, Toshio/Mary R. Gillmore/Karen S. Cook, 1988: Network Connections and the Distribution of Power in Exchange Networks. *American Journal of Sociology* 93, 833–851.

Yarbrough, Beth V./Robert M. Yarbrough, 1985: Free Trade, Hegemony, and the Theory of Agency. *Kyklos* 38, 348–364.

Young, H. Peyton, 1991: Negotiation Analysis. In H. Peyton Young, ed., *Negotiation Analysis,* 1–23. Ann Arbor: University of Michigan Press.

Young, Oran R., 1982: Regime Dynamics: The Rise and Fall of International Regimes. *International Organization* 36, 277–297.

———, 1995: System and Society in World Affairs: Implications for International Organizations. *International Social Science Journal* 144, 197–212.

Zintl, Reinhard, 1992: Kooperation und Aufteilung des Kooperationsgewinns bei horizontaler Politikverflechtung. In Arthur Benz/Fritz W. Scharpf/Reinhard Zintl, *Horizontale Politikverflechtung: Zur Theorie von Verhandlungssystemen,* 97–146. Frankfurt am Main: Campus.

———, 1995: Der Nutzen unvollständiger Erklärungen: Überlegungen zur sozialwissenschaftlichen Anwendung der Spieltheorie. Discussion Paper 95/2, Max Planck Institute for the Study of Societies, Cologne.

Zolo, Danilo, 1992: *Democracy and Complexity: A Realist Approach.* Cambridge: Polity Press.

Zürn, Michael, 1992: *Interessen und Institutionen in der internationalen Politik: Grundlegung und Anwendungen des situationsstrukturellen Ansatzes.* Opladen: Leske & Budrich.

# About the Book and Author

*Games Real Actors Play* is a book about conceptual tools that social scientists could and should use in comparative case studies of complex policy interactions. Given that standard methods of theory testing will not work well for complex and potentially unique cases, the framework of "actor-centered institutionalism" shifts the emphasis from testing to the development and evaluation of theoretically disciplined and empirically grounded hypotheses. Since valid explanations must reconstruct the interactions among intendedly rational (individual, collective, and corporate) actors, Scharpf argues throughout that empirical researchers should, and could, rely on the logic of game-theoretic explanations. But to be empirically viable, such explanations must systematically exploit the information about actor orientations, capabilities, and constraints that is contained in the institutional settings within which policy interactions take place.

In the context of policy research, Scharpf argues that substantive policy problems need to be mapped onto the constellations of policy actors involved, and he shows how these constellations can be represented by relatively simple and transparent game-theoretic models. Next he argues that for any given actor constellation, policy outcomes are directly affected by institutional structures and the modes of interaction that these allow. Hence the explication of the policy implications of various modes of interaction—such as non-cooperative games, negotiations, majoritarian and hierarchical decisions, and the frequently encountered combinations of these—constitutes the major part of the book. Throughout, the theoretical and methodological discussion is enriched by frequent references to, and some extensively presented, examples from comparative policy research in Europe and in the United States.

Beyond that, *Games Real Actors Play* addresses the need to integrate the positive and normative aspects of policy studies without violating the integrity of either empirical research or normative discourse. Scharpf shows how the criteria of "good" policy, which must inevitably be used in assessing the empirical effects of institutional arrangements, can be formulated in such a way that idiosyncratic value judgments can be ruled out within the context of interaction-oriented policy research.

Fritz W. Scharpf is codirector of the Max Planck Institute for the Study of Societies in Cologne, Germany, and a former director of the International Institute of Management and Administration, Wissenschaftszentrum, Berlin. He has taught at the Yale Law School, the University of Chicago Law School, and the University of Konstanz. He has published widely on constitutional law, democratic theory, policy formation and policy implementation, political economy, negotiation theory, and game theory.

# Index